THE LAST UTOPIANS

The Last Utopians

FOUR LATE
NINETEENTH-CENTURY
VISIONARIES
AND THEIR LEGACY

Michael Robertson

PRINCETON UNIVERSITY PRESS

PRINCETON & OXFORD

Copyright © 2018 by Princeton University Press

Published by Princeton University Press,
41 William Street, Princeton, New Jersey 08540

In the United Kingdom: Princeton University Press,
6 Oxford Street, Woodstock, Oxfordshire OX20 1TR

press.princeton.edu

Jacket art: Paul Signac, *Au temps d'harmonie: l'âge d'or n'est pas dans le passé,
il est dans l'avenir*, 1893–95. Oil on canvas, 310 x 410 cm (122 x 161.4 in)

ISBN 978-0-691-15416-9
Library of Congress Control Number: 2018931636

British Library Cataloging-in-Publication Data is available

This book has been composed in Miller

Printed on acid-free paper. ∞

Printed in the United States of America

10 9 8 7 6 5 4 3 2 1

CONTENTS

ACKNOWLEDGMENTS

UTOPIA IS A PROCESS as much as it is a destination; the generosity I've encountered and the pleasure I've had in writing this book have been truly utopian.

The book had its origins in a lunch with Hanne Winarsky. The sushi was so-so, but the conversation was inspiring. I had the chance to try out ideas in a number of settings, including two conferences of the Society for Utopian Studies and a Politics Forum at The College of New Jersey. My presentation at the forum led to some wonderful conversations with colleagues; my thanks to Juda Bennett, Tim Clydesdale, Piper Kendrix Williams, and Kim Pearson. I also shared work-in-progress with colleagues in the Religion in the Americas workshop of the Princeton University Department of Religion, where I spent a happy and productive year as a visiting fellow; special thanks to Wallace Best, Jessica Delgado, and Judith Weisenfeld.

Three brilliant writer-editors read every word of this book in draft and showed me the way forward; I'm immensely grateful to David Blake, Lynn Powell, and Michelle Preston. Jonathan Greenberg, another superb writer-editor, offered to read the manuscript at a crucial moment and provided invaluable help. Dan Rodgers shared his knowledge and wisdom when I was at the start of this project and, at the end, read the entire manuscript. Florence Boos read the finished book and saved me from many errors.

Steve Jendrysik, chair of the Chicopee Historical Commission, showed me around the Edward Bellamy house. Sally Goldsmith and Rony Robinson served as guides in Derbyshire, and Jo Magee allowed me to poke around the grounds of Carpenter's Millthorpe cottage. David Capron joined me at Red House, and Helen Elletson, curator at Kelmscott House, introduced me to the William Morris Society collections. Special thanks to John Baker, who took an interest in this project from its inception, shared his vast knowledge of Edward Carpenter, connected me with his large network of friends, rode along to Kelmscott Manor, and hosted me at his Hammersmith flat.

Exploring the varieties of contemporary utopianism was a particularly pleasurable form of research. My concluding chapter names some of the people who went out of their way to host my visits, answer my questions, and share their visions of a better world. People who aren't named there include, at Erraid, Britta and her fellow residents and all my fellow visitors: Alison, Neal, Roz, Chris, Julia, Andy, Liz, Chris, and Melanie. At Findhorn, Carin Bolles arranged for me to talk with some of the community's most interesting, knowledgeable residents: Mari Hollander, Graham Meltzer, and Lisa and Michael Shaw. Steve Bremner, Peter McAlinden, and David Wray took me under their wing at an Edward Carpenter Community retreat. I am also grateful to David Adler, Peter Davey, Will Iles, and Ted Vidler for sharing their experiences in the community. I'm grateful to everyone I met at Faerie Camp Destiny. David Edleson made it possible, and he and Joey Cain made me feel at home. Stephen Duncombe encouraged me to visit Occupy Wall Street. Diane Barlow and Nancy Lemmo welcomed me to Waldorf School of Princeton. Marty Johnson of Isles shared his years of experience with Trenton's community gardens. Though I never attended Burning Man, I appreciated Ethan Dunn's invitation and our long conversation about Burning Man while hiking in the Oakland hills.

A Rodney G. Dennis Fellowship from the Houghton Library at Harvard made it possible for me to spend a month there researching the Edward Bellamy papers; Fiona Carr, Silvia Chiang, and Parker Van Valkenburgh made my time in Cambridge a joy. The sabbatical and SOSA committees at The College of New Jersey supported this project from inception to conclusion. Dean Ben Rifkin supported two research trips to the U.K. The students in my "Utopia" course at The College of New Jersey were valued collaborators, as were the students in "The Utopian Tradition in Western Literature" at Northern State Prison.

It has been a pleasure to work with friends old and new at Princeton University Press, Kathleen Cioffi, Thalia Leaf, and Anne Savarese, and with copyeditor Daniel Simon and indexer Steven Moore.

Miranda Robertson was unfailingly supportive during the years I was writing, as was my companion in many of the adventures described in these pages, Mary Pat Robertson. My life with them proves that utopia can be found in the here and now.

THE LAST UTOPIANS

Introduction

ONE SUMMER RECENTLY, I made a twelve-hour trip from London—by train, ferry, bus, and dinghy—to Erraid, a tiny island in the Scottish Hebrides that lies close by the southwestern tip of the larger island of Mull. Erraid was uninhabited until the late nineteenth century, when the Stevenson engineering firm built cottages for the families of lighthouse keepers. Robert Louis Stevenson, son and nephew of the firm's proprietors, stayed in one of the cottages before he wrote *Kidnapped*, his adventure tale set partly on Erraid. That summer I too stayed in one of the Stevensons' cottages, its thick, beautifully crafted granite walls apparently impervious to the passage of time. The cottages now house a commune—or, to use the currently preferred term, an *intentional community*. I had come to stay for a week with the dozen people who inhabit the island year-round, supporting themselves in frugal but comfortable fashion by gardening, fishing, tending livestock, making candles, and hosting visitors attracted by the chance to experience a Hebridean version of the simple life.

Each morning the residents and guests gathered in one of the cottages to choose work assignments for the day: splitting firewood, cleaning out the chicken coop, painting a room, cooking a meal. Most days, I chose gardening. The residents are justifiably proud of their gardens, which occupy several large, handsome plots just in front of the cottages, surrounded by low stone walls built by the lighthouse keepers to shelter their crops from grazing sheep and the harsh North Atlantic winds. That summer the weather was glorious, and every time that I stood up from thinning carrots or picking beans and looked about, I gasped involuntarily at the beautiful vista before me. Directly across was the sparsely settled Ross of Mull, its deep-green, sheep-flecked meadows rising toward rugged Ben More mountain. To the northeast, a mile across the sound, I could just make out the squat, dark tower of the abbey of Iona, the island where Christianity first established a foothold in Britain in the sixth century. There was seldom anyone in sight. I could hear nothing but the bleating of sheep, the cry of gulls, and occasionally—if the wind was right—the bell of the ferry between Iona and Mull. Bathed in sunshine, breathing in the cool, salt-tinged air, I couldn't help saying to myself, "This *is* utopia!"

⊰⊱

I knew that, temporarily intoxicated by the salt air and the stunning landscape, I was being foolishly extravagant. I was well aware of the term's etymology: coined by Thomas More in his book of the same name, *utopia* is a Latin term for *no place*. I'd come to Erraid not on an impossible quest to find perfection but because of my interest in the legacy of four once-celebrated writers of the late nineteenth and early twentieth centuries—a group that I'd come to think of as the "last utopians."

These four writers—Edward Bellamy, William Morris, Edward Carpenter, and Charlotte Perkins Gilman—lived and wrote near the end of an extraordinary period of utopian writing and social experimentation in Great Britain and the United States, dating from roughly 1825 to 1915. Not coincidentally, this period also represented the triumph of industrial capitalism in both countries. Nineteenth-century utopian writers and the founders of the era's communal experiments were among the intellectuals both impressed and dismayed by the era's changes: the disruption of traditional modes of agricultural and artisan labor; the rapid spread of new technologies and the accompanying damage to the natural environment; the immense growth of urban centers; the vast, and vastly unequal, increases in wealth; the alterations to traditional family structures and conceptions of women's and men's roles in the world. The disruptions of industrial capitalism provoked a variety of intellectual and cultural responses, ranging from Karl Marx's predictions of capitalism's imminent demise to British philosopher Herbert Spencer's embrace of the era's savage inequalities as a necessary feature of an ultimately beneficent social evolution. Along with Marxian socialism and Spencerian social theory, utopianism provided hundreds of thousands of people in nineteenth-century Britain and the U.S. with a means of understanding and responding to the era's wrenching changes.

Marx was particularly aware of the parallels between his own intellectual project and those of utopian writers. He devoted a section of the *Communist Manifesto* to the earliest and most influential of the nineteenth-century utopian writers, Claude Saint-Simon, Charles Fourier, and Robert Owen, labeling them as "utopian" socialists. He intended the epithet to be dismissive; these writers had failed to attain the insight of Marx, a "scientific" socialist.[1] Despite Marx's disdain, two of the utopian socialists, Fourier and Owen, were enormously influential in the U.S. and U.K. Both writers imagined that society could be transformed through the establishment of utopian communities, and over a period of three decades, beginning in the 1820s, dozens of Fourierist and Owenite communities were founded in North America and Great Britain.[2]

The enthusiasm for utopian social experiments waned after mid-century, but during the later nineteenth century, utopian literature—both works of social theory and imaginative romances in the vein of More's *Utopia*—proliferated. The self-taught economist Henry George's visionary *Progress and Poverty* (1879) was wildly popular in both the U.S. and U.K., while novelists such as Marie Howland and John Macnie published utopian fictions that reached small but appreciative audiences.[3]

Then, in 1888, the American novelist Edward Bellamy published *Looking Backward 2000–1887*, narrated by a Bostonian who time-travels 113 years into a utopian future. Before the book's publication, Bellamy was a midlist author of cleverly plotted romances with a reputation as a lightweight Nathaniel Hawthorne. By the early 1890s, *Looking Backward* had become one of the most successful books of the century, and Bellamy was transformed from a reclusive

New England writer into an international political figure. The novel was hailed as the *Uncle Tom's Cabin* of the industrial era, a comparison meant to suggest that just as Harriet Beecher Stowe's novel had inflamed the movement against slavery and helped spark the Civil War, *Looking Backward* might well inspire a massive reaction against industrial capitalism. The book in fact sparked a short-lived political movement in the U.S. with the now-unfortunate name of Nationalism, intended to signify its appeal to all sectors of society. In the U.K., where *Looking Backward* was also widely popular, it was embraced by Fabians and others on the political left. Moreover, the book initiated a vogue for utopian fiction that continued for the next twenty-five years. More English-language utopian works— over five hundred—were published in the quarter-century following the appearance of Bellamy's novel than had appeared in the nearly four hundred years between More and Bellamy. Many of these novels directly proclaimed their debt to Bellamy, with titles such as *Looking Forward, Looking Further Forward,* and *Looking Further Backward.*[4]

Most of these derivative fictions reached few readers and quickly receded into well-deserved obscurity. However, one of the novels written as a direct response to *Looking Backward* was widely read when it appeared in book form in 1891 and has come to be regarded as one of the classics of the genre, equal in its imaginative power to Thomas More's foundational text: William Morris's *News from Nowhere.* Morris is the most widely known of the last utopians, although relatively few of the millions of people around the world who recognize his name are aware that he wrote a utopian novel. They know him as a designer of high-end interiors and an inspiration for the Arts and Crafts movement, a sort of Victorian lifestyle guru. During his lifetime, however, Morris was as famous for his poetry and his politics as for his design work. During the 1880s and 1890s, Morris became one of England's most prominent socialists, and he regarded his designs, his narrative poetry, and his prose fictions as elements of an integrated utopian vision. From childhood, Morris had been influenced by Victorian medievalism—the renewed interest, after centuries of neglect, in Gothic architecture, medieval craftsmanship, and tales of courtly love and adventure. In his maturity, he transformed what was often a nostalgic turning aside from present realities into a critique of capitalism, and he imagined a postindustrial future in which unalienated artisans produced works of beauty while living in a pastoral landscape where labor was indistinguishable from play.

Morris's vision of a de-urbanized future was shared by his acquaintance Edward Carpenter, who was active in the same socialist circles as Morris. Carpenter was England's most famous apostle of the simple life, a British Thoreau whose essays and poems denouncing middle-class civilization led George Bernard Shaw to nickname him the Noble Savage. Morris was more sympathetic to Carpenter. An 1884 chat about Carpenter's farm in rural Derbyshire caused Morris to ruminate, "I listened with longing heart to his account of his patch of ground, seven acres: he says that he and his fellow can almost live on it: they grow their own wheat, and send flowers and fruit to Chesterfield and Sheffield markets: all that sounds very agreeable to me."[5] Morris admired not only Carpenter's nearly self-sufficient rural life but also his partnership with his "fellow," Albert Fearnehough, a former Sheffield ironworker. Morris had no idea that the two men were lovers.

In the 1880s, when the word "homosexual" was unknown in the English language, Carpenter's relationships with a succession of young working-class men were widely admired in his socialist circles as models of cross-class friendships. Carpenter took advantage of the era's conceptual fuzziness about human sexuality to write a series of increasingly bold essays and books about what he called "homogenic love" and the "intermediate sex." He united his contemporaries' interest in utopian projections of the future with his own armchair-anthropologist theorizing to argue that men-loving men and women-loving women constituted the utopian vanguard. In the long-distant past, he believed, members of the intermediate sex had rejected the conventional roles of warrior, hunter, and gatherer and served instead as tribal healers, priests, artists, and visionaries, making possible the advance of civilization. Now, with nineteenth-century civilization breaking down into antagonistic camps—class against class, men against women—people of the intermediate sex could again lead humanity into a transformed future. From their positions on the margins of patriarchal capitalist society, homogenic lovers were uniquely suited to model more fluid and equal human relationships and to envision an egalitarian future.

On her first visit to England in 1896, Charlotte Perkins Gilman sought out both Morris and Carpenter. Now best known as author of the protofeminist short story "The Yellow Wallpaper," Gilman's reputation at the time rested on her work as an activist and speaker in the Nationalist political movement inspired by Bellamy's *Looking Backward*. Following her return from England, she wrote a series of utopian fictions that climaxed with the novel *Herland* (1915). Like Bellamy's *Looking Backward*, Gilman's novel portrays an egalitarian socialist society; in accord with Morris's and Carpenter's ideas, it depicts a largely agrarian land in which people in comfortable tunics and leggings enjoy days of agreeable labor punctuated by vegetarian meals and wholesome recreations. Unlike the utopias of her male colleagues, however, Gilman's is populated exclusively by women, who reproduce by parthenogenesis, bearing only daughters. Carpenter imagined that homogenic lovers could serve as the utopian vanguard; Gilman believed that emancipated women would play that role.

Edward Bellamy, William Morris, Edward Carpenter, and Charlotte Perkins Gilman are the subjects of this book, which is centered on the flourishing of utopian literature and social thought in the United States and Great Britain from the mid-1880s until 1915. These four figures were not the only significant utopian writers of the period, and, although there were intellectual and personal connections among them, they did not think of themselves as a group. I focus on them because their particular strain of utopianism seems to me not only admirable but also relevant to our current political moment.

Utopia is notoriously difficult to define. In the popular imagination it signifies an impossibly perfect ideal—*no place*. But Thomas More's neologism is a bilingual pun; *utopia* is a Latinization not only of the Greek *ou-topos*, no place, but also of *eu-topos*, good place. Utopia is not necessarily a fantasy of perfection, and utopianism can be seen simply as *the envisioning of a transformed, better world*, which is how I use the term in this book.[6] That's a capacious definition. What unites the utopianism of Bellamy, Morris, Carpenter, and Gilman are four distinctive elements.

First, all four writers were democratic socialists. Appalled by the widespread poverty and misery engendered by late nineteenth-century industrial capitalism, they sought an egalitarian alternative. Their socialism had distinctive Anglo-American roots. With the exception of Morris, they had little use for Marx. They derived their socialist ideals from a mix of Robert Owen's and Charles Fourier's communal theorizing, Emersonian Transcendentalism, Walt Whitman's proclamations of comradeship, Thomas Carlyle's reactionary anticapitalism, and John Ruskin's aesthetically influenced attacks on the industrial system. Marx and Engels frequently expressed their exasperation at what they saw as the naïve and unscientific nature of this strain of late nineteenth-century British and American socialism, but it was the dominant form of socialist thought at the time.[7]

Late nineteenth-century socialism's roots in Owenite and Fourierist communalism led many adherents, including the last utopians, to a critique of the patriarchal family that was rare among orthodox Marxists, most of whom believed that radicalizing the working class was paramount. The last utopians emphasized women's economic independence as crucial to a transformed society, and they imagined new forms of family and community.[8] Edward Bellamy was the sole exception. He was unable to conceive that women's economic equality might disrupt the insular privacy of the Victorian family. All the others imagined—and in the case of Carpenter and Gilman, lived out—alternatives to lifelong heterosexual marriage. Their works portray a future marked by gender equality and by fluid, alternative forms of romance, family, and community.

All four writers' egalitarianism was shaped by their religious ideas, which constitute the last utopians' third distinctive feature. At heart they were religious more than political thinkers. Bellamy, Carpenter, and Gilman espoused a post-Christian liberal spirituality that was common among late nineteenth-century cultural progressives, while Morris, who claimed to be an atheist, referred frequently to the "religion of socialism." Influenced by a distinctly nineteenth-century combination of Christian evangelicalism, Transcendentalism, and concepts borrowed from Asian religions, the last utopians believed that the self was an illusion, that everyone was united in an inclusive divine spirit, and that humanity was destined to realize its oneness. They believed that the utopian future would be achieved through a nonviolent process of mass conversion, not violent proletarian revolution. Political change depended on a process of evangelization. Even Morris, a self-proclaimed atheist and revolutionary, typically spent his Sundays on London street corners addressing passersby, offering them the good news of socialism.[9]

Their immanentist theology—that is, the idea that the divine is immanent within humanity and nature—influenced the last of their distinctive ideas: their reverence for the natural world and commitment to elements of a Thoreauvian simple life. Carpenter, who threw over successive careers as a Cambridge don and a university extension lecturer for life as a market gardener in rural Derbyshire, served as a model. He built a small writing hut for himself, with one side open to the elements, and claimed that he could not have written "Towards Democracy," his breakthrough poetic masterwork, had he not composed it in the open air.[10] Only Bellamy, who preferred not to venture outside the Massachusetts house where he had lived since birth, was immune to the call of the wild. Yet even Bellamy shared the last utopians' concern for the environment, their horror at the unchecked and increasingly severe pollution of late nineteenth-century cities.

<hr />

Their visions of a socialist, egalitarian future of simple living in harmony with nature qualify Bellamy, Morris, Carpenter, and Gilman as *utopians*. Why were they the *last*? I don't want to suggest that the utopian imagination suddenly dried up after 1915; utopian novels continued to be produced throughout the twentieth century. What's indisputable, however, is that following World War I, the once-large audience for utopian fiction diminished drastically. If *Looking Backward* and *News from Nowhere* were major texts of the 1890s, Aldous Huxley's *Brave New World* (1932) and George Orwell's *Nineteen Eighty-Four* (1949) were heralded as masterworks of the twentieth century. Twentieth-century speculative fiction turned from imaginative depictions of better worlds to descriptions of horrors to come. What accounts for literature's dystopian turn?

To take only the most obvious explanation, the massive violence of two world wars, which climaxed with the Holocaust and Hiroshima, seemed to mock the faith in inevitable progress that lay at the heart of nineteenth-century utopianism. The last utopians were all born during the Victorian era, when an optimistic version of evolutionary theory dominated historical understanding. Human history, it was believed, lay on an upward trajectory, and progress—including its industrial and technological varieties—promised a better world. In the words of novelist Richard Powers, "The nineteenth century . . . held to the doctrine of perfectibility. . . . Most thinkers of the . . . century believed in the upward spiral of rationality, which would at last triumph over the imperfections of nature."[11] World War I seemed, to many, to knock the upward spiral permanently askew. Human rationality and technological progress had led to the industrialized slaughter of the European battlefields, with more than seventeen million deaths during the course of the four-year war.

In addition, the totalitarian political regimes of the twentieth century seemed attributable, at least in part, to utopian imaginings. The Bolshevik Revolution was arguably a utopian project intended to turn tsarist Russian into an ideal Marxist nation; Stalin's brutal repression and murder of those perceived to be enemies of the state could be seen as deriving from his utopian conception of the Soviet Union; and Cambodia under the Khmer Rouge could be regarded as the most powerful, deliberately planned attempt in world history to realize utopia. When Pol Pot assumed power in 1975, he declared it to be the Year Zero. Cambodia would begin anew, and the Khmer Rouge would create a perfect state, a project that would eventually require the elimination of more than one million of their fellow citizens.[12]

Philosopher Karl Popper famously argued in *The Open Society and Its Enemies* (1945) that utopian thinking is inherently violent. He identified an "aesthetic" strain in utopianism, a desire to wipe the slate clean and begin society afresh. Popper traced the aesthetic approach to statecraft back to Plato, whose *Republic* lays out a perfect, and perfectly beautiful, society. The idea that a perfect society could be crafted like a work of art leads inevitably, Popper argued, to repression and violence. Popper, whose attack on utopianism appeared in 1945, drew directly on his personal experience: in 1938 he had fled his native Austria for New Zealand, just ahead of the Nazi Anschluss. Popper advocated, in opposition to the utopian social engineering that animated Stalin, Hitler, and other despots, what he called "piecemeal engineering," the slow, incremental reforms of liberal democracies.[13]

In the twenty-first century Popper's anti-utopian theories have been amplified and updated by philosopher John Gray in his brilliantly argued polemic *Black Mass: Apocalyptic Religion and the Death of Utopia* (2007). Writing after the collapse of the Soviet Union, Gray is less concerned with the discredited utopian left than with what he regards as the utopian right, exemplified by Margaret Thatcher and George W. Bush. Thatcher possessed a utopian faith in the transformative potential of free-market economics; Bush imagined that he could impose liberal democracy on Iraq, a project that Gray regards as utopian in its blindly grand hubris. Gray locates the philosophical origins of the American invasion of Iraq in the French Revolution, when Jacobin radicals conceived of violence as an instrument for remaking humanity. The Jacobins' successors, according to Gray, include not only the Bolsheviks, the Nazis, George Bush, and Tony Blair but also the Taliban and al-Qaeda. Utopias, Gray writes, "are dreams of collective deliverance that in waking life are found to be nightmares." Gray's gift for the memorable apothegm is shared by the French political philosopher Frédéric Rouvillois, who writes, "All utopias are totalitarian. . . . And, conversely, all totalitarian states are fundamentally utopian."[14]

Many defenders of utopia argue that the twisted visions of a Stalin, Hitler, or Pol Pot cannot be labeled utopian, but my own definition—the envisioning of a transformed, better world—can be applied to these murderous tyrants. If you believe, as I do, that the utopian imagination is crucial to shaping a better future, it's important to acknowledge that attempts to impose utopia from above can have devastating consequences. That's why the nonviolent, egalitarian, and democratic values at the heart of the last utopians' visions are so important. The modest playfulness to be found in the utopian imaginings of Bellamy, Morris, Carpenter, and Gilman is antithetical to the totalitarian spirit. What G. D. H. Cole identified as the implicit invitation extended in Morris's *News from Nowhere*—

"Here is the sort of society I feel I should like to live in. Now tell me yours."—is present in the work of all four.[15] That is not to say that disturbing authoritarian elements are totally absent from their work, and in what follows I explore their many shortcomings. I argue, however, that their imaginative visions are particularly valuable for contemporary progressive political thought and practice.

The early twenty-first century may not seem a propitious moment to revive the work of four utopian writers. Utopian fiction has few readers, but dystopian fiction and film are surging. The wildly successful *Hunger Games* and *Divergent* book series and films are the most obvious examples, but dystopian writing is proliferating in serious literary fiction as well, with critically and commercially successful recent works by Margaret Atwood, Gary Shteyngart, Howard Jacobson, and many others.[16] Defining features of twenty-first-century life in the U.S. and U.K.—terrorism, massive state surveillance, police brutality, widening inequality, ethnic hatred, climate change, life-altering technology—have provided fertile soil for the growth of the coruscating, monitory critiques found in dystopian literature.

Contemporary fiction has little use for the utopian visions of Bellamy, Morris, Carpenter, and Gilman, and I don't argue for a continuing literary legacy. Instead, in my concluding chapter I suggest that their utopian visions are currently manifested in *lived utopianism*, which I define as the effort to live out some portion of a transformed future in the here and now.[17] Utopian studies scholars interested in the contemporary scene often turn to ethnographic case studies, as in Davina Cooper's *Everyday Utopias*, which analyzes six contemporary sites that she calls "hot spots of innovative practice." Cooper's sites include Hyde Park's famous speakers' corner and Summerhill, the celebrated progressive school, as well as "prefigurative practices" including public nudism, which its advocates regard as a means of living out a radical conception of equality. Cooper argues that in contemporary society, with utopian objects such as novels and buildings and communities in relatively short supply, utopianism needs to be reconceived as an orientation, "a way of engaging with spaces, objects, and practices that is oriented to the hope, desire, and belief in the possibility of other, better worlds."[18]

My final chapter explores contemporary everyday utopias that embrace the last utopians' central values—institutions, sites, and practices that are committed to political, sexual, and spiritual egalitarianism; that promote simplicity and sustainability; and that explore new forms of family and community. The intentional community on the isle of Erraid where I spent a week is one such site. In my last chapter, I describe my visits to Erraid and to two other long-established intentional communities, one in northern Scotland and another in rural Virginia. I also visited a community that was highly intentional but also intentionally temporary: Occupy Wall Street. On a bitterly cold day in October 2011, I stood in the rain and participated in a "mic check" among dozens of people repeating and amplifying a speaker's words. The ritual had been generated by necessity—loudspeakers were not permitted on the site—but it became central to this temporary community's democratic praxis. The Occupy movement was limited to a particular moment, but other temporary utopias repeatedly come together and dissolve. I visited two such contemporary communities inspired by Edward Carpenter: the Edward Carpenter Community, a British gay men's group that holds regular retreats, and the Radical Faeries, a group established by gay American activist Harry Hay that traces its lineage to Carpenter and Walt Whitman.

Progressive schools constitute another site of contemporary utopianism. I spent two days at the Waldorf school in my town, where children devote as much time to gardening, cooking, and knitting as to more conventional academic pursuits. Rudolf Steiner, the early twentieth-century Austrian intellectual who founded the first Waldorf school, was unfamiliar with William Morris, but the schools he inspired would fit easily into the landscape of Morris's antihierarchical Nowhere, where the ability to weave a garment or cook a meal is as valued as any intellectual accomplishment. Waldorf schools are particularly noted for their emphasis on gardening. Steiner advocated what he called "biodynamic" gardening, which goes beyond organic principles to align agriculture not just with the four seasons but with the natural cycles of the moon.

Biodynamic gardening is one part of contemporary food movements, which may be the most widespread form of progressive utopianism in the twenty-first century. Farmers and consumer activists in a variety of sites across North America and Great Britain, from inner-city gardens to suburban farmers' markets to rural communities, are working toward a transformed food system. Contemporary food movements envision a future in which profit-driven food conglomerates and massive industrial farms are supplanted by small-scale, community-oriented, sustainable agricultural systems.

The Last Utopians is the first book to focus on the distinctive strain of transatlantic utopianism found within the work of Bellamy, Morris, Carpenter, Gilman, and their contemporary heirs. It builds on a substantial body of work on late nineteenth-century utopianism. Much of this work, influenced by the idea that the United States itself represents a utopian experiment, deals exclusively with American writers: Bellamy and Gilman, certainly, but also William Dean Howells, who wrote a trilogy of novels about the imaginary land of Altruria, along with many lesser-known contemporaries.[19] Other works take a transnational perspective on the period, placing American and British writers in dialogue, as I do here.[20] All these books reflect the vibrancy of the academic field of utopian studies, which has flourished over the past forty years, with its own professional associations and journals.

The Last Utopians differs from earlier studies in significant ways. First, it brings Edward Carpenter into the discussion of utopianism. Carpenter never wrote a utopian novel, so he has been excluded from studies that focus on narrative fiction. I take inspiration from Dohra Ahmad, who in *Landscapes of Hope* analyzes political manifestos alongside novels, and who defines as utopian any text that "proposes and enacts a better order that does not yet exist anywhere."[21] Using this criterion, much of Carpenter's poetry and prose can be understood as utopian discourse that celebrates a not-yet-existing better order. Carpenter, who fell into obscurity following his death in 1929, has received much attention since the 1970s from queer theorists and historians of sexuality. I place his celebration of the "intermediate sex" in the context of works by his utopian contemporaries.[22]

The Last Utopians has fundamentally different purposes from the earlier books I've cited, which are literary and intellectual histories intended for a specialist audience. This book is concerned with lives as well as texts, and it centers on a series of narrative biographies that detail the ways these writers tried to live out their utopian commitments. Following the unexpected success of *Looking Backward*, the deeply private Bellamy ventured outside his comfortable haven in Chicopee Falls, Massachusetts, to drum up political support for the Nationalist political party and, later, for the Populist movement. The Oxford-educated Morris turned his back on his comfortable upper-middle-class upbringing to speak for socialism on street corners and, donning a workman's smock, to labor as a jack-of-all-trades artisan. Carpenter threw over his prestigious post as a Cambridge don and moved to England's industrial north, working first as a lecturer and then as Derbyshire's most highly educated market gardener. Gilman braved scandal to divorce her husband, giving him custody of their young daughter, in order to tour the country as a lecturer for Nationalism and women's rights. Later, she again defied convention by marrying her younger cousin, an attorney who unreservedly supported her career.

This book combines biography and literary analysis in an effort to understand the ways that, just over a century ago, utopianism not only animated important works by Bellamy, Morris, Carpenter, and Gilman but also shaped their lives. I set these writers and their works within the context of their tumultuous times in order to understand why, for a period of some thirty years from the 1880s until the First World War, utopian fiction had an unprecedented success, utopian speculation suffused the era's intellectual life, and a wide variety of cultural radicals experimented with ways to live out their utopian beliefs.

The Last Utopians does not attempt a comprehensive survey of utopianism in either the late nineteenth and early twentieth centuries or today. H. G. Wells, for example, produced multiple works of speculative fiction, both utopian and dystopian, around the turn of the twentieth century; however, Wells's utopian vision, articulated most clearly in *A Modern Utopia* (1905), has little in common with the works of the last utopians. His ideal future is technocratic, authoritarian, and hierarchical, with power centered in the hands of an elite class of intellectuals descended from Plato's Guardians. Similarly, my final chapter does not consider twenty-first-century techno-utopianism. Belief in the power of technology and computer science to deliver a transformed future is widespread, but the every-day utopians whom I discuss are suspicious of what they see as tech-nological hubris, preferring to emphasize the values of simplicity, sustainability, and community.

These contemporary utopians insist, even if implicitly, on the value of imaginative visions of the future. Milan Šimečka, a philoso-pher and dissident under Czechoslovakia's Communist regime, pub-lished an essay on utopianism during the 1980s, when he was work-ing as a laborer after having been expelled from his university teaching position. Šimečka railed, understandably, against the Marxist utopia, yet he went on to argue that "a world without uto-pias would be a world without social hope, a world of resignation to the status quo and the devalued slogans of everyday political life." The utopian visions of Bellamy, Morris, Carpenter, and Gilman have not, more than a century later, been realized, but elements of their transformative visions—environmentalism, economic justice, equal-ity for women and sexual minorities—remain central to progressive politics today. Utopian studies theorists and scholars argue that imagined utopias are best understood as heuristic devices, useful tools that serve the dual purpose of critiquing the present and of-fering possibilities for the future. In the words of Lucy Sargisson, "The function of Utopia is not its own realization." Rather, the pur-pose of utopia is to stimulate critical thinking and to promote the political imagination. In Karl Mannheim's apt aphorism, "The im-possible gives birth to the possible."[23]

In mapping the utopian contours of two historical moments—the period from the 1880s to 1915 and the early twenty-first cen-tury—this book implicitly interrogates its own title. After World War I, utopianism never regained the importance it held during the previous century, but neither did it disappear. The title is intended to be provocative, to raise questions about the place of utopian thinking today and to stimulate readers' own utopian imaginings. *The Last Utopians* plunges deeply into the lives and works of four writers active at a high point for utopian fiction and speculation in both the United States and Great Britain, and it briefly surveys some of the varieties of contemporary utopianism in the two nations. In writing about utopianism both then and now, I strive for a stance of sympathetic distance. That is, I acknowledge the flaws in the last utopians' grand visions, the ways in which authoritarianism and racism and gender essentialism are woven into the fabric of their dreams, but at the same time I try to avoid the scolding tone of much recent writing about these authors, which seems aimed at demonstrating the current academic community's intellectual and moral superiority. The last utopians, imperfect creatures of their time, dared to publish their dreams, and millions of people in the U.S. and U.K. were thrilled by their visions. A hundred years later, we're rightly fearful of grandiose schemes, and the audience for conventional utopian fiction has shrunk toward the vanishing point. Nevertheless, lived utopianism—contemporary manifestations of what Ernst Bloch called "the principle of hope"—is widespread.[24] Visions of social transformation remain essential to progressive political thought and practice. Millions of people in the U.S. and U.K. are demonstrating through their daily actions the truth of Oscar Wilde's characteristically witty observation: "A map of the world that does not contain Utopia is not worth even glancing at."[25]

CHAPTER ONE

Locating Nowhere

The Worst of Times

For more than two decades during the late nineteenth century, from 1873 to 1896, both the United States and Great Britain experienced what was called, until the 1930s claimed the title, the Great Depression. Historians have debated the accuracy of the label: the American economy underwent a cycle of recurrent booms and busts, while in Britain, despite a macroeconomic decline, working-class living standards actually improved. Nevertheless, as Mark Bevir has pointed out, people of that era perceived themselves to be living through exceptionally hard times, and there is ample evidence of high levels of poverty and unemployment. When the wealthy former industrialist Charles Booth began his famous survey of poverty in London in the 1880s, his aim was to disprove a survey conducted by socialists which claimed that 25 percent of Londoners earned below the minimum amount necessary for satisfying basic needs. Instead, he found out that the figure was too low, and that fully 30 percent of the population of Europe's largest city was living in abject poverty. Booth believed that London was a special case, but B. Seebohm Rowntree, another industrialist-turned-investigator, found that poverty in the provinces was equally severe, with 28 percent of York's inhabitants unable to meet basic needs. Although accurate statistics for U.S. poverty during this period are difficult to obtain— Booth was the first person to define a "line of poverty," and the concept was not employed in the United States until 1904—the Iowa commissioner of labor statistics commented in his 1891 report that 88 percent of working-class Iowa families earned less than the amount determined to be "the necessary living expenses of laboring men with families."[1]

Statistics about late nineteenth-century poverty levels may be inexact, but there is no shortage of journalistic accounts of human misery. Robert Blatchford, editor of the popular *Clarion* newspaper published in Manchester, collected a number of his articles about poverty in England's industrial north in his book *Dismal England* (1899), its very title a challenge to Victorian self-satisfaction. His article about the metalworking shops of Cradley, near Birmingham, offers a grimly poetic litany of outrage: "At Cradley I spoke to a married couple who had worked 120 hours in one week and had earned 18s. [18 shillings, less than one pound sterling] by their united labour; at Cradley I saw heavy-chain strikers who were worn-out old men at thirty-five; at Cradley I found women on strike for a price which would enable them to earn twopence an hour by dint of labour which is to work what the battle of Inkerman was to a Bank Holiday review. At Cradley the men and the women are literally being worked to death for a living that no gentleman would offer his dogs." Jacob Riis, the pioneering investigator of New York City's tenements, quoted from a report of the Association for the Improvement of the Condition of the Poor in his celebrated *How the Other Half Lives* (1890): "In the depth of winter the attention of the Association was called to a Protestant family living in a garret in a miserable tenement in Cherry Street. The family's condition was most deplorable. The man, his wife, and three small children shivering in one room through the roof of which the pitiless winds of winter whistled. The room was almost barren of furniture; the parents slept on the floor, the elder children in boxes, and the baby was swung in an old shawl attached to the rafters by cords by way of a hammock. The father, a seaman, had been obliged to give up that calling because he was in consumption, and was unable to provide either bread or fire for his little ones."[2]

The economic desperation of the working class during this period is evident also in the unprecedented level of strikes and labor violence. Conditions in the United States were particularly severe.

In July 1877, four years into the nation's worst economic crisis up to that point, workers on the Baltimore & Ohio Railroad went on strike when the railroad's president announced simultaneously a 10 percent dividend for shareholders and a 10 percent wage cut for workers, on top of cuts already enacted in previous years of the depression. The ensuing strike was ruthlessly repressed by state and federal troops, setting off a nationwide chain of strikes, which involved most of the nation's railroad workers and at least half a million other laborers. The Great Strike, as it came to be known, did little to better workers' pay or conditions, but it highlighted America's class divisions and the willingness of business and government to use force against labor activists. By the summer's end, over one hundred strikers across the U.S. had been killed and many hundreds wounded. The rest of the century was marked by frequent clashes between capital and labor, climaxing in 1886 during what was called the Great Upheaval, when some 1,400 strikes occurred nationwide, again involving close to half a million workers. On a single day, May 1, nearly two hundred thousand people took part in a work stoppage in support of the eight-hour day; forty thousand marched in Chicago alone. Three days later, at a mass labor rally in Chicago's Haymarket Square, someone threw a bomb at a line of policemen, killing eight officers and setting off a paroxysm of violence on the part of the police, who fired into the crowd, killing several people and wounding scores of civilians and fellow officers. The bomb thrower was never identified, but the Chicago authorities nevertheless indicted eight prominent anarchists for murder, even though six of them were not at the Haymarket on May 4. Seven of the men were sentenced to death, five were hanged, and one committed suicide before the governor of Illinois commuted the sentences of the two still living.[3]

Many middle-class observers in both the U.S. and Great Britain became convinced that their societies were on the verge of violent revolt. Some welcomed the cathartic purging that seemed to them certain to arrive. "The great social revolution of the nineteenth century has already begun," crowed H. M. Hyndman, leader of England's most prominent socialist organization, in 1885. American novelist William Dean Howells was less triumphal in his tone but no less certain that enormous changes were in the making. Two years after Haymarket he wrote to his friend Henry James, "After fifty years of optimistic content with 'civilization' and its ability to come out all right in the end, I now abhor it, and feel that it is coming out all wrong in the end unless it bases itself on a real equality."[4]

At the moment that Howells was writing to James, Edward Bellamy's *Looking Backward* had recently appeared. Its publication in 1888 set off a literary chain reaction, with hundreds of utopian novels being published over the next twenty-five years, including three by Howells himself. This proliferation of utopian fiction had multiple causes, including authors' and publishers' desire to ride the coattails of Bellamy's commercial success, but the economic and social upheavals resulting from nineteenth-century industrial capitalism were at the heart of the era's utopian turn. Only a hundred years earlier, both the United States and Great Britain had been primarily agricultural societies. Now, with what seemed dizzying speed, cities were exploding in population, filled with internal immigrants from the countryside and foreigners from continental Europe. The newly enlarged cities laid bare the increasing inequalities of wealth, with squalid slums in close proximity to the mansions of the newly rich. Long-established rhythms of labor—the seasonal ebb and flow of farmwork, the irregular, self-determined hours of the independent artisan, the long but varied workday of the housekeeper—were replaced by the mechanical, disciplined regularity of the factory. In addition, an increasingly democratic political sphere provided space for protest movements that agitated, sometimes violently, to overturn the system of laissez-faire capitalism that lay beneath the rough, dynamic, unequal realities of the new urban industrial societies.

Industrial capitalism also underlay the multiple challenges to patriarchal family structure. As John Tosh points out, the Victorian middle-class family seems so modern in many ways because it was the first to grapple with the separation of the domestic sphere from the world of work.[5] Modernity challenged normative gender roles for both women and men and led to the nineteenth-century movements for women's equality. The institution of marriage was destabilized, as new middle-class ideals of companionate marriage came into conflict with long-standing beliefs in inherent and absolute sexual differences. And the emergence of sexual science and theorization of the concept of homosexuality offered new opportunities for self-definition and understanding at the same time they created regimes of sexual discipline and oppression.

In response to the turbulence of their era, with its oppressive realities and tantalizing possibilities, Bellamy, Morris, Carpenter, and Gilman—along with hundreds of their now-obscure peers—offered their visions of peaceful and egalitarian future worlds. The sheer number of utopian works produced in the twenty-five years before World War I was unprecedented, and the urgency of these works—the sense that civilization was on the brink of violent disaster, and only a radical reordering of society could save it—is unquestionable. As Frank and Fritzie Manuel point out in their magisterial history of utopian thought in the Western world, most epochs in the West have been turbulent, and every era has produced its share of utopian speculations.[6] Nevertheless, certain periods in particular countries have proven especially favorable for the production and reception of utopian literature. The late nineteenth century in the United States and Great Britain was one such period; early sixteenth-century England was another.

A Brief History of Nowhere

Thomas More, born in 1478, was an adolescent at the time of Christopher Columbus's first voyage in 1492; he was a young man when Amerigo Vespucci explored the Americas at the turn of the century. More came to maturity during Europe's great age of exploration, when Europeans were dazzled by new possibilities, when wild surmise about what might yet be discovered became commonplace. It was a time also of massive economic upheaval, with mercantile capitalism overturning the feudal order. The human costs of the mercantile revolution were particularly evident in England. The great nineteenth-century Marxist scholar Karl Kautsky wrote, "Nowhere else in Europe . . . were the unfavourable reactions of the capitalist mode of production upon the working classes so immediately obvious as in England; nowhere did the unhappy workers clamour so urgently for assistance." Rising rents for land, changes in the wool industry, and rural enclosure combined to catastrophic effect for English peasants and workmen. Enclosure, the practice of fencing off common lands cultivated by peasants in order to use them for the more profitable purpose of grazing sheep, was particularly disruptive, throwing families off the land and resulting in homelessness, unemployment, and poverty on a massive scale. In the words of Raphael Hythloday, sheep, those formerly placid creatures, "apparently developed a raging appetite, and turned into man-eaters. Fields, houses, towns, everything goes down their throats."[7]

Hythloday is the principal character in More's *Utopia* (1516), which purports to be the transcription of a conversation held at Antwerp in 1515 and conducted in Latin—the lingua franca of educated Europeans—among More, who was at the time a well-connected lawyer and public official, dispatched to the Low Countries by Henry VIII as part of an English mission to negotiate treaties; Peter Gilles, the town clerk of Antwerp; and the fictional Hythloday, a Portuguese mariner who had supposedly accompanied Amerigo Vespucci on his voyages to the New World. More goes to considerable trouble to establish the verisimilitude of his account: *Utopia* opens with a flourish of proper names, recounting the actual itinerary that More followed in the Low Countries and naming Gilles along with other people whom he actually knew. More explains that Gilles introduced him to Hythloday, who then talked at length about his visit to the previously unknown isle of Utopia.

The documentary-like details of *Utopia* are intermixed with elaborate scholarly jokes: Hythloday's name is a bilingual pun, a Latin surname combining two Greek roots that together signify *spouter of nonsense*. Utopia's capital city of Amaurot lies on the River Anyder—that is, *Dream-town* is next to the river *Nowater*. The elaborate humanist banter that opens *Utopia* also includes a poem, supposedly by the island's poet laureate. The poem claims that Utopia deserves to be called Eutopia, *good place*; the pun is built into the name of More's imaginary island, which can be construed as a Latinization of either *ou*(no)-*topos* or *eu*(good)-*topos*. This foundational ambiguity shaped the next five centuries of commentary on More and other utopian writers: is utopia to be taken as purely imaginary or as an ideal? More declines to say, but in the same poem he points to a completely serious predecessor: "Plato's *Republic* now I claim / To match, or beat at its own game."[8]

The Republic (ca. 375 BCE) is not exactly a utopian work; in essence, it's a philosophical inquiry into the nature of justice. However, in parts of *The Republic* Plato speculates about an ideal state. Most famously, he advances the ideas of the philosopher-king and of a ruling class of "Guardians." The Guardians, who include both women and men, live together in community without either private property or conventional family structures—concepts that would be central to modern utopian literature. Plato's egalitarianism, however, is limited to an aristocratic elite. The subordinate classes live quite differently from the Guardians, and everyone in the Republic grows up being taught what Plato calls a "noble lie," or "magnificent myth," that all people, far from being created equal, are composed of either gold, silver, or iron and bronze.[9]

Utopia builds on the classical era's preoccupation with the nature of the ideal ruler and the perfect city-state. As Krishan Kumar points out, More's work was also created in dialogue with three other literary traditions: stories of the Golden Age, of the Christian millennium, and of Cokaygne, a creation of medieval folklore.[10]

The earliest Golden Age narrative appears in Hesiod's *Works and Days* (ca. 700 BCE), which describes the long-gone era when men lived like gods, "their hearts free from sorrow." The Golden Age became a frequent subject of Latin poets. Ovid's *Metamorphoses* (8 CE) has a famous description, and Pindar, Horace, and Virgil all touched on the subject as well. The biblical Garden of Eden is the ancient Hebrews' version of the Golden Age, while the Christian concept of heaven relocated paradise from the mythic past to the afterlife.[11]

The New Testament book of Revelation added the idea of the millennium, the thousand-year reign of Christ. Most Christians have conceived of the millennium as the sequel to Christ's second coming, but beginning in the Renaissance a "postmillennial" interpretation of Revelation took hold among a significant minority, who believed that Christ would return after the millennium, a thousand-year period of peace and plenty established by human effort. This strain within Christian thought intersected with utopianism, the idea that humans could create an ideal society; Christian postmillennialism and utopianism intermingled productively from the Renaissance on.[12]

If the millennium was a moral paradise dependent, at least for some, on conscious human effort, Cokaygne stood, in folk culture, for an effortless, sensual paradise. The most famous of its literary expressions is "The Land of Cokaygne," an anonymous fourteenth-century English poem, which is part soft-core pornography—the land's abbeys and convents are filled with lusty monks and nuns—and part glutton's dream:

> There are rivers broad and fine
> Of oil, milk, honey and of wine;
> Water serveth there no thing
> But for sight and for washing.
>
> . . . .
>
> Yet this wonder add to it—
> That geese fly roasted on the spit,
> As God's my witness, to that spot,
> Crying out, "Geese, all hot, all hot!"

The sensual satisfactions of Cokaygne continue to be an important part of popular utopian imaginings, as in the famous American tramp song "The Big Rock Candy Mountain," which tells of the land where "the sun shines every day / On the birds and the bees and the cigarette trees, / And the lemonade springs where the bluebird sings."[13]

Thomas More's Utopia is devoid of both cigarette trees and sexual license; adultery is punishable, on second offense, with death. Yet it has some elements of the dreams of escape and freedom seen in tales of the Golden Age and Cokaygne. At a time when most Europeans lived in poverty despite long hours of grinding labor, the inhabitants of Utopia work only six hours a day. Moreover, everyone's needs—if not their desires—are fully met by the state. More's *Utopia* is a distinctly modern work, neither a philosophical meditation on justice nor a fantasy of paradise lost, neither chiliastic religious vision nor folk dream of unlimited sensual satisfaction. Instead, at its heart it combines a cry of outrage at poverty and inequality with a conviction that human reason can devise a better world. Throughout the classical and medieval eras, poverty had been seen as inevitable and ineradicable, as much a fact of nature as floods or drought. With the dissolution of the feudal order came new intellectual, as well as economic and social, possibilities, and for the first time it was possible to imagine that a world without want might actually be achieved. *Utopia* stands as one of the first and greatest expressions of the modern conception of social justice. There is a direct line from Raphael Hythloday's outrage that life for the poor means toiling "like cart-horses" to Robert Blatchford's anger at Cradley metalworkers being worked to death for a living that no gentleman would offer his dogs.[14]

Generations of readers and critics have debated whether More's utopian state can be taken as a model of perfection—a doubly fruitless argument, not only because the answer will vary depending on how one weighs the benefits of equality against freedom, but also because More's own intentions are unknowable, hidden behind multiple screens of elaborate banter, wordplay, and the narrative's Chinese-box construction. John Ruskin, throwing up his hands, proclaimed it "perhaps the most really mischievous book ever written." Stephen Duncombe argued more recently that *Utopia* is best seen as a generative tool, a sort of Renaissance technology whose point is not to provide definitive answers to questions about the ideal society but to encourage further speculation.[15]

As a generative tool, *Utopia* was to prove wildly successful. Numerous utopian works followed during the Renaissance, the most notable of which, Tommaso Campanella's *City of the Sun* (1623), owes much to Thomas More. Like *Utopia*, *City of the Sun* is a playful traveler's tale that offers a serious protest against the poverty and inequality of contemporary society. In addition, it describes a form of primitive communism, with no money and an equal distribution of goods. Along with *Utopia*, *City of the Sun* demonstrates how, from its origins, utopian fiction constituted a literature of protest, offering an alternative model of the good life centered on equality and simplicity. Both works challenged the existence of a leisure class and insisted on the worthiness of labor. They also challenged, to some extent, their era's gender inequalities, opening up education— including, remarkably, military training—to women and incorporating women into the workforce, even if limiting them to suitably "womanly" tasks.[16]

Utopia and the City of the Sun are alike also in being tightly controlled and static societies, with virtually no opportunity for growth and change. More's and Campanella's conceptions of an ideal society that is simple, egalitarian, and static was challenged by Francis Bacon's *New Atlantis* (1627), a brief and unfinished work that was published after Bacon's death and that proved to be highly influential. Bacon's work departs significantly from the utopian tradition established by More. Following the traveler's tale convention, *New Atlantis* is narrated by a sailor who happens upon the unknown island of Bensalem. Bacon, however, was uninterested in issues of social equality. Bensalem is fully as hierarchical as Europe, distinguished only by the virtue of its rulers and their subjects' unquestioning submission to authority. Bacon's primary interest lies in Bensalem's most distinctive institution, known as Salomon's House. The heart of *New Atlantis* is a monologue by one of the Fathers of the House, who describes its aim as "the knowledge of Causes, and secret motions of things; and the enlarging of the bounds of Human Empire, to the effecting of all things possible." Salomon's House, in other words, is the prototype of a scientific research institute. Bacon was interested in the dynamic possibilities of the emerging scientific method, and *New Atlantis* can be seen as an origin point of technological utopianism, the belief that science and engineering can create a better world.[17]

The eighteenth century produced countless scientific works that would have delighted Bacon, but it yielded no utopian fictions with the lasting influence of the Renaissance utopias. The most notable fictional utopia of the era is Louis-Sébastien Mercier's *The Year 2440* (1771), narrated by a Parisian who falls asleep in 1768, only to awaken 732 years in the future.[18] Mercier's work was immensely popular; it went through at least twenty-five editions in France and was widely translated. It was also among the first works to depart from the traveler's tale convention and to locate utopia in the future. By placing their alternative societies in the future, Mercier and his successors implicitly announced that a better world was historically achievable, transferring the idea of utopia from "an undiscovered *somewhere* to a forthcoming *somewhen*," in Chris Jennings's apt phrase.[19]

Mercier's work turned out to be remarkably prescient. He imagined a postmonarchical French republic, and his narrator, soon after awakening, finds that the Paris Bastille, the prison that represented the Bourbon kings' absolute power, has been destroyed. Mercier's republican vision was effectively realized less than twenty years afterward in the French Revolution. The revolution, which radically reimagined not only the system of government but many details of everyday life, can be seen as the most ambitious utopian experiment in history up to that point. Like the authoritarian utopian experiments of the twentieth century, it involved considerable bloodshed and terror and, after a period, fell apart; however, the revolution's temporary success, its demonstration that dramatic social change could be effected in a remarkably brief time, inspired visionaries across Europe and America. As the industrial revolution surged, simultaneously upsetting old hierarchies and creating new inequalities, radical intellectuals in Europe and the United States devised schemes for the total reconstruction of society. The earliest and boldest of these thinkers were the utopian socialists.

Nowhere in the Worst of Times

Henri de Saint-Simon, Robert Owen, and Charles Fourier did not regard themselves as "utopian socialists"; that label was affixed to them retrospectively by Marx and Engels. The three earlier writers did not consider themselves to be a group—each was too enamored of his individual genius for that. They wrote their major works before the term "socialism" entered the French and English languages in the 1830s, and they would have rejected the label "utopian." The famous utopians of the past wrote speculative fiction, while they saw themselves as the discoverers of new, scientifically demonstrable social truths.[20]

Saint-Simon, an aristocrat who threw in his lot with the common people during the French Revolution, was relatively modest in his aims compared to Owen and Fourier. They imagined a radical transformation of daily life; Saint-Simon wanted merely to revolutionize politics and government. Born in 1760, he came of age in a system dominated by the nobility, clergy, judiciary, and military. Fired by the ideals of liberty, equality, and fraternity, he spent the last two decades of his life outlining an elaborate system that would put government in the hands of men of genius: scientists, artists, and industrialists. Under their benign meritocratic direction, poverty would be eliminated and class hostility would disappear.[21] Saint-Simon's writings had relatively little influence during his lifetime, but in the decade after his death in 1825 a coterie of energetic disciples spread Saint-Simonian doctrines throughout France. Saint-Simon's fame, however, never approached that of Owen and Fourier, whose ideas reached millions in Europe and the United States.

During the early nineteenth century, Robert Owen was famous throughout Europe as the managing partner of a model factory in New Lanark, Scotland. Thousands of visitors toured the cotton mill each year, drawn by Owen's benevolent reforms and by his genius for self-promotion; however, Owen's ambitions extended far beyond New Lanark. In 1817 the forty-six-year-old Owen began a series of lectures and publications aimed at transforming his entire society. His program was based on the establishment of what he called "Agricultural and Manufacturing Villages of Unity and Mutual Cooperation." He imagined reorganizing society into villages of one to two thousand people, housed together in a grandiose structure that he called a "parallelogram." These villages would counter the philosophy of "individual interest" that dominated British society and foster a culture of communalism. Thanks to the system of education to be instituted in the villages, human nature would be transformed. "It is of all truths the most important, that the character of man is formed FOR—not BY himself"—this was Owen's Great Truth, which for the rest of his life he repeated in countless variations. The villages of mutual cooperation were the means by which human character was to be remade, and during the 1820s he withdrew from active management of the New Lanark mill in order to devote himself to realizing his utopian scheme.[22]

In 1824 he embarked for America on an apostolic mission. He had determined that he could institute a model village in the U.S. for a fraction of the price it would cost in Britain, and soon after arriving he purchased the extensive property of a religious community that was relocating from its site of Harmony, Indiana. Early in 1825, the first Agricultural and Manufacturing Village of Unity and Mutual Cooperation, renamed New Harmony, began receiving settlers. Within two years, the settlement had fallen apart. Nevertheless, New Harmony served as one of the most important utopian experiments in history. The first nonsectarian socialist community to be founded in either the U.S. or Europe, it inspired the founding of almost thirty other communities in North America and Great Britain during the three decades after 1825. The last Owenite community folded in 1863, but Owenism remained a major force in nineteenth-century reform. Late in the century Friedrich Engels claimed that Owen was, for a time, "the most popular man in Europe," and he said that "every social movement, every real advance in England on behalf of the workers links itself on to the name of Robert Owen."[23] In addition, numerous women in Britain and America were inspired by Owen, recognizing the liberatory potential within Owenite communalism. The shared approach to cooking, housework, and childcare promised to free women from the bounds of the patriarchal nuclear family, and Owen suggested that women could be full political actors in communal decision-making. The reality never lived up to the promise; nevertheless, utopian socialist communities provided at least a partial refuge for women seeking release from the straitjacket of nineteenth-century gender ideology, and the Owenite communal movement served as a training ground for a generation of women's rights activists.[24]

In the United States, Owenism's considerable influence on feminist, working-class, and social reform movements was exceeded by the enormous popularity of the concurrent movement of Associationism, the name American adherents gave to the doctrines of Charles Fourier. Fourier, born to an affluent middle-class family in southern France in 1772, lost his inheritance when he was imprisoned after the French Revolution and his family property was confiscated. The experience gave him a visceral foundation for views that were shared by millions in America and Britain: an optimistic sense of the possibilities for profound change in political and social arrangements combined with a profound distaste for revolutionary violence as a means to that end. Following the revolution, Fourier became a traveling salesman for a Lyon cloth merchant, and for most of his life he continued to work as a salesman and clerk. Externally, Fourier's life was meager. He never married or, so far as is known, had any significant romantic relationship; he lived in modest circumstances for his entire adult life; and he was so secretive and suspicious of others that, though he attracted disciples, he had few real friends.[25]

Fourier possessed, however, an extraordinarily rich social imagination, which was expressed in an outpouring of idiosyncratic writing, beginning in 1803 and continuing until his death in 1837. A legend in his own mind, he compared himself to Isaac Newton; Newton had explained the laws of gravitational attraction, while Fourier had discovered the laws of "passionate attraction." Fourier's grand theory, like Owen's, combined psychological and social/communal dimensions; however, whereas Owenite psychology rested on the single insight that human character was determined by the environment, Fourier's theory of personality had all the baroque elaboration of the Palais de Versailles. He believed that humans were actuated by twelve different drives, or "passions," and he determined, through a "calculus of passionate attraction," that humanity could be divided into 810 distinct personality types. Fourier's name for his utopia was "Harmony"—an understandably popular place name among nineteenth-century utopians. Employing an analogy with musical harmony, Fourier arranged his personality types on a scale from Solitones (people dominated by a single passion, such as ambition or love) to Heptatones (a more sophisticated mixture of seven of the twelve passions).[26]

Fourier's hatred of contemporary civilization in part resembled Owen's and Saint-Simon's; all three men were appalled by the poverty, inequality, and wretched working conditions of early industrial Europe. Fourier's theory of personality, however, led him toward a more extensive critique. It was not enough, he believed, to end poverty and improve working conditions; work itself had to be radically reconceived. Applying his concept of human passions, he elaborated a theory of "attractive" labor. Owen's utopian imagination did not extend beyond a reduction of hours for his village workers and early retirement at sixty. Fourier, in contrast, imagined a world in which labor became inseparable from pleasure; in which workers were matched with tasks depending on their personality types; in which work was performed alongside like-minded fellows, with leadership rotating among the group; and in which no one worked at a task for more than two hours before switching to another. This method, he wrote, "is dictated by the eleventh passion, the *Butterfly*, which impels men and women to flit from pleasure to pleasure, to avoid the excesses that ceaselessly plague the people of [current] civilization

who prolong a job for six hours."[27] Since all people had some element of the Butterfly passion, the multiplicity of a workday in Harmony would ensure happiness for all.

In the utopian future of Harmony, citizens would perform their
work in communal settlements called "phalanxes." The ideal number of people in each phalanx was 1,620, allowing for two representatives of each personality type. With uncharacteristic laxness, Fourier suggested that if around 1,800 people were randomly assembled,
the phalanx would function well enough. Working independently of
Owen but along similar lines, he envisioned that inhabitants of the
phalanx would live communally in a single large building, called a
phalanstery, laid out on harmonious geometrical principles.

With his theory of personality settled, the phalanx envisioned,
work schedules settled, and the phalanstery designed, all that was
needed was a wealthy benefactor to fund the first Fourier-inspired
community. During the last decade of his life, Fourier made sure to
be available at noon each day in his Paris apartment, ready to receive
a philanthropic millionaire. His Maecenas never arrived. Instead,
in 1832 he received a visit from Albert Brisbane, an intellectually
curious young American who had been traveling around Europe,
calling on men of genius. Fourier, fearful that this foreigner wished
to steal his ideas, wanted nothing to do with Brisbane. The resource-
ful American hit on the idea of offering the elderly philosopher five
francs an hour for tutorials in his ideas. Following his return to
America in 1834, Brisbane became a full-time propagandist for Fourierism or, as he decided to call it, Associationism.[28]

Americans were introduced to Fourier through books and newspaper columns by Brisbane, since no English translation of Fourier's
works was available until the 1850s. This was just as well, since Brisbane emphasized Fourier's ideas about labor and community and
downplayed the sexual dimensions of the Frenchman's theories of
the passions. Fourier had imagined a "new amorous world" com-
plementing his "new industrial world," and he described this world
of erotic satisfaction in exuberant detail. He believed that every
person deserved not just a satisfying work life but a satisfying sexual life, and he had no patience for what he saw as the stultifying
bourgeois institution of marriage, which he, along with many
other nineteenth-century radicals, regarded as a form of legalized

prostitution. Fourier believed that, once women received the same legal and economic rights as men, they would have no reason to marry and would prefer to participate in the nightly amorous adventures that he envisioned as a vital part of life in the phalanx. Fourier used the term "orgy" to describe these nightly rituals, but he imagined a sort of Higher Orgy, in which community elders would facilitate the sexual couplings, relying on their knowledge of citizens' personality types. In the Fourierist phalanx, no one would be poor, no one would toil at detestable labor, and no one would be left lonely and sexually frustrated.[29]

Brisbane gingerly detoured past the sexual dimensions of Fourier's utopian vision, though more cosmopolitan Americans understood the erotic implications of the theory of passionate attraction; Ralph Waldo Emerson dismissed Fourierism as "a calculation how to secure the greatest amount of kissing that the infirmity of the human constitution admitted."[30] Kissing aside, many other reform-minded intellectuals, along with idealistic working-class women and men, were attracted to the notion of establishing a Fourierist phalanx. Nearly thirty Fourierist communities were founded in the United States during the 1840s, amidst an enthusiasm for communal utopian experiments that was unequaled until the 1970s. Emerson, skeptical of the movement but nevertheless impressed by its force, quipped to Thomas Carlyle in 1840, "We are all a little wild here with numberless projects of social reform. Not a reading man but has a draft of a new Community in his waistcoat pocket."[31]

Emerson was directly familiar with one new community, Brook Farm, located not far from Boston. Founded in 1841 by George Ripley, a fellow Transcendentalist, Brook Farm originally had no formal connection with the fledgling Associationist movement, but three years into its existence it declared its allegiance to Fourierist principles. Brook Farm is the best known of the antebellum American utopian communities, in part because of its connection to Emerson and other eminent intellectuals, in part because of *The Blithedale Romance* (1852), a novel about a lightly disguised version of Brook Farm, written by former resident Nathaniel Hawthorne. Remarkably, Hawthorne, whose fundamentally conservative view of society is evident in all his mature fiction, was one of the first members of Brook Farm, arriving only weeks after its founding. In the novel he published a decade after his seven-month experience at Brook Farm, he labeled it an "exploded scheme for beginning the life of Paradise anew"; however, Hawthorne moved to Brook Farm with great expectations, and while he was there he wrote his sister, without irony, that "such a delectable way of life has never been seen on earth, since the days of the early Christians." Hawthorne never fully renounced his youthful idealism and enthusiasm; the narrator of *Blithedale Romance*, seemingly speaking for the author, says, "Whatever else I may repent of, . . . let it be reckoned neither among my sins nor follies that I once had faith and force enough to form generous hopes of the world's destiny."[32]

Other Brook Farm residents were even more positive about the experience, despite the community's dissolution after only six years. Rebecca Codman Butterfield concluded her memoir of her four years at Brook Farm with a list of its many advantages over "our present isolated imperfect form of social organization." The list includes "Superior Educational Advantages for All," "The Doing Away with the False Relation of Employer and Employed," and "The Full Recognition of the Equality of the Sexes." Fourierism promoted values and reforms that were widely embraced by nineteenth-century progressives. Carl Guarneri has estimated that perhaps one hundred thousand Americans were affiliated with the movement in some way, and F. O. Matthiessen wrote that the period he labeled the "American Renaissance" could as well be called the "Age of Fourier."[33]

The enthusiasm for transforming society through model communities, whether inspired by Owen, Fourier, or some other visionary, peaked during the 1840s. Both secular and religious communities continued to be established throughout the nineteenth century in the U.S. and Great Britain, though not at the same rate, and none achieved the prominence of Brook Farm. As Krishan Kumar observed, late nineteenth-century communes were generally considered a retreat from mainstream society rather than a means of transforming it.[34] What was behind this shift? There were many factors, though the principal one is doubtless the increasing pace of industrialization and urbanization. Owen and Fourier came to maturity during the late eighteenth century, when the majority of people in both Europe and North America lived on farms or in villages and small towns. Massive industrialization did not seem inevitable. It was possible to imagine a modern future in which the current patchwork of small landholdings and workshops was replaced by rationally planned villages with common agricultural plots and communally managed small-scale industries. By the late nineteenth century, however, it was clear to most observers that the pace of change was irreversible, and it became more difficult to envision a future without big cities and massive factories.

Yet far from killing off utopian longings, the urbanized, technologically advanced civilization of the late nineteenth century spurred a new wave of utopianism that was fully as grand and optimistic as the visions of Owen and Fourier. These new utopians, however, rejected their predecessors' idea that the path to utopia would be blazed by small, self-contained communities. Model communities had not changed the world; a different approach was needed. The new utopian thinkers, born more than sixty years after the utopian socialists, were raised in a world where industrial capitalism and new technologies of transportation and communication fostered the growth of an interdependent, unified nation—a process that, in the United States, was violently accelerated by the Civil War. Plans for model communities were superseded by concepts of transformation at the national level.

No one better exemplifies the ambitious national reach of late nineteenth-century utopian thinkers than Henry George. George, a self-educated journalist who dabbled in Democratic Party politics, led a hand-to-mouth existence in San Francisco until he turned forty. That year he published *Progress and Poverty* (1879), a long-winded book that purported to revolutionize economic theory. Remarkably, the book became an enormous international sensation, selling over two million copies and making George a celebrity. British newspapers called him "George the Fifth" and "the prophet of San Francisco"; George Bernard Shaw claimed that five out of six British socialists in the early 1880s had been swept into the movement by Henry George. In 1886, at the height of his popularity, he ran for mayor of New York as a third-party candidate and nearly won, trailing the Tammany Hall Democrat but outpolling the Republican candidate, a young rising star named Theodore Roosevelt.[35]

George's career as a messianic economic crusader began ten years before the publication of *Progress and Poverty* when a casual conversation with a stranger led to an epiphany: all economic distress had a single cause, the private ownership of land. With this flash of insight, George believed that he had solved the greatest conundrum of the nineteenth century: why, in spite of industrial progress and rising wealth, did low wages, poverty, and unemployment persist? The answer was that the share of wealth due to workers was instead going to landlords. With the economic problem identified, the solution was simple: not public ownership of land, which smacked of Continental socialism, but the appropriation of all profits on land through taxation. A tax on land values would generate so much revenue and so increase productivity that all other taxes could be eliminated—hence the label "Single Tax" affixed to George's program.

Economically, George's analysis was shaky, a problem concealed in *Progress and Poverty* by masses of verbiage, some adroit mathematical formulas, and a flurry of references to classical economists such as Adam Smith, David Ricardo, and John Stuart Mill that few readers were in a position to dispute. However, the appeal of the book was never its economic rigor but the simplicity of its proposals, its evangelical style, and its utopian vision. George promised that modern society's problems could be solved without class warfare or even class rancor. In his view, there was no reason for conflict between capital and labor; the venturesome capitalist and the honest workingman were united in their interests against the landowner. Once the landowner's unjustly earned wealth was appropriated through the Single Tax, society would advance effortlessly toward utopia. This "simple yet sovereign remedy," he promised, "will raise wages, increase the earnings of capital, extirpate pauperism, abolish poverty, give remunerative employment to whoever wishes it, afford free scope to human powers, lessen crime, elevate morals, and taste, and intelligence, purify government and carry civilization to yet nobler heights." In the penultimate chapter of the book, George's rhetoric soared even higher as he described the Single Tax future: "It is the Golden Age of which poets have sung and high-raised seers have told in metaphor! It is the glorious vision which has always haunted man with gleams of fitful splendor! ... It is the culmination of

Christianity—the City of God on earth, with its walls of jasper and its gates of pearl! It is the reign of the Prince of Peace!"[36] George's Christian millennial rhetoric appealed to countless readers in both the U.S. and Great Britain who, even if they were not themselves evangelical Christians, had come of age in a mid-nineteenth-century culture permeated by evangelical idealism. George offered a simple, tranquil path to utopia, negotiating between, on one hand, a seemingly rapacious plutocracy and, on the other, the working-class violence that was feared in the U.K. and vividly exemplified in the U.S. during the years following the Great Strike of 1877.

George's popularity declined rapidly following his near-win in the 1886 New York City mayor's race. In Britain, his support dissipated as Irish activists turned their attention from issues of land ownership to Home Rule, political leftists abandoned the Single Tax for a broader socialist program, and academic economists humiliated George at debates that exposed his shaky understanding of the field. In the U.S., he lost working-class support when his distrust of labor union activism became obvious, and his progressive credentials were permanently tarnished when he declared support for the execution of the Haymarket anarchists. By the late 1880s, the Single Tax crusade had become a fringe movement.

Yet the utopian longings that made Henry George a hero had not dissipated. Millions of people in both the United States and Great Britain remained convinced that their societies were on the brink of disaster, with class antagonism ready to explode into violence. Influenced by a waning but still powerful culture of Christian evangelicalism, they were eager to believe that a simple, nonviolent solution could usher in the millennium, that a brutally competitive capitalist system could be transformed into a "cooperative commonwealth"—a phrase that served as the title of an influential economic tract of 1884.[37] They were prepared to embrace a prophetic utopian vision pointing the way toward a peaceful, harmonious future. They were ready, in other words, for Edward Bellamy's *Looking Backward*.

CHAPTER TWO

Edward Bellamy's Orderly Utopia

NOT LONG AFTER HIS THIRTY-SEVENTH BIRTHDAY, in 1887, Edward Bellamy was handed one of those opportunities for self-assessment that people at midlife often welcome. The occasion was a questionnaire from his college fraternity, which was compiling a biographical directory of alumni. It had been exactly twenty years since Bellamy joined the fraternity, and he seized the chance to review the past two decades, carefully answering the four-page questionnaire even though, as he admitted, he had been in college only a few months. Union College, in upstate New York, had been a last-minute choice. Since boyhood, he had been planning to attend West Point. He easily passed West Point's entrance exam but, when he arrived at the military academy, failed the physical; the doctors may have detected the tuberculosis that was to kill him three decades later. He turned to Union for lack of a better alternative. His older brother Fred was there, and he could enter at the last minute as a nonmatriculated student and study English literature, his only passion aside from the military. It did not work out, and he left college after a semester.

Still, Bellamy remembered Union College fondly enough, and the fraternity questionnaire gave him an excuse to review the past twenty years. He noted that after leaving college he had studied law and was admitted to the bar but never practiced. His current profession was "writing books, contributing to magazines, newspaper work, general scribbling." In answer to a question about publications, he wrote simply that he had published "three or four romances in book form and an indefinite number of magazine contributions." Bellamy was being modest; two of his books had won the praise of William Dean Howells, the era's most eminent man of letters. In a review of Bellamy's most recent novel, Howells had compared him to Hawthorne. Still, Bellamy knew he was scarcely a household name; he was a midlist author, earning just enough to support his family in comfortable middle-class style.[1]

Bellamy had no idea that, within two years, he would become one of the most famous authors in the world. *Looking Backward*, the utopian romance that appeared just a few months after he completed his fraternity questionnaire, became an enormous international best-seller. It sold half a million copies in the U.S., two hundred thousand copies in Great Britain, and was soon translated into fifteen foreign languages. It was hailed as the *Uncle Tom's Cabin* of the industrial era and, like its predecessor, had effects far beyond the world of literature. *Looking Backward* inspired a political movement, Nationalism, that had adherents across the U.S. and Great Britain and that, in America, presented candidates for office, sponsored legislation, and had a significant influence in the presidential election of 1892. Edward Bellamy, an intensely private man, was transformed into an international political figure.

Bellamy had located his utopia in the year 2000. In the euphoria of his early success, he claimed that a century was needlessly generous; the great change would come within fifty years. It did not, although there was a revival of interest in *Looking Backward* in the 1930s, and "Bellamy Clubs" were established across the U.S. and Europe. Then the novel sank largely out of sight, only to be revived in the 1980s, as its hundredth anniversary approached and historians turned their attention to the once-famous book. What they found there appalled them: Bellamy's utopia was an academic's nightmare, a highly regimented state that seemed closer to Stalin's Soviet Union than to Shangri-La. In 1982 a historian published a major revisionist study of Bellamy that set the tone for dozens of subsequent analyses; its title was *Authoritarian Socialism in America*.[2]

FIGURE 2.1 Edward Bellamy. Arthur E. Morgan, *Edward Bellamy*
(New York: Columbia University Press, 1944).

The title is dramatic but not entirely unjustified; Bellamy's utopian envisionings have an authoritarian tinge. Yet his book inspired
hundreds of thousands of readers in the late nineteenth century and
had an effect on political movements that were embraced by millions. It fueled a vogue for utopian fiction that persisted for a
quarter-century after its appearance, with the publication of more
than five hundred English-language works between 1889 and 1914.[3]
Viewed in the context of Bellamy's generally quiet life and frequently
turbulent times, *Looking Backward* becomes a more complex text
than either its contemporary admirers or subsequent critics would
allow, and Bellamy's utopian vision reveals depths both abysmal and
profound.

Edward Bellamy's father, Rufus, was a Baptist minister, but the religious tone of the household was set by his wife, Maria Putnam Bellamy—fair, delicate, and fiercely pious. Rufus was her opposite: easygoing, rotund. A neighbor in the industrial mill town of Chicopee Falls, Massachusetts, described him as "a chunky fellow who could roll endwise as easily as over and over." Young couples sought him out to officiate at their weddings. He was known for palming the fee the groom gave him and immediately turning it over to the bride: "Some pin-money for you," he would whisper confidentially. Maria was a more formidable figure. "I was scared to death of her," one of Rufus's female parishioners recalled. "She was very critical. She would go at things the hardest way and expected others to do the same." Edward's brother Fred said that her chief concern, "next to revealed religion," was "a high aim in life." The letter she wrote to Edward on his twenty-first birthday reveals her moral and spiritual earnestness: "May the best of blessings be yours, and chiefest among them a heart to consecrate yourself a 'living sacrifice' to your God and Saviour."[4]

As an adolescent, Edward fully embraced his mother's religious intensity. An earnest boyhood essay that he—or more likely his mother—saved for posterity begins, "That there is an almighty, ever-existing, overruling God, the Source of all created things animate and inanimate, . . . who among sane men can doubt?" When he was fourteen, he followed the pattern set for good Baptist youth: he had a conversion experience and was baptized into the church. Of course, for most young people conversion and church membership were largely pro forma; for Edward, however, the experience was overwhelming. He would hurry home from school so that he could pray—not that he was petitioning God for anything, but simply so that he could feel absorbed in the divine. He wondered how he had ever gotten along without Christ being constantly in his heart, and he pitied others their prayerless, godless state. His prayers at night roused him to ecstatic visions of heaven, and he fell asleep with a feeling of exultation at the thought that he might die before morning.[5]

This heroic Christianity proved only a phase. The dreams of military heroism were more constant. As a ten-year-old, he compiled a list of the qualities he thought necessary to a soldier: self-control, obedience to orders, bravery, attention—this last "in order to learn and know more, besides it looks better." He made meticulous lists of the battles of the Revolutionary War and of Napoleon's twenty-six marshals, signing the latter "E. S. Bellamie," transforming his surname into one more likely to appear on some future list of Napoleonic officers. The Civil War erupted when he was eleven; for four years he was immersed in daily reports of the struggle to save the Union. Once the war was concluded, he pored over military histories, read biographies of Napoleon and Admiral Nelson.[6] When, at seventeen, he was rejected from West Point, he was at a complete loss. He would have to rewrite the narrative of his future life, which had seemed so firmly scripted.

His semester at Union College failed to provide any alternative vision of the future. He was at loose ends in Chicopee Falls when he was invited to join his cousin William in Germany. The two young men settled in Dresden, where they lodged with a German family and studied at the university. Years later, Bellamy glibly claimed to an interviewer that the only thing he learned in Germany was to drink beer, but his letters home to his brother Fred recorded his shock at European poverty, his dismay at his first glimpses of urban slums and peasant hovels. He and William debated the socialist theories that abounded in 1860s Germany without coming to any resolution, but they were both obsessed with the problem of inequality.[7]

When he returned to Chicopee Falls in 1869, Bellamy looked at his hometown with new eyes. He had viewed it as a village without extremes of either wealth or poverty, where anyone willing to work was sure of a fair living. In fact, it was not the bucolic Yankee village of Bellamy's recollection. Chicopee—the town comprising the contiguous settlements of Chicopee Falls and Chicopee Center—had become an industrial center in the early nineteenth century. The Chicopee River provided the power for cotton mills and armament factories, and young women and men left marginal New England farms for employment in the rapidly expanding factories. Later they were replaced by impoverished Irish immigrants, and by 1858 two-thirds of the workers were Irish. The workday was twelve hours, six days a week; the median earnings of mill girls in the 1850s were between two and three dollars a week. The ten-hour workday was not established until 1874, and it applied only to women and children.[8]

The Bellamy family lived in a handsome Victorian wood-framed house on a rise overlooking the river and mills. They were not rich, but Rufus Bellamy was more comfortable than the average minister, receiving rents from a block of commercial buildings that he owned. The family's professional and social circles were centered in the Baptist church, whose members were solidly middle class and native-born; the Irish millworkers were looked after by Catholic priests.

Before he went to Europe, Bellamy was oblivious to the class differences in his town. On his return, he recognized that, even in Chicopee, an "inferno of poverty" surged beneath the seemingly placid surface.[9] His experience in Europe had defamiliarized his hometown, and the young man struggled to express his newfound dismay at the inequality of social conditions. He found an outlet in the local lyceum, the adult education forum of small-town America during the nineteenth century. Two years after his return from Europe, Bellamy delivered at least three short addresses to the Chicopee Falls Lyceum. One of them, on the topic of popular education, was little more than an exercise in high-style Victorian oratory, but two of the addresses, although filled with grandiose rhetoric, reveal a young man's genuine shock at the poverty and inequality surrounding him and his certainty that something must be done. The first address, "The Barbarism of Society," harkened back to the abolitionist rhetoric of the antebellum years in its condemnation of industrial slavery: "a slavery whose prison is the world, whose shackles and fetters are the unyielding frame of society, whose lash is hunger, whose taskmasters are those bodily necessities for whose supply the rich who hold the keys of the world's granaries must be appealed to, and the necks of the needy bowed to their yoke as the price of the boon of life."[10] The stiff diction and furbelowed syntax show a young man perfecting his oratorical skills, but there is no reason to think that Bellamy was not in earnest.

Several weeks later, Bellamy took up the same topic again, but this time he named a remedy: socialism. He was vague about what a socialist system would entail, but he promised that it would introduce "an era of a more perfect liberty and happiness than the world has ever known." In the 1870s, with Owenite and Associationist communitarianism a generation in the past, few of Bellamy's listeners in Chicopee Falls would have had any direct knowledge of socialism. At the time, the only declared socialists in North America were a few thousand German immigrants familiar with the works of Karl Marx. In small-town New England, the signifier "socialism" was available for appropriation, and Bellamy used it as a synonym for "utopia," promising that the socialist future would be a "new world of ... peace and liberty and happiness." Bellamy's youthful enthusiasm for a vaguely delineated socialism demonstrates the applicability of social theorist Zygmunt Bauman's argument that, starting with its origins in the early nineteenth century, socialism served as a counterculture to capitalism, a future-oriented imaginative possibility inextricably connected with utopian thinking.[11]

Bellamy, who was probably twenty when he made his lyceum speeches, may have been trying on roles. Defending socialism could serve as a nineteenth-century equivalent of showing up at a family reunion with a pierced nose or prominent tattoo. Still, the two lyceum speeches show his estrangement, to at least some degree, from the social and economic status quo of post–Civil War New England, his dismay at poverty and inequality, and his longing for a better, transformed world.

In the meantime he had to make a career for himself. The military was out; he had tried and abandoned college; perhaps he should follow the example of his brother Fred and take up the law. In 1869, when Bellamy returned from Germany and was casting about for a profession, it was still possible to become a lawyer through an apprenticeship system, and that fall he began to "read law" at a firm in Springfield, the city adjacent to Chicopee. Less than two years later, he was admitted to the bar and opened his own office in Chicopee Falls.

In an unpublished autobiographical novel that Bellamy worked on during his twenties, the central character decides to study law, imagining that he will be engaged in "the arguing of great constitutional questions, the chivalrous defense of the widow and orphan, ... and the vindication of accused and sorely beset innocence." In reality, Edward Bellamy's first case involved the prosecution of a widow for nonpayment of rent. It was also his last case; he quit the law in disgust. He used his novel to record a tirade against "the dirty trade of a local pettifogger."[12]

At twenty-one, he found himself with an unused license to practice law and no profession. Soon enough, he found his way into journalism with a position on the *Daily Union* in nearby Springfield, Massachusetts. During his five years with the *Daily Union*, Bellamy turned out hundreds of book reviews and editorials. Thankfully, the editorials lack the linguistic ornateness of his lyceum addresses, but they reveal a young man still trying on roles. The voice he adopted as editorial writer was that of a mature, judicious Victorian patriarch, a mild progressive who consistently tempers his positions with on-the-other-hand gestures. He supported women's suffrage but ridiculed efforts to change laws pertaining to divorce or property rights. He decried economic inequality but considered communism to be "lunacy." He deplored a Saratoga's hotel exclusion of Jews but criticized Jewish "vulgarity."[13] During his twenties, Bellamy played the role of solid New England Republican in his professional life. His unpublished writings of the 1870s, however, reveal a conflicted and unconventional young man with a deep and intriguing spiritual life and a Napoleonic sense of his own destiny.

❧

During his twenties, Bellamy turned his back on his adolescent conversion and his parents' Protestant beliefs. His reasons were in part theological and in part stemmed from the gender anxiety common among middle-class men of his era. Theologically, Bellamy found himself in agreement with the many American religious liberals who regarded the Judeo-Christian conception of God as divine sovereign as a fundamentally feudal notion, unsuitable for a modern, democratic age. "Ordinary religion is different in degree (not as it should be, in kind) from loyalty to earthly sovereigns," Bellamy wrote in his journal. He was equally uncomfortable with the conventional conception of Jesus. "The relation established by Christianity between the believer and Christ makes a woman of the former, tending as it does peculiarly to cultivate the feminine graces of trustfulness and confidence in protection to be paid by love," he wrote. "It is better adapted to women than men on whose minds it has an effect to degenerate the masculine virtues of self-reliance and valor."[14]

Bellamy's comment illustrates one of the major crises of nineteenth-century American Protestantism: the perceived "feminization" of religion. Starting with the Great Awakening of the eighteenth century, American Calvinism was challenged by an emotionally fervent evangelicalism that stressed the necessity of ecstatic conversion, a "surrender" to Jesus. By the 1860s, when Bellamy was converted, evangelical emotionalism permeated New England Protestantism. In the conventionally gendered thinking of the era, "male" Calvinist rationalism had been superseded by "female" emotion.

The postwar years proved to be an anxious time for middle-class American men. The relatively stable antebellum class structure and the masculine ideals it supported were subjected to intense stresses by the era's rapidly increasing urbanization and industrialization. As a new class of industrialists amassed enormous wealth during the era that Mark Twain and Charles Warner labeled "the Gilded Age," middle-class intellectuals saw their cultural authority and prestige diminish. American manhood was being redefined, and Bellamy was representative of countless middle-class men who, in an anxious attempt to shore up their masculinity, rejected a conventional Christianity that they saw as both outmoded and feminized.[15]

Bellamy turned to alternative modes of spirituality. His notebooks and unpublished writings reveal that he spent his twenties earnestly working out, on paper, his religious beliefs. He generally wrote as if he were the first person ever to grapple with what a post-Christian, nontheistic spirituality might entail, but his notebooks offer a classic example of late nineteenth-century liberal spirituality fed by multiple streams. Bellamy acknowledged only two influences: Auguste Comte, the French intellectual who stripped Catholicism of its theological base but adapted its elaborate ritualistic superstructure for what he called the "Religion of Humanity"; and Henry Ward Beecher, the charismatic Congregational preacher who rejected the Calvinist emphasis on original sin and salvation of the elect in favor of a liberal theology that emphasized a loving God who offered redemption to all.[16]

Bellamy's religious musings echo the humanistic strains in both Comte and Beecher, but they also reveal the much more powerful influence of Ralph Waldo Emerson. Bellamy never mentions Emerson, yet his incomplete, unpublished essays on religion are Emersonian in both substance and style. It seems as if Bellamy did not acknowledge Emerson not because the older writer's influence was small, but because it was so large. Bellamy's essays don't simply show a debt to Emerson; it's as if they are trying to *be* essays by Emerson.[17]

Almost all the essential Emersonian themes are prominent in Bellamy's writings about religion. A mystical apprehension of the natural world is at the center of both writers' religious experience. Bellamy wrote in "The Religion of Solidarity," the longest and most complete of his youthful essays, that "there are times in the experience of most persons of emotional temperament in which this desire (I had almost called it lust) after natural beauty amounts to a veritable orgasm." He went on to interpret this orgasmic yearning for union with nature as a sign that we are "homesick for a vaster mansion than the personality affords, with an unconquerable yearning, a divine discontent tending elsewhere."[18] If this "yearning" had feminine elements, his sexual imagery of a feminized nature subjected to male lust laid to rest any masculine anxieties.

Both Emerson and Bellamy rejected orthodox religion in favor of a humanistic creed that located the divine within individuals as well as in the natural world. Both identified a dual life within each person: the individual consciousness and a larger self that includes all creation. Emerson called the larger self the "Over-Soul"; Bellamy labeled it the "Universal soul." He succinctly summed up his philosophy of the dual life with his claim that "the co-existence of this Universal soul with the certain soul of individuality makes up human life and explains its riddle."[19]

Bellamy, however, differed significantly from Emerson in the moral conclusions he drew from Transcendentalism. Believing that each human soul is divine, Emerson encouraged his readers' individualism: "Trust thyself; every heart vibrates to that iron string," he wrote in "Self-Reliance." He revealed that when his "genius"—his individual spirit—called, he shunned father and mother and wife and brother. Bellamy rejected individualism. He defined genius as

"the vivid partaking of the soul of solidarity. . . . To be possessed of
his genius, the man must be unconscious of his personality; he must
be beside himself, even as the Delphic priestess was required to be
before the oracle spoke through her."[20] Bellamy's religion of solidarity did not involve self-denial so much as self-abandonment, a rejection of the concept of individuality as anything more than a phe-
nomenal manifestation of the universal soul. As Bellamy saw it,
selfishness is possible only if one believes in one's unique selfhood.
Once one realizes that any individual life is only a transitory expression of the universal soul, a morality of unselfishness and self-
sacrifice will naturally follow.

In 1887, the year he completed *Looking Backward*, Bellamy returned to "The Religion of Solidarity," his most substantial early
essay. Writing an addendum on the final page of the manuscript, he
solemnly instructed, "I should like this paper to be read to me when
I am about to die. This tribute I may render without conceit to the
boy of twenty-four who wrote it. This paper . . . represents the germ
of what has been ever since my philosophy of life."[21] The morality
of solidarity suffuses *Looking Backward*. In a chapter of the novel
that has probably been skimmed over by most readers but that Bellamy regarded as the key to his utopian vision, a minister of the
future world delivers a lengthy sermon that restates Bellamy's
youthful essay. Bellamy may have rejected his father's religion, but
he clearly longed for the role of preacher.

⟨⟩

The roots of *Looking Backward* lie not only in Bellamy's religious
musings but also in "Eliot Carson," an unpublished novel with multiple drafts scattered among the young writer's notebooks. "Eliot
Carson" allowed Bellamy to fulfill the fantasy of preaching a new
gospel to a worshipful audience. The novel has two principal versions. In the first, Eliot is the prophet of a new liberal religion that
he enunciates in a series of lengthy monologues delivered to his love
interest Edna. The second focuses on Eliot's vocational crisis at the
age of thirty. He is in line to become manager of the mills in the
town of Hilton—a stand-in for Chicopee Falls—but resigns his position in order to live as a sort of junior Thoreau by his own lake in

the woods. Bellamy never saw any of his "Eliot Carson" drafts through to completion, but the manuscripts provide the single most useful tool for understanding Edward Bellamy in the years leading up to *Looking Backward*. Bellamy's utopian novel is usually interpreted as a political document in the tradition of More's *Utopia*, but it is more revealing to interpret it as a sequel to "Eliot Carson," which in its two principal versions focuses on what Bellamy saw as the two central tasks of modern life: the need to find a single, unifying religion to replace the multiple competing versions of an outmoded Christianity, and the search for a satisfactory balance of labor and leisure.

The first, religiously centered version of "Eliot Carson" sheds fascinating light on Bellamy's utopian imaginings. In part, the novel repeats at greater length the doctrine spelled out in "The Religion of Solidarity": our individuality is an illusion, a trap to be escaped, and freedom is to be found in recognition that one's true self is the universal soul shared by all. This core doctrine is spiced with episodes of nature mysticism and attacks on Christianity, which Eliot calls nothing more than "a little earthly kingdom, set on high." In the peroration of one of several sermons that he delivers to Edna, Eliot offers both a dismissal of all existing religions and a summary of his own good news: "This is the new religion I have to offer you. A religion which, instead of adding one to the vain attempts to explain the deity of God, tells you that you are more god than man, and makes your manhood a trifling thing, compared with the cultivation of your godhead."[22]

For long stretches of the novel, Edna has little to do but listen appreciatively, "with heaving heart and wet eyes," to Eliot's neo-Emersonian sermons.[23] In the earliest drafts, however, Edna is a much more interesting character. Critics generally refer to "Eliot Carson" as an autobiographical novel, but it is more accurately an autobiographical fantasy. Eliot Carson represents Edward Bellamy as he wished to be: an inspired, self-confident person whose manly life in the woods embodies the optimistic religious philosophy that he preaches. Edna represents Bellamy as he actually was: doubtful, questioning, unable to sustain a joyous certainty in the godhead that Eliot assures her is within.

The journals that Bellamy kept in his twenties, while drafting multiple versions of "Eliot Carson," at times reiterate that novel's optimistic spirituality, but they also record Bellamy's black moods, personal anguish, and heavy drinking. Edna is not a tippler in any of the novel's versions, but she is, like Bellamy, a spiritual seeker who painfully disengages from her parents' faith. As a young adult, Bellamy resigned his membership in the Baptist church, and a long section of "Eliot Carson" involves Edna's conversation with her minister, as she confesses her loss of faith and, in the face of his protests, boldly tenders her resignation. The narrator refers to Edna's "reckless spirituality," and she squarely faces the social consequences of her action, acknowledging that, as a female freethinker, she will be ostracized more severely than a man would be. "It is deemed wicked for a man to be an unbeliever in the popular faith," she tells the minister, "but for a woman to be one . . . is thought not only wicked, but unseemly and unwomanly, almost indecent."[24]

In these early drafts of "Eliot Carson," Bellamy revealed a remarkable ability to leave behind not only the dominant religious assumptions of his era but also its gender conventions. He embodied his own religious revolt in an intellectually bold woman who defies her town rather than assent to a creed she no longer believes. Bellamy was, however, unable to sustain his protofeminist insights for even the length of the manuscript. Later in the same version of "Eliot Carson" his protagonist goes off on a conventionally misogynistic rant about women's inability to embrace the true, selfless religion because they are mired in the personal. Nevertheless, the first "Eliot Carson" reveals Bellamy's ability to adopt, if only temporarily, a woman's point of view and foreshadows the profeminist activism that he adopted in the 1890s.

In the second "Eliot Carson," Bellamy abandons both his attention to women's consciousness and his preaching of a post-Christian spirituality in order to focus on the problem of vocation. The Eliot of this version is undergoing an early midlife crisis. Ten years out of college, Eliot is a successful and eminently eligible young bachelor. Paymaster of the woolen mills in Hilton, he is in line to be named the mills' chief manager and is engaged to the lovely Nelly Dona. However, his fiancée's name—a near-rhyme for the poisonous *belladonna*—points to the darker side of Eliot's situation. In an outburst to Nelly, he explains his sense of entrapment: "It is ten years that I have been at work since I left college. In that time I have not read ten books, I have not thought ten hours upon the underlying problems of life without some understanding of which life is a stupidly crazy farce. I have not grown an inch morally or mentally. . . . [If I keep on] I shall have forgotten that there are or ever were any books to read, or any world beyond woolen. As to thinking about anything so impractical as the mystery of existence, the nature of the soul, or the relation of the island of humanity to the great tract of infinity, why I shall have left all that to the parsons."[25]

Most of the novel consists of Eliot's variations on this theme of the conflict between labor and intellectually fruitful leisure. In one of his diatribes to the remarkably forbearing Nelly, Eliot says that every intellectually curious young man faces the same quandary as he: "It is a law of society . . . that at the age of twenty-one or thereabouts mental culture shall cease and the mind be thenceforth be used merely as a tool . . . to weave woolen, to spin cotton, or keep books, or grind off editorials at so much a column." The reference to journalism lays bare the novel's autobiographical heart: Edward Bellamy was grinding off editorials instead of performing the "great work" that, he confided to his journal, awaited him.[26] In 1877, after five years on the *Springfield Daily Union*, Bellamy resigned his position and set off with his brother Fred on a voyage to Hawaii. The brothers were supposedly traveling for their health, but Edward clearly saw the trip as a chance to change his profession; the notebook he kept during his travels is filled with ideas for short stories. When the brothers returned the next year, Edward Bellamy began his career as a fiction writer.

Bellamy's first novel, *Six to One* (1878), was lightweight commercial fiction, a courtship story set on Nantucket, where during the summer season unmarried women supposedly outnumbered men six to one. He soon hit his stride with *Dr. Heidenhoff's Process* (1879), an elaborately plotted romance about a physician who has invented a machine that can extirpate painful memories. William Dean Howells praised the novel and its creator, comparing Bellamy to Hawthorne. Howells, who delighted in nurturing young writers, was being generous; *Dr. Heidenhoff's Process* has little of the metaphoric and psychological power of "The Birthmark" or Hawthorne's other romances of human imperfection. However, Bellamy had found his genre, and during the 1880s he continued to produce high-concept romances that move between contemporary social reality and the realms of dream and fantasy.

Looking Backward, Bellamy claimed, began as one more romance. "I had, at the outset, no idea of attempting a serious contribution to the movement of social reform," he later wrote. "The idea was of a mere literary fantasy, a fairy tale of social felicity." He had an idea for a story set in the year 3000: it would begin with a grand parade of the "industrial army," a workforce of the future that conscripted every young male citizen into its ranks.[27] It was only as he began to write his tale that the fantasy world of the thirty-first century turned into utopia—not merely an imagined *no place* but a *good place* capable of future realization. Excited by his own vision of a peaceable kingdom, Bellamy dialed back the date of his novel by a thousand years; its full title is *Looking Backward, 2000–1887*.

Published in 1888, *Looking Backward* was the first widely popular English-language utopian novel of the nineteenth century. Of course, it had a long foreground. As a well-read journalist and writer, Bellamy would have been familiar with the utopian socialists and the antebellum communal experiments of the Owenites and Associationists. In addition, he almost certainly read John Macnie's *The Diothas* (1883), a fantasy in which, thanks to mesmerism, the narrator is transported to ninety-sixth-century New York, whose inhabitants travel in proto-automobiles that reach the staggering speed of twenty miles per hour. Macnie imagined an egalitarian future in which citizens work only a few hours a day, but his critique of nineteenth-century New York is centered not on the era's poverty and exploitation but on the nefarious influence of Catholic immigrants.[28]

It's likely that Bellamy took the idea of mesmeric time-travel from *The Diothas*, but the spirit of *Looking Backward* is very different from the earlier book's reactionary nativism. *Looking Backward* owes more to Henry George's utopian economic tract *Progress and Poverty* (1879). The novel echoes George's Jeremiah-like condemnation of poverty and social injustice, his belief that a relatively simple economic change could utterly transform a conflict-ridden nation, and his evangelical emphasis on individuals' conversion to the new gospel as a precondition for the transition to utopia. George thought that the Single Tax would open the door to utopia; Bellamy imagined that an industrial army was the key.[29]

The notion of conscripting all workers into a single military-style national organization, so appealing to Bellamy, has horrified his critics, who focus on the authoritarianism inherent in military hierarchies and on the suppression of individualism. Bellamy believed that he had devised safeguards against any abuse of power by the officers of the industrial army. As for the suppression of individualism—that was precisely the point. The nineteenth century was an era, a character in *Looking Backward* remarks, of "excessive individualism."[30] The industrial army is a means of realizing the religion of solidarity that Bellamy had sketched out as a young man. *Looking Backward* combined his lifelong infatuation with the military with his religious yearnings for self-suppressing spiritual unity.

Bellamy was scarcely alone in his admiration for the military. Historian Jackson Lears has argued that a "regenerative militarism" was among the dominant ideologies of post–Civil War America.[31] The countless monuments to the Civil War dead, located in virtually every city hall and town square and university campus across the United States, silently championed the virtues of selfless devotion to a greater cause. When the narrator-hero of *Looking Backward* is abruptly pulled back into the nineteenth century, the only positive sight he encounters is a military parade. "Here at last were order and reason," he exclaims, "an exhibition of what intelligent coöperation can accomplish."[32] In imagining the industrial army of the year 2000, Bellamy created an institution marked not only by order and reason but by a spiritualized solidarity. Soldiers' experience of brotherhood could, he reasoned, be realized within the entire society.

Bellamy's unpublished novel "Eliot Carson" had been an attempt to put the religion of solidarity into fictional form, but the manuscript is all telling and no showing. The utopian romance form of *Looking Backward* enabled Bellamy to depict a world in which his self-invented religion has permeated society. As he worked on the book, he dropped the opening scene of the industrial army marching in a grand review. However, in a nod to his original conception, the novel opens on Decoration Day, 1887—the late nineteenth-century holiday devoted to remembering the fallen soldiers of the Civil War. The valor and self sacrifice of the Union dead serve as implicit contrast to inhabitants of Gilded Age Boston.

Looking Backward's narrator-protagonist, Julian West, is one of the idle rich, a young man whose most strenuous exercise consists of cursing the workmen whose frequent strikes are delaying completion of the house into which he intends to move with his future wife, Edith Bartlett. Julian spends Decoration Day with his fiancée, then returns home, where he retires to a specially built sleeping chamber in his basement. Julian is an insomniac, and on this evening he summons, as he frequently does, a mesmerist who can infallibly put him to sleep. Julian cannot awaken from this mesmeric sleep on his own, but his servant has been trained to break the trance. On this night, however, Julian's house burns down, the servant is killed, and Julian is buried beneath the rubble in his secret subterranean sleeping chamber.

He awakens in the year 2000. Another house has been built on the site, and while digging in the garden, the family living there, the Leetes, discover Julian's buried bedchamber with Julian still asleep inside it. Dr. Leete, a retired physician, brings Julian out of his trance, and the rest of the novel consists principally of conversations between the twentieth-century doctor and his nineteenth-century guest.

Much of their discussion centers on the industrial army, the central institution of Bellamy's utopia. Private enterprise has disappeared, replaced by a comprehensive state socialism. All citizens, both women and men, are conscripted into the workforce army at the age of twenty-one and serve until forty-five, at which point they continue to receive the same salary that they had during their working life—as well as before. In Bellamy's scheme, everyone is allotted an annual stipend at birth and receives this unvarying amount for life. Child or adult, woman or man, worker or retiree, physician or coal miner, able-bodied or not—in the twentieth-century utopia, everyone is economically equal.

Julian is quickly enamored by Dr. Leete's descriptions of the new society. Subtle, or even consistent, characterization was not Bellamy's strong point, and his protagonist, a privileged young man, is almost immediately converted to the utopian point of view. Julian is delighted by the advantages associated with the industrial army: poverty and unemployment have disappeared, class differences have vanished, women have achieved economic parity with men. And there's more: since everyone is equal, crime has been eliminated; since most laws were devoted to regulating commercial transactions and protecting private economic interests, the legal system has withered away; and since class divisions are unknown, political differences do not arise, and party politics have been replaced by a system of efficient, impartial administration.

Julian can see no flaw in this future world nor, evidently, could thousands of Bellamy's nineteenth-century readers. More than a century later, the problems are more evident. *Looking Backward* can seem less a forecast of utopia than a precursor of Orwell's *Nineteen Eighty-Four*. Bellamy's future world seems to leave no room for individualism, for difference, for dissent. The static economic structure provides little opportunity for innovation. In the absence of political and legal systems, there is no institutional avenue for addressing abuses of power or selecting among competing proposals for change. In Chris Ferns's terms, Bellamy's dream of order has eclipsed the human dream of freedom.[33]

Reading *Looking Backward* in the twenty-first century, it's impossible not to recollect the dystopian horrors of the past hundred years: the Soviet gulag, China's Cultural Revolution, Cambodia's Year Zero. Bellamy's contemporary readers, however, approached the novel with experience of different horrors: recurrent financial crises, appalling urban slums, widespread rural poverty, child labor, twelve-hour workdays in dangerous conditions, near-constant labor violence, the Great Strike, the Great Upheaval, the Haymarket affair. The 1880s were an era of apocalyptic imaginings; Julian speaks for many of his contemporaries when he tells Dr. Leete that he would not have been surprised to awaken in a landscape of "charred and moss-grown ruins."[34] The United States seemed to be lurching toward one of three horrific alternatives: repressive plutocracy, lawless anarchy, or a war of total destruction between the two. The society depicted in *Looking Backward* offered a way out.

The regimentation of Bellamy's future society may have seemed unimportant to his readers compared to its utter calm. Their own era's violent antagonism between capital and labor has given way to a tranquil classless society. Moreover, the novel promised that the transition to utopia could be achieved peacefully. Explaining to Julian how their ideal society was achieved, Dr. Leete tells a tale not of violent revolution but of a peaceful process of unfolding evolution. Like other progressive thinkers of his era, Bellamy rejected Herbert Spencer's "social Darwinism," which validated survival of the fittest within a laissez-faire economic system. Instead he embraced Lamarckism, which relied on the pre-Darwinian work of French biologist Jean-Baptiste Lamarck. Lamarck argued that mutations were not random but directed and that evolution led inevitably toward improvement. Nineteenth-century social Lamarckism held that society was similarly evolving toward perfection. Bellamy's contribution was to apply Lamarckian theory to the economic system. In his view, the nineteenth-century trend toward monopolies, trusts, and other forms of business combinations was not something to be attacked but applauded, a necessary step to the nationalization of the entire economic system. As Dr. Leete explains, the concentration of capital was part of "a process of industrial evolution that could not have terminated otherwise. All that society had to do was to recognize and coöperate with that evolution." As he sums up this evolutionary process, "The epoch of trusts . . . ended in The Great Trust." In the witty phrase of Jean Pfaelzer, Bellamy differed from Karl Marx in believing that capitalism contained the seeds of its own perfection.[35]

According to *Looking Backward*'s account of evolutionary change, everyone from workers to plutocrats quickly embraced the new system. As numerous critics have pointed out, however, the book had a particular appeal to the late nineteenth-century middle class.[36] Julian West awakens in the year 2000 in the midst of a family that exactly resembles a Victorian upper-middle-class household, and for the rest of the book he has almost no contact with anyone outside this family. Dr. Leete is an articulate retired physician; his daughter Edith is a beautiful young woman whose only obvious labor is falling in love with Julian; and Mrs. Leete fulfills the role of perfect wife by absenting herself for virtually the entire novel. *Looking Backward* suggested that once class differences disappeared, everyone would naturally conform to Victorian middle-class norms.

The Leetes have little contact with anyone in their community. The citizens of twentieth-century Boston eat in communal dining halls, but each family has a private room within the hall, and the only person Julian meets is their young male waiter, who is so thoroughly middle-class in appearance and manner that he reminds Julian of the nineteenth-century college boys who waited on tables during summer vacation. Julian's only other excursion outside the Leetes' home is when he accompanies Edith on a shopping expedition. Her father calls her an "indefatigable shopper," but it is difficult to see the appeal of shopping as depicted in the novel. Retail stores have been replaced by giant merchandise centers, and salespeople have been replaced by informational placards that describe the sample goods on display. Once the consumer decides on a purchase, she hands an order form to a clerk, who sends it off in a pneumatic tube; some hours later, the goods are delivered to the consumer's home. The process is rational, efficient, and completely impersonal.[37]

Looking Backward's avoidance of the public sphere and narrow focus on the middle-class nuclear family derive partly from Edward Bellamy's personal preferences, his extreme reticence and evident agoraphobia. He called himself a "home body," a label that scarcely covers his mania for private life.[38] Except for brief periods, he spent his entire life in the house where he was born. At age thirty-two, he married his foster sister Emma Sanderson, the daughter of one of Rufus Bellamy's parishioners, whom his parents had taken in when she was thirteen and Edward was twenty-four. The newlyweds remained in the house where both had been living with Edward's parents and stayed there for the rest of their marriage, except for a few months after the birth of their second child in 1886. When Bellamy's father died late that year, they returned to the family house, rejoining Bellamy's mother.

As a former newspaper editor, Bellamy was something of a public figure in Chicopee Falls, but he was adept at avoiding social invitations or even conversations with neighbors met on the street. At home, he had a standard line that he would utter as darkness fell, both humorous and completely sincere: "Pull down the curtains," he would say. "Don't put a light in the front hall, for it might lure someone in to call upon us." His brother Fred said that he "dreaded the sound of the door bell [announcing] the casual caller as if it forebode an earthquake." Associates regarded Bellamy as a witty companion, but at home, when he was in the midst of writing, he would retreat to his study for days, scarcely speaking to his wife and two children and emerging only for meals. Prone to depression and troubled by dyspepsia, he would carve the meat for the rest of the family but ask the servant girl to bring him a raw egg in a glass of milk or, occasionally, just a tumbler of whiskey.[39]

Looking Backward is in part Bellamy's personal fantasy of a perfectly private and tranquil family life, but it also reflects a broader yearning among middle-class Americans for privacy and tranquility in an era of massive population growth and surging urbanization. In a study of the dozens of utopian novels published on the heels of *Looking Backward*'s success, Neil Harris found that many of them portray a future in which urban crowds have disappeared and utopians enjoy an undisturbed private life.[40] Early nineteenth-century American utopians emphasized communitarian living, variations of the Fourier phalanx that redefined and expanded the family to include the entire community. Their late nineteenth-century successors, in contrast, tended to reduce the notion of community to its smallest possible unit, the nuclear family.

A tension exists at the heart of Bellamy's conception of solidarity. In existential and spiritual terms, the self seemed to him too small and isolated, and his youthful writings describe moments of mystical unity when the self seemed to dissolve in union with nature and the all-pervading divine. In political terms, Bellamy wanted to live in a society of perfect equality. Yet owing to both his reticent temperament and his class position, he was disposed to fear humanity en masse. In *Equality*, the sequel to *Looking Backward*, a character praises the proto-radio that enables people to enjoy music, lectures, and sermons in their own home and says to Julian that "being in a crowd, which was the matter-of-course penalty you had to pay for seeing or hearing anything interesting, would seem too dear a price to pay for almost any enjoyment."[41] The comment reveals the quintessentially private, middle-class social perspective that shapes Bellamy's utopia. Yet, in a seeming paradox, *Looking Backward* won a vast readership beyond the educated middle class, appealing to thousands of industrial workers and farmers.

It was evidently easy enough for readers outside the middle class to ignore the novel's class-bound limitations and to focus on the economic program explained by Dr. Leete, which takes up four-fifths of the book. At the heart of that program is absolute economic equality and a stress on the dignity of labor. *Looking Backward* fit easily into what historians have termed the "producerist" ideology common among the nineteenth-century working class. In contrast to the widespread Gilded Age admiration for successful capitalists as the creators of wealth, producerist ideology celebrated workers and regarded their labor as the foundation of society. Although it had its origins in antebellum republicanism, producerist thought paralleled Marxism in its emphasis on the labor theory of value. For most American workers, however, the desired end result of produce-rism was not dictatorship of the proletariat but higher wages and better working conditions.[42]

Bellamy took the ideas of producerism to another level. All labor, he argued, is so dignified that to sell it in the marketplace for whatever price it will fetch is "sordid," turning labor into a mere commodity. In Bellamy's utopia, everyone receives the same salary, regardless of what labor she or he performs. In his view, taking work out of the marketplace revealed its essential quality as an act of service to the nation as a whole. Recognizing that people worked for status as well as income, Bellamy replaced monetary rewards with military-like honors. A paean to this system delivered by Julian stresses Bellamy's two central ideals of humanistic spirituality and military sacrifice: "By requiring of every man his best you have made God his taskmaster, and by making honor the sole reward of achievement you have imparted to all service the distinction peculiar in my day to the soldiers."[43]

The system of military conscription, instituted in the U.S. for the first time during the Civil War, presumably helped readers accept the idea of compulsory service in the industrial army. Moreover, Bellamy's system has attractive features that offset its compulsory nature. The work week is shorter than the sixty to seventy-two hours common in the late nineteenth century—considerably shorter for the most difficult trades, such as mining, in order to attract workers. Workers' freedom to choose their trade is preserved; if there is an oversupply of applicants for one field and not enough in another, the bureaucrats in charge of the labor system adjust the working hours and offer unspecified incentives until there is a perfect balance of supply and demand. And with the retirement age set at forty-five, most people spend half their adult life at leisure. The stable and secure society described in *Looking Backward* appealed to countless economically distressed workers and farmers during the late nineteenth century's long depression.

It also had a wide appeal for women. That appeal may seem surprising, since in many ways the novel simply reinforces Victorian gender norms. Mrs. Leete is self-effacing to the point of invisibility. Edith never leaves home except to go shopping, and the only labor she performs in the novel is the emotional work of supporting Julian. Dr. Leete reveals that although women are also members of the industrial army, they serve in a separate-but-equal branch. The many women's movement activists who admired *Looking Backward* presumably looked past its benevolent paternalism and embraced its remarkably radical critique of nineteenth-century capitalism's sexual double standard. The novel suggested that, just as it was wrong for workers to be dependent on a private employer, it was immoral for women to be economically dependent on men. In his professional life, Bellamy wrote stories celebrating conventional courtship and marriage, and in his personal life, he addressed his wife Emma as "little girl."[44] But in constructing his utopia he drew upon the nineteenth-century women's movement's most radical critiques: in a system in which women lack economic independence, marriage is essentially a barter, with women offering their persons in exchange for economic support. In love matches, he wrote in *Looking Backward*, affection may have made women's dependence on men "endurable," though he added that "for spirited women . . . it must always have remained humiliating." His spokesman Dr. Leete continues, "What, then, must it have been in the innumerable cases where women, with or without the form of marriage, had to sell themselves to men to get their living?"[45] The bland diction cannot conceal the radical assumption that underlies Dr. Leete's rhetorical question: unless women have economic independence and equality with men, there is no real difference between marriage and prostitution.

Given Bellamy's brief but powerful defense of women's right to economic equality, it is not surprising that *Looking Backward* was embraced by many women's movement activists and leaders. The young Charlotte Perkins Gilman got her start as a writer and speaker spreading the Bellamy gospel, and Frances Willard, leader of the nation's largest and most powerful women's organization, the Women's Christian Temperance Union, was heavily influenced by the book, which she originally thought must have been written by a woman. Never having heard of Edward Bellamy, she wrote to an associate, "Some of us think that Edward Bellamy must be Edward*ina*—i.e., we believe a great-hearted, big-brained *woman* wrote the book. Won't you please find out?"[46]

Looking Backward contains elements that appealed directly to American women, workers, farmers, political radicals, and a large portion of the middle-class reading public, yet the novel's appeal went beyond those groups, and in the years after its publication it found a broad international audience. What made the book so appealing to so many? In part, the answer is to be found in the marriage plot that Bellamy imported from his commercial fiction. The Julian West–Edith Leete courtship is in many ways as formulaic as the love story in Bellamy's apprentice-work novel *Six to One*. Yet as David Bleich points out, this seemingly prim romance has a powerful erotic undercurrent.[47] Julian's relationship with Edith Bartlett, his nineteenth-century fiancée, remains unconsummated for years after their engagement because the workmen building the couple's new home frequently go on strike, delaying their marriage. The era's economic system proves to be not merely chaotic and unjust but sexually repressive. In Bellamy's egalitarian utopia, by contrast, Julian's romance with Edith Leete builds to a climax in a matter of days. Edith tells Julian that she loves him at the same moment that he declares his love for her. She tells him that unlike the women of the nineteenth century, she sees no need to hide her feelings, "conceal[ing her] love like a fault." The contrasting romances with the two Ediths suggest that a transformed system will have erotic as well as economic advantages. Moreover, the interactions between Julian and Edith Leete provide a break from Dr. Leete's socioeconomic monologues and offer readers a familiar and popular plot device; Bellamy himself compared the book's structure to a "sugar-coated pill."[48]

Thematically as well as structurally, *Looking Backward* is designed for broad appeal. The word "socialism" is never mentioned.

Instead, Dr. Leete insists throughout the book that their system of state ownership of the means of production represents nothing more than the extension to the economic sphere of the equality already established in America's political system. Bellamy's genius lay in his ability to make his utopia seem both plausible and unthreatening. Before the publication of *Looking Backward*, most Americans' image of radical social change was defined by the revolutionary anarchism behind the bombing at Chicago's Haymarket Square. *Looking Backward* suggested that society could be transformed peacefully and gradually, and the end result would be not a dictatorship of the proletariat but universal equality and a reassuring continuity of social norms.

Critics frequently place *Looking Backward* in the tradition of scientific utopias established by Bacon's *New Atlantis*. However, that's a mislabeling. The new technologies on display in the Boston of 2000 unquestionably added to the book's appeal, but Bellamy's utopia does not depend on technology. The most significant innovation in the story is one that Julian observes during an excursion with the Leetes: when it rains, a system of continuous awnings is extended over the sidewalks. Dr. Leete points up the contrast: "in the nineteenth century, when it rained, the people of Boston put up three hundred thousand umbrellas over as many heads, and in the twentieth century they put up one umbrella over all the heads." This is not so much science fiction as metonymy: the awning signifies the ethic of solidarity that suffuses twentieth-century society.[49]

Bellamy's youthful essay "The Religion of Solidarity" is at the heart of his utopian vision. The world of the future easily gives up the democratic political process—in this egalitarian paradise, there are no significant social disagreements—but religion proves indispensable. On Julian's first Sunday morning in utopia, the Leete family listens to a sermon—not in a church, which would entail mixing with crowds, but in the comfort of home, clustered around the marvelous proto-radio. Bellamy, in the didactic style that characterizes the entire novel, recounts the sermon in full. The sermon cleverly disguises the full extent of Bellamy's religious radicalism; its mentions of Jesus Christ and the fatherhood of God are designed to appeal to conventionally religious readers. In its essence, however, the sermon conveys the humanistic spirituality that Bellamy embraced in his twenties. Humans are not naturally sinful and self-ish, the utopian preacher Mr. Barton proclaims. It was only an un-just, competitive economic system that, in the pre-utopian past, made them act in self-interested ways. Now that competition has yielded to cooperation, the "social and generous instincts of men" can blossom.[50]

Looking Backward appealed to the Romantic belief in human goodness still common in the late nineteenth century, the conviction that human nature had been perverted by the unjust institutions of contemporary society. Reform society, and human nature will spring back to its naturally benign form. Dr. Leete informs Julian that dur-ing the hundred years of his mesmeric sleep, prisons were entirely eliminated, replaced with a handful of institutions housing the in-curably insane. Not only have criminals disappeared, but so have the greedy and acquisitive. Early on in the great transformation, the wealthiest members of society recognized the superiority of the new system of equality and willingly gave up their wealth and privilege.

Before Julian West begins his narrative of awakening in the twentieth century, he offers his readers—supposedly citizens of the modern utopia—a parable to explain the long-ago world of the late nineteenth century. Society, he says, was like a "prodigious coach" to which humanity was harnessed. Those pulling the coach—the vast majority—were miserable, while the lucky few seated on the top traveled in a luxury undermined by its precariousness, since the coach frequently lurched, sending some of the passengers sprawling into the dirt. The parable highlights the injustice and absurdity of the era's class-divided economic system, but its most remarkable aspect is that the figure driving the coach is "hunger."[51] In other words, no one is responsible for the unjust system; everyone is equally a victim; the coach was not designed but simply sprang into existence.

As an explanation of late nineteenth-century capitalism, the par-able is obviously inadequate, but it appealed enormously to readers uneasy with more radical analyses. Bellamy's decision to open the novel with this simple analogy reveals his belief that if people could only view their society with new eyes—could see, as if from a distant vantage point, its cruelties and absurdities—they would want to change it. The parable of the coach is a literary device designed to defamiliarize contemporary society, as is the entire novel. That defamiliarization reaches its climax in the novel's penultimate chapter.

The chapter begins with Julian being awakened in his sleeping chamber by his servant. Disoriented, he soon realizes that his journey to the twentieth century has been a dream. A glance at the masthead on the newspaper by his bedside confirms that the year is 1887, as does the front page, which is filled with news of war, poverty, corruption, and crime. Julian leaves his house and walks about the city, passing through a fashionable shopping street, the manufacturing district, and a slum. The day before, the walk would have been completely routine; now, it is a journey through Hell. He is "shocked . . . at every step" by the waste and inefficiency of the commercial system, the economic competition that fosters a callous individualism, and, above all, the juxtapositions of wealth and poverty. Julian's dream of utopia has defamiliarized his surroundings, and he suffers the "cognitive estrangement" from everyday reality that theorist Darko Suvin argues is the ultimate goal of utopian fiction. Overwhelmed by the wretchedness of the poor, Julian runs out of the slum with a self-accusing voice wailing in his head: "I found upon my garments the blood of this great multitude of the strangled souls of my brothers. The voice of their blood cried out against me from the ground. Every stone of the reeking pavements, every brick of the pestilential rookeries, found a tongue and called after me as I fled: What has thou done with thy brother Abel?" The biblical language signals Julian's complete conversion to the religion of solidarity. The poor are no longer a spectacle to be viewed but brothers to be loved.[52]

Julian's return to the nineteenth century highlights his role as a stand-in for the reader. For the time that it takes to complete the novel, readers of *Looking Backward* have accompanied Julian on his journey to utopia. If the novel has had its intended effect, upon closing the book readers should share his sense of estrangement from contemporary reality and undergo a similar conversion to the religion of solidarity. The only question is: What is to be done?

Julian's answer is to assume the role of prophet calling his contemporaries to righteousness. Fleeing the slums, he heads straight to the home of his fiancée, Edith Bartlett, where she and her family are hosting a dinner party, the men in formal wear, the women in gowns and jewels. Queried by his friends about his distressed looks, he bursts out, "I have been in Golgotha. I have seen Humanity hanging on a cross!" Seeing that they are obviously repelled by his passion, he restrains himself and speaks calmly, explaining the irrationality of the current economic system and how easily it can be transformed. As he finishes his oration, he eagerly searches his friends' faces for a positive response. Instead, he sees only scorn, and the scene culminates with Edith's father ordering the men to throw him out of the room as they shout, "Madman!" "Fanatic!"[53]

At that moment, Julian wakes up. His previous awakening was only a dream. Utopia is reality, and the novel ends as Julian joins the twentieth-century Edith in the garden—a man and woman together in an edenic paradise. Bellamy, ever the canny commercial writer, deftly achieves his happy ending. As Jonathan Auerbach points out, it is as if Bellamy anticipated and refuted James Joyce: history is a nightmare from which you *can* awake. Yet if the ending clicks satisfyingly into place, there remains a sense of poignancy. Julian's failure to convert his friends enacts Edward Bellamy's own worst fear: that his novel would have no effect on readers, would convert no one. Readers would regard him as a shrill lunatic and toss him—or at least his book—aside. As Jean Pfaelzer notes, in its conclusion *Looking Backward* demonstrates its own inadequacy, showing that humanity cannot renew itself through literature. After the novel was published in January 1888, Edward Bellamy had to face the same question that Julian did in his dream of returning from utopia to the nineteenth century: Now, what is to be done?[54]

{⸺⸻}

Bellamy's immediate answer was to continue writing fiction. In the year following the appearance of *Looking Backward*, Bellamy published five short stories, none of them dealing with the social issues he had addressed in his utopian novel. *Looking Backward* sold respectably—twenty-two thousand copies in its first year—but it appeared that nothing significant had changed, either for Edward Bellamy or the nation he had imagined could be transformed. Then the book took off. Over two hundred thousand copies were sold in 1889; magazine writers hailed it as the *Uncle Tom's Cabin* of the industrial age; clubs sprang up to spread Bellamy's ideas; requests to translate *Looking Backward* into other languages poured into Bellamy's home in Chicopee Falls; a magazine promoting the book's scheme was started; and Edward Bellamy, the man who kept the lights off and shades drawn so that nobody would call on him, was transformed into a national political figure.

Initially, Bellamy was squeamish about translating his utopian vision into a practical program. In the months after *Looking Backward*'s publication, several readers wrote to him suggesting that a political organization be founded to advance the book's program. Bellamy agreed with them that "Nationalism" was a good designation for a movement that aimed, in his words, "at a national control of industry with the resulting changes." He was reluctant, however, to be seen as the founder of a new political party. "Nationalism is not a party but a breaking of light," he wrote eloquently but vaguely. He was afraid of being lumped together with socialists. "The word socialist is one I never could well stomach," he told William Dean Howells. "It smells to the average American of petroleum, suggests the red flag, with all manner of sexual novelties, and an abusive tone about God and religion." When he was approached about starting a Nationalist club, he approved of the idea so long as the organizers reached out only to the "cultured and conservative class." He wanted to take the subject of economic reform "out of the plane of the beer saloons and out of the hands of blatant blasphemous demagogues and get it before the sober and morally minded masses of the American people."[55] In *Looking Backward,* he had dared to imagine a world utterly transformed, but when readers approached him about translating his ideas into action, he clung to the ideal of Victorian respectability. If change were coming, it had best keep its jacket on and its tie tightly knotted.

He had no need to worry. The group that gathered in Boston in December 1888 to found the first Nationalist club was eminently respectable. There were some journalists, several retired military officers, and a few literary men, including Howells. Their mood was buoyant. When one of the newspaper men moved to appoint a committee to draw up by-laws, elderly Edward Everett Hale, the distinguished author, Unitarian minister, and former abolitionist, rose and said, "I had hoped that once before I died I might be a member of a body that had no by-laws to squabble over." Howells, seated on an upturned wooden box, his short legs dangling over the edge, kicked his heels against the box in delighted approval, creating a racket and causing the room to erupt in laughter. The Nationalist movement was launched.[56]

Though they made no by-laws, they decided to limit the membership to 250 people. They wanted the "best men" of Boston—"men who had been successful in the present fierce competitive struggle," one member wrote. "They were not the weak, crying for mercy; they were the strong, demanding justice. They were not the crank or uneducated foreigner, importing ideas declared to be 'exotics'; they were men of position, educated, conservative in speech and of the oldest New England stock."[57] When they began a monthly journal, the *Nationalist*, in 1889, they modeled it on E. L. Godkin's prestigious *Nation* magazine. The motto on its cover proclaimed its goals as "The Nationalization of Industry and the Promotion of the Brotherhood of Humanity." The club had no trouble promoting the brotherhood of humanity; it was full of Unitarians and Theosophists eager to expound on the theme. The nationalization of industry proved more of a problem. Within months a second, competing Nationalist club was formed in Boston. The second club had no limitations on membership and no concerns about members' genealogical stock; instead, it served as a gathering point for activists interested in immediate political reform.

The Nationalist movement spread quickly after its establishment in Boston: by 1890 there were 127 clubs in 27 states, from New England to California. For its entire existence, the movement contained within it the tensions seen between the two Boston clubs and within Bellamy himself. Should the movement stress spiritual development of the individual, or should it work for social reform? If reform was the goal, should it pursue immediate political measures or promote the utopian vision of a transformed society?

Bellamy initially allied himself with the most class-bound and cautious elements within the Nationalist movement. He continued to churn out marketable short stories and preferred to think of Nationalism as a form of enlightenment, not a mere political party. Yet over the course of the two years following the publication of *Looking Backward*, Bellamy changed. His clear distinctions between the respectable and disreputable began to crumble as he came into increasing contact with the political and cultural radicals attracted to his utopian vision. Charles F. Willard, a newspaperman who seized the role of Nationalist historian, claimed that the movement was founded by Boston Brahmins, but Willard himself was a complicated and interesting figure, a Theosophist who spent much of his time in beer halls talking politics with radical German immigrants. Agnes A. Chevaillier, another founding member of the first Boston club, was a radical feminist who made her living as a mind-cure practitioner. As Charles Postel points out, Nationalists may have claimed that the movement was made up of respectable professionals and businessmen, but in reality the Nationalist clubs attracted a cross-class bohemian subculture.[58]

Rubbing shoulders with this diverse group and immersing himself in the reform literature of the period, Bellamy underwent a transformation almost as remarkable as Julian West's. By the summer of 1890, when he received an invitation to write a lucratively compensated serial novel for the *Atlantic*, the nation's most prestigious literary magazine, he turned it down. "It would indeed be a delight to me to revert to those psychologic studies and speculations which were the themes of my earlier writings," he told editor Horace Scudder. "But since my eyes have been opened to the evils and faults of our social state and I have begun to cherish a clear hope of better things, I simply 'can't get my consent' to write or think of anything else. As a literary man I fear I am 'a goner,' and past praying for." Caught up in the tumultuous, thrilling political atmosphere of the early 1890s, Bellamy was convinced that the millennium was imminent. "I don't know what part I am to play in the great deliverance," he wrote to a Nationalist friend, "but I am daily more convinced that it is at hand."[59]

Bellamy soon found the part he was to play. Within a year after its founding by the elitists in the first Boston club, the *Nationalist* magazine was struggling for subscribers. New Nationalist clubs continued to be formed, but the movement as a whole was not growing, since established clubs frequently collapsed, unable to bridge divisions between spiritual liberals interested in promoting the religion of solidarity and those committed to immediate political reform. Overcoming his earlier political and organizational timidity, Bellamy decided to start a new publication. The *Nationalist* was a quality monthly intended for Nationalist club members; the *New Nation* would be an inexpensive weekly newspaper aimed at the widest possible audience. Aware that he could not issue a national newspaper from Chicopee Falls, Bellamy left the comfort of his birthplace and started living out of a hotel room in Boston. For such an intensely private man, the sacrifice was not inconsiderable. He was resolved to realize his utopian vision by turning himself into a political activist.

The first issue of the *New Nation*, edited and published by Edward Bellamy, appeared in January 1891. In the prospectus Bellamy announced his intention to seek alliances with the women's movement, progressive churches, labor unions, and farmers' organizations. The paper's motto read, "The industrial system of a nation, as well as its political system, ought to be a government of the people, by the people, for the people." With its patriotic appropriation of Abraham Lincoln's famous phrase, the slogan highlighted Bellamy's evolutionary philosophy of political change. The United States' founders had firmly established the principle of political equality, and if universal suffrage had not yet been fully achieved, the nation had nevertheless moved steadily toward that ideal. The inevitable next step, in Bellamy's view, was economic equality.

Bellamy believed, counterintuitively, that the essential precondition for economic equality was the growth of capitalist monopolies. In his thinking, monopolies were the first step along the evolutionary road toward a centralized national economy. Once the American economy was under the control of a small number of corporations, the transition to a truly national economy controlled by the state could be easily accomplished. Every issue of the *New Nation* featured a roundup of news items about the growth of private monopolies, headlined "Nationalistic Drift." As far as Bellamy was concerned, the spread of trusts counted as good news. Twentieth-century Progressives were known as "trust-busters," but Nationalists celebrated monopolies as precursors of the economic equality to come.

The *New Nation* also featured news about the People's Party in every issue. The populism of the 1890s is usually seen as a rural movement, and there is no question that the party's strength lay in the rural South and Midwest. However, a small but vibrant Populist movement existed in the urban Northeast, particularly in Massachusetts, where the People's Party was composed almost entirely of Nationalist club members. Elections for the Massachusetts legislature and governorship were scheduled for November 1891, and in the months leading up to the election, Bellamy cheered on the Populist campaign. For several weeks he reprinted in every issue a summary of the Massachusetts People's Party platform, which offers the clearest statement of the immediate reforms that Nationalists embraced as preliminary steps on the road to utopia. The platform mixed bold steps advocated by socialists—nationalization of railroads and telegraphs—with milder proposals favored by a wide range of reformers, including female suffrage, the eight-hour day, civil service reform, and extension of public education.

The reticent Bellamy, who had declined the dozens of speaking invitations he received soon after the publication of *Looking Backward*, now took to the platform on behalf of the Massachusetts People's Party, speaking at a rally in Boston's famed Faneuil Hall in October 1891. He found the location particularly appropriate, noting that it had been the inaugural site of America's first two great emancipation movements: emancipation of the colonists from British rule and the emancipation of black Americans from slavery. Now the third great movement was under way: emancipation of the poor from the rich.

Bellamy turned out to be a surprisingly effective speaker, lacing his oration with red-meat applause lines. Speaking of the Civil War, he said, "While the men of the people had been saving the republic at the south the men of money had been stealing it away at the north. The soldiers came home to find that the slave-holding oligarchy had been driven out of power only to give place to a moneyed oligarchy." Bellamy rejected Marxist ideas of class warfare, but during the 1890s he became increasingly willing to attack the wealthy as destroyers of American democracy. In his speech's conclusion, he championed public ownership of industry as the only means of averting a political apocalypse. "America is to-day imperiled because it is a house divided against itself," he shouted out to the crowded hall. "Unless we shall carry the republican idea into industry we must abandon it in politics."[60] Nationalist candidates failed at the Massachusetts polls in 1891, but nationwide the People's Party experienced enormous growth. Bellamy cautioned that Nationalists should not let themselves be absorbed into the People's Party—they had utopian goals that not all Populists shared—but he continued to champion the Populists, and in 1892 he was selected as a delegate to the national People's Party convention in Omaha, Nebraska.

Ill health kept him from traveling to Omaha, but his ally Frances E. Willard, the temperance leader who joined the Nationalists despite her disappointment that Edward Bellamy was not actually Edwardina, served as the convention's chair. Historians tend to discount the Nationalist influence within the People's Party, and it's true that despite the prominence of the Nationalist chair, the number of Nationalists at the convention and within the People's Party was relatively small. However, *Looking Backward* was immensely popular among Populists. During the early 1890s, Populist newspapers throughout the rural South, Midwest, and West offered paper-covered copies of the novel for fifty or even twenty-five cents. Many elements in *Looking Backward* and Nationalism fit smoothly with Populist values: the celebration of the dignity of labor; the patriotic insistence that economic equality was the logical consequence of America's political equality; the religious rhetoric and nods to Christian belief; the rejection of violent revolution and promotion of an evolutionary model of political change.[61]

Bellamy's belief that the United States was poised at a historical turning point, with Nationalism as the only alternative to either plutocracy, anarchy, or violent destruction, found a powerful echo in the famous preamble to the 1892 People's Party platform adopted in Omaha. Written by Ignatius Donnelly, a politician and novelist who had published his own utopian novel, the preamble reflected Donnelly's fondness for inflammatory rhetoric and apocalyptic imaginings. "We meet in the midst of a nation brought to the verge of moral, political, and material ruin," Donnelly began. He continued, "A vast conspiracy against mankind has been organized on two continents, and it is rapidly taking possession of the world. If not met and overthrown at once it forebodes terrible social convulsions, the destruction of civilization, or the establishment of an absolute despotism."[62] The platform itself was, by comparison, tame, little different from the platform that Massachusetts Nationalists put forward in 1891 during their unsuccessful campaign for the statehouse: it included calls for nationalization of the telephone, telegraph, and railroads, for the eight-hour workday, the secret ballot, and a graduated income tax.

The Populists nominated former Union general James B. Weaver for president and ran slates for U.S. Congress and state officials in almost every state. Weaver received over one million votes in the election of 1892, carrying four Western states. Eleven Populist candidates were elected to Congress, and numerous Populist candidates were elected at the state level. It was one of the most successful third-party campaigns in American history. Writing in the *New Nation*, Bellamy claimed victory. "On every hand," he wrote, "the ground is broken up and ready for the seed." The Nationalist movement was the "advance guard" of the People's Party, which he predicted would win the presidency in 1896. If he avoided Donnelly's violent rhetoric, he shared the widespread sense that the nation was at a historical turning point. "Human destiny," he wrote, "is turning as on a hinge."[63]

The optimistic Bellamy was wrong about the 1896 election for the presidency. After a bitter internal fight, the Populists endorsed the Democratic candidate for president, William Jennings Bryan, who transmuted the Populists' economic concerns into the single, fiscally simplistic issue of the gold standard. Privately, Bellamy said that the dissolution of the People's Party after 1896 was "a good riddance," since the party had "fallen into bad hands."[64] By that point, the *New Nation* had folded. Early in 1894, battered by yet another economic depression and with circulation sliding from its high of eight thousand subscribers, the journal issued its last number. Bellamy's health was worsening, and he gratefully returned to Chicopee Falls. His political career had been an attempt to realize his utopian vision, but it had in turn altered his vision. He decided that, in the short time left to him, he would write a sequel to *Looking Backward*.

Equality (1897) begins where *Looking Backward* leaves off, with Julian joining Edith in her garden. Bellamy evidently intended a seamless integration of his two utopian novels into one larger work, but the differences between the two books are striking. *Equality*

reflects Edward Bellamy's immersion in Nationalism's radical bohemian subculture during the years following the publication of
Looking Backward.

When *Looking Backward* first appeared, Bellamy wanted nothing to do with socialism, dismissing its foreign associations and
whiff of petroleum and trying to purge socialists from the Nationalist clubs. However, he soon acknowledged that national ownership
of the means of production and distribution as depicted in *Looking
Backward* was a form of socialism. In the *New Nation* he called
Nationalism "the American socialism" and even claimed that it was
"the most radical form of socialism," since it insisted on absolute
economic equality, with every citizen receiving the same stipend.
Members of the Socialist Labor Party (SLP), the principal Marxist
organization of the early 1890s, attacked Nationalists as "middle
class faddists" who refused to recognize the role of the working class
as revolutionary vanguard, but Bellamy refused to return the vitriol,
instead writing in the *New Nation* about goals that, as socialists, the
SLP and Nationalists held in common.[65]

Bellamy did not use the term "socialism" in *Equality*, but the
book appropriates socialist language to offer a much more radical
critique of the American economic and political system than *Looking Backward* contained. *Equality* directly attacks capitalism in a
way that *Looking Backward* had avoided. In its first chapter, Bellamy writes that American politicians were nothing more than "vas-
sals and tools of the capitalists," and he later calls American democracy "merely a mask for plutocracy."[66] The famous parable of the
coach in *Looking Backward* highlighted the irrationality and injustice of America's economic system, but it suggested that no one was
at fault. In contrast, the most famous passage in *Equality* is a
lengthy chapter entitled "The Parable of the Water Tank." In this
parable set in a dry land, a class of men known as "capitalists" seize
all the water sources, force the people to haul water to a central tank
called "the Market," then sell the water back to them for a profit.
The parable so clearly illustrates Marxist class analysis that after the
Bolshevik revolution the Soviet authorities published it as a pamphlet, distributing over a quarter million copies.[67]

Equality reveals Bellamy's political radicalization in the years
following the publication of *Looking Backward*, and it shows as well

his changing ideas about gender. The Nationalist party brought Bellamy into contact with numerous women's movement activists, who were attracted by *Looking Backward*'s promise of economic equality between women and men. However, they presumably pointed out to him that despite what the novel says about gender equality, what it shows is a conventional Victorian household in which women are always available to cater to men's emotional needs. Bellamy heavily revised his portrayal of Edith in *Equality;* as Kenneth Roemer points out, she is essentially a different character.[68] The Edith of *Looking Backward* is an angel of the house, but *Equality*'s Edith is an active, independent young woman. One of her first actions in the later novel is to shed her long skirt and appear before Julian in androgynous trousers. Attired in a version of the bloomers advocated by female dress reformers, Edith strides to the local gymnasium, where she competes alongside men in footraces and other events.

Looking Backward had envisioned a separate-but-equal industrial army for women, sequestering them in lighter employments, but *Equality* abandons that idea. Edith, like all other youths, is a common laborer during her first three years in the workforce; after that, she will have a choice of any profession. She mentions the women who are "machinists, farmers, engineers, carpenters, iron workers, builders, [and] engine drivers," and then takes Julian to tour a factory where they are escorted by a female superintendent. *Looking Backward* attacked women's economic dependence on men, but *Equality* lays out a much fuller critique of capitalist patriarchy. Dr. Leete decries the "triple yoke" that subjugated nineteenth-century women. The first yoke is "class rule of the rich," a bondage that women share with men, but the next two problems are unique to women. Women are subjected to the rule of the individual man, whether husband or father, on whom they depend economically, and they are also subject to what the normally soft-spoken Dr. Leete denounces as a "slave code" of gendered behavior. "The main hope of a comfortable life for every woman consisted in attracting the favorable attention of some man who could provide for her," he explains. Trained from an early age to please men, women had "to repress all that was spontaneous and individual." Dr. Leete praises female individualism, and he also criticizes the mainstream women's movements of the late nineteenth century as insufficiently radical.

He explains that they worked to gain women the vote and to reform male morality but failed to challenge women's economic subordination.[69]

If *Equality* radically advanced the cause of gender equality, it took a step back on race. *Looking Backward* is virtually silent on the topic of race. Its one black character, Julian's servant, disappears from the novel once Julian awakens from his century-long sleep. *Equality* ends the earlier novel's silence. Dr. Leete assures Julian that despite the new nation's full economic equality, racial segregation is enforced in the geographical areas that prefer it. He regrets this segregation as a necessary concession to "bigoted local prejudices," but it is clear that, at least in the South, utopia is a whites-only club. Bellamy insisted in the *New Nation* that Nationalism was "color-blind," but in his zeal to infuse his economic ideas into the growing People's Party, he felt bound to assure southern Populists that Nationalism would not disturb the region's Jim Crow laws.[70]

The gesture was probably futile. It's doubtful that more than a handful of white southern readers—or readers of any race or region—got far enough into *Equality* to reach the chapter on "The Colored Race and the New Order." The book is more than twice as long as *Looking Backward* and many times duller. Bellamy dispensed with even the slight framework of plot that he employed in *Looking Backward* and relied almost entirely on monologues delivered by the indefatigable Dr. Leete. Bellamy, his body riddled with tuberculosis, clearly rushed to finish the book, packing in every argument he could think of in favor of Nationalism. Absent any organizing plot, the book simply peters out rather than concluding; the final chapter is a grab bag of Nationalist talking points.

Edward Bellamy died in 1898 at the age of forty-eight, a year after publishing *Equality*. The obituaries that appeared in newspapers across the United States and Great Britain noted the popularity of *Looking Backward* and the impact of the Nationalist political movement, but they discussed Bellamy's influence largely in the past tense.[71] Of course, die-hard Nationalists disagreed. John Clark Ridpath, editor of the liberal *Arena* magazine, titled his tribute to Bellamy "Is the Prophet Dead?" and answered his own query in the negative. He concluded his essay with the grandiose declaration, "Had we the courage to clear away sometimes, to lay a new foundation, . . . then we should all become apostles of Edward Bellamy."[72]

It is not clear how many readers took up this apostolic challenge. Yet it's possible to call the years between 1888 and 1914 the Age of Bellamy, in the same way as the quarter-century before 1850 can be labeled the Age of Owen and Fourier. Of course, Bellamy's utopian ideas were not realized in practice, any more than society was transformed by the dozens of communities founded by followers of Owen and Fourier. However, the issues raised in *Looking Backward* dominated public discussion during the late nineteenth and early twentieth centuries and animated reform movements in both the United States and Great Britain. Economic inequality, the labor question, the relation between government and industry, women's rights, urban planning, environmental pollution—all were at the center of what historian Daniel Rodgers has shown to be a transnational Progressive movement.[73]

Utopian speculation was at the center of what Richard Hofstadter called "the Age of Reform."[74] Oscar Wilde said that a map of the world that does not include Utopia is not worth glancing at because "it leaves out the one country at which Humanity is always landing. And when Humanity lands there, it looks out, and, seeing a better country, sets sail. Progress is the realisation of Utopias."[75] In his epigrammatic way, Wilde was suggesting that all political reform depends on a vision of utopia. Not every one of the five hundred utopian fictions published in the U.S. and Great Britain during the twenty-five years after *Looking Backward* contributed to that era's reforming zeal, but collectively they inspired activists' visions of the future. *Looking Backward* decisively turned utopian fiction away from geographical romance—the traveler's-tale convention employed by Thomas More and his successors—and toward the emerging genre of science fiction and the device of time travel. Setting utopia in a possible future instead of in the geographical imaginary emphasized that it was achievable by human effort. Moreover, Bellamy's insistence that utopia could be achieved through a peaceful process of evolutionary change appealed to those who rejected calls for the revolutionary violence of class warfare.

Looking Backward had a lasting effect on British and American reformers throughout the early twentieth century. The historian

R. C. K. Ensor stressed that Edward Bellamy, along with Henry George and *Cooperative Commonwealth* author Henry Gronlund, laid the intellectual foundations of the British Fabian movement. Ebenezer Howard, the pioneering English urban planner, paid tribute to Bellamy, as did prominent Americans including labor activist and socialist politician Eugene Debs and novelist Upton Sinclair, author of *The Jungle*. Bellamy's influence continued into the 1930s, when both philosopher John Dewey and historian Charles Beard ranked *Looking Backward* as the second most influential book of the past fifty years, surpassed only by Marx's *Capital*. The book was embraced by New Deal intellectuals, most notably Arthur Morgan, who served as founding director of the Tennessee Valley Authority while simultaneously researching his biography of Bellamy, a hagiographic volume that describes the author as one of the greatest men in history.[76]

Bellamy's influence extended into the 1950s, as demonstrated by the example of a student at the New England Conservatory of Music who gave a copy of *Looking Backward* to her earnest young suitor from Atlanta in April 1952. Three months later, Martin Luther King Jr. wrote to Coretta Scott, thanking her "a million times for introducing me to such a stimulating book." "There can be no doubt about it," he wrote. "Bellamy had the insight of a social prophet. . . . I welcomed the book because much of its content is in line with my basic ideas. I imagine you already know that I am much more socialistic in my economic theory than capitalistic. . . . I would certainly welcome the day to come when there will be a nationalization of industry. Let us continue to hope, work, and pray that in the future we will live to see a warless world, a better distribution of wealth, and a brotherhood that transcends race or color."[77]

Looking Backward played a role, however minor, in shaping Martin Luther King's utopian dream. The brilliant young minister no doubt saw clearly the book's limitations, including its obliviousness of difference—not only racial difference, but all the diverse and sometimes chaotic ways in which people choose to express their creativity, to satisfy their sexuality, to create a family, to further community, to find meaning in labor, to worship the divine. Human desires are larger and messier than Bellamy's orderly utopia allowed for. Yet King must have been drawn to the book's essential sweetness, its conviction that surely everyone is appalled by poverty in the midst of wealth, by the violence and greed inherent in a competitive economic system which demands that people fend for themselves and their families and close their eyes to others' suffering. Julian West's dream-return to the nineteenth century, in the novel's penultimate episode, brilliantly estranges readers from contemporary social realities, raising a host of radically simple questions: Why should slums exist within sight of great wealth? Why should streets be dirty and skies dark with pollution? Why should people willing to work be unemployed? Why should the well-being of children and the elderly be dependent on the caprice of their family circumstances?

The passage of time has uncovered the authoritarian dimensions of Edward Bellamy's utopia, but it has also confirmed his book's value. *Looking Backward* disturbed readers' complacency, fueled their outrage at inequality, and spurred their desire for change. It also led directly to a quarter-century's flood of utopian fiction. Some of those works were obvious imitations of Bellamy, some borrowed only his idea of a journey to a transformed future, and others were direct rejections of his ideas. As it turned out, the greatest of the fictional responses to *Looking Backward*, William Morris's *News from Nowhere*, fell into the final category.

CHAPTER THREE

William Morris's Artful Utopia

EDWARD BELLAMY'S *Looking Backward* was wildly popular in Great Britain, going into seventeen printings in the first year of its appearance and selling some two hundred thousand copies. No one was more disturbed by its success than William Morris. Early in 1889 he fumed about the book to a friend, saying thank you very much but *he* wouldn't care to live in such a "cockney paradise" as Bellamy imagined. "Cockney" was Morris's epithet for anything vulgar or philistine or, worst of all, middle class. Morris himself was born into the higher reaches of the middle class, and he spent his entire adult life in revolt against its values. Bellamy seemed to him the epitome of the middle-class reformer, "perfectly satisfied with modern civilization, if only the injustice, misery, and waste of class society could be got rid of." Morris wrote that the leading passion of his own life, "apart from the desire to produce beautiful things," was "hatred of modern civilization." He wanted to expose the narrow, complacent, and authoritarian dimensions of *Looking Backward*. The best way to do that, he decided, was to write his own utopian novel.[1]

Within a few months of reading *Looking Backward*, Morris began writing *News from Nowhere*, which was serialized in the socialist magazine *Commonweal* in 1890. Bellamy had fussed over the details of getting his hero into the utopian future a century hence, but Morris didn't give a damn about plausibility. *News from No-*

where is frankly presented as one man's dream. "The only safe way of reading a utopia," Morris wrote in his review of *Looking Backward*, "is to consider it as the expression of the temperament of its author." Bellamy had invented a protagonist with few obvious similarities to himself, but Morris's first-person narrator is remarkably similar to Mr. William Morris. The man who calls himself William Guest (he coyly declines to give his real name) is fifty-six years old—Morris's age at the time he was writing—and lives at the same location on the River Thames where Morris had his London home. Over the course of the book, the narrator travels up the Thames to a house identifiable as Kelmscott Manor, Morris's country retreat, where he is greeted by a "tall handsome woman" who calls to mind Morris's famously tall and beautiful wife, Jane.[2]

Edward Bellamy had stumbled into utopianism. Prior to *Looking Backward*'s publication he appeared to be an unexceptional journalist and author, a middle-class family man notable only for his mania for privacy. It surprised everyone, including Bellamy himself, when he produced a wildly popular utopian novel. Morris had been journeying toward utopia his entire life. From childhood, he rejected the world as it is in favor of an idealized, antimodern realm. As a boy, he devoured the romances of Walter Scott. As a young man, he plunged into the Pre-Raphaelite movement, which set out to reclaim artistic approaches superseded since the Renaissance. Next he turned to design and inspired what became known as the Arts and Crafts movement, which rejected machine-made products in favor of traditional handicrafts. At the same time as he carried out his design work, he produced volumes of narrative verse that turned their back on the modern world and celebrated the heroism of ages past. Then, at the height of his career, he risked his reputation as an esteemed artist and poet by joining Britain's first socialist political party and agitating for a working-class revolution.

Morris crafted his very personality into a dismissal of the world as it is. He was given to passionate enthusiasms for the unconventional and to titanic rages against modern civilization, with its worship of technology and efficiency, its infatuation with the mass-produced, its focus on money as the measure of the good life, and its complacent acceptance of massive accumulations of wealth in the hands of a few accompanied by poverty for the many.

Looking Backward was the beginning of Edward Bellamy's utopianism. *News from Nowhere* served as climax of the utopianism that William Morris had been engaged in for decades. Throughout his adult life he rejected central Victorian beliefs—not only religious belief but also the belief in progress, the embrace of technology, and the divisions between work and leisure, art and design, literature and politics, intellectuals and workers. He lived a life devoted to labor in the service of beauty and to struggle in the cause of equality. One of history's great utopian dreamers, he managed with remarkable success—if not without a measure of contradiction—to live out his ideals.

Born in 1834, William Morris had a childhood radically different from that of Edward Bellamy in the New England mill town of Chicopee Falls. When Morris was six, his father, a wealthy London financier, leased a mansion set within a fifty-acre park adjacent to Epping Forest, some twenty miles from the City. William, one of nine children, was free to explore the area. He roamed the forest with his younger brothers, fishing and sighting birds that, even as a boy, he knew the names of. He knew the forest "yard by yard," he claimed, and it was "always interesting and often very beautiful." He had a deep love for nature in all its forms and, as a small boy, had a garden of his own where he cultivated flowers.[3]

He spent as much time reading as exploring the outdoors. He claimed that he began reading Walter Scott's novels when he was four and had finished them all by the time he was seven. He continued reading the Scottish romancer as an adult; Scott, he said, meant more to him than Shakespeare. Scott's novels are filled with bold action, cunning villains, self-sacrificing heroes, doomed love affairs, and lovingly detailed depictions of the Middle Ages—all characteristics of Morris's own narrative poems and prose romances. His indulgent parents stoked his passion for the Middle Ages by giving the boy a child-sized suit of armor and a pony, which he employed in imagined knightly adventures. His love for all things medieval included architecture. When he was eight, his father took him to visit Canterbury Cathedral, parts of which date from the twelfth century.

The impressionable boy thought that the gates of heaven had been opened to him. Such raptures were a surprise to other members of the Morris family; none of them was at all artistic. The Morrises lived, William later wrote, "in the ordinary bourgeois style of comfort" and followed the religious strictures of the evangelical wing of the Anglican church.[4] The Morris children were not allowed to mix with dissenters, although an exception was made for Quakers, who played a prominent role in the banking sector on which the Morris family fortune depended.

William was sent to Marlborough College, a recently founded public school in the mold of Eton and Harrow, shortly before he turned fourteen. "I think I may fairly say I learned next to nothing there, for indeed next to nothing was taught," he claimed. The experience left him with a distaste for conventional education and a hostility to authority, which at Marlborough proved itself to be at once harsh, capricious, and ineffectual. The one saving grace was the school's location in rural Wiltshire, surrounded by prehistoric monuments. "I set myself eagerly to studying these and everything else that had any history in it," Morris later recalled.[5]

Morris's love for history and ancient buildings was fulfilled when he entered Oxford in 1853. Oxford in the 1850s remained, in large part, a medieval town; the intensive Victorian development that now strikes any visitor would not come until later in the century. Morris fell in love with the place. Throughout his life he regarded it as "the most important town of England," not because of the university—academically, he found it no more congenial than Marlborough—but because of the architecture.[6] Morris, always given to enthusiasms, would drag new acquaintances off to see the Merton College tower.

He quickly found himself at the center of a group of friends who shared his interests. Immediately upon his arrival, he met Edward Burne-Jones, who was to gain fame as a painter. At the time, however, both of the earnest young men, swept up in the Victorian Anglo-Catholic revival, assumed they would enter the ministry after graduation. Through Burne-Jones, Morris fell in with a group of high-minded students who called themselves the Set. Oxford undergraduates in the 1850s were roughly divided into two groups: the "fast" men, absorbed in sports and drinking, and the reading men.

The members of the Set fell firmly into the latter group. There were a half dozen of them, all except Morris chums since their schooldays in Birmingham. Morris relished being part of this community of male friends, and throughout his life he would seek out equivalent groups. He quickly gained a reputation as one of the Set's most formidable intellects—"How Morris seems to know things, doesn't he?" one member remarked to another. He was also its designated clown. He talked incessantly, showed off his strength, and happily answered to the nickname Topsy, bestowed on him in honor of his unruly mop of tangled dark hair. Burne-Jones thought Morris "one of the cleverest fellows I know." Describing Morris to a boyhood chum, he wrote that his new friend was "full of enthusiasm for things holy and beautiful and true, and, what is rarest, of the most exquisite perception and judgment in them. . . . If it were not for his boisterous mad outbursts and freaks, which break the romance he sheds around him—at least to me—he would be a perfect hero." Morris's outbursts and freaks became legendary among the Set. "A little more *piano*, sir," Madox, the college servant assigned to Morris, would deferentially suggest, encouraging the young man to lower his voice.[7]

The members of the Set liked to read aloud to one another in the evenings: religious works, Shakespeare, and, above all, Tennyson. They were particularly taken with Tennyson's early verse narratives of the Middle Ages: "The Lady of Shalott" (1832) ,"Sir Galahad" (1842), "Morte d'Arthur" (1842), "Sir Launcelot and Queen Guinevere" (1842). The Set was not alone in its enthusiasm for Tennyson and the Middle Ages; by the 1850s a sort of medieval mania was in full force among the British reading public.

A vast number of Victorians embraced the era's medieval revival, and their motivations varied widely. For many, medievalism served as a comforting alternative to modernity, a refuge and escape from the radical changes of the industrializing nineteenth century. Conservatives celebrated the seemingly stable social hierarchy of the feudal past, enraptured, in the words of historian Charles Dellheim, by a "dream of order." Yet liberals and radicals also turned to the Middle Ages for inspiration, finding there a "vision of liberty." Victorian progressives subscribed to what Dellheim calls the "myth of

Saxon liberty," focusing on the small-scale democracy of the village community.[8]

John Ruskin, the great Victorian sage, drew his own distinctive lessons from the Middle Ages. His masterwork *The Stones of Venice* (1851–53) was completed the same year Morris entered Oxford. Morris and Burne-Jones laid hold of the book immediately upon its publication and became enamored of the chapter on "The Nature of Gothic." This essay had a lifelong influence on Morris; he was to call it "one of the very few necessary and inevitable utterances of the century."[9] "The Nature of Gothic" is essentially an essay in art history, but Ruskin, with a nineteenth-century intellectual's disdain for disciplinary boundaries, was not content to define Gothic art in purely aesthetic terms. Influenced by recent histories that offered a positive interpretation of medieval guilds, Ruskin argued that the appealing roughness of Gothic art came from the freedom of medieval workmen. A Victorian bricklayer worked under rigid supervision, but a medieval stonemason was free to bring all his individuality and creativity into the shaping of a gargoyle. A medieval cathedral was not the creation of an individual architect whose vision was executed by unthinking workers but a communally created work of art.

In defining the nature of Gothic, Ruskin felt compelled to define the nature of Victorian industrialism, and he found the contrast appalling. Gothic buildings were "signs of the life and liberty of every workman who struck the stone," whereas Victorian workmen were treated like commodities, "sent like fuel to feed the factory smoke." Railing against nineteenth-century economists who praised the modern division of labor, Ruskin eloquently cried, "It is not, truly speaking, the labour that is divided; but the men." He continued, "The great cry that rises from all our manufacturing cities, louder than their furnace blast, is . . . that we manufacture everything there except men." Years before the Marxist concept of the alienation of labor was available to English readers, Ruskin independently developed a comparable idea. He also, tentatively, sketched out a solution. Unlike Marx, he had no interest in a workers' revolution. Instead, he called for "healthy and ennobling labour," and he attacked the nineteenth-century distinction between the manual laborer and the gentleman: "It would be well if all of us were good handicraftsmen in some kind."[10]

William Morris's entire career, including his vision of utopia, is presaged by Ruskin's essay. "To some of us when we first read it, . . . it seemed to point out a new road on which the world should travel," Morris wrote. Fascinated since childhood by architecture and design, by buildings and furnishings and illuminated manuscripts, Morris took from Ruskin an ennobling vision of labor and the conviction that craftsmanship, far from being an adjunct to more significant historical forces, could itself drive social change. Inspired by Ruskin's tribute to Gothic architecture, Morris made two pilgrimages to the Gothic cathedrals of northern France during his time at Oxford. The journeys were transformative. Years later, he said that his visit to Rouen, with its medieval town center and massive, beautifully preserved cathedral, was "the greatest pleasure I have ever had."[11] Morris loved Gothic buildings with an intensity that most people bring only to their romantic lives. Among his first published works was an essay about the cathedrals he visited in France, its opening sentences suffused with his passion:

> Not long ago I saw for the first time some of the churches of North France; still more recently I saw them for the second time; and remembering the love I have for them and the longing that was in me to see them during the time that came between the first and second visit, I thought I should like to tell people of some of those things I felt when I was there. . . . And I thought that even if I could say nothing else about these grand churches I could at least tell men how much I loved them. . . . For I will say here that I think those same churches of North France the grandest, the most beautiful, the kindest and most loving of all the buildings that the earth has ever borne.[12]

The adjectives are startling: these buildings are not only *grand* and *beautiful* but also *kind* and *loving*. Morris anthropomorphizes the cathedrals, turning buildings that strike many viewers as awesome and imposing into intimate companions with the ability to solace and endear the visitor.

Morris's deeply affectionate tribute to the French cathedrals reveals his extraordinarily acute aesthetic sensibility; the essay reveals also that by the time he wrote it, during his final months at university, aesthetics interested him far more than theology. Near the end of his second trip to France in the summer of 1855, walking on the quay in Le Havre one night, he and Burne-Jones determined that they would not take holy orders after graduation, as their families expected of them, but would instead dedicate themselves to art: Burne-Jones would become a painter and Morris an architect. The usual path for would-be architects in the mid-nineteenth century was apprenticeship with a practitioner. Accordingly, in January 1856, immediately after his graduation, Morris joined the firm of G. E. Street, a prominent Gothic revival architect in Oxford. It seemed the perfect position for him. He left the firm within a year, however, lured away by the powerful influence of a painter and poet who would become both a close friend and a tormenting figure: Dante Gabriel Rossetti.

{⚬⚬⚬}

Gabriel Charles Dante Rossetti, six years older than Morris, was the son of distinguished and well-connected Italian expatriates living in London. Gabriel—as he was known throughout his life to his family and friends—showed great talent as a painter early on, and he was only twenty in 1848 when, with fellow painters William Holman Hunt and John Everett Millais, he founded the Pre-Raphaelite Brotherhood and assumed the name Dante Gabriel. The members of the brotherhood, which soon attracted other painters, wanted nothing less than to change the course of English painting. Their idea was to recapture the truth to nature exemplified in the Italian painters of the *Quattrocento*. To their mind, painters of the High Renaissance and later, starting with Raphael, were all mannerists to some degree, copiers not of nature but of other artists.[13]

Taken as a historically based theory of Western art, the Pre-Raphaelite credo is eccentric, but as a rallying cry for young artists intent on establishing themselves as their generation's avant-garde, it was enormously effective. The Pre-Raphaelite Brotherhood quickly attracted comment. Not all of it was favorable, but that was no matter; the point was to get themselves noticed. Eventually they gained the attention of John Ruskin, who devoted one of his famous 1853 Edinburgh lectures to interpreting and praising the young artists.

Morris got hold of Ruskin's lecture immediately after its publication in 1854, while he was still at Oxford. He ran into Burne-Jones's room one morning, waving the book, insisting that his friend put everything aside and listen to him read Ruskin's encomium. "For many a day after that," Burne-Jones recalled, "we talked of little else but paintings which we had never seen."[14]

On his graduation from Oxford two years later, Burne-Jones moved to London to become a painter and sought out Rossetti. The older painter befriended Burne-Jones and, soon after, Morris, who joined Burne-Jones in London. The two young men were primed for discipleship. For his part, Rossetti was eager for acolytes. Pre-Raphaelitism was flourishing, but the formal brotherhood had disbanded during the early 1850s, and Rossetti—flamboyant, charming, generous, and hungry for both fellowship and praise—eagerly took up the pair. "Two young men . . . have recently come to town . . . and are now very intimate friends of mine," he wrote in a letter. "Their names are Morris and Jones. They have turned artists instead of taking up any other career to which the University generally leads, and both are men of real genius."[15]

Burne-Jones had already demonstrated his genius for painting. Morris's only artistic endeavor to date, aside from writing poetry, was making rubbings of brass tombs in medieval churches around Oxford. No matter—Rossetti was certain that he could be a painter. Morris wrote to a friend in the summer of 1856, "Rossetti says I ought to paint, he says I shall be able; now as he is a very great man, and speaks with authority and not as the scribes, I *must* try. I don't hope much, I must say, yet will try my best."[16] By the end of the year, Rossetti had convinced Morris to throw over his fledgling career as an architect and the next summer enlisted him in a scheme to paint murals in the debating chamber of the Oxford Union. Neither Rossetti nor any of the young men he enlisted to help him had experience with murals, and they botched the job. The designs soon darkened into near invisibility. However, Morris's return to Oxford yielded more than wall paintings; it was during this time that he met his future wife.

Rossetti needed models for the Oxford Union murals, which depicted scenes from Malory's *Morte d'Arthur*. The artists could pose for one another as King Arthur and his knights, but that would not do for the women characters. There were no professional models to be had in Oxford, so Rossetti started looking about for attractive women. He called it trolling for "stunners." He had done it in London, which was how he met Elizabeth Siddal, a young working-class woman who was his model and companion throughout the 1850s and whom he later married. In Oxford, he came upon the perfect stunner in the audience at a theater one evening: Jane Burden, the seventeen-year-old daughter of a stable hand. She posed for Rossetti, then Morris; within a few months, Morris proposed marriage.

It was not the marriage Morris's family—perhaps even Morris himself—had expected. Burne-Jones, as a painter, may have been something of a bohemian, but he was courting a young woman he had known since childhood, Georgiana (Georgie) Macdonald, daughter of an eminent clergyman. Jane Burden came from the lower reaches of the working class. She was, however, an intelligent woman, an avid reader who listened contentedly as Morris, during their unconventional courtship, read aloud to her from Dickens's *Barnaby Rudge*. She was, moreover, startlingly beautiful: tall, thin, with elegant features and masses of dark, wavy hair. She was exotic looking, not typically English; people speculated that she had gypsy blood. Morris's portrait of her as Iseult, Tristan's lover, is awkwardly executed—it was one of Morris's first oil paintings, and he soon abandoned the medium—but it conveys Burden's strange, angular beauty. Morris supposedly scribbled on the canvas, "I cannot paint you but I love you."[17]

The young couple's feelings about their impending marriage cannot be known with certainty, but they must have been complicated. Judging from her later comments, Burden had no great passion for Morris, but marriage to the wealthy young artist would have been a means of lifting herself, at a stroke, out of her impoverished surroundings. For his part, Morris was no doubt infatuated with his striking young model, but the marriage also constituted a declaration of independence from middle-class conventionality. Moreover, there was the example of Rossetti's relationship with Elizabeth

FIGURE 3.1 William Morris, *La Belle Iseult* (1858). Tate, London.

Siddal. Marrying Burden was a way of simultaneously breaking from his smotheringly respectable background and linking himself with his artistic idol. No member of Morris's family attended the wedding on April 26, 1859. Immediately after the ceremony, the bride and groom left for an extended honeymoon in Europe.

Morris was well able to afford it. At twenty-one, he had come into an independent income thanks to a gift of stock from his widowed mother. Morris was financially comfortable enough that, in the months before his marriage, he began negotiations with Philip Webb, a talented young architect he had met when both were working for G. E. Street in Oxford. He asked Webb to design a house for him and Burden, something out of the ordinary. Morris wanted a house that would stand as an embodiment of the ideals that he had been developing since he entered Oxford: forward-looking medievalism, artisanal authenticity, communal fellowship. Once returned from his honeymoon, he and Webb began working in earnest. By the next summer the house was ready.

⊰⚘⊱

Rossetti called Red House "a real wonder of the age, more a poem than a house." He was given to hyperbole, but Red House is unquestionably extraordinary, an aesthetically distinguished building and an exuberant expression of Morris's developing utopian ideals. It was at once a shelter for a growing family (the Morrises' two daughters were born within two years of their arrival at the house), a workshop that recalled the integrated labor and living of the past, an experiment in new conceptions of decorative art, and a center of convivial fellowship. The house is located in Bexleyheath, Kent, now an hour's Tube ride from central London, though in Morris's day the journey by rail could take twice as long. Its name came from its red brick exterior and red tile roof—unusual at a time when suburban villas were uniformly stucco and slate. Morris described the house as "very mediaeval in spirit," and Webb's austere black-and-white elevations highlight the house's Gothic elements, with pointed arches over windows and doors, steeply pitched gables, and small round windows piercing the second floor. The warm red brickwork

FIGURE 3.2 Red House, Bexleyheath, London. Designed for William and Jane Morris
by Philip Webb in 1859. National Trust Images / Andrew Butler.

of the finished structure softens the austerity, making the house
seem invitingly eccentric.[18]

Morris was very happy at Red House, playing with his two young
daughters, working in his studio, serving as bountiful host. A friend
recalled, "It was the most beautiful sight in the world to see Morris
coming up from the cellar before dinner, beaming with joy, with his
hands full of bottles of wine and others tucked under his arms."[19]
Red House enabled Morris, still in his twenties, to re-create the
bonhomie he had enjoyed with the Set at Oxford, gathering friends
about him for food and wine and games. There are stories of them
shrieking with laughter at hide-and-seek, pelting one another with
the apples that grew in profusion in the orchard just outside the
windows.

Morris and his friends threw their youthful energies into decorat-
ing Red House. The house began to fill with massive pieces of
wooden furniture, constructed to Morris's specifications, and
painted by Morris and Burne-Jones and Rossetti with scenes from
medieval life. For his murals in the drawing room, depicting the
wedding of Sir Degravant and Lady Melidor, Burne-Jones gave the

bridal couple the faces of William and Jane Morris, collapsing the centuries between medieval legend and contemporary life and creating a visual enactment of the young artists' desire to bring the lost virtues of the medieval era—its courtliness and heroism; its earnest, imperfect art and craftsmanship—into the modern world. Burne-Jones said at the time that they were "slowly making Red House the beautifullest place on earth," but Morris's aims went far beyond the aesthetic. "All the minor arts" of mid-Victorian England, he said, "were in a state of complete degradation." By "minor arts," he meant the arts of daily living—the design of dinnerware and furniture, of fabrics and wallpaper. He had a sense that the path to a better future began with the transformation of the material conditions of everyday life. So, he said, "with the conceited courage of a young man I set myself to reforming all that."[20] His reforming zeal led, the year after the completion of Red House, to the establishment of the Firm—officially Morris, Marshall, Faulkner & Co.—which would soon become one of the most celebrated design companies in history.

The Marshall of the Firm's formal name was Peter Paul Marshall, a civil engineer and minor painter with excellent connections among Pre-Raphaelite patrons. Charles Faulkner was an Oxford friend from the days of the Set, a mathematician who became the Firm's first business manager. The other partners were all accomplished artists: Rossetti, Burne-Jones, architect Philip Webb, and Pre-Raphaelite painter Ford Madox Brown. Early in 1861, the Firm issued its first circular seeking commissions, describing the partners as "Fine Art Workmen in Painting, Carving, Furniture, and the Metals."[21] The primary audience for the circular was clergymen. The Firm's most important early commissions were for the renovation of churches, and it quickly gained a reputation for its superb stained glass. Later, its wallpapers sold widely to private clients, and now, more than 150 years later, most people familiar with Morris's name know him as a designer of wallpapers and fabrics.

Morris's designs remain fresh and, on first glance, even startling: bold and deeply colored. Most wallpaper is designed to be unassuming and tasteful, to form a decorous background to furniture and framed pictures. Morris's wallpapers are closer in effect to the murals he and his friends were painting at Red House, works of art that

FIGURE 3.3 William Morris and Philip Webb, "Trellis" wallpaper (1864).
Victoria and Albert Museum, London.

dominate a room, drawing attention to themselves. His first design
was "Trellis," based on a rose trellis in the Red House garden. It is a
brilliant design, one of Morris's greatest. The repeated squares of
the trellis are simultaneously beautifully realistic and frankly meta-
poetic, acknowledging the mechanically repeating nature of wallpaper design and manufacture and echoing the square shapes of the
woodblocks that the Firm used to print its papers. It is as if Morris

FIGURE 3.4 Edward Burne-Jones, caricature of William Morris
at a weaving demonstration. William Morris Gallery, London
Borough of Waltham Forest. UK / Bridgeman Images.

wanted to dissolve the boundary between the domestic and the natural and turn the sturdy masonry of his clients' houses into living forms. His wallpapers are imbued with a utopian desire for harmony with nature that suffuses his work in every medium.

With extraordinary zeal, Morris set out to master every aspect of the Firm's production. He not only designed wallpapers and fabric but also taught himself to carve woodblocks for printing, to dye fabric, and to weave. Burne-Jones drew a series of caricatures of Morris at work, intended to raise a chuckle among their friends. In all of them, Burnes-Jones emphasizes Morris's corpulence, his great mane of curly hair, and his intense focus on his work. Part of the fun, though, was simply the idea of this brilliant Oxford graduate and distinguished poet working at such humble occupations. Burne-Jones's own profession of painting may have had bohemian associations, but it was nevertheless a gentlemanly pursuit. Morris, how-

FIGURE 3.5 William Morris in a workman's smock. William Morris Gallery, London Borough of Waltham Forest.

ever, was likely to show up at a dinner party with his hands colored blue from the dyeing vats. He had himself photographed in his workman's smock, and outside the workshop he took to wearing rough blue serge suits, with no cravat. Fourteen years after founding the Firm, Morris deliberately sat on this top hat, crushing it—a physical declaration of independence from the gentleman's code. Just as the Firm challenged nineteenth-century industrial methods, in his own life Morris challenged divisions between art and labor, gentleman and worker.

The Firm was quartered in central London, a distressingly long commute from Bexleyheath. In 1864 Morris and Burne-Jones came up with a plan to move the works near Red House and to expand the house itself. Webb drew up a design, an L-shaped addition that would create a quadrangle. Morris and Burne-Jones were wildly enthusiastic. They playfully named the expanded building-to-be the Palace of Art, after Tennyson's allegorical poem in which the narrator builds a "lordly pleasure-house" for his soul. The Palace of Art would vastly expand not only the living space of Red House but also its utopian dimensions. The design recalled an Oxford college or a medieval cloister, both utopian spaces in Morris's imagination, and it held a promise of perpetual community and fellowship among the two families. Then disaster struck: Georgie Burne-Jones, pregnant with her second child, caught scarlet fever and delivered prematurely; the infant died three weeks later. Burne-Jones's own health was poor and, too distracted to work, he saw his income plummet. In November he wrote Morris to say that they would have to abandon the plans for Red House. Morris was devastated, writing in return, "As to our palace of Art, I confess your letter was a blow to me at first, though hardly an unexpected one—in short I cried." Within a few months, Morris decided to leave Red House himself. He had contracted a crippling rheumatic fever, which made his daily commute impossible for a time, and his independent income was suffering from a fall in his investments. With great reluctance, he put Red House up for sale, leased a new building for the Firm in London, and moved his family into quarters above the shop. Once they left the house in November 1865, he never set eyes on it again. The sight of it, he said, would be more than he could bear.[22]

The move from Red House had one positive effect: with the three to four hours gained daily by eliminating his lengthy commute, Morris resumed writing poetry. He had begun writing poetry as a teenager, greatly increased his output while at Oxford, and at twenty-three published his first volume, *The Defence of Guenevere* (1858), a collection of narrative poems on medieval subjects. Reviews were largely negative, and the volume sold poorly. Morris, stung, set poetry aside. Now, with time on his hands and his customary store of creative energy, he turned again to poetry. He planned out a collection of narrative poems modeled on Chaucer's *Canterbury Tales*. Like Chaucer, he invented a narrative frame: a group of fourteenth-century Norsemen set sail to find a fabled earthly paradise. After decades of fruitless search, they land in an unnamed land, where they and their hosts entertain one another by telling long stories: twenty-four in all, drawn from classical and medieval sources. *The Earthly Paradise*, published in three volumes between 1868 and 1870, was an enormous success. Reviews were highly favorable, and the entire work was reprinted multiple times in both Great Britain and the United States, turning Morris into one of England's most popular poets.

{⚜⚜}

The combination of his literary success and the rising fortunes of the Firm meant that Morris could think of getting a country house. In the spring of 1871, he wrote Charley Faulkner an elated letter:

> I have been looking about for a house for the wife and kids, and whither do you guess my eye is turned now? Kelmscott, a little village about two miles above Radcott Bridge—a heaven on earth; an old stone Elizabethan house like Water Eaton [a manor house near Oxford], and such

a garden! ... I am going there again on Saturday with Rossetti and
my wife: Rossetti because he thinks of sharing it with us if the thing
looks likely.[23]

Morris's description of the village and house as heavenly was perfectly sincere; his comment about Rossetti, as Faulkner well knew,
was disingenuous.

Morris assumed joint tenancy of Kelmscott Manor with Rossetti soon after their visit only partly in order to secure a country
house for his family. Just as important was the need to find a place
where Jane and Rossetti could carry on their love affair away from
the intensive scrutiny and quick-running gossip of London. Rossetti and Jane had been close since he first encountered her in
Oxford as a seventeen-year-old stunner. Their relationship intensified during the 1860s, following the death of Rossetti's wife, Elizabeth Siddal, in 1862 and the Morrises' move from Red House to
central London in 1865, when Jane was twenty-five and Rossetti
thirty-seven. That year he invited her to pose for a series of photographs in the garden of his home in Chelsea—the site of the
famous menagerie kept by the flamboyant, self-mythologizing artist, which included at various times a wombat, kangaroos, and
armadillos as well as owls, hedgehogs, peacocks, and an assort-
ment of other mammals, birds, and lizards. In the photographs,
Jane is wearing one of the demure, high-necked, vaguely medieval
gowns she preferred, but her languorous poses carry an erotic
charge. Rossetti described her that summer as the "very Queen of
Beauty."[24]

Over the next few years Rossetti made dozens of drawings and
numerous paintings of the Queen of Beauty, works that create a
uniformly idealized image of Jane Morris—elongating her neck,
slimming her cheeks, sharpening her nose, and turning her lips ro-
seate and plump, as if begging to be kissed. All those characteristics
can be seen in the famous 1868 portrait known formally as *Mrs.
William Morris in a Blue Silk Dress*. Morris commissioned and paid
for the portrait, and Rossetti's Latin inscription on the frame acknowledges that his subject is the wife of a famous poet. But it also
cheekily praises her great beauty and boasts that her fame will live
on in his painting.

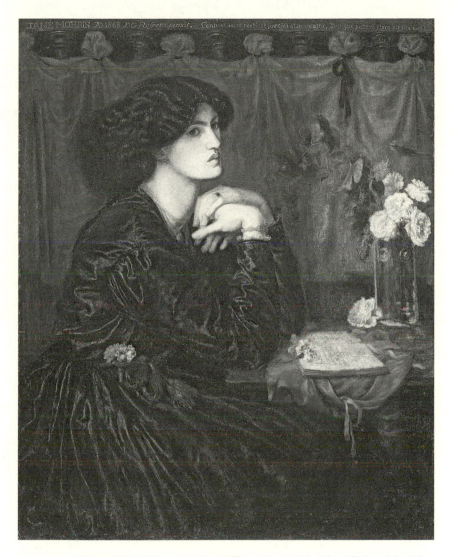

FIGURE 3.6 Dante Gabriel Rossetti, *Mrs. William Morris* (*The Blue Silk Dress*) (1868).
Society of Antiquaries of London: Kelmscott Manor, UK / Bridgeman Images.

In the spring of that year Rossetti drew a design of linked rosettes in a notebook and wrote two dates: September 1857—the month he met Jane—and April 14, 1868. It is not known what occurred between the two on the latter date. Jan Marsh, biographer of both Rossetti and Jane Morris, thinks it unlikely that they had sexual intercourse then—or indeed at any time, given a physical problem that may have rendered Rossetti impotent. She suggests that the two declared their love for each other.[25] In any case, the relationship was passionate, and their mutual infatuation was clear to everyone in their circle.

Morris's reaction to the love affair was remarkably muted. He suffered, as Florence Boos writes, in "stoic silence," expressing his anguish only in a series of unpublished poems.[26] The tone of his many letters to Jane remained consistently affectionate throughout their long marriage, even during the height of her affair with Rossetti. None of Jane's letters to Morris survive. They lived together, according to observers' accounts, in unbroken if somewhat distant amity. Morris acknowledged, in a letter to his close friend Philip Webb, that he was inept at expressing affection: "I am something of an Englishman and the words wont flow."[27] Rossetti, in contrast, was famously smooth-tongued with women. It is not surprising that Jane fell in love with him. And it is understandable that Morris decided to avoid a scandal and keep intact his marriage and, at least for a time, his business partnership.

By 1871, however, Morris was keen to get his wife and Rossetti out of London. The latter two spent the summer together at Kelmscott, along with the Morris children, while Morris traveled to Iceland. The next summer Rossetti and Jane were again at Kelmscott while Morris dropped in occasionally, but the lovers' relationship was permanently altered by the severe mental breakdown Rossetti experienced that year. His attempt at suicide was not successful, but his turn to alcohol and drugs succeeded all too well. He spent much of the remaining ten years of his life physically ill, mentally disturbed, and befuddled by whiskey and chloral. He gave up his share of the Kelmscott Manor tenancy in 1874, and the next year Morris became the Firm's sole proprietor, ending his business association with Rossetti. Rossetti protested bitterly, but Morris was clearly relieved, not least because he had Kelmscott to himself.

Kelmscott Manor is not a grand country house of the sort beloved by BBC period dramas. It is a gray stone house that began as the relatively modest home of a prosperous Oxfordshire farmer in about 1600. The front of the three-story house is marked by two high gables that flank the entrance; to the right is a large later addition, set perpendicular. The interior layout is eccentric, with mismatched floor and ceiling heights, and a first-floor sitting room opening directly into a bedroom. Outside runs a small stream that feeds into the Thames, a short walk away. Morris loved the house intensely. It seemed to him almost a living thing, as if it were not constructed but had "grown up out of the soil and the lives of those that lived on it." He thought Kelmscott Manor "the type of the pleasant places of the earth, and of the homes of harmless simple people not overburdened with the intricacies of life; and as others love the race of man through their lovers or their children, so I love the earth through that small space of it."[28]

The house was a retreat, but it also inspired Morris with visions of a utopian future. In March 1874, less than three years after he first saw Kelmscott, he wrote a friend from London, where he was immersed in work despite his longing to get out to the country. He began by grumbling about the city: "Surely if people lived 500 years instead of three score & ten they would find some better way of living than in such a sordid loathsome place." Then he turned to speculation: "But look, suppose people lived in little communities among gardens & green fields, so that you could be in the country in 5 minutes walk, & had few wants; almost no furniture for instance, & no servants, & studied (the difficult) arts of enjoying life, & finding out what they really wanted: then I think one might hope civilization had really begun."[29] Kelmscott Manor served as foundation for Morris's later utopian imaginings of a simple life in harmony with nature.

His imagination was spurred also by the two trips he made to Iceland in the early 1870s, soon after acquiring Kelmscott. Iceland was not, at the time, on the itinerary of the typical English tourist. Getting there required a five- or six-day voyage on a small ship over rough seas. Once there, visitors encountered a poor island nation, its economy based on fishing. There were no hotels or inns—visitors had to find accommodation with locals or pitch a tent—and the transportation infrastructure consisted of ponies. What drew Morris to this forbidding destination was heroism: the deeds of ancient heroes recorded in the Icelandic sagas and his own need for stalwart stoicism in the face of private difficulties.

Morris had always been attracted to Old Norse literature, which he found a bracing corrective to what he called the "maundering side" of medievalism. When he encountered Eiríkr Magnússon, an

Icelandic scholar living in London, in 1868, he immediately arranged to meet three days a week with his new friend. Magnússon
would teach him the Icelandic language, and the two would write
translations of medieval works. Morris fell in love with the old
stories: "The delightful freshness and independence of thought of
them, the air of freedom which breathes through them, their worship of courage (the great virtue of the human race), their utter
unconventionality took my heart by storm," Morris wrote.[30] Within
two years, the two men completed translations of several major
sagas. When the opportunity arose to travel to Iceland with Magnússon in 1871, Morris seized it. Filled with energy, he set about
making arrangements for what he knew would be a difficult two-
month journey at the same time as he arranged to install his family
and his wife's lover in Kelmscott Manor.

The journey was as difficult as he anticipated: long miles astride
the ponies, mountainous terrain, rough camping, and lashings of
rain and snow. On his first day out of Reykjavík, Morris found the
scenery disconcertingly barren and forbidding. "Most strange and
awful the country looked to me," he wrote in his journal, "in spite of
all my anticipations: a doleful land at first with its great rubbish
heaps of sand, striped scantily with grass sometimes." Yet Morris
also found it exhilarating, to the point that he made a second trip to
Iceland two years after the first. After that journey, he wrote to a
friend that "the glorious simplicity of the terrible & tragic, but beautiful land with its well remembered stories of brave men, killed all
querulous feeling in me."[31] Morris brought back from Iceland an
ethic of stoic courage and experience of a society based in simplicity
and equality. Both the ethical and social ideals would prove crucial
to Morris in the remaining two decades of his life, when he rein-
vented himself, turning from popular artist and poet into a controversial political writer and activist animated by an unyielding
utopianism.

William Morris's transformation from one of England's most celebrated artist-writers into its sole public artist-writer-socialist began
in the late 1870s, prompted by the unlikely combination of the

Ottoman Empire and old buildings. The Victorian political crisis known as the "Eastern Question" first drew him into public activism. The Eastern Question was a shorthand term for the long-running tension between western European nations and Russia, which jostled for influence in eastern Europe as the Ottoman Empire unraveled. In 1876 it seemed as if England might be drawn into a war between Turkey and Russia when the government of Conservative prime minister Benjamin Disraeli threw its support to Turkey as a means of countering Russian expansionism. British liberals, appalled by sensationalized newspaper accounts of Turkish atrocities against Bulgarian Christians, opposed any alliance with the Ottoman Empire. Former Prime Minister William Gladstone rallied Disraeli's liberal opponents, and William Morris became deeply involved in the antiwar movement as treasurer of the Eastern Question Association (EQA). Morris threw his formidable energy into the cause, and his letters of the time show him obsessively following the intricate political maneuvering within Parliament. The liberals were successful—Britain stayed out of the Russo-Turkish War of 1877–78—but the experience left Morris with a fundamental distrust of parliamentary politics.[32]

At the same time as he was active in the EQA, Morris founded the Society for the Protection of Ancient Buildings, known familiarly as "Anti-Scrape." Enamored as he was with Gothic architecture, he became dismayed by a series of clumsy restorations of medieval churches, and early in 1877 he sent a letter to the *Athenaeum* magazine proposing a new society for architectural preservation. "What I wish for," he wrote, is an association "to keep a watch on old monuments, to protest against all 'restoration' that means more than keeping out wind and weather, and . . . to awaken a feeling that our ancient buildings are not mere ecclesiastical toys, but sacred monuments of the nation's growth and hope." The society's manifesto, published the next month, was even blunter. Morris wrote that the past fifty years of so-called "Restoration" had done more damage to ancient buildings "than all the foregoing centuries of revolution, violence, and contempt."[33]

Morris's love of ancient buildings was so strong that, on occasion, he would erupt into one of his legendary rages at the sight of an ill-conceived restoration. On his first visit to Glasgow's magnificent twelfth-century cathedral, he spied a modern memorial in white marble that had been erected against the building's exterior. "What the hell is that?" he yelled to the consternation of Glaswegian pass-ers-by. "What infernal idiot has done *that*?" He kept up his high-volume rant for some minutes. His host, a buttoned-up Scot, was mortified, although he noted with relief that after a while the on-lookers, "believing they were witnessing the distraction of some unfortunate fellow creature bereft of his reason, resumed their way, remarking compassionately about him to one another."[34]

Drawing on his reading of Ruskin and of recent historians of the Middle Ages, Morris began working out a unified theory that could explain the aesthetic decline from medieval to modern times and bring together his love for Gothic architecture, his work in handi-crafts, and his recent engagement in political activism. You can see him formulating his theory in the lectures on art that he began de-livering in 1877. His ideas were anchored in his radical interpreta-tion of medieval history. The dominant Whig historians of the nine-teenth century had a progressive view of British history: the Middle Ages, a time of gross ignorance and brutal violence, had been suc-ceeded by the glories of the Renaissance, which was succeeded by the Age of Enlightenment, which gave way to the nineteenth cen-tury—an era of scientific and technological achievements, increased wealth, rapid growth of political democracy, and unsurpassed levels of education, refinement, and taste. Morris turned the conventional Whig histories on their head. In his view, the nineteenth century was notable not for its supposed achievements but for the ugliness of its cities and the destruction of the countryside, for the misery of the mass of industrial workers juxtaposed to the vulgar luxury of the rich. In the Middle Ages, by contrast, the worker was a crafts-man—which is to say, an artist—who was free to produce items of beauty. His work was a joy to him, and he lived in a simple and beautiful house, worshipped in a grand and beautiful church, and was surrounded by beautiful, handmade objects. Morris did not deny the tyranny and violence of the Middle Ages, but he argued that the violence was occasional, while the work—creative and sat-isfying—was ongoing. "Not every day, you may be sure, was a day of slaughter and tumult, though the histories read almost as if it were so," he lectured; "but every day the hammer chinked on the anvil, and the chisel played about the oak beam, and never without some beauty and invention being born of it, and consequently some human happiness."[35]

Morris threw out conventional historical periodization in favor of two broad labels that could explain British history from the eleventh century to the present: Feudalism and Commercialism. He had little interest in the conventional historical subjects of kings, queens, parliaments, and wars; instead, he gave his attention to the intertwined issues of art and labor. In the Feudal era, the artisan was his own master, and his labor "was sweetened by the daily creation of Art," but in the postmedieval Commercial epoch, the division of labor resulted in the "complete destruction" of the worker's individuality and his "enslavement to his profit-grinding master." In Morris's earliest lectures, delivered to audiences attracted by his reputation as a designer, he put his hopes for change in a transformation of the decorative—or "lesser"—arts, such as furniture, fabrics, and ceramics. "Only let the [lesser] arts . . . beautify our labour," he told the hearers of an 1877 lecture, "and there will be pretty much an end of dull work and its wearing slavery." A return to handicrafts could, he believed, fundamentally transform the nature of labor in the modern world. He went on, "There is nothing that will aid the world's progress so much as the attainment of this; I protest there is nothing in the world that I desire so much as this, wrapped up, as I am sure it is, with changes political and social, that in one way or another we all desire."[36]

Initially, Morris was uncertain about the nature of the political and social changes that were, he intuited, bound up with his ideas about the transformation of labor. Over the next few years, however, his aesthetic concerns became connected to his increasing discomfort with the economic and social disparities of class-bound British society. His awareness of class differences was spurred by his move to the London borough of Hammersmith in 1879. Morris, forty-five years old and at the height of his success as a designer, needed larger quarters for his household, which included not only his wife, Jane, and daughters, Jenny and May, but also three servants and a nurse for Jenny, who had epilepsy. He settled on a large eighteenth-century mansion with an unobstructed view of the Thames from the front windows and a spacious garden in back.

The situation might have been idyllic, except for the proximity of the Hammersmith slums. Sitting in his study, Morris frequently found his concentration interrupted by the yells and shrieks of his working-class neighbors. The disturbances aroused his explosive temper, filling him, by his own admission, with a "fierce wrath." Yet Morris had the self-awareness to curb his anger and to reflect that it was only his good luck in being born "respectable and rich" that put him in his luxurious study "among delightful books and lovely works of art" and not in the streets, among "drink-steeped liquor-shops [and] foul and degraded lodgings." Another successful, middle-aged artist and business owner might have stopped there, with the acknowledgment of his good luck and compassion for those less fortunate. But the disparity gnawed at Morris, and he chafed as his consciousness of his class position increased, poised as he was between a brutalized lower class and the self-satisfied milieu of his wealthy clients, the only ones who could afford the exquisite hand-made productions of Morris & Co. In one famous incident, Morris turned suddenly on one of his most loyal customers, Sir Isaac Low-thian Bell, who came upon Morris stamping about and talking to himself and inquired if anything was wrong. "It is only," Morris exploded, "that I spend my life in ministering to the swinish luxury of the rich." Morris was maddened by the contradictions in his own life. He believed that the decorative arts could beautify and ennoble the lives of every person—"I do not want art for a few," he said in an 1877 lecture, "any more than education for a few, or freedom for a few"—yet the Firm's products were priced beyond the reach of the working class. He hated class hierarchy and believed in absolute human equality, yet he lived with his family in a grand house, attended by servants.[37]

Tormented by these contradictions and convinced that society must be entirely remade, Morris began a self-transformation from Gladstonian liberal to revolutionary socialist. The process was not simple. As in the United States at the time, there was virtually no organized socialist movement in Great Britain. As Fiona MacCarthy writes, at the beginning of the 1880s left-wing politics in Britain were "a confused amalgam of the London working-men's and Radical clubs, the remnants of the Chartists, and the more recent influx of foreign refugees."[38] Karl Marx had been living in London since

1849, but little of his work had been translated into English, and his immediate influence in England was limited to a small circle of German-speaking émigrés. Yet when a friend stopped by the Morris & Co. shop in Oxford Street one day in 1882, Morris declared to him, "I'm going in for socialism."[39]

Absent Marx, Morris was converted to socialism through his reading of an eclectic group of authors: Ruskin, Thomas More, Robert Owen, Charles Fourier, Henry George. At some point not long after its publication in 1881, he also read H. M. Hyndman's *England for All*, the notorious book that introduced Marxist ideas to a broad English readership. Hyndman was definitely not the person his Cambridge classmates would have voted Most Likely to Establish English Socialism. Son of a wealthy businessman, his chief distinction at university had been his ability on the cricket pitch. After graduation, he became a journalist and then in 1880 a candidate for Parliament—an unsuccessful one, since his political views were an awkward mix of social radicalism and Tory jingoism. Soon afterward he read Marx's *Capital* in a French translation and converted to socialism. He published *England for All* in 1881 and the same year founded a new political organization, the Democratic Federation, which later became the Social Democratic Federation (SDF). The book championed British imperialism but also borrowed heavily from *Capital* in its economic analysis. Hyndman coyly acknowledged his debt to "a great thinker and original writer" but never mentioned Marx's name. Marx was outraged. He and Engels regarded Hyndman as an unprincipled, opportunistic careerist. They were exactly right. The SDF was for a time, however, the only socialist organization in Great Britain, and by January 1883 Morris felt himself duty-bound to join it.[40]

Morris's friends and acquaintances could not believe that he was truly serious about socialism. When a group of Oxford students, with undergraduates' delight in provocation, invited Morris and Hyndman to address them, the authorities vetoed Hyndman but approved Morris, eminent Oxonian and celebrated poet. Morris protested against Hyndman's exclusion—"I am quite as much a socialist as he is"—but it did no good. In November 1883 Morris proceeded to Oxford to lecture on "Art and Democracy."[41] He began his lecture on familiar ground: the relation between art and labor and the historical change from the artistic apogee of the Middle Ages to the brutal commercialism of the present. He then went on to declare that he was "one of the people called Socialists," and he urged his listeners to "renounce their class pretensions and cast in their lot with the working men." The college masters were aghast. In the words of J. W. Mackail, Morris's first biographer and himself an Oxford man, they had continued "with a sort of obstinate innocence" to believe that dear old Morris was not actually a socialist. "When they found that he had really meant what he said, their feeling was one which approached consternation."[42]

The letters and diaries of eminent Victorians are filled with exclamations of wonder at what had gotten into William Morris. When novelist George Gissing read newspaper accounts of Morris's September 1885 arrest in a mêlée associated with a socialist demonstration, he wrote to his brother, "Do you see the report of the row the Socialists have had with the police in the East End? Think of William Morris being hauled into the box for assaulting a policeman! . . . Alas, what the devil is such a man doing in that galley? It is painful to me beyond expression. Why cannot he write poetry in the shade? He will inevitably coarsen himself in the company of ruffians."[43]

What the devil *was* William Morris doing in such company? Morris was fully aware of the oddity of his position. At the time he joined the SDF it had only a few members, all of them, with the possible exception of Hyndman, trailing far behind Morris in terms of education, wealth, and prominence. Conscious that most of his peers regarded him as simultaneously a class traitor and a laughingstock, he spoke of enduring "the inconveniences of martyrdom, though without gaining its dignity." His most powerful explanation of his decision to cross what he called "the river of fire" and become a revolutionary socialist comes in an 1883 letter. Morris explained that he couldn't help asking how he himself would feel if he had happened to be born poor instead of rich. The question made him "ashamed" of his own position. "Nothing can argue me out of this feeling, which I say plainly is a matter of religion to me," he wrote. "The contrasts of rich and poor are unendurable and ought not to be endured by either rich or poor. Now it seems to me that, feeling this, I am bound to act for the destruction of the system which seems to me mere oppression and obstruction."[44] Morris seems to have been harkening back to his visits to Iceland and his translations from the Icelandic. The heroes of the Norse sagas had not quailed from facing their foes, no matter how fearsome. Neither would he.

Given that capitalism must be destroyed, the only question was how best to effect its destruction. Morris's answer was to *"make Socialists."*[45] This formulation of the task distinguished Morris from two other camps within the small British socialist movement. On one side were the parliamentary reformers, who put their faith in electing socialist MPs. Elect enough of them, the thinking went, and Great Britain would experience a second Glorious—and bloodless—Revolution, with capitalism eliminated through the legislative process. In the U.S., Edward Bellamy and the Nationalists followed this "parliamentary" path, supporting Nationalist and then Populist candidates as a practical method of moving toward a socialist utopia. In the U.K., the Fabian Society, founded in 1884, advocated a similar strategy. Opposed to these gradualists were the proponents of revolutionary violence, who believed that violence directed against emblems of the ruling class, or against its members, would hasten the coming of the open class warfare necessary for the destruction of capitalism. The British left contained relatively few activists committed to immediate violence, but Britons had only to look to Europe and Russia to see examples of the philosophy in action.

Morris rejected both alternatives. He acknowledged that violence might be necessary at some point in the struggle to overthrow capitalism, but he rejected bombings and assassinations as futile; they played into the hands of reactionaries and could not spark a revolution, since few British workers had any knowledge of alternatives to capitalism. As for the parliamentary strategy, he had seen enough political maneuvering during his work for the EQA to be convinced that the few socialist representatives who might conceivably be elected would be swallowed by the institutional leviathan and quickly dissolved in the acidic juices of endless committee meetings, reports, and legislative compromise.

Given his aversion to both immediate acts of violence and conventional activism within the parliamentary system, Morris embraced the strategy of making socialists through propaganda, a term he used frequently. "Propaganda" had no negative connotation in the late nineteenth century and perfectly expressed Morris's commitment to spreading the socialist faith through writing and, in particular, through speaking. He lectured throughout England and Scotland to whoever would have him: SDF branches, the Fabians, Secular Societies, workingmen's clubs. In good weather, he frequently spoke on street corners to passersby. Conditions were often difficult—he wrote to his daughter May that in Birmingham he'd had to compete for an audience with a troupe of performing fleas— and the work was exhausting. He had to shout to attract hearers, deal with hecklers, and endure harassment by the police. Yet for years, whenever he was in London he devoted his Sundays to socialist lecturing, though occasionally, and understandably, with reluctance. "It is a beautiful bright autumn morning here," he wrote to a friend early one Sunday, "and I am not over-inclined for my morning preachment at Walham Green, but go I must also to Victoria Park in the afternoon. I had a sort of dastardly hope that it might rain."[46]

Morris lectured tirelessly for the SDF from the time he joined the organization in January 1883 until his resignation two years later. The break came because of Hyndman, whose autocratic nature made him increasingly difficult to work with. In the most diplomatic expression of his reasons for leaving the SDF, Morris cited Hyndman's "unfortunate spirit of political ambition"; at his frankest, he called the man a "precious rascal."[47] The difficulties within the SDF did nothing to lessen Morris's certainty that socialism was the path to a utopian future. Three days after his resignation, he and nine other former SDF members founded the Socialist League, for which he served as speaker, writer, editor, organizer, treasurer, and funder-of-last-resort over the next six years.

Morris co-wrote the founding manifesto of the Socialist League, which was published on the front page of the first issue of the new organization's journal, *The Commonweal*, in February 1885. The manifesto begins as a primer on socialism; Morris clearly did not expect his British readers to know anything about the movement's basic tenets. By its end, the manifesto becomes a utopian document, moving from a critique of current conditions and an explanation of socialism to a forecast of the world to come: not only will labor and the economy be transformed, but also marriage and education, along with all other personal and social relationships. "Mere work," Morris writes stirringly, "would no longer be proposed as the end of life, but happiness for each and all."[48]

Morris would sorely need this utopian vision of the happy world to come during the next few years, when the Socialist League became as riven by dissension and factionalism as the SDF had been. On Morris's right flank were the parliamentarians, who wanted to advance socialism by introducing legislation and running candidates for Parliament. Morris repeatedly argued that this strategy was futile, since Parliament's fundamental purpose was "the preservation of society in its present [capitalist] form."[49] Any changes introduced through the parliamentary process would be a matter of tinkering with the political machinery in order to keep it running more efficiently—thus delaying the necessary socialist revolution.

To Morris's left were the anarchists. During the late nineteenth century, two strains of anarchism competed for dominance. On one hand was the "mutualist" strain of anarchism promoted by the Russian political theorist Peter Kropotkin. Morris became friendly with Kropotkin after the latter moved to London in 1886, and he had few disagreements with the Russian's political philosophy. Kropotkin argued, contra Darwin, that cooperation, not competition, was the driving force in evolution, and he imagined a future society made up of what he called "free federations": small, decentralized associations of individuals for mutual aid and collective action.[50] In contrast to Kropotkin, most of the anarchists in the Socialist League fell into the movement's "individualist" wing. The individualists rejected all notions of authority, no matter how democratically conceived. On a theoretical level, Morris thought they were wrong; he believed that, even in the ideal future community, decisions would have to be made by majority rule. On a practical level, their individualist ethics made them extremely difficult to work with. Morris's daughter May described an "atmosphere of constant quarrel" within the Socialist League.[51]

Morris remained active in the Socialist League throughout the 1880s in spite of the constant quarrels. His political speeches and essays of these years are filled with denunciations of the brutality and ugliness of contemporary civilization, but a few also contain a future-oriented utopian dimension. Marx famously disdained utopian speculation, saying that he had no interest in writing "reci-pes . . . for the cook-shops of the future."[52] However, Marx, in Mor-ris's terminology, was an "analytical" socialist, while he himself was a "visionary."[53] Morris's utopian essays of the 1880s center on five principal characteristics of his utopian vision. Most fundamental is the eradication of class difference. Morris delighted in envisioning a time when the words "poor" and "rich," though they might still be found in the dictionaries, would be virtually incomprehensible in the egalitarian society to come.[54] Next is the transformation of labor, which in Morris's mind was intimately connected with the creation of art. "Art is the expression of man's pleasure in labour"— this, Morris believed, was the heart of John Ruskin's message, and Morris devoted his entire career to defining and enacting pleasur-able labor.[55] In his ideal society, craftsmanship would take prece-dence over the division of labor. Morris was no Luddite, however, and his utopian vision made room for machinery. Machines, he ar-gued, should be utilized to perform society's most distasteful tasks, leaving workers free to perform meaningful labor, by which he meant the production of objects of utility and beauty.

Education was central to Morris's discussions of future society, but he had little interest in reforming schools. Instead, he wanted to replace the "class" education of the present, designed to sort peo-ple into the categories of worker or manager, with a truly "liberal"— that is, liberatory—education that would equip everyone for both pleasure and productivity.[56] Morris's idea of a liberal education in-cluded instruction in reading and writing, but his real interest was in the "arts of life," among which he included swimming, riding, boating, carpentry, cooking, baking, and sewing.[57] Morris did not directly address gender equality in his utopian essays, yet his belief that everyone should learn to build and bake and sew upset conven-tional hierarchies based on women's and men's supposedly "natural" tendencies and pointed toward an egalitarian future.

Along with education, Morris demanded health for everyone, which to him meant the elimination, as far as possible, not only of disease but also of asceticism. He advocated a healthy sensuality, the extinction of any shame associated with sexuality and the body. Insofar, he said, as "we feel the least degradation in being amorous, or merry, or hungry, or sleepy, we are so far bad animals, and therefore miserable men."[58] Finally, Morris believed that a better future demanded a restored natural world. He had spent his childhood in Epping Forest, sighting birds and climbing trees; as an adult, he lived in the industrialized London borough of Hammersmith, with its skies darkened by smoke and the river Thames, which ran in front of his home, filled with poisonous waste. Enamored of the art and craftsmanship of the Middle Ages, he imagined a future in which the city could be returned to its medieval condition, with "a few pleasant villages on the side of the Thames" in place of "that preposterous piece of folly once called London."[59]

During the same period in the 1880s when he was writing his utopian essays, Morris published two serialized fictions in *Commonweal*, the Socialist League journal that he edited. Both works nod toward utopia. *The Pilgrims of Hope* (1885–86), the first of the *Commonweal* fictions, is a long narrative poem about the Paris Commune. At the time of the Commune in 1871, years before his own turn to socialism, Morris had paid scant attention to the events in Paris, when for ten weeks a radical coalition of socialists, anarchists, and communists had ruled the city. Following his conversion to socialism, however, he, like many British socialists, came to regard the Paris Commune as an emblem of utopian possibility. The narrator of *Pilgrims of Hope* is an English socialist who, despairing of any possibility of revolution in his own country, travels to Paris to join in the Commune. Once there, he finds a populace suffused with joy: "I saw what few have beheld, a folk with all hearts gay."[60] This utopian moment is short-lived, however, both for the Commune and the narrator. The French national army invades Paris and, in what became known as the "Bloody Week," slaughters thousands of Communards and seizes power. The narrator's wife and best friend are killed in battle, and he retreats to England.

A Dream of John Ball (1886–87), the second *Commonweal* fiction, is a prose novella set during the English Peasants' Revolt of 1381. The unnamed narrator, a present-day socialist and obvious stand-in for Morris, dreams himself into a fourteenth-century Kentish village on the eve of the revolt. Morris's deep love for the built environment of the Middle Ages suffuses the tale's early pages. A village church, so new that the stone carvers' dust still lies on the grass beneath the windows, "ravishe[s his] heart with its extreme beauty, elegance, and fitness." Every building in the village is equally beautiful, and though the gaily attired people may be "rough," they are "merry and good-tempered."[61] As in *Pilgrims of Hope*, the utopian moment is fleeting; the men of the village are about to go into battle against the king's forces. They win the skirmish, but the narrator, like his readers, knows that the revolt will soon be put down and its leaders, including the saintly John Ball, will be executed in London.

The year after Morris completed *A Dream of John Ball*, Edward Bellamy's *Looking Backward* was published in England and quickly became a best-seller. Morris felt compelled to address Bellamy's utopian romance in *Commonweal;* his review is a polite but efficient evisceration. He begins by examining, with clear distaste, what he calls Bellamy's "temperament." That temperament, he says, "makes its owner (if a Socialist), perfectly satisfied with modern civilization, if only the injustice, misery, and waste of class society could be got rid of; which half-change seems possible to him." Morris believed that injustice, misery, and waste were at the center of so-called "modern civilization," of which he was an avowed enemy. Bellamy's ideal society, Morris pointed out, involved little more than a change in economic arrangements. As an example, he pointed out that Bellamy's "only idea of making labour tolerable" was "to decrease the amount of it by means of fresh and ever fresh developments of machinery," whereas his own view was that "the true incentive to useful and happy labour is and must be pleasure in the work itself." Morris insisted that he did not want to quarrel with Mr. Bellamy's vision of the future, since that, he said, "must always be more or less personal to [an author]." Nevertheless, he saw the book as a threat, since it was "sure to be quoted as an authority for what Socialists believe."[62] The prospect clearly rankled Morris. His review implies the need for an alternative vision of the socialist future. Who better to provide it than himself?

{~~~⟩⟨~~~}

Only six months after Morris's review of *Looking Backward* was published in *Commonweal*, the magazine's January 1890 issue featured on its first page the opening installment of *News from No-*

where: or, An Epoch of Rest. Being Some Chapters from a Utopian Romance. The novel begins in a Socialist League meeting room where the members are arguing vehemently about what the society of the future, following the socialist revolution, will be like. The first-person narrator, William Guest—a thinly disguised stand-in for William Morris—leaves fuming. He mulls over the clever ripostes he should have used at the time, berates himself for having lost his temper, then turns to a note of pure longing for the world to come: "If I could but see a day of it," he says to himself; "if I could but see it!" Back home in the "shabby" London borough of Hammersmith, he falls asleep on a cold winter's night.[63]

He awakens on a glorious June morning sometime in the twenty-first century, in a future world that resembles Morris's beloved Middle Ages. The industrial works along the Thames riverbanks have disappeared, replaced by graceful cottages. The Hammersmith bridge, a technological marvel of nineteenth-century ironwork, has ceded place to a graceful stone structure resembling the Ponte Vecchio in Florence. And the first person he meets is a Thames ferryman who is beautifully dressed in a medieval-style tunic cinched by a broad leather belt with an elaborate handworked clasp.

The ferryman rows Guest out for a midriver swim in a miraculously pristine Thames, free of its Victorian-era industrial pollution. The narrator's immersion in the cool, clear water functions as a baptismal rite that ushers him into the edenic paradise that England has become. London, Guest soon learns, is now a collection of villages separated by open countryside. Some areas are more densely populated, to accommodate people who like to live among a crowd, but England as a whole has undergone de-urbanization. We learn that the place called Manchester, England's third-largest city, has disappeared. The railroads have disappeared as well, and although there are "force vehicles" on land and "force-barges" on the river, most people prefer to travel by premodern modes. The characters in the book go by horse cart or, on the river, by rowboat. In its physical aspects, all of England now resembles Morris's two favorite places on earth, Oxford and Rouen, largely restored to what they were in the fourteenth century.

Critics often exaggerate the science fiction dimensions of *Looking Backward*—the novel actually contains few technological marvels—but Bellamy's utopia is built upon central agents and values of modernity: science and technology, mechanization, urbanization, and centralized bureaucratic administration. Bellamy's vision of the good life depends on machine production and specialization of labor within the city beautiful. *News from Nowhere* displays William Morris's lifelong revolt against modernity. The technological, political, and economic accomplishments of which the Victorians were so proud have been jettisoned in favor of a pastoral simplicity. Government, politics, money, schools—even labor as conventionally understood—have disappeared.

In the opening chapters of *News from Nowhere*, William Guest plays the role of wide-eyed visitor in the utopia of his creator's imagination. His initial guide is Dick Hammond, the ferryman. Yet it is a mistake to identify Dick with his work ferrying people across the Thames. In utopia, the specialization of labor that distinguishes the modern era is no more, and virtually everyone Guest meets does multiple forms of work. Dick does fine metalworking when he is not on the river, and he volunteers to serve as Guest's guide over the course of the next few days, since he was already planning to head upstream on the Thames to join in the haying in Oxfordshire, for the sheer pleasure of using his muscles in a spell of what he calls "easy-hard work." During his absence from London, his friend Robert—a weaver and mathematician—will take over the ferry. The distinction between labor and recreation has disappeared in Nowhere. On a walk about London, Dick and Guest pass a group of road-menders. Guest is eager to see how people "would set to on a piece of real necessary work." They do so with the same casual joy that infuses every other activity in utopia, looking more like "a boating party at Oxford" than like the rough navvies who mended roads in Victorian England. The road-menders are handsome, finely dressed young men who chat with a group of attractive women as they work. Dick envies them: "It's right down good sport trying how much pick-work one can get into an hour," he says before reluctantly moving on.[64]

Edward Bellamy constructed his utopia on the assumption that work was a distasteful necessity. All employments in his future world require only a few hours a day, and the least desirable tasks lure workers by requiring the fewest hours. Moreover, all workers, whatever their occupation, retire at forty-five. Morris was horrified at this idea. "Heavens! think of a man of forty-five changing all his habits suddenly and by compulsion!" he wrote in his review of *Looking Backward*. He attacked Bellamy's idea that the egalitarian society of the future would have to devise incentives besides the fear of poverty in order to induce people to labor: "It cannot be too often repeated that the true incentive to useful and happy labour is and must be pleasure in the work itself." Ten years before reading *Looking Backward*, he had attacked the idea of improving workers' lot by increasing their leisure: "Shall all we can do with [toil] be to shorten the hours of that toil to the utmost, that the hours of leisure may be long beyond what men used to hope for? and what then shall we do with the leisure, if we say that all toil is irksome? Shall we sleep it all away?—Yes, and never wake up again, I should hope, in that case."[65]

William Morris, moving indefatigably from writing romances to designing wallpaper to weaving tapestry, imagined a utopia in which everyone likes working as much as he does. "Fancy people not liking to work!—it's too ridiculous," Dick exclaims.[66] Another character explains that they would as soon think of devising extrinsic rewards for the work of copulation as for other forms of labor. In the future according to Morris, road-mending would be as pleasurable as sex.

Everyone Guest encounters seems suffused with something akin to postcoital euphoria. As Dick escorts him around London, he marvels at the inhabitants' youthful good looks and their openly joyous expressions. Even the act of procuring material necessities has become a pleasure. When Guest enters a shop in order to obtain a pipe and tobacco, he is enchanted by the two children in charge of the establishment; in utopia, shopkeeping is literally child's play. He is befuddled when he tries to pay and with difficulty understands that people in this society have no notion of commercial exchange or even of money. The pipe they give him is magnificent: hand-carved wood with decorations of gold and gems. Guest worries that it is far too fine for everyday use, but Dick can scarcely understand his concern. Someone made the pipe for the sheer pleasure of crafting it, and now it is his to enjoy.

Even before they reach the shop, Guest expresses his surprise that the children he sees are not in school. Dick is unfamiliar with the word *school*, and likewise with *education*. In response to Guest's alarm at this discovery, Dick reassures him. "Our children learn," he says, "whether they go through a 'system of teaching' or not. Why, you will not find one of these children about here, boy or girl, who cannot swim. . . . They all of them know how to cook; the bigger lads can mow; many can thatch and do odd jobs at carpentering; or they know how to keep shop. I can tell you they know plenty of things." It is only when prodded by Guest that Dick acknowledges that "book-learning" also takes place in this de-schooled society, although Dick has little interest in talking about his fellows' intellectual accomplishments. He and his neighbors discourage "bookishness" in favor of "genuinely amusing work, like house-building and street-paving, and gardening."[67]

For all his interest in the manual arts, Morris himself was bookish, a voracious reader and prodigiously prolific writer. In his depiction of the future, however, he playfully inverts conventional values, challenging modern civilization's most cherished hierarchies: mind over body, the ideal over the material. Morris reacted viscerally against the idea that a knowledge of Latin grammar was more valuable than skill in carpentry, or the plate we eat from less important than the ideas we absorb.[68]

On Guest's first day in Nowhere, Dick hands the visitor off to his great-grandfather, an antiquarian who resides in what used to be the British Museum. The middle third of *News from Nowhere* consists of Guest's conversation with old Hammond, a fount of information on the new society and how it arose from the old. The loquacious Hammond describes for Guest the utopia's government—or rather, the absence of anything resembling nineteenth-century British institutions. "We no longer have anything which you . . . would call a government," he tells Guest. The nation-state has disappeared, replaced by autonomous local communities that conduct their business at a Mote—a Germanic term for an assembly of the folk and a word Morris loved, coming as it did from "the times before bureaucracy." The social structure envisioned in *News from Nowhere* is best described as a form of anarcho-communism, despite Morris's insistence that "I am not an Anarchist as I understand the word." For him the word was inescapably associated with the maddening individualists of the Socialist League. The local Motes, however, perfectly embody the decentralized, antiauthoritarian "free federations" that Kropotkin, the theorist of mutualist anarchism, advocated. Kropotkin welcomed the publication of *News from Nowhere* and wrote that, in spite of Morris's professed hostility to anarchism, the book was "the most thoroughly and deeply anarchist conception of future society . . . ever . . . written."[69]

Morris and Kropotkin both foresaw the eventual withering away of the state, and they imagined that politics would disappear along with it. A witty, flagrantly brief chapter of *News from Nowhere* begins with Guest's query, "How do you manage with politics?" Hammond replies, "We are very well off as to politics,—because we have none."[70] That concludes the chapter.

Hammond also tells Guest that the Houses of Parliament, still standing, are used to store manure. Morris, not normally given to scatological humor, could not resist this joke. Hammond explains further that there are no law courts. With the abolition of private property, civil law has been abandoned, and in an egalitarian world no longer divided into rich and poor, crime has been virtually eliminated.

Guest is equally entranced by what he has observed of the new society and by old Hammond's disquisition on its libertarian structure. One thing remains puzzling to him, however, and after they share a meal in a nearby, beautifully decorated communal dining hall, he poses a question to his host: How did the change come about? Morris devotes two lengthy chapters to a history of the revolution that overthrows capitalism and eventually leads to his twenty-first-century socialist utopia. Bellamy and the Nationalists imagined that socialism could be achieved through the general diffusion of their progressive middle-class values, but Morris saw this as pernicious nonsense. He embraced the orthodox Marxist view that the path to socialism lay through class conflict and a workers' revolt.

Old Hammond describes in detail the history of the revolution, which began when workers' peaceful demonstrations were met with violent government repression, leading to a bloody but brief civil war in which the workers triumphed. In contrast, his description of the period from the war's end to the peaceful anarcho-communism of the present day is notably brief and vague. Morris's vision of the transition to utopia is remarkably like Bellamy's, after all. Bellamy used the religious metaphor of a "Great Revival" to explain the change in consciousness that made possible a smooth and peaceful path to utopia. Morris similarly finessed the transition from bitter civil war to halcyon peace by referring to the new "religion of humanity" and using the implicitly spiritual language of the world's "second birth." Concluding his account of the civil war, old Hammond's tone shifts from sober Marxist historian to poetic evangelist: "The spirit of the new days, of our days, was to be delight in the life of the world," he tells Guest, "intense and overweening love of the very skin and surface of the earth on which man dwells, such as a lover has in the fair flesh of the woman he loves; this, I say, was to be the new spirit of the time."[71]

Hammond's eroticized description of the new spirit of the time forms a sharp contrast with the political/military history that precedes it, but the chapters on revolution are the exception in *News from Nowhere* and Hammond's sensual language the rule. As many critics have observed, the book is marked by a pervasive sensuality; there's an erotic heat to Guest's experiences of the new world. "For a political blueprint, *News from Nowhere* is a surprisingly sexy book," Jan Marsh observes. The sexiness begins with Guest's first sight of three utopian women, all youthful-looking, all dressed in simple medieval style, all "comely" and "shapely."[72] The prettiest of the three joins Guest at his first meal after he awakens in Hammersmith, standing behind him and laying her hand on his shoulder, in which she holds a fragrant herb. The woman's touch, the smell of the balm—the sensuousness of Morris's utopia persists throughout the book.

The sensuousness functions in part as a deliberate challenge to middle-class Victorian prudery. Morris was influenced by Fourier's doctrine of attractive labor, and *News from Nowhere* reveals that he also shared to some extent Fourier's interest in the free expression of sexual desire. However, he had little of the Frenchman's rage for order, which led Fourier to lay out precise rules for the conduct of sexual orgies. Morris possessed an Englishman's untheorized confidence that people could find attractive sexual partners on their own. Nevertheless, he agreed with Fourier that the passions were inherently positive and that the ideal society must gratify rather than repress them.

If the sensual aspects of *News from Nowhere* have an ideological dimension, at the same time they are intensely personal. Guest is fifty-six, exactly Morris's age when he was writing the book, and the tale is marked by a middle-aged man's melancholy-tinged sexual desire. His appreciation of female beauty is as strong as ever, but he is perpetually doubtful that his desire for an attractive younger woman is returned. The comely Annie may provocatively lay her hand on his shoulder and then kiss him on seeing him again, but Guest tells himself that it does not mean anything: "it was clear that so delightful a woman would hardly be without a due lover of her own age." As Jan Marsh notes, Guest is "sexually on the make," and the entire book is "imbued with the feeling and imagery of male desire."[73]

Yet at the same time as he imbued his utopia with his own desires, Morris acknowledged female sexuality as a healthy, natural force. Annie flushes red when she kisses Guest, but it is from "friendly pleasure," not from shyness. Dick's lover Clara similarly flushes with pleasure when Dick engages in a bit of sexual banter, talking about how they will fall into bed after a day of haying, "and you will look so beautiful with your neck all brown, and your hands too, and you under your gown as white as privet."[74] *News from Nowhere* is written from an exclusively male point of view, but the women characters are sexually desiring subjects and not simply objects of male lust.

Morris takes care to portray Clara, who joins Guest and Dick at old Hammond's quarters, as an autonomous sexual actor. While Clara and Dick are out of the room, old Hammond explains that she and Dick were formerly partners and had two children. Then Clara fell in love with another man and left Dick and the children. Now, she has decided to quit the other man and reunite with Dick. Their reunion provides old Hammond an opportunity to explain that society has left behind what he calls "such lunatic affairs" as marriage contracts and divorce courts in favor of free unions.[75]

Morris was committed to the concept of free unions both personally and ideologically. In his own life, he accepted his wife's love affair with Rossetti. As a socialist, he believed that in a capitalist system where women lacked property rights, marriage was a form of "legal prostitution," and he attacked the idea that "once two people have committed themselves to one act of copulation they are to be tied together through life no matter how miserable it makes them[,] their children or their children's children." He acknowledged however, that the free unions he envisioned in *News from Nowhere* could not eliminate "all the trouble that besets the dealing between the sexes."[76] The book demonstrates the perpetually disruptive power of sexuality. The socialist utopia in *News* may have eliminated crimes against property, but crimes of passion still exist. Soon after his arrival, Guest hears about a double murder and suicide resulting from a love triangle. Later he learns of another murder, again the result of a love triangle. The doubling is peculiar, as if Morris felt compelled to repeat himself: the dealing between the sexes could, even in Arcadia, lead to madness and violent death.

Still, *News* stresses that the combination of ending poverty and abolishing the legal system will eliminate most of the crime and misery associated with sex, marriage, and the family. Economic equality between men and women was a crucial part of Morris's program. During the 1880s Friedrich Engels, August Bebel, and Eleanor Marx and Edward Aveling all published major works about the economic condition of women under capitalism. A consensus developed among British socialists that women's economic dependence on men made egalitarian relationships between the sexes virtually impossible. Morris agreed, and he wrote that he did not "consider a man a socialist at all who is not prepared to admit the equality of women as far as condition goes." His qualifying phrase about "condition," however, reveals the limits of his views on gender equality. "You must not forget," he lectured a younger colleague, "that child-bearing makes women inferior to men, since a certain time of their lives they must be dependent on them. Of course we must claim absolute equality of condition between women & men, as between other groups, but it would be poor economy setting women to do men's work (as unluckily they often do now) or vice versa."[77]

News from Nowhere reflects Morris's skeptical views about gender equality. The women of Nowhere may have a sexual independence far in advance of their nineteenth-century counterparts, but in their working lives they are, with one exception, confined to the domestic realm. When Guest wakes up in the future, he soon meets Dick the ferryman-metalsmith and Robert the mathematician-weaver, but all the women he encounters are engaged in some form of domestic service, cleaning or cooking or serving food. The sole exception is a woman met on the voyage up the Thames, a stone-carver working on a new house whose daughter works alongside her. Given the respect in which Morris held stone-carving, this is no small accomplishment. Philippa, the carver, is carrying on the tradition of the fourteenth-century masons who created what Morris believed to be the world's greatest works of art. However, Philippa and her daughter stand in contrast to all other women described in the book, who are content to labor in the home.

Old Hammond defends women's domestic labor against the nineteenth-century devaluation of any form of manual work, attacking the notion that housekeeping is "an unimportant occupation, not deserving of respect." Ruth Levitas argues that this is a more progressive opinion than that held by Edward Bellamy, who wanted to get rid of domestic labor by delegating it to machines.[78] It is not possible to fit Morris's and Bellamy's ideas about women into neat progressive vs. conservative slots, however. Bellamy's *Equality*, the sequel to *Looking Backward*, is remarkably progressive in some respects: the Edith of that novel is a farm laborer, and she reveals that women of the future fill many arduous occupations, including ironworker and engine-driver. On the other hand, Bellamy's characters, however liberated, reproduce conventional Victorian family relationships, and *Looking Backward* adopts the marriage plot of countless nineteenth-century novels, ending with Edith's and Julian's union-for-life. Morris believed that women were naturally suited to domestic labor and child-rearing, yet *News from Nowhere* includes women characters far more independent and interesting than Edith Leete, who has no discernible personality beyond what is required of an ingénue destined for the altar.

The most important of *Nowhere*'s women characters is Ellen, whom Guest meets on his journey up the Thames. The last third of the novel is devoted to a four-day journey by boat from London to the countryside, where Dick is eager to join in the haying. In the years before writing the book, Morris made the same journey multiple times, traveling up the Thames from his house in Hammersmith to Kelmscott Manor. At its heart, *News from Nowhere* is a journey-book—more specifically, a river-book—and recalls the greatest of all river-books, published six years earlier: *Adventures of Huckleberry Finn*. Like Mark Twain, Morris—whom Bernard Shaw described as "an incurable Huckfinomaniac"—knew intimately his country's iconic river, and he intuited the metaphoric power of a river voyage.[79] Huck and Jim's raft trip down the Mississippi provides the framework for some of Mark Twain's most savage satire, as the two travelers stop along the way at settlements invariably marked by some combination of greed, corruption, cowardice, and violence. Yet their trip is also the occasion for some of the most lyrical writing in Mark Twain's body of work, utopian moments on the raft when Huck and Jim shed their clothes along with every other marker of civilization, lounging in a state of perfect innocence and equality, at one with the big muddy river and the warm cloudless sky. The river trip in *Nowhere* is all idyll, a *Huckleberry Finn* with the satire removed. In Morris's dream of the future, water and shore are equally pure and innocent.

Guest encounters Ellen at the close of his first day on the river, when he and his traveling companions, Dick and Clara, pull up near the cottage where the youthful Ellen lives with her grandfather. The old man is a "grumbler"—a sort of designated skeptic in this happy land who complains about everything and longs for the more exciting world of competition and strife that he has read about in nineteenth-century novels.[80] The old man serves as a comic foil, demonstrating that only cranks could prefer the nineteenth century to the anarcho-communist epoch of rest. His granddaughter Ellen, in contrast, serves as the embodiment of the new age. In this era of beautiful women, Ellen is the most beautiful of them all, and Guest falls in love with this wise young beauty. Ellen joins his party as they row upriver, and she becomes simultaneously his love-interest, his muse, and his guide to the new society.

Ellen is as clear-sighted and articulate as old Hammond, and in her scenes with her grandfather she eloquently defends the new world against his grumbling. Critics have called her a Virgil to Guest's Dante, but she is closer to the allegorical figure of Liberty in Eugène Delacroix's famous painting *Liberty Leading the People* (1830). Like the woman in a phrygian hat with a musket in one hand and the French flag in the other, fearlessly striding barefoot over the barricades, Ellen is less a realist character than an allegory of the

FIGURE 3.7 Eugène Delacroix, *Liberty Leading the People* (detail; 1830).
Musée du Louvre, Paris. RMN–Grand Palais / Art Resource, NY.

new society. She has nothing of the martial about her, however; she is more of a nymph, identified with the beauty and fecundity of the English countryside in which the last part of Morris's romance is set. She resembles Liberty also in her overt sexuality. Delacroix's figure is bare-breasted, at once maternal—she nourishes the nation—and an object of desire. *News* repeatedly mentions Ellen's desirability to men, and at one point she makes to Guest a startlingly suggestive promise: "This evening, or to-morrow morning," she tells him, "I shall make a proposal to you to do something which would

please me very much, and I think would not hurt you."[81] This in-
nuendo leaves the reader's mind racing: Did she just say what I
think she did? It seems as if the book is about to veer in a radically
different direction, until we learn that Ellen's proposal is for Guest
to come live with her and her grandfather when they move to Cum-
bria in a few weeks' time. Her proposal turns out to be more innocent than it first appears, but it heightens our awareness of both
Ellen's sexuality and the narrator's frustrated desire for her.

Guest's desire for Ellen cannot be consummated for many reasons: he is more than three decades older than she; almost as soon
as they meet, hints are dropped that his visit to the future will not
last much longer; and Ellen herself occupies a liminal status between realist character and allegorical figure. At the end of their
four-day journey up the Thames, the travelers alight at a lovely village adjacent to a handsome old house. As they disembark, Ellen
takes Guest by the hand and whispers, "Take me on to the house;
we need not wait for the others: I had rather not." It might be the
suggestion of a lover, the prelude to private embraces. Instead, Ellen
embraces not the man but the house, laying "her shapely sun-
browned hand and arm on the lichened wall," then crying out, "O
me! O me! How I love the earth, and the seasons, and weather, and
all things that deal with it, and all that grows out of it,—as this has
done! . . . The earth and the growth of it and the life of it! If I could
but say or show how I love it!"[82] In this, the book's ecstatic climax,
Ellen transcends not only her relationship with Guest but her
human identity and becomes the voice of the utopian future, the
epoch of rest when humans have ceased from striving to conquer
nature and instead have become as intimate as lovers with the earth
and its growth—not just the organic growth of field and forest but
the human-made growth of handcrafted buildings constructed by
artisans freely expressing their creative joy.

Shortly after completing *News from Nowhere*, Morris established
the Kelmscott Press, devoted to producing beautiful letterpress editions of his own books and those of his favorite authors. Among its
early productions was an edition of *News*, with a frontispiece that
shows Morris's beloved Kelmscott Manor. The legend below the picture reads, "This is the picture of the old house by the Thames to
which the people of this story went." The frontispiece brilliantly

THIS IS THE PICTURE OF THE OLD HOUSE BY THE THAMES TO WHICH THE PEOPLE OF THIS STORY WENT HEREAFTER FOLLOWS THE BOOK ITSELF WHICH IS CALLED NEWS FROM NOWHERE OR AN EPOCH OF REST & IS WRITTEN BY WILLIAM MORRIS

FIGURE 3.8 Kelmscott Manor. Frontispiece of Kelmscott Press edition of *News from Nowhere* (1892). Rare Book Division, Department of Rare Books and Special Collections, Princeton University Library.

complicates our understanding of *News from Nowhere*. The book's subtitle declares it to be a "utopian romance," but the picture of Morris's own house blurs the boundaries between romance and reality. The building that prompts a fictional character's ecstatic praise is not a product of the author's imagination but an actual, existing structure. Inserting Kelmscott Manor into the book brings utopia tantalizingly close. Elements of an ideal future are already among us, Morris suggests; it is within our power to make the entire world as beautiful as this corner of it.

Guest's time alone with Ellen at the beautiful old house is fleeting; Dick arrives and pulls him away to take a swim in the river before dinner. The dinner is held in what used to be the village church and is now a fellowship hall. The scene allows Morris once again to blur the line between utopian romance and present reality; the building he describes is the Kelmscott village church, a medieval building close by Kelmscott Manor. The building has been filled with tables and festooned with flowers; in place of the cross hang two scythes, symbols of the simple agricultural labor that has drawn together in rural Oxfordshire this group of handsome, joyous people. Guest pauses at the threshold to admire the simple and beautiful room, its long tables filled with gaily dressed women and men, chatting animatedly in anticipation of the pleasurable labor to come on the morrow. But suddenly, wrenchingly, he realizes that no one can see him. Dick walks past him into the hall and joins Clara and Ellen, who glance in his direction but turn away. Guest, sick at heart, retreats and plunges into the darkness. The next thing he knows he is awakening in his bed in "dingy" Hammersmith.[83]

Guest cannot partake of the final communal feast; the scene of perfect harmony and fellowship is unattainable. Yet in the book's brief epilogue after he awakens in nineteenth-century London, he refuses to call Nowhere a dream, for that would be to identify it as a merely personal projection. *News from Nowhere* is not one man's imaginings but a public document, appearing in the pages of *Commonweal*, a journal read by socialists struggling for a better future. "If others can see it as I have seen it," the narrator concludes his tale, "then it may be called a vision rather than a dream."[84] With these final words, Morris insists that utopia is not a diversion to read about but a goal to win.

More than one hundred years after its publication, *News from No-where* remains the most widely admired of nineteenth-century uto-pian fictions—with good reason. It is that century's greatest dream of freedom, the only imagined utopia that escapes completely from the regimentation of Bellamy's industrial army, the forced fellow-ship of the Fourierist phalanstery, the benevolent but omnipresent paternalism of the Owenite community. Morris's is the most liber-tarian of the era's utopias, a peaceful realm devoid of state coercion. The inhabitants of Nowhere are free of compulsory education, con-scription, taxes, jury duty, marriage licenses, and passports; they live in a land without schools, prisons, police, or army. They labor at work they love, pursuing multiple occupations at the same time, while living in beautiful buildings and surrounded by a natural world that has been restored to its pre-industrial purity. In this world of ease and plenty, people live long and healthy lives and glow with beauty, their interactions with one another tinged with a wholesome sensuality. *News from Nowhere* offers an alternative to capitalist modernity, a vision of non-ascetic simplicity, fulfilling labor, and full individuality combined with loving fellowship.

Nowhere also offers an optimistic assessment of the human ca-pacity to change. Morris rejected both theological notions of origi-nal sin and popular Darwinist conceptions of inherent human competitiveness in favor of the Romantic conception of a plastic human nature shaped for good or ill by its environment. When Guest, in conversation with Hammond, puts forward the generally accepted notion that political strife is "a necessary result of human nature," the old man snaps back at him, "Human nature! . . . what human nature? The human nature of paupers, of slaves, of slave-holders, or the human nature of wealthy freemen? Which? Come, tell me that!"[85] Guest quickly folds, for he sees around him the truth of Hammond's claim: the wealthy freemen of Nowhere ami-cably cooperate with one another in their small-scale, leaderless communities.

Morris's *Nowhere* has proven attractive to so many people not only because of its inherent qualities but also because, more than any other nineteenth-century writer on utopia, he acknowledged the difficulty of achieving it. Owen, Fourier, and Bellamy finessed the transition to utopia, suggesting that a rational recognition of the greater good would lead all classes to embrace radical social transformation. Morris, in contrast, devotes nearly a sixth of his book to the sanguinary civil war necessary for the new world to be born. "How could that [second birth] take place without a tragedy?" old Hammond asks rhetorically.[86]

Tragedy followed by reconciliation: *News from Nowhere* follows a compelling narrative arc, landing us in an attractive, beautifully realized future. Even among Morris's many admirers, however, the book has its critics. The most wittily devastating is Graham Hough, who highlights the irreconcilable contradictions of Morris's vision of utopia. For example, he points out that the central problem for an ideal society such as Morris's is how a large population can be supported at a decent level without significant industrialization. Morris's answer is by doing without things. However, Morris also believed that in a socialist state no one would have to do without anything she wanted, a conundrum he could solve only by positing, in Hough's words, that "people don't really want all the things they would have to do without."[87]

The novel contains other glaringly unresolved contradictions. For example, it portrays a world in which all labor is carried out joyously, never acknowledging that some tasks may be inherently unpleasant. Admittedly, Morris addressed the topic in his utopian essay "The Society of the Future" (1888). There he argues that distasteful work—he mentions "sewer-emptying, butchering, letter-carrying, boot-blacking, hair-dressing"—will "come to an end: we shall either make all these occupations agreeable to ourselves in some mood or to some minds, who will take to them voluntarily, or we shall have to let them lapse altogether."[88] It's easy enough to imagine a society letting butchering and boot-blacking simply lapse—but sewer-emptying? Bellamy at least was willing to acknowledge that unpleasant tasks had to be done, and he devised a system, involving a diminished work week, designed to attract volunteers to difficult occupations such as mining. *News from Nowhere* depicts a world in which people are drawn to difficult but necessary labor such as harvesting a field by the desire to exercise their bodies with a group of friends. It seems not to have occurred to Morris, who was no athlete himself, that people might prefer to satisfy their desire for exercising in company by joining a hiking club or playing sports.

Even after granting Morris his point that "the only safe way of reading a utopia is to consider it as the expression of the temperament of its author," he seems remarkably loathe to acknowledge temperaments different from his own. The world of *News from Nowhere* affords little room, for example, to those who might be driven to conduct scientific research or develop improved technologies. Like most other utopians of his era, Morris gave little thought to difference. He is somewhat better than Bellamy in this regard, since he does include one "grumbler," Ellen's grandfather, who rejects Nowhere's egalitarian premises and claims to prefer the competitive society of old. Yet this grumbler is at heart a lovable old coot, easily silenced by his articulate granddaughter.

Morris's denial of fundamental differences between people lies behind his rejection of politics. To Morris, politics was exclusively concerned with the clash of interests, and interests were the creation of class society. In a classless society, he believed, competing interests would disappear. Morris could not envision an egalitarian world in which people would come into conflict because of basic differences in defining the good life, where they might fall into contending camps over the tensions between fundamental values such as innovation and preservation, privacy and publicity, or family and community.

Yet as Alice Chandler suggests, to criticize Morris in this way may be to miss the point. "It is like criticizing a myth," she writes. Her comment raises the question, What is the ultimate purpose of *News from Nowhere*? Krishan Kumar points out that the novel can be interpreted in two fundamentally different ways, as either an affirmation of an existing possibility in society or as an evocation of a state of innocence by which the present is to be judged. If it is the former, Morris is offering us a portrait, however loosely sketched, of an ideal future; if the latter, *News* is best understood as a heuristic tool for critiquing the present and imagining alternatives.[89]

Of course, the two interpretations are not mutually exclusive; the book can be seen as both a partially realizable blueprint and a challenge to readers' imagination. The conversation with old Hammond is pure blueprint, a lengthy disquisition on women, marriage, the family, property, governance, law, technology, labor, and the nation-state. However, the loquacious Hammond does not, thankfully, dominate the book. Much of the novel consists of imaginative descriptions of daily life in a transformed world. For all their attractiveness, these sections do not seem to function as a utopian blueprint since, as Stephen Arata points out, Guest's frequent uneasiness makes it clear that even William Morris would not be fully content to live in the world he describes. E. P. Thompson best captured this aspect of *News from Nowhere* in his famous formulation that the novel's true function is *the education of desire*, "to teach desire to desire, to desire better, to desire more, and above all to desire in a different way."[90] In the twenty-first century, amidst a culture saturated with advertising and entertainments that relentlessly stimulate consumer appetites, the value of this sort of educative function is more apparent than ever.

Morris himself was unconcerned with precisely how readers understood his utopian fiction. Bellamy devoted the years following the appearance of *Looking Backward* to elaborating the details of his utopia and to devising strategies and tactics for its eventual realization. *News from Nowhere* occupied a different position in Morris's career; it was simply one aspect of the utopianism he lived out his entire life. The medievalism he embraced from childhood gave him a vision of a heroic society of intense fellowship, joyful labor, a beautiful built environment, and harmony with the natural world. Red House represented an attempt to create a Palace of Art, both refuge from a cockneyfied world and model of a future in which the creation and enjoyment of the decorative arts suffused every moment of life. His designs for the Firm exemplified a union of art and nature, of craft and design. His myriad activities, from writing poetry to designing wallpaper to dyeing cloth to weaving tapestries, served to obliterate distinctions between gentleman and worker, between intellectual and artisan. His first forays into political activity were efforts to end war and to preserve the beauty of the past for the benefit of the future. And the tireless socialist activism of his last fourteen years of life was William Morris's attempt to create, as best he saw how, a joyous, peaceful, and egalitarian *eu-topia*—not *nowhere* but a *good place*.

CHAPTER FOUR

Edward Carpenter's Homogenic Utopia

IN THE AUTUMN OF 1913, E. M. Forster slipped away from the northern English spa town of Harrogate, where he was accompanying his mother while she took the cure, to visit Edward Carpenter in the village of Millthorpe, some sixty miles distant. The thirty-four-year-old Forster was already a professional success—both *A Room with a View* (1908) and *Howards End* (1910), his third and fourth novels, had been well received—but he felt himself blocked both creatively and sexually. He had published little over the past three years, and he was desperately lonely, tormented by his desires and unsuccessful in establishing a lasting relationship with another man. He hoped that a pilgrimage to meet the personage known as the Sage of Millthorpe could help him.

Edward Carpenter, the Sage of Millthorpe, was sixty-nine years old at the time of Forster's visit. He had been living at Millthorpe, in rural Derbyshire, for thirty years, and his seven-acre holding had been attracting pilgrims for nearly that long. They were drawn there for multiple and overlapping reasons. All were familiar with Carpenter's reputation as a British Thoreau, a former Anglican clergyman and Cambridge don who had jettisoned Victorian respectability in favor of a vegetarian, sandal-wearing version of the simple life. Many had read his poetic masterwork "Towards Democracy" (1883), a long, spiritually fervid free-verse poem that attacks British

FIGURE 4.1 Edward Carpenter (*right*) and George Merrill.
Carpenter Collection, Sheffield City Archives.

materialism and forecasts the coming millennium. Some were inspired by his socialist activism, which dated to the earliest days of
the British movement. A select few were drawn by his pioneering
writings about same-sex love and by his cross-class relationship
with George Merrill, an adventurous younger man from the Sheffield slums.

Forster was drawn to Millthorpe for all these reasons, but it was
seeing Carpenter's and Merrill's famous partnership that "touch[ed]
a creative spring" in him, he later wrote. He added, "George Merrill
also touched my backside—gently and just above the buttocks. I
believe he touched most people's. The sensation was unusual and I
still remember it, as I remember the position of a long vanished
tooth."[1] That touch on the backside freed Forster's imagination and
led directly to *Maurice*, his swooning idyll of a novel about the love
affair between Cambridge graduate Maurice Hall and gamekeeper
Alec Scudder.

Forster wrote that he had undertaken his visit to Carpenter in
the spirit of "one [who] approaches a saviour."[2] The religious lan-

guage was not chosen carelessly. Carpenter was widely regarded as a utopian prophet. In many respects, his vision resembled that of his friend William Morris. Both were conscientious objectors to industrial modernity who looked forward to an anarcho-communist future of small farms and joyous labor. However, whereas Morris described an ideal future achieved through working-class revolution, Carpenter believed that the path to utopia would be blazed by Uranians. During the years before the word "homosexual" became fixed in the English language, Carpenter wrote about the "homogenic" sentiment and settled on the term "Uranian," or "Urning," to describe the man-loving men and women-loving women who he believed were the advance guard in the march to utopia. As he saw it, conventional men and women, whatever their class, were too fully entangled within the materialistic, competitive individualism of capitalist patriarchy to transform British society from the ground up. Uranians, occupying as they did a liminal space, could view the dominant ideology from a critical distance and envision more humane alternatives. They constituted, Carpenter believed, an "intermediate sex," combining what he saw as the best of both genders: women's tender, loving nature and men's energy and capacity for action.[3] From the mid-1880s until his death in 1929, Edward Carpenter promoted his vision of a utopia toward which the intermediate sex was leading the way.

{≈≈≈≈≈≈≈}

Three years before Edward Carpenter's birth in Brighton in 1844, the railway to London was completed, turning the seaside resort into a popular destination. Brighton had been fashionable since the late eighteenth century, when the Prince of Wales began construction of a seaside villa that eventually metamorphosed into the rococo Royal Pavilion. Now the Victorian middle class surged in, drawn in part by the chance to glimpse the young Queen Victoria and her family during their summer residence. The queen, dismayed by the influx, soon abandoned Brighton for the Isle of Wight, but commoners were undeterred. Over the next twenty years the population grew by more than half.[4] Edward Carpenter lived in Brighton throughout the years of its surging popularity as a stylish resort. For a certain sort of young man, it would have been an

attractive place to grow up, filled with crowds of visitors and boom-
ing with new construction. But Edward Carpenter was not that
young man. Serious and sensitive, he felt out of place. "At home," he
recalled decades later, "I never felt really at home."[5]

His father, Charles, the son of an admiral, had abandoned careers in the navy and the law and lived off his investments. Edward
grew up in a large household of ten children and a small brigade of
servants. Later on he would be contemptuous of the small-minded
upper-middle-class culture among which he lived in Brighton, but
at the time he took it all—its dread of "appearances," its concern
about what others would think of one's clothing or one's speech—
terribly seriously and felt unable to come up to the mark. His refuge
was the outdoors: the sea, just yards from his front door, and the
miles of downs that stretched outside the town. He would return
from his rambles to spend time with his sisters, with whom he was
close. There were six of them, three of whom never married, and in
his loneliness and unsatisfied longing Edward identified with them.

Unlike his sisters, however, he had a means of escape. At twenty,
after a year of study in Germany, he entered Cambridge. Still under
the influence of fashionable Brighton standards, he chose Trinity
Hall because it was a "gentlemanly" college, and once there he fell
in with the boating set. His rowing mates were genial young men
who seldom opened a book. The days slid by, he recalled, "with
games and wine parties and boat suppers."[6] Rather to his surprise,
Carpenter found himself at the head of his class at the end of his
first year. He became academically ambitious, studied for the famously difficult mathematical tripos examination, and graduated
with first-class honors. The Trinity Hall authorities approached him
about remaining at the college. Leslie Stephen—famous at the time
for his mountaineering exploits in the Swiss Alps, now better known
as the father of Virginia Woolf—had recently resigned his teaching
fellowship. Would Carpenter be interested? It was a clerical fellowship, but surely Carpenter would not object to ordination as an Anglican priest?

He would not. Carpenter had been raised in an atmosphere of
Anglican religious liberalism. His father read deeply in the works of
F. D. Maurice, the celebrated liberal theologian and Christian social-
ist, and emerged a sort of Broad Church mystic, a label that fit his

son as well. Carpenter prepared confidently for his ordination, foreseeing a comfortable career as a clergyman and don. Then, on the eve of his ordination, the bishop called him into his study. One of the questions on the written examination concerned Abraham's sacrifice of Isaac. Carpenter, eager to demonstrate his advanced ideas, had explained it as a relic of pagan Moloch worship. The bishop was aghast. Did not Carpenter understand that the episode was a prefiguration of Christ's self-sacrifice? The bishop talked for hours with the youthful candidate for ordination, declaring at the end of their conversation that although he could not follow Carpenter's ideas, he was certain that they were *not* the doctrine of the Church of England. The bishop then left him alone, no doubt expecting the young heretic to withdraw gracefully. Instead, Carpenter went ahead, allowing the apostolic hands to rest, however uncertainly, on his head.

Once ordained, he became curate, or assistant priest, at St. Edward's church in Cambridge. He assisted at services, visited parishioners, tutored undergraduates in mathematics, and, on the side, wrote poetry. These early works, published as *Narcissus and Other Poems* in 1873, while Carpenter was still in his twenties, are thoroughly conventional poems, indistinguishable from the verse of other accomplished, highly educated Victorian rhymesters. The title poem, a verse retelling of the Narcissus and Echo story, contains a hint of homoeroticism in its description of the eponymous hero:

> ... day by day the boy in form and face
> Grew fairer, by the myriad waving grace
> Of slender arms encircled—grew to be
> More comely than the gods did e'er decree
> To mortal man before. His beauty was
> The beauty of a tall flower in the grass
> Where-o'er the golden hours glide one by one,
> Steeped in sweet slumbers of the golden sun,
> A dream-fed beauty.[7]

This sort of extravagant tribute to male beauty was a common trope in nineteenth-century poetry, unlikely to raise a reader's eyebrow, particularly when contained within a retelling of Greek myth. The volume as a whole is eminently respectable, with subjects taken from ancient mythology and the Bible, along with lyrics inspired by nature and music. Any social criticism is muted, expressed in the sort of decorous blessed-are-the-meek rhetoric that parishioners might expect to hear delivered from the pulpit of a Sunday.

Meanwhile, Carpenter was becomingly increasingly uncomfortable with both Anglican doctrine and his pastoral duties. On the surface, his situation seemed ideal: his immediate superior, the vicar of St. Edward's, was none other than F. D. Maurice, the great theological liberal and social progressive whom Carpenter's father admired. Maurice may have been no more orthodox than Carpenter himself, but the old man had made his peace with the Anglican establishment, and in any case had perfected a homiletic style that left hearers baffled as to where he stood theologically; one wit said that listening to him preach was "like eating pea-soup with a fork."[8] For his part, Carpenter was appalled by the congregation of tradesmen in their sleek Sunday best who took everything in a spirit, as he saw it, of mere superstition, and by the old ladies who would hastily shuffle a prayer book onto the table when they saw the curate approaching. Four years after his ordination, tortured by religious doubts and feeling himself a hypocrite, he told the Trinity Hall dean that he had to resign his orders. The dean told him not to be silly. They all knew that Anglican doctrine was tomfoolery; he should bite his tongue and get on with it. Carpenter rather hoped that he might abandon the priesthood while still retaining his teaching fellowship, but the college made clear that this was impossible. In 1874, at the age of thirty, Carpenter tendered his resignation. He knew nothing of life beyond the safely circumscribed realms of Brighton and Cambridge. He was determined to find out more.

At the same time as Carpenter experienced his vocational crisis, Cambridge was expanding and institutionalizing the program of university extension lectures begun in the previous decade. Carpenter became taken with the idea that he must throw in his lot with the working classes, and he agreed to teach a course on astronomy in Leeds, located in England's industrial north. Once he arrived, he discovered that he had undertaken the work under a twofold misapprehension. First, few workers wanted anything to do with the extension classes; he found himself lecturing to audiences composed almost entirely of middle-class women. Next, the skies over Leeds were so polluted that the stars were virtually invisible, making his subject purely theoretical; he might as well have been teaching paleontology.

He was, moreover, terribly lonely. Carpenter identified so strongly with his unmarried sisters because his desires, so similar to theirs, were similarly unfulfilled. His sisters may have longed for intimacy with a man, but Victorian courtship codes gave no way for them to fulfill or even express their desire. Carpenter found himself in the same situation. Since adolescence he had been infatuated with various boys and men, but so far as he knew no other male shared his desires. Convinced that he was a "hopeless monstrosity," he felt himself at times "on the brink of despair and madness with repressed passion and torment."9

Carpenter was caught in the bind experienced by virtually every other middle-class man-loving Englishman during the era before the conceptualization of "homosexuality" at the end of the nineteenth century. The moral code promulgated in both church and home insisted that same-sex desires were an abomination, and the era's rigid class segregation meant that respectable young gentlemen were unlikely to come into contact with working-class cultures, such as among sailors and soldiers, where same-sex liaisons were common. Bookish youths such as Edward Carpenter turned by default to a small number of literary texts that valorized love between men: the biblical story of David and Jonathan, Plato's *Phaedrus* and *Symposium*, the sonnets of Shakespeare and Michelangelo. Yet these centuries-old texts were inadequate. All left readers wondering if a satisfying, ennobling love between men existed only in the past, and all were frustratingly vague about the physical dimensions of male love. Where, tortured young Victorians couldn't help asking, was the *body* in all this?10

Then in 1868 literary critic William Michael Rossetti, brother of Dante Gabriel and Christina, published a selection of Walt Whitman's poems in England. Until this time, Whitman's books had been difficult to obtain in Great Britain. His verse was widely regarded as primitive and his subject matter as scandalous. Only a small elite of well-connected literary intellectuals in Great Britain had read Whitman; nevertheless, they believed that there was an audience for his work, so long as it was carefully selected. Rossetti set about tidying up Whitman's work for the British public. He removed offensive words—*prostitute* and *womb* had to go—and cut entirely the poems that celebrated sexual love between men and women. However, he left intact the poems from the "Calamus" section of *Leaves of Grass*, which are about love between men. The "Calamus" poems fit easily into the tradition of the English friendship poem, such as Milton's "Lycidas" and Tennyson's *In Memoriam,* and Rossetti regarded them as unexceptionable.

Thus in 1868, when a Cambridge don came by his room and casually dropped off a copy of Rossetti's *Poems by Walt Whitman,* Carpenter was able to read such "Calamus" poems as the following:

> . . . when I thought how my dear friend, my lover, was on his way
>   coming, O then I was happy;
> O then each breath tasted sweeter—and all that day my food nourished
>   me more—and the beautiful day passed well,
> And the next came with equal joy—and with the next, at evening, came
>   my friend;
> And that night, while all was still, I heard the waters roll slowly
>   continually up the shores,
> I heard the hissing rustle of the liquid and sands, as directed to me,
>   whispering, to congratulate me;
> For the one I love most lay sleeping by me under the same cover in the
>   cool night,
> In the stillness, in the autumn moonbeams, his face was inclined
>   toward me,
> And his arm lay lightly around my breast—and that night I was
>   happy.[11]

Carpenter was thrilled. Here was a poet who regarded male love as idealistically as did Plato, yet imbued it with a chaste but pervasive sensuality expressed in a direct modern idiom.

Buoyed by reading Whitman, Carpenter gradually came to discover that there were other men like him. "I made a few special friends," he wrote, "and at last it came to me occasionally to sleep with them and to satisfy my imperious needs by mutual embraces and emissions."[12] Yet even as he found physical outlets for his sexual desires, Carpenter clung to an idealizing Whitmanesque view of male love. Once he resigned his Cambridge fellowship in 1874, he reached out to Whitman in a remarkable letter: "Yesterday there came (to mend my door) a young workman with the old divine light in his eyes . . . and perhaps, more than all, he has made me write to you." He continued, "Because you have, as it were, given me a ground for the love of men I thank you continually in my heart. (—And others thank you though they do not say so.) For you have made men to be not ashamed of the noblest instinct of their nature. Women are beautiful; but, to some there is that which passes the love of women."[13]

The letter reveals a number of the themes that were to remain constant in Carpenter's writing about same-sex love for the next fifty years. His phrase "the noblest instinct" ennobled male love and at the same time identified it as natural and innate—in contrast to the doctrine of the Anglican church, which regarded sex between men as a sinful acquired vice. Carpenter skillfully turned Anglican doctrine on its head: male sexual desire figures as a "divine light," and his reference to the love passing the love of women echoes the language of the biblical story of David and Jonathan. Newly out of orders and still living in his Cambridge rooms, the young ex-clergyman appropriated religious language and texts to sanctify his desires for men. In addition, Carpenter allied himself to Whitman's democratic project. In his masterpiece "Song of Myself," Whitman identified himself as "one of the roughs," connecting his poetic persona to the working class.[14] Carpenter, writing his letter to Whitman from the gardens of Trinity Hall, could scarcely make the same claim, but he identified the object of his (spiritualized) desire as a workingman, suggesting that love between men could transcend class barriers.

The ideas about same-sex love articulated in the letter to Whitman would eventually form the basis of Carpenter's utopian theorizing. In the meantime, a variety of experiences during the decade after he left the church would transform him from an obscure former clergyman into a hero of the British political and spiritual left.

Carpenter's most significant experience during the years immediately following his resignation from Cambridge was his visit to Walt Whitman in America, three years after writing his initial letter. If

Carpenter valued most of all the validation of his love for men that he found in *Leaves of Grass*, he also seized on the book's religious and political dimensions. Whitman never intended *Leaves of Grass* to be received as a purely aesthetic creation; he envisioned it as a new bible of democracy. Carpenter understood the "Calamus" poems' underlying premise that affection between men is the foundation of democracy, and he saw that Whitman's ecstatic mystical expressions of divine unity and of love for all creation demanded an egalitarian polity. During the 1870s, Carpenter began to conceive of himself as a potentially Whitman-like figure who could bring the good news to British shores. He wrote Whitman a long, ecstatic letter early in 1876 in which he proclaimed, "I feel that my work is to carry on what you have begun. You have opened the way: my only desire is to go onward with it." His goal was nothing less than a complete transformation of society. As he explained the next year to Whitman in unabashedly grandiose terms, "What must be done—and what you have largely (for a foundation *entirely*) done— is to form a new organic centre for the thought growth of this age." Shortly after writing the latter letter, Carpenter set sail for America, arriving in May 1877.[15]

He and Whitman hit it off famously. The handsome young Englishman was given to adulation, and the fifty-seven-year-old poet, prematurely aged by a severe stroke four years earlier, was hungry for praise. As they sat together on the front porch of the Philadelphia house where Whitman was staying, Carpenter thought he looked like "some old god" with his disciples clustered about his feet.[16] Carpenter was equally impressed by Whitman's unaffected manner. As they walked about Philadelphia, tram conductors, truck drivers, and street vendors would greet Whitman by name, drawn to him not by his reputation but by simple personal affection. Whitman seemed to embody the democratic comradeship he wrote about in his poetry, and Carpenter fell in love with the grand old man. They stayed together in the home of Whitman's Philadelphia friends for a week; the two men may have become lovers.

The evidence is ambiguous. In a letter sent from Philadelphia to an English friend, full of praise for Whitman, Carpenter wrote, "He has taken me to himself." Does the phrase prove a sexual encounter? Ninety years later the American memoirist Gavin Arthur, who met

Carpenter when the latter was elderly and he was a young visitor to England, claimed to have asked Carpenter directly if he had slept with Whitman. "Oh yes—once in a while—he regarded it as the best way to get together with another man," Carpenter supposedly replied before taking Arthur upstairs to show him how Whitman made love. There is reason to doubt Arthur's account: he wrote differing versions of his encounter with Carpenter, varying the dialogue and actions each time. However, Allen Ginsberg, who knew Arthur, believed the story and constructed a gay lineage connecting himself to Whitman: Ginsberg had slept with Neal Cassady, who had slept with Gavin Arthur, who had slept with Edward Carpenter, who had slept with Walt Whitman.[17]

In a letter to Whitman after his visit, Carpenter professed his love for the poet and revealed his utopian vision resting upon a foundation of Whitmanesque fellowship: "For a long time I have cherished the thought that . . . I might be the beginning, or at least one of a small band of followers who by the force of personal intercourse and attachment might have the strength (which is so hard to have alone) to move the world, or rather to form the nucleus—you being at the heart of it—for all that great vitalized organization of human love and fellowship which must be—without which modern civilization will be merely nothing."[18] Carpenter's earlier ordination as an Anglican clergyman had proven unsatisfactory. The apostolic connection with Whitman seemed, in contrast, to have the potential to revitalize modern civilization.

Returning to his lectures in Sheffield, Carpenter searched for some way to realize his ambitions. His university extension lecturing had come to seem as futile as his clerical career, and his health began to break down. Fortunately, at that point a good-looking young ironworker named Albert Fearnehough began attending his lectures and struck up a friendship. Fearnehough (pronounced *fernuff*) lived with his wife and two children on a farm outside Sheffield, and Carpenter began leaving the city as often as he could to help out on the farm or to ramble about the countryside with his new friend. "In many ways he was delightful to me," Carpenter wrote, "as the one 'powerful uneducated' and natural person I had as yet, in all my life, met with." The quoted phrase is from Whitman; Carpenter viewed Fearnehough through Whitmanesque lenses as a sort of unsullied representative of both working-class authenticity and the natural world. In his autobiography, Carpenter interpreted his life in Dantean as well as Whitmanesque terms: his years in Brighton, Cambridge, and the industrial North had been spent wandering in a "*selva oscura*," a dark wood. Fearnehough was the Virgil who would lead him to a new life, one "close to Nature and actual materials, shrewd, strong, manly, independent, not the least polite or proper, thoroughly human and kindly, and spent for the most part in the fields and under the open sky."[19]

At the same time that his intimate friendship with Fearnehough deepened, Carpenter underwent a personal crisis when his mother and father died in quick succession. At this emotionally precarious moment, he experienced a spiritual illumination. "I became . . . overwhelmingly conscious," he wrote afterward, "of the disclosure within of a region transcending in some sense the ordinary bounds of personality, in the light of which region my own idiosyncrasies of character . . . appeared of no importance whatever—an absolute Freedom from mortality, accompanied by an indescribable calm and joy." In later years, Carpenter would describe the experience as the onset of "Cosmic Consciousness," a mystical state transcending the normal individual consciousness. Concurrent with this illumination, he "became conscious that a mass of material was forming within me, imperatively demanding expression."[20] By that point, Carpenter had moved into Fearnehough's farmhouse. Using skills he had picked up as an informal apprentice at a Brighton carpentry shop, he knocked together a tiny writing shed with one side open to the air. There, looking out over open fields, he began writing a long poem that was published in 1883 as "Towards Democracy." The poem, regarded by readers and by Carpenter himself as his masterpiece, formed the foundation of the utopian project that he was to pursue for the remainder of his life.

{⟨▰▰▰⟩⟫⟨▰▰▰⟩}

With "Towards Democracy," Carpenter turned his back on the conventional, decorous, and technically proficient poetry of his Cambridge years in favor of emotionally charged free verse. Whitman's influence pervades the poem. When Havelock Ellis, a physician and

FIGURE 4.2 Edward Carpenter in his writing hut at Millthorpe. Clara Barrus,
Whitman and Burroughs, Comrades (Boston: Houghton Mifflin, 1931).

rising young writer, was handed a copy of Carpenter's newly published book by an acquaintance, he glanced through it and handed
it back with a witty dismissal: "Whitman and water." Ellis later re-
canted this judgment, but there's more than a grain of truth in the
assessment: "Towards Democracy" is in many ways a watered-down
version of Whitman's "Song of Myself." Like "Song of Myself," "Towards Democracy" is a long poem in numbered sections. Both are
in free verse, but Carpenter's lines frequently expand into small
paragraphs, making the verse prosy in comparison to Whitman's
singing, lyrical lines. Like Whitman, Carpenter revised his work
multiple times over his career: after its initial publication in 1883,

"Towards Democracy" became the title piece of a collection of poems that appeared in 1885 and that was reissued in ever-expanding editions in 1892 and 1905.[21]

"Towards Democracy" resembles "Song of Myself" in content as well as form. Both poems have a protean speaker, an "I" who occasionally represents the poet but frequently assumes other identities, changing age, sex, class, race, and nationality at will, and sometimes transmuting into an all-seeing supernatural figure able to transcend space and time. Both speakers desire to forge intimate connections with the reader. And both poems are centered on the poet's mystical apprehension of unity, an algebra of the divine in which poet equals reader equals every human being equals the entire natural world.

Where the two poems differ fundamentally—what earned Carpenter his reputation as the *English* Walt Whitman—is in their political projects.[22] Whitman believed that the American nation needed only to recognize the perfection already inherent in its people and its land in order to realize the democratic promise of its foundations. "Song of Myself" is above all a poem of celebration, a loving inventory of the American people and landscape. Writing thirty years after Whitman, amidst the savage inequalities of late-Victorian England, Carpenter had no desire to sustain a similarly celebratory tone. Although parts of "Towards Democracy" are suffused with a love of the English landscape and people, the speaker just as often assumes the excoriating tone of a Hebrew prophet, attacking "the puppet dance of gentility" that Carpenter hated in Brighton. The speaker recoils from the dirt and poverty of the industrial slums and charges that the "gaunt women" and "thin joyless . . . children" he observes are the "necessary obverse and counterpart" of "deadly Respectability sitting at its dinner table, quaffing its wine, and discussing the rise and fall of stocks."[23]

The speaker of "Towards Democracy" is simultaneously a lover of the English countryside, a scourge of the wealthy and respectable, and the prophet of a utopian future. The poem's first words are "Freedom at last!"—as if the millennium were already realized. The opening sections are filled with exclamations of "Freedom!" and "Joy!"—Carpenter had a weakness for exclamatory abstractions—and in the third section the speaker explains exactly what is behind his happiness: "I conceive a millennium on earth—a millennium not of riches, nor of mechanical facilities, nor of intellectual facilities, nor absolutely of immunity from disease, nor absolutely of immunity from pain; but a time when men and women all over the earth shall ascend and enter into relation with their bodies—shall attain freedom and joy."[24]

The real interest of this prosy mission statement is in its definition of the millennium as a time when people shall "enter into relation with their bodies." Throughout the poem Carpenter remains enticingly vague about the nature of the "Democracy" toward which he is pointing, but early on he makes clear that it does not have to do with institutions: "Democracy in States or Constitutions [is] but the shadow of that which first expresses itself in the glance of the eye or the appearance of the skin."[25] Writing in a culture that privileged mind over body, Carpenter insisted that both personal and political salvation depended on a healthy physicality.

In "Towards Democracy," the first work written after the mystical illumination that transformed his life, Carpenter did not insist on the homosexual dimensions of this salvific physicality; he had not yet formulated his ideas about a Uranian vanguard. Rather, he slipped acknowledgments of same-sex passion into the midst of Whitmanesque catalogs that celebrate multiple forms of love, as in the following passage:

> Young Men and Women, I—though not of myself alone—call you: the time is come. (Is not the sweet rain falling?) [. . .]
>
> Spreaders of health (better than any doctor) to individuals, to the diseased prostrate nation, sustainers of ridicule, clearers of the ground laden with the accumulated rubbish of centuries,
>
> Lovers of all handicrafts and of labor in the open air, confessed passionate lovers of your own sex,
>
> Arise!
>
> Heroes of the enfranchisement of the body (latest and best gift long concealed from men), Arise![26]

Within the syntactically democratic form of the catalog, the passionate lovers of their own sex are no more central to the ideal democracy than the spreaders of health and lovers of handicrafts—yet neither are they any less so.

"Towards Democracy" attracted thousands of readers during the 1880s and 1890s, when a vibrant and variegated socialist counter-culture was forming in late-Victorian Britain. The activist Fenner Brockway, who called *Towards Democracy* the bible of the socialist movement, voiced the sentiments of countless other readers at the fin de siècle. In Brockway's recollection, "We read it aloud in the summer evenings when, tired by tramping or games, we rested awhile before returning from our rambles. We read it at those moments when we wanted to retire from the excitement of our Socialist work, and in quietude seek the calm and power that alone gives sustaining strength. We no longer believed in dogmatic theology. Edward Carpenter gave us the spiritual food we still needed."[27]

Carpenter's utopianism was a central element of his appeal to Victorian socialists. Like all utopian writing, "Towards Democracy" both fosters cognitive estrangement from present realities and offers an appealing vision of a transformed future. The poem attacks the "smooth-faced Respectability" that "grind[s] cheap goods out of the hard labor of ill-paid boys" but also imagines the coming millennium "when men and women all over the earth . . . shall attain freedom and joy."[28] "Towards Democracy" does not offer a fully realized model of utopia in the manner of *Looking Backward* or *News from Nowhere*, but in its very abstractness, its repeated invocations of a future of strategically undefined "Democracy," "Freedom," and "Joy," it appealed to readers across a broad spectrum of the British left.

The poem brilliantly anticipated the reform movements that would attract numerous activists in the decades following its publication. Vegetarians and antivivisectionists found support for their views ("Do you batten like a ghoul on the dead corpses of animals, and then expect to be of a cheerful disposition? Do you put the loving beasts to torture as a means of promoting your own health and happiness?") as did the middle-class members of the growing women's movement (the poem laments the "young girls and women, with sideway flopping heads, debarred from Work, debarred from natural Sexuality, weary to death with nothing to do").[29]

In Great Britain as in the U.S., the political left broadly overlapped the spiritual left, and "Towards Democracy" offers a vague but appealing post-Christian mystical spirituality. It begins with the speaker's mystical awakening:

I arise out of the dewy night and shake my wings.

Tears and lamentations are no more. Life and death lie stretched
below me. I breathe the sweet aether blowing of the breath of God.

Deep as the universe is my life—and I know it; nothing can dislodge
the knowledge of it; nothing can destroy, nothing can harm me.

Joy, joy arises—I arise. The sun darts overpowering piercing rays of
joy through me, the night radiates it from me.

Insofar as the poem has a plot, it concerns the speaker's identifica-
tion with the earth and all living beings following this moment of
enlightenment. Like Edward Bellamy with his concept of the "dual
self," the speaker shares an Emersonian conviction that the individual can shed his limited perspective and embrace his higher self,
the oversoul: "Apart from all evil—from all that seems to you evil—
your Soul, my friend, that towards which you aspire, which will become you one day—your true Self—rides, / Above your phantasmal
self continually." For all its indignation at the state of contemporary
England, the poem is profoundly optimistic, assuring readers that
they have the power to shake off the deadly illusions of Victorian
respectability, assume their true selves, and participate in a broad
and joyous movement toward the democratic utopian future.[30]

At the same time that "Towards Democracy" appeared in print, Carpenter moved to rural Derbyshire. Upon his father's death, he had
inherited £6,000, a considerable fortune in 1883. He used a portion
of it to buy a seven-acre plot near the hamlet of Millthorpe, some
nine miles south of Sheffield. A local builder, working fast, put together a plain stone cottage that, in a departure from the local style,
showed its unornamented back to the road. However, once one entered the gate and walked around to the house's front, the eccentric
siting justified itself: the front door opened onto a beautiful meadow
sloping down to a clear, swift stream. Carpenter's friend Albert
Fearnehough, along with his wife and two children, joined Carpenter at Millthorpe, and the two men worked ferociously hard, plant-
ing fruit trees and laying out beds. By the next year, Carpenter had
acquired a wagon, painted "Ed. Carpenter—Market Gardener" on

its side, and was taking fruit, flowers, and vegetables into the markets at Sheffield and Chesterfield.

Carpenter was, it seems safe to say, the only honors graduate of Cambridge selling goods in the markets of those two northern cities. Yet his back-to-the-land career was not as surprising as it would have been earlier in Queen Victoria's reign. Martin Green has called the 1880s a British "New Age."[31] Edward Carpenter became one of the leading figures of the developing counterculture and Millthorpe a prominent stopping-place on the New Age circuit. Like William Morris's Red House and Kelmscott Manor, Carpenter's cottage at Millthorpe assumed utopian dimensions. That was not, however, because of its design. Discerning guests found the house ugly and inconvenient; it was laid out railcar-fashion, one room leading directly to the next without a corridor. What made Millthorpe so appealing were the people who gathered there, although it took some years to establish the right mix. For the first ten years, with the Fearnehough family in residence, their two children demanded much attention, and the taciturn Fearnehough and his wife mingled uneasily with Carpenter's bohemian friends. Once they departed, George and Lucy Adams, working-class socialists who were friends of Carpenter, arrived in order to help keep the place running; unlike Morris, Carpenter was unwilling to employ servants. It was not until 1898 that the Adamses departed, and Carpenter's lover and companion George Merrill moved in. Merrill's arrival initiated Millthorpe's glory years. Carpenter's reputation as poet, polemicist, and political activist was at its height, and the combination of his kindly warmth and George Merrill's saucy friendliness attracted men and women of diverse backgrounds and interests. In his autobiography, Carpenter boasted of the variety of his guests: "Architects, railway clerks, engine-drivers, signalmen, naval and military officers, Cambridge and Oxford dons, students, advanced women, suffragettes, professors and provision-merchants, came into touch in my little house and garden; parsons and positivists, printers and authors, scythesmiths and surgeons, bank managers and quarrymen, met with each other. Young colliers from the neighboring mines put on the boxing-gloves with sprigs of aristocracy; learned professors sat down to table with farm-lads."[32]

Like Morris and many others in their overlapping circles, Carpenter believed that late nineteenth-century England was on the

FIGURE 4.3 Millthorpe, ca. 1900. George Merrill is standing at left, Edward Carpenter seated at far right. Carpenter Collection, Sheffield City Archives.

path to a classless utopia. He hailed "the inception of a number of new movements or enterprises tending towards the establishment of mystical ideas and a new social order." He cited the Theosophical Society, the Vegetarian Society, the antivivisection movement, "and many other associations of the same kind," which collectively marked "the coming of a great reaction from the smug commercialism and materialism of the mid-Victorian epoch, and a preparation for the new universe of the twentieth century."[33] Carpenter prepared for the new universe to come through his participation in a remarkable number of political and social movements, centering on a combination of simple living, socialism, sexual theorizing, and spirituality.

Carpenter's spiritual experiences and beliefs were crucial to his utopian program. Following his resignation from the Anglican priesthood, he immersed himself in the heady atmosphere of cosmopolitan spirituality that flourished in late nineteenth-century Great Britain and the United States. The ground had been prepared by the American Transcendentalists. Both Walt Whitman and

Henry David Thoreau, whose *Walden* Carpenter greatly admired, were intrigued by Asian religions. Thoreau, in particular, pored over the few Indian religious texts that had been translated from the Sanskrit, and he boasted in *Walden,* "I bathe my intellect in the stupendous and cosmogonal philosophy of the Bhagvat Geeta."[34] When Carpenter's Cambridge friend Ponnanbalam Arunachalam sent him a copy of the Bhagavad Gita in 1881, Carpenter was highly receptive to its religious message. Earlier that year Carpenter's mother had died, placing him in a psychologically labile state. Just at this moment, the Bhagavad Gita arrived, and "all at once I found myself in touch with a mood of exaltation and inspiration—a kind of super-consciousness—which passed all that I had experienced before." This was the mystical illumination that resulted in *Towards Democracy*, a book that, like *Leaves of Grass* and *Walden,* is studded with references to Hinduism.[35]

Less than ten years after first reading the Bhagavad Gita, Carpenter received an invitation from his friend Arunachalam, who upon graduation from Cambridge had returned to his native Ceylon (now Sri Lanka) and begun studying with a Hindu holy man. Arunachalam, genuinely eager to see his friend and eager also to fan Carpenter's interest in Hinduism, pressed him to visit with an irresistible mixture of enticement and flattery. "Your life," he wrote in a letter, "seems to have been a preparation for the high stages [of Hinduism]. You of all friends are most ripe. So come out to the East and seek the truth. You must work out your evolution with the zeal of a hero."[36] In 1890 Carpenter sailed for Ceylon and India. Decades before the spiritual seekers of the 1960s and later made the passage to India commonplace, Carpenter was determined to find his own guru.

He found him in Ceylon. Carpenter spent more than a month in daily study with Ramaswamy, his friend Arunachalam's spiritual teacher. Carpenter described the guru's teachings in detail in the book he published about his journey, *From Adam's Peak to Elephanta* (1892). The heart of the teachings, in Carpenter's view, was the concept of "nondifferentiation," a frontal attack on Western conceptions of individuality. One's self, according to this doctrine, is an illusion, and every living person is simply an aspect of Brahman, the all-pervading divinity. Ramaswamy placed the doctrine of nondifferentiation at the center of his contemplative spiritual practice; Carpenter appropriated it for his own purposes, linking it to his democratic utopianism. Writing in a bluff British tone very different from that of the Hindu holy texts, Carpenter exhorted the readers of *From Adam's Peak*, "You have to learn to live in a world in which the chief fact is *not* that you are distinct from others, but that you are a part of and integral with them. . . . Difficult as this teaching is for us in this day to realise, yet there is no doubt that it must lie at the heart of the Democracy of the future, as it has lain, germinal, all these centuries in the hidden womb of the East." Hindu philosophy can be turned to a variety of political uses; Carpenter was certain that its teachings of divine unity led straight to socialism. He called Ramaswamy "a Socialist [at] heart"—a description that must have nonplussed the Hindu sage.[37] During the years after his mystical illumination and the publication of *Towards Democracy*, Carpenter united spirituality and socialism in a distinctive synthesis.

When Edward Carpenter became interested in socialism in the early 1880s, the movement had a few hundred adherents who were split into a number of competing and frequently hostile factions. The politically curious Carpenter investigated most of them and managed, remarkably, to stay on good terms with them all. As was the case with William Morris, his first exposure to socialist ideas came through reading H. M. Hyndman's manifesto *England for All* (1881). On a visit to London, Carpenter dropped in a meeting of Hyndman's Social Democratic Federation (SDF) not long after Morris joined the group. Hyndman, sensing an opportunity, soon afterward divested Carpenter of £600, which he used to fund the new SDF journal *Justice*. Carpenter was willing to bankroll *Justice*, even though he declined to join the SDF. Instead, the journal became one of the many socialist causes he supported. He attended meetings of the Fellowship of the New Life, a spiritually inflected group dedicated to social reform through "the cultivation of a perfect character in each and all."[38] When the more politically minded members of the fellowship broke away to found the Fabian Society, Carpenter attended meetings of both organizations. When Morris broke with

Hyndman and established the Socialist League, Carpenter remained on good terms with both men, and then helped found the Sheffield Socialist Society, an independent group. Carpenter wrote for *Commonweal* when it was edited by Morris and continued to do so after Morris resigned and anarchists took over the journal. When John Creaghe, an anarchist who attacked Morris in the pages of *Commonweal*, turned his sights on Carpenter, excoriating him for supporting Fabians and trade unionists, Carpenter wrote him a good-humored reply: "Certainly, comrade Creaghe, I stick up for Fabians and Trade Unions just as much as I do for the Anarchists. . . . We are all travelling along the same road. Why should we be snarling at each other's heads?" Comrade Creaghe remained unconvinced by Carpenter's political ecumenism; so did George Bernard Shaw. When Carpenter invited Shaw to contribute to a volume of essays, the Fabian playwright responded with an essay that ridiculed "the cherished illusion that all Socialists are agreed in principle though they may differ as to tactics."[39]

For Shaw, tactics and principles were indistinguishable, and it was absurd to claim that there was no real difference between Fabians interested in permeating the parliamentary system of government and anarchists committed to the violent overthrow of the state. Creaghe and Hyndman would have agreed. All of them were vitally concerned with questions of power: who would lead England on its journey to the socialist future? Carpenter, in contrast, was remarkably indifferent to political power. His utopianism not only shaped his vision of the future but also suffused his day-to-day political involvement. It was Morris who wrote that "fellowship is life," but socialist fellowship remained for Morris a largely unrealized ideal; his political life during the 1880s was filled with battles for control of the SDF and the Socialist League.[40] Carpenter, cheerfully promiscuous in his political commitments and aloof from internecine strife, tried to live out utopian fellowship in the here and now.

Carpenter's unified politics of means and ends was in part a self-created program, but it was fashioned within the context of the diffuse political movement that historians have labeled "ethical socialism." The two other dominant varieties of British socialism, Marxism (represented by the SDF) and Fabianism, were centered in London;

ethical socialists predominated in northern industrial cities not far from Millthorpe such as Sheffield, Manchester, and Leeds. Robert Blatchford, arguably the most influential British socialist of the fin de siècle—his *Clarion* magazine, published in Manchester, claimed a circulation of nearly 84,000, which was 81,000 more than Morris's *Commonweal* had at its peak—said that the London socialists looked to Marx, while those in the rest of the country took their doctrine from an eclectic group of nineteenth-century reformers and visionaries: Darwin, Carlyle, Ruskin, Dickens, Thoreau, and Whitman.[41] Marxist socialists placed their hope for social change in a class-conscious revolutionary proletariat; ethical socialists believed that a better future would be achieved once enough individuals had rejected the individualistic, competitive ethic of capitalism in favor of the communal, cooperative socialist ideal. Like Morris, ethical socialists were committed to "making Socialists," but for them the making of socialists had less to do with educating workers about the class struggle than with awakening individuals to the ethic of fellowship. Marxists dismissed religion as a tool of the ruling class, but ethical socialists insisted on the religious foundations of their work for reform. Ethical socialists were more likely to talk about conversions than either elections or revolutions; they tended to be skeptical of all conventional political activities. "It is of much more importance to teach and live socialism than it is to elect socialist representatives," claimed a leading ethical socialist. "A million theoretical socialists are of less real and ultimate value than one earnest soul whose socialism is the expression of his heart's religion and life."[42]

Edward Carpenter became the poet laureate of ethical socialism. *Towards Democracy*, in its multiple editions, sold thousands of copies, while Carpenter's poem "England, Arise!", set to music, became the unofficial anthem of the British labor movement. Along with Morris and Shaw, Carpenter was one of the most popular political lecturers in late nineteenth-century Britain. Morris was best known for his connections of art and labor, his evocations of a future in which laborers would joyfully create products that were also works of art. Shaw preached "gas-and-water socialism," the Fabian strategy of moving gradually from municipalized services to public ownership of all means of production. Carpenter advocated the

"Larger Socialism," an integrated political and cultural program that accommodated every progressive movement in late-Victorian Britain, including vegetarianism, antivivisection, women's rights, environmentalism, sex reform, anticolonialism, naturism, and multiple varieties of post-Christian spirituality. Carpenter's big-tent approach to socialism thrilled ethical socialists and unaffiliated bohemians, but it brought him into conflict with sober-minded Marxists and Fabians.

The conflict reached its climax in 1889, when Carpenter delivered a lecture in London to an audience of Fabians and prominent members of the Social Democratic Federation. The lecture, provocatively entitled "Civilisation: Its Cause and Cure," was based on a witty premise; it is no surprise that Oscar Wilde read it with pleasure.[43] Carpenter argued that modern civilization—the entire superstructure of Victorian society—was in essence a disease. Carpenter had been reading intensively in nineteenth-century anthropology, and he found in the work of American scholar Lewis H. Morgan an outline of human history that fit easily into his socialist outlook. Morgan's theory of social development—like that of his British contemporary Edward B. Tylor—centered on a transition from savagery to barbarism to civilization. Resisting the predominant nineteenth-century narrative of progress, Morgan, who claimed that he had been adopted by the Iroquois Indians of upstate New York, romanticized the savage state and predicted that civilization would be superseded by a more egalitarian form of society, with the "revival, in a higher form, of the liberty, equality and fraternity of the ancient gentes," or clan.[44]

Carpenter, embracing Morgan's view that modern civilization was only a stage through which humanity must pass, used the American's observations of the Iroquois, along with other anthropological studies, to literalize the metaphor of civilization-as-disease. Modern Britons were far less healthy than primitive peoples, Carpenter argued, and their poor physical and mental health came precisely from elements within the civilization of which they were so proud. Physically, they had forsaken the "nature-life" of savages, muffled their bodies "in the cast-off furs of the beasts," hidden themselves from the sun in houses that were nothing but "boxes with breathing holes," and darkened the sky with the smoke of factories. Socially, they had replaced "the unity of the old tribal society" with the impersonal and divisive institution of "Government," designed to protect private property. And spiritually, they had lost sight of the "cosmic self," worshipping the false idols of individualism and materialism.[45]

After diagnosing the disease, Carpenter offered both the means of cure and a vision of the postcivilized future. His prescription involved a return to community and to nature. Reflecting his contacts with the anarchist philosopher Peter Kropotkin, he argued that the coming society would be a stateless utopia of voluntary "mutual help and combination." Like Kropotkin, he predicted that humans in the new society would live in harmony with animals and give up meat-eating. However, he went considerably further in his valorization of the "natural." He imagined people coming out of their houses, living outdoors as much as possible, and throwing off their clothing, the better to bask in the sunlight of unpolluted skies. And there was more: once the "Civilisation-period has passed away, the old Nature-religion . . . will come back." Before Christianity, humans worshipped the powers of generation and the heavens above; in the coming utopia, "the meaning of the old religions will come back to [Man]," and "on the high tops once more gathering he will celebrate with naked dances the glory of the human form and the great processions of the stars."[46]

This ecstatic peroration was a bit much for the Fabians. A socialist journal reported that the address was greeted by a "chorus of adverse criticism" and that a "nettled" Mr. Carpenter "defended himself with considerable smartness." From this point on, Shaw began referring to Carpenter as the "Noble Savage," while Hyndman complained, "I do not want the movement to be a depository of odd cranks: humanitarians, vegetarians, anti-vivisectionists, arty-crafties and all the rest of them." Carpenter was undeterred. A few months later he included "Civilisation: Its Cause and Cure" as the title essay of a new collection that became, along with *Towards Democracy*, one of his most popular books: it went into eighteen editions between 1889 and 1938 and was translated into seven foreign languages, including Bulgarian, Danish, and Japanese.[47]

The success of *Civilisation* and *Towards Democracy* was rivaled by that of *Love's Coming-of-Age*, originally published in 1896 by a small left-wing press and then issued in multiple expanded and revised editions by commercial publishers in England and the U.S. The book, which falls into the genre of Victorian marriage manuals, might well have won readers on the basis of its first chapter, enticingly titled "The Sex-Passion." If that is indeed the case, then thousands of copies must have been left unread. Anyone expecting racy prose encountered instead passages such as the following: "How intoxicating indeed, how penetrating—like a most precious wine—is that love which is the sexual transformed by the magic of the will into the emotional and spiritual!"[48] Carpenter fell easily into the cadences of an Anglican clergyman at a prenuptial counseling session.

Yet despite its prim diction, *Love's Coming-of-Age* is at heart a subversive book that employs the marriage-manual genre to advance a radical sexual and political agenda. Throughout the book, Carpenter denounces asceticism and challenges the idea that the primary purpose of sex is procreation. He celebrates sex as a source of pleasure and a means of intimacy, and he questions lifelong monogamy as the sole model for sexual relationships. Moreover, *Love's Coming-of-Age* attacks the interconnected institutions of patriarchy, capitalism, and imperialism, and it identifies the oppression of women as the most urgent problem facing Victorian society.

The book's title hints at Carpenter's central metaphor: love—along with the associated realms of marriage and sexuality—is at a fundamentally immature stage and can grow to maturity only within conditions of freedom in a transformed society. His second chapter, "Man, the Ungrown," contains the heart of his argument. Reinterpreting the story of the Garden of Eden, the ex-clergyman makes "Private Property" the serpent that, rather than seducing Eve, bites Adam, infecting him with a "craze for property and individual ownership" that culminates in "the enslavement of women." Carpenter rails against the "beefy self-satisfaction" of the middle-class Englishman and, in his book's most powerful passage, abandons his usually genial authorial voice to rant against the English patriarchy:

> It is certainly very maddening at times to think that the Destinies of the world, the organisation of society, the wonderful scope of possible

statesmanship, the mighty issues of trade and industry, the loves of Women, the lives of criminals, the fate of savage nations, should be in the hands of such a set of general nincompoops; men so fatuous that it actually does not hurt them to see the streets crammed with prostitutes by night, or the parks by day with the semi-lifeless bodies of tramps; men, to whom it seems quite natural that our marriage and social institutions should lumber along over the bodies of women, as our commercial institutions grind over the bodies of the poor, and our "imperial" enterprise over the bodies of barbarian races, destroyed by drink and devilry.

Carpenter repeatedly connects the presumably private realm of personal relationships to broad public issues of capitalism, imperialism, and gender inequality. He argues that Victorian civilization is the product of ungrown men who believe the emotions and passions—not to mention the body and sexuality—to be shameful, and whose mania for owning things leads them to treat others in purely instrumental terms. They reduce women, children, the working class, and imperial subjects to means of satisfying the individual greed that is at the core of England's "commercial civilisation." In the "free society" to come, men will learn that love is paramount, thus transforming all personal relationships—not only those between men and women but between men of different classes and races.[49] Carpenter used the genre of the Victorian marriage manual for utopian purposes. Like every utopian tract, *Love's Coming-of-Age* offers both a vision of a transformed future and a critique of contemporary society, promoting readers' cognitive estrangement from the world about them.

Women's rights are central to the social critique of *Love's Coming-of-Age*. Carpenter argued that under current conditions a woman faced two equally distasteful choices: either to sell her body outright and be scorned as a prostitute or to dispose of herself to one man for life and be forced into the role of either the working-class "household drudge" or the vapid, idle "lady." He linked the predicament of women under patriarchy to the situation of workers under capitalism: just as the wage-worker had no means of livelihood except by the sale of his bodily labor, women had no means of livelihood except by the surrender of their bodily sex. The emancipation of women, he argued, is inextricably linked to the struggle for socialism: "Not till our whole commercial system, with its barter and sale of human labour and human love for gain, is done away" with, he wrote, "will women really be free."[50]

Love's Coming-of-Age cemented Carpenter's position among the greatest profeminist male writers of the Anglo-American nineteenth century, along with John Stuart Mill, Walt Whitman, and Friedrich Engels. Like his predecessors, Carpenter was unable to escape entirely the gravitational pull of the Victorian gender system. His work mixes forward-thinking egalitarian principles with nineteenth-century gender essentialism. He argued that the institution of marriage depends on women's freedom, that it can survive only as a union of equals, yet he also asserted that women are "more primitive, more intuitive, [and] more emotional" than men. Carpenter shared his culture's sentimental reverence for "the depth and sacredness of the mother-feeling in woman," and since a mother's life is bound up with the life of her child, it follows that "she is nearer the child herself, and nearer to the savage."[51]

Carpenter was writing in an age of transition, and his ideas about women are inconsistent, veering among reverence, condescension, and exhortations to women to be "strong and courageous." Nevertheless, Carpenter's female contemporaries regarded him as a valued ally. Carpenter was in correspondence with virtually every leading feminist in fin-de-siècle England, and their letters testify to the inspiration they found in his writing. The radical women's rights activist Isabella Ford, a close friend, gushed to Carpenter, "I believe you were a woman in some other incarnation." Carpenter's reply to this compliment is unknown. What's clear is that he combined his utopian theorizing with work on immediate reforms and was one of the earliest members of the Men's League for Women's Suffrage. Eve Kosofsky Sedgwick notes Carpenter's remarkable ability to "focus erotically on the Male, sentimentalize intermittently about the Female, and yet work relatively unswervingly for the rights of actual women."[52]

Carpenter believed that his sympathy for women's rights came precisely from his erotic attraction to men. As a youth he had seen his older unmarried sisters become trapped in a state of "enforced celibacy" and suffer from nervous illnesses. He wrote that most men—"for whom the physical side of sex, if needed, is easily accessible"—have no comprehension of women's predicament. But as a young man uninterested in sex with women, strongly attracted to men, but without any idea that his desires might be reciprocated, Carpenter realized "in my own person some of the sufferings which are endured by an immense number of modern women, especially of the well-to-do classes." Later on, he theorized that "homogenic" men have a special affinity with women. He argued that most men, shaped by the conventions of commercial civilization, are absorbed in commerce and career, their emotional lives stunted. Homosexual men, in his view, resembled women, in that for both, "Love—in some form or other—is the main object of life." Carpenter believed in a natural alliance between male homosexuals and women, since both suffered within "a state of society which has set up gold and gain in the high place of the human heart." Even if one has doubts about the inevitability of political alliances between women and gay men, there is no question that Carpenter was keenly aware both of women's suffering and of his own male privilege. He knew he was lucky. Miserable in Brighton, he was, unlike his sisters, able to escape—first to Cambridge and then to the North, where he found a rich "world of the heart," a subculture of men from all classes who valued comradeship above all else.[53]

Carpenter's comment about the homosexual world of the heart is typical of his advocacy. From 1883, when "Towards Democracy" first appeared, through the publication of his final book in 1927, Carpenter did more than any other English-language writer to advance the cause of homosexual men and women. However, his campaign bears virtually no resemblance to the work of twenty-first-century LGBTQ activists. Carpenter had no interest in the language of "rights" or even of "equality." Instead, he argued that homosexuals are less sensual and more spiritual than other men and women; that they have been responsible for the origins and furtherance of art, science, and religion in the course of human history; and that they are the vanguard of the utopia to come.

⁘

Carpenter's sexual theorizing, which seems now both courageous and peculiar, came out of the particular circumstances of fin-de-siècle Britain. When he began writing about same-sex passion in the

1880s, the word *homosexual* did not exist in English. The most widely available term was *sodomite*, a word employed in police reports, judicial proceedings, and studies of the insane, which were at the time the only existent English-language writings about sexual relationships between men. Sodomy was considered to be a perverse expression of male lust, a crime of opportunity that was potentially committable by any man who failed to keep himself pure. Michel Foucault famously distinguished between the sodomite and homosexual in *The History of Sexuality:* "The sodomite had been a temporary aberration; the homosexual was . . . a species."[54] Foucault dated the creation of the homosexual—a person known less for specific sexual acts than for a particular sexual sensibility—to 1870; however, in England the distinction between sodomites and same-sex lovers did not come about until the 1890s. Edward Carpenter was at the center of the cultural shift.

If homosexuals were nonexistent in British discourse until the 1890s, sodomites were rarely present. Sodomy was a capital offense until 1861 and punishable by life imprisonment thereafter, but the charge was rarely brought and even more rarely reported by journalists. That changed in 1895, when Oscar Wilde charged the Marquess of Queensbury with libel for labeling him a "somdomite." (The marquess had a weak grasp of orthography.) Wilde lost his case and was prosecuted under the Criminal Law Amendment Act of 1885, which got around the weaknesses of the difficult-to-prove sodomy statute by criminalizing all acts of "gross indecency" between men. The Wilde trials made male homosexuality visible in British and American culture, and they set off a wave of homophobic reaction. The animosity surrounding Wilde and homosexuality was so intense that as late as 1916, in his autobiography, Carpenter was careful to specify that he had never met Wilde personally.[55] Carpenter was so intent on distinguishing himself from Wilde, from gross indecency, and from an association with sodomy because by 1916 he had been working for more than twenty years to construct an alternative model of homosexuality and homosexual men and women—or, rather, Urnings.

Carpenter took the term *Urning* (pronounced *earning*) from Karl Heinrich Ulrichs, a German lawyer and civil servant who in the 1860s began publishing works in defense of same-sex love. The word *homosexual* had not yet been coined. Ulrichs looked to Plato for a conceptual model and found the term *Urning* in a discussion about love in the *Symposium*. Writing in opposition to the reigning legal discourse that regarded sexual acts between men as instances of criminal perversion, Ulrichs argued that same-sex attraction was an inborn trait and that sexual relations between consenting Urnings were morally blameless. He theorized that Urnings' sexual desires were the result of *anima muliebris virili corpore inclusa*—a female soul in a male body.[56]

Ulrichs was a precursor of the Continental physician-scientists who came to be known as "sexologists."[57] Carpenter, fluent in European languages, was familiar with the sexologists, and in his own work he relied particularly on three writers on homosexuality: Richard von Krafft-Ebing, author of *Psychopathia Sexualis* (1886); Albert Moll, author of *Perversions of the Sex Instinct* (1891); and Havelock Ellis, who co-authored *Sexual Inversion* (1897). As Krafft-Ebing's and Moll's titles make clear, they regarded homosexuality as a perverse form of sexuality, to be classed alongside pedophilia and bestiality. However, their work included nonjudgmental case studies of homosexual men and women, and Carpenter took from them three ideas favorable to his own position. First was the concept that same-sex desire was a congenital trait in a certain segment of the population; next, that this trait was more widespread than had been supposed; and finally that, aside from their sexual object-choice, homosexuals were little different from the general population.[58]

Sexual Inversion was even more useful to Carpenter. The book was a collaboration between Ellis, a heterosexual physician and writer, and John Addington Symonds, a highly regarded poet and critic who had circulated his privately published works about same-sex love among his wide circle of acquaintances. The erudite Symonds had long been aware of Ulrichs's work, and he accepted the notion of "inverted" desire as an accurate and nonpejorative description of his own sexual nature. However, he rejected Ulrichs's etiology of a female soul in a male body; he felt himself to be entirely masculine in disposition. Following Ulrichs, he and Ellis asserted that sexual inversion was innate, a variation from the norm akin to color blindness. Symonds went on to argue that given sexual inversion's status as an inborn disposition rather than an acquired vice,

British laws against consensual relations between men should be repealed.[59]

Carpenter was in correspondence with Symonds during the 1890s, and he was well aware of the latter's argument that since sexual inversion was a harmless variation, the repeal of laws against same-sex relations would not "be absolutely prejudicial to social interests."[60] Carpenter also campaigned for a change in British law, but his arguments for reform went considerably beyond Symonds's. Carpenter linked his sexual theorizing to his socialist politics and argued that inverts, far from being merely harmless, were uniquely positioned to lead the transformation of capitalist society into an egalitarian utopia.

Carpenter first aired his ideas in *Homogenic Love*, an 1894 pamphlet printed "for private circulation only." By that point, the word *homosexual* had been introduced into English discourse, but he, like Symonds, preferred *homogenic*, a compound of two Greek roots. *Homosexual*, which combined a Greek and a Latin root, grated on the nerves of these classically trained Englishmen like fingernails on slate. Whatever its title, the timing of *Homogenic Love* could scarcely have been worse. The next year, Oscar Wilde was convicted of gross indecency, and Max Nordau's *Degeneration* was translated into English. Discourses of perversion and degeneration fed into one another, creating an image of the homosexual as a threat not only to public order but to civilization itself.

Carpenter did not shrink from his defense of homogenic love, but it was not until 1906 that he was able to adapt his 1894 pamphlet for inclusion in a new edition of *Love's Coming-of-Age*. Two years later, he expanded his ideas into *The Intermediate Sex*, issued by a major British publisher and widely circulated. Carpenter was able to place *The Intermediate Sex* with a commercial publisher despite Britain's post-Wilde-trials homophobia in large part because of the work's sweet, calm, surely-we-can-all-agree tone. The book is studded with footnotes to scientific tomes in German, French, and Italian, but in place of the dominant "medico-forensic" model of Continental sexology, Carpenter took the tone that he must have used as a Broad Church parson, genially addressing his parishioners on a Sunday morning.[61]

Carpenter took great pains to distinguish "Urnings," respectable men and women who happened to be born with a love for their own sex, from the mere sensualists and curiosity-seekers who appeared in police reports. He argued that male Urnings were actually less sensual than other men, and that far from being the product of fin-de-siècle degeneration, they represented advanced types on the evolutionary scale. He treated with skepticism Ulrichs's theory that male Urnings possessed a female soul, with the reverse being true for females, but he did argue that Urnings were naturally more androgynous. This was all to the good. The extreme sex differentiation promoted by Victorian society meant that men and women were "wont to congregate in separate herds, and talk languages each unintelligible to the other." Urnings, with their unique insights into both sexes, had "a special work to do as reconcilers and interpreters of the two sexes to each other."[62] Carpenter memorably expressed this view of Urnings' unique social role in his 1902 poem "O Child of Uranus," which begins:

> O Child of Uranus, wanderer down all times,
> Darkling, from farthest ages of the Earth the same
> Strange tender figure, full of grace and pity,
> Yet outcast and misunderstood of men—
> Thy Woman-soul within a Man's form dwelling,
> [Was Adam perchance like this, ere Eve from his side was drawn?]
> So gentle, gracious, dignified, complete,
> With man's strength to perform, and pride to suffer without sign,
> And feminine sensitiveness to the last fibre of being;
> Strange twice-born, having entrance to both worlds—
> Loved, loved by either sex,
> And free of all their lore![63]

The poem portrays the androgynous Urning as a mythic hero free of the conventional cultural constraints of gender—the straitening "lore" of social expectations. The poem goes on to depict the Urning as a Christ-figure, a redemptive lord of love who combines "Mother-love" and "sex-emotion."

In *The Intermediate Sex,* Carpenter granted that "ordinary [i.e., heterosexual] love" has an important role to play in the propagation

of the race, but he argued that Urnings, possessed of a "double nature," were disproportionately represented among humanity's great
artists and leaders. The Uranian temperament, he wrote, "is exceed-
ingly sensitive and emotional," and Urnings place love ahead of the
motives that animate the ordinary person, such as devotion to family or business success. Linking his sexual theorizing to his utopian
socialist commitments, Carpenter argued "the Uranian spirit" had
the potential to lead to "a general enthusiasm of Humanity," and
that "the Uranian people may be destined to form the advance guard
of that great movement which will one day transform the common
life by substituting the bond of personal affection and compassion
for the monetary, legal and other external ties which now control
and confine society." Carpenter saw the "Cash-nexus" as supreme in
contemporary society; Uranians were poised to help love take "its
rightful place" as the dominant force in a utopian future.[64]

Carpenter emphasized the potential of homogenic love to transcend class barriers. "Eros," he wrote, "is a great leveller." He believed that Uranian love breached class barriers more easily than
conventional heterosexual unions: "It is noticeable how often Uranians of good position and breeding are drawn to rougher types, as
of manual workers, and frequently very permanent alliances grow
up in this way."[65] Carpenter was no doubt thinking of his own relationships with Albert Fearnehough and George Merrill. Moreover,
he was attuned to cross-class relationships formed by men and
women in his own circle, which he depicted in his long utopian
poem "A Mightier Than Mammon" (1902). The poem describes a
number of these relationships: a "young heir" who falls in love with
a coal-shoveller, a Cambridge alumna who lives with a working-
class woman from the East London slums, a "Cinghalese coolie"
who loves a European officer on a merchant ship. Carpenter writes
that these lovers constitute "the Outline and Draft of a new order"
and portrays them as avatars of a future society knit together by
love, "rather than by the old Cash-nexus."[66]

Carpenter was undoubtedly sincere in his belief in the inherently
democratic dimensions of same-sex love, yet as a member of the
upper-middle-class British intelligentsia, he was oblivious to the
enduring inequities of power within these cross-class relationships.
As William Pannapacker has pointed out, Carpenter's long relation-

ship with Merrill may have been widely regarded as a model of democratic comradeship, but Merrill was listed on the local tax rolls as Carpenter's servant. Eager to celebrate Uranians' cross-class relationships as harbingers of the coming utopia, Carpenter ignored the ways in which human desires are shaped by social class. As Ruth Livesey pithily observes, "in his haste to go barefoot into Utopia," Carpenter failed to address basic issues of inequality. He could not conceive that a Cambridge graduate's eagerness to jettison civilization might not be shared by working-class men and women who had yet to enjoy many of its benefits.[67]

Moreover, no matter how much Carpenter might have wanted to eliminate class differences, his writings on homogenic love inscribe a novel hierarchical distinction between different types of same-sex passion. Carpenter realized that many Britons and Americans, even among the progressives who formed his readership, associated homosexuality with the criminal and sordid, and he acknowledged the existence of "debaucheries," "scandals," and "abuses." He insisted, however, that there is an important distinction between such instances of "mere carnal curiosity" and the "genuine heart-attachment" among what he calls the "superior" type of Urnings. Eager to escape the taint of scandal associated with homosexuality, Carpenter constructed a sexual hierarchy with superior Urnings at the top and "extreme" types at the bottom. The latter, he asserts, are "not particularly attractive." Men of this type are "distinctively effeminate," he charges, and he goes on to plaster them with stereotypically feminine attributes: they are "sentimental, lackadaisical, mincing in gait and manners, something of a chatterbox." The "extreme type of the homogenic female" is similarly caricatured as "markedly aggressive," with "masculine manners and movements." Carpenter opposed these extreme types, which he claimed to be relatively rare, to "the more normal and perfect types" of homogenic men and women. The normal homogenic man is thoroughly masculine in appearance and manner but has "the tenderer and more emotional soul-nature of the woman," while the typical homogenic woman is "thoroughly feminine and gracious" yet possesses a "masculine" temperament—namely, one that is "active, brave, [and] originative."[68]

It is as if Carpenter took to heart the dictum of his mentor Walt Whitman: "Be radical—be radical—be not too damn radical!"[69]

Carpenter tried to advance a radical sexual project while leaving intact conventional definitions of gender. It's not that Carpenter approved of the Victorian ideology of "separate spheres," which relegated men to the public sphere and women to the home; the central point of *Love's Coming-of-Age* is that the masculine world of government and commerce depends on the exploitation and oppression of women, workers, and imperial subjects. He accepted, however, his culture's conventional distinctions between masculine and feminine traits and qualities. Rather than trying to dismantle gender distinctions, Carpenter argued that the trail leading beyond a system based on patriarchal dominance would be blazed by homogenic men and women who combined "man's strength to perform" and "feminine sensitiveness to the last fibre of being," in the words of his Uranian poem.

⟨⟩

Carpenter's vision of Urnings as utopian trailblazers was bound up in his evolutionary view of human history. After the turn into the twentieth century, at the same time as he elaborated his ideas about Uranians' utopian potential, he became absorbed in anthropological speculation about homosexuals' role in the origins of human civilization. He published an article on the topic in 1911 in the *American Journal of Religious Psychology*, which became part of his book *Intermediate Types among Primitive Folk* (1914). Carpenter wrote in the waning moment of the gentleman amateur, before the discipline of anthropology had become fully professionalized. *Intermediate Types among Primitive Folk* has been called "a gay *Golden Bough*"—a synthesis of carefully footnoted ethnographic material and unbridled speculation.[70]

The book's central thesis is that Urnings were responsible for the rise of civilization in prehistoric times. In the earliest human societies, most men were warriors and hunters, while women engaged in agriculture and domestic work. Absent some motive force, human society might have remained indefinitely in this primitive phase. It was the Urnings, or "intermediate types," who made human progress possible. Uranian men, less interested in hunting and warfare, and Uranian women, not content to remain in the home, turned to other activities: they composed songs, studied nature, or speculated about the supernatural. "They became students of life and nature," Carpenter theorized, "inventors and teachers of arts and crafts, or wizards . . . and sorcerers; they became diviners and seers, or revealers of the gods and religion; they became medicine-men and healers, prophets and prophetesses."[71] Intermediate types, he concluded, laid the foundation of art, science, literature, and religion. Far from being the social outsiders that most Britons regarded them as, homosexuals were responsible for the rise of civilization.

Carpenter's anthropological theories were bound up with his religious ideas. His studies with the Hindu sage Ramaswamy had led him to the concept of "cosmic consciousness," a mystical apprehension of universal unity. During the early twentieth century, as he developed his sweeping views of human history, he theorized that cosmic consciousness was not simply a transitory state accessible to a few spiritual adepts but rather the end-stage of an evolutionary process. The earliest humans had possessed "simple consciousness," the unmediated awareness of the world seen in animals and young children. Next came civilization and "self consciousness," which Carpenter regarded as a "fatal split" between self and world. Self consciousness led to individualism, which over the centuries had resulted in the economic exploitation and environmental devastation of present times. However, he believed that the West was poised at a moment of transition. "Finally," he wrote, "with the complete antagonism of subject and object, of 'self' and 'matter,' . . . and the terrible disruptions of life and society which ensue—comes the third stage." Cosmic consciousness arrives, "the long process of differentiation comes to an end, and reintegration takes its place."[72] This third stage of consciousness, in which differences between women and men, lower and upper classes, and humanity and the natural world are reconciled, was not yet widely dispersed. However, thanks to the blending of male and female elements in their psyche, intermediate types had special access to the new consciousness and were uniquely qualified to lead humanity in the next phase of human evolution.

Carpenter's evolutionary theory of society and social change was both spiritual and political in nature. He believed that the experience of nondualistic unity achieved in cosmic consciousness led to

an understanding that the individual ego was merely a manifestation of "the great Self," the transcendental oversoul.[73] Once people
recognized that they were spiritually connected to all other selves,
they would want to return to the communal order of society that
was humanity's natural state prior to the institution of civilization
and its attendant self-consciousness and possessive individualism.
This communal order was the "Democracy" toward which Carpenter had devoted his life since the publication of *Towards Democracy*
in the 1880s. Carpenter never argued that cosmic consciousness was
limited to Uranians—his utopian vision depended on the widespread diffusion of the new order of perception—but he believed
that homogenic lovers were already modeling the democracy of the
future and would lead humanity to its perfected destiny.

Like Bellamy, Carpenter imagined that in the perfect democracy
to come, diverse forms of religion would be united in one great
world-religion. Carpenter's vision of utopian religion was more ecstatic and physical than Bellamy's—no listening to sermons for him
when one could be out dancing naked under the sun or stars—but
they shared a sense that all hitherto existing religions were simply
imperfect expressions of a single spiritual truth. Bellamy and Carpenter were convinced that the new religious consciousness, closely
linked to socialist idealism, was spreading. Bellamy placed the Great
Revival, enunciated in *Equality*, in the early twentieth century. Carpenter cannily forbore to offer a firm date, but he argued that humanity was on the cusp of the great Transformation. "The human
race is arriving . . . at one of the most fruitful and important turning-
points in [its] history," he wrote, on the verge of embracing "a Consciousness which shall have Unity as its foundation-principle."[74]

Understanding Carpenter's religious ideas clarifies both his utopianism and his political ecumenism. Carpenter could claim that
Fabians, anarchists, and trade unionists were all "travelling along
the same road" because their differing political programs were of
little interest to him. What mattered was that all the socialist group-
ings were alike in their rejection of commercial society and their
"glowing and vital enthusiasm towards the realization of a new society." Utopia would not be achieved by a political mass movement,
as his friend William Morris imagined, but through the spread of a
new consciousness of unity. Carpenter's fundamentally religious

conception of social change also explains his lack of interest in offering a utopian blueprint in the mode of *News from Nowhere* or *Looking Backward*. He acknowledged that the society of the future would have to work out details of land and labor and industry, "questions of taxation, representation, education, etc." These "complex affairs" could not, however, be worked out in advance; they would have to be decided by trial and error. It was useless to try to determine the details of utopia; instead, one needed to promote the coming revolution in human consciousness. Rather than writing fully realized romances of the future, Carpenter offered suggestive poems and essays that constitute a tutorial in cleansing the doors of perception. He gave his money and time to socialist causes not because he agreed with every part of their political programs but because he saw in the movement as a whole a hunger not just for betterment of material conditions but for "betterment of social life and a satisfaction of the needs of the heart fully as much as an increased allowance of bread and butter."[75]

And who better than Uranians understood the needs of the heart? Their androgynous temperament gave them insights into the emotional nature of both sexes. "It is probable," he wrote, "that the superior Urnings will become, in affairs of the heart, to a large extent the teachers of future society." And thanks to the surveys compiled by the scientific sexologists, Carpenter was able to assure his readers that Urnings formed a much larger proportion of the population than had previously been imagined. Before the work of researchers such as Havelock Ellis, the sexual invert was considered to be a rare aberration. Ellis, however, estimated that homosexuals might constitute as much as 5 percent of the population. In any case, Carpenter was certain that "thousands and thousands" of men and women of the intermediate type existed in England, and he theorized that their numbers might be increasing.[76] The growing band of Uranians was leading the way toward the utopian future.

{≈≈≈≋≈≈}

For almost four decades, the pilgrims flocked to Millthorpe. They were drawn by Edward Carpenter's published visions of a transformed world, but they were equally attracted by the example of his lived utopianism. Stories about this Arcadian corner of Derbyshire circulated widely among British and American progressives. Carpenter himself was not above spreading such stories. In his autobiography, he recounted the time a Christian missionary tried to press a tract on George Merrill. "Keep your tract," Merrill told him. "I don't want it." "But don't you wish to know the way to heaven?" the man persisted. "No, I don't," Merrill replied with some heat. "Can't you see that *we're in heaven here*?"[77]

Carpenter's writings were an expression of his utopianism, but so was the writing of them. Composing outdoors in the hut he had built himself, using the skills he had developed during a stint in a Brighton joiner's shop; thinning carrots and radishes in the garden or picking ramps by the stream; taking early strawberries into the market at Sheffield; having a pint at the local pub, amidst hard-drinking, taciturn Derbyshire farmers; playing Schubert *lieder* on the piano of an evening, while George Merrill sang; chatting with working-class friends who frequented the café that he and the other Socialist Society regulars had opened in the Sheffield slums—all were part of Carpenter's utopianism. He always insisted that he went into the countryside and took up manual labor not out of some idealistic purpose but simply in order to please himself. Yet once there, he saw that his mode of life might point to something more. He "began to wonder if the most sensible and obvious thing to do were not just to try and keep at least one little spot of earth clean," to do honest work and grow pure food. "It would not be much," he reflected, "just a little glimmer . . . in the darkness; but if others did the same, the illumination would increase, and after a time perhaps we should all be able to see our way better."[78]

Carpenter's work never received the attention given to Bellamy's *Looking Backward* or Morris's *News from Nowhere*. His utopian vision is spread across poems and essays and contained within anthropological treatises and sex-reform pamphlets, virtually all of them out of print by the time of his death in 1929. Yet more than any other British or American figure of his generation, Carpenter successfully combined a prophetic vision of an ideal future with everyday utopianism. It was that combination of the visionary and the practical, the fervid belief in the revolutionary potential of Uranian love and the long-term relationship with working-class George

Merrill, that drew so many visitors to Millthorpe—Edward Morgan Forster among them. After Carpenter's death, Forster wrote coolly distanced appraisals of his former mentor, but at the time they met he was overwhelmed, making multiple visits to Millthorpe after his first encounter. Carpenter seemed to the emotionally constrained novelist to be living out the ideals he admired but had been unable to realize in his own life: unashamed sensuality, democratic comradeship, and a deep connection to nature. On December 31, 1913, about to turn thirty-five the next day, Forster turned to his journal for his annual summing up. For once, the supremely articulate writer could only burble: "Forward rather than back. Edward Carpenter! Edward Carpenter! Edward Carpenter!"[79]

CHAPTER FIVE

Charlotte Perkins Gilman's Motherly Utopia

CHARLOTTE PERKINS GILMAN is best known today for "The Yellow Wallpaper," a widely anthologized and frequently taught short story that mixes gothic conventions with feminist insights—a chilling dissection of patriarchy that seems as if it could have been coauthored by Edgar Allan Poe and Gloria Steinem. Yet when the story was published in 1892, no one—including Gilman herself—thought of her as a fiction writer. Her contemporaries knew her as a speaker and writer on behalf of Nationalism, the political movement inspired by Edward Bellamy's *Looking Backward* (1888). Bellamy may have conceived his utopia as a thought experiment, but Nationalists regarded it as a feasible political blueprint. They chose the name of their movement not as an expression of American exceptionalism but as a tribute to the national scale of Bellamy's economic model, in which the state served as the sole producer of goods and employer of labor. Nationalists were, for the most part, middle-class socialists who were dismayed by both the plutocratic excesses of Gilded Age America and the violence that attended many of the working-class strikes and demonstrations of the period. They were drawn to *Looking Backward*'s vision of a near-future America of absolute equality, a utopia achieved through a peaceful process of quasi-religious individual conversion.

Many were also drawn to Nationalism by Bellamy's stance on women's economic independence; in the society depicted in *Looking Backward*, every woman and man earns an equal salary. A substantial proportion of Nationalists were women, and a surprisingly large number of women played leading roles in the movement.[1] Gilman, for example, was Nationalism's unofficial poet laureate, publishing numerous poems in support of the cause—bouncy light verse that poked fun at conservatives and made an egalitarian future seem tantalizingly possible. Her first lecture to a Nationalist club, "Human Nature," was characteristic of her distinctive approach. Gilman lauded Nationalism's challenge to laissez-faire capitalism, saying that it had "struck at a great taproot in striking at our business system, the root of the struggle between man and man." However, she added, there was another root as deep, or possibly deeper: "the struggle between man and woman."[2]

Edward Bellamy was certain that, once his version of socialism was established, gender equality would follow. Gilman took a different approach. She believed that women's independence was a precondition of socialism and that the realization of utopia depended on women's distinctive contributions. Gilman's immediate goal throughout her career was to end both women's economic dependence on men and the middle-class ideal of domestic femininity, in which the obedient daughter left the protection of her father only to assume a supporting role to her breadwinning husband. Other women's rights activists shared this goal, but for the most part they lobbied for women's freedom to compete alongside men in the capitalist marketplace. Gilman argued instead that once women were liberated from compulsory domesticity, they would be free to bring their unique perspective as mothers into the social sphere. Edward Carpenter spoke for the larger socialism; Gilman advocated what she called the "larger motherhood." She believed that women's "mother instinct" could save the world and usher in utopia. As she wrote in her poem "Mother to Child," "For the sake of my child I must hasten to save / All the children on earth from the jail and the grave." Gilman argued that women's motherly impulses were only waiting to be freed from the constraints of conventional domesticity and extended into society as a whole. Her life's work centered on the concept of what she called the "World's Mother"—the selfless, nurturing woman-spirit who loves, protects, and teaches the entire human race.[3]

The all-embracing World's Mother was especially attractive to Gilman given her disastrous experience within the conventional nuclear family. After the birth of her daughter in 1885, when Gilman was twenty-four, she was plunged into a horrendous depression, an episode that she drew on for "The Yellow Wallpaper." When her daughter was three, Gilman separated from her husband; six years later, she divorced him and gave up custody of their child. Gilman's actions, at a time when divorce was socially abhorrent and paternal custody almost unheard of, required considerable courage. Against enormous cultural odds, she chose to live out her commitment to women's independence. During the early years of the twentieth century, Gilman went on to write a series of utopian fictions, including *Herland* (1915), a witty portrait of an ideal all-female society. Her entire adult life and work can be seen as an extended utopian experiment, an effort to imagine and enact women's transformative powers under conditions of gender equality.

Charlotte Perkins Gilman was a *Beecher*. She was immensely proud of the fact, quick to let acquaintances know of her connection to the distinguished New England family. Lyman Beecher, the celebrated Calvinist preacher, was her great-grandfather. Among her great-aunts were the reform writer Catherine Beecher, women's rights activist Isabella Beecher Hooker, and novelist Harriet Beecher Stowe. She believed that she had inherited "the Beecher urge to social service," along with their "wit and gift of words." She was also aware, though she confided the fact only to a few, that she had probably inherited the Beecher tendency toward mental illness. Lyman Beecher was almost certainly manic-depressive, and at least seven of his twelve children suffered from serious depression or other ailments; two sons committed suicide.[4]

Her father, Frederick Beecher Perkins, was sane enough, and certainly brilliant—he studied at Yale, knew nine languages, and had a distinguished career as a writer, editor, and librarian. However, he was also morose and selfish; even his daughter had to admit that he had a "small moral sense." After a doctor warned him that having another child would kill his wife, who had borne three children in as many years, he abandoned his family, and Charlotte saw little of him growing up. Her mother, Mary Westcott Perkins, was pretty, petite, nervous, and emotionally smothering. By the time Charlotte was a young adult she coolly judged her mother to be an exaggerated example of the "so called 'feminine'" woman, with the typical woman's love for home and family raised to the level of mania.[5]

Mary Perkins was a difficult woman, but she was trying to raise Charlotte and her son (the third child had died in infancy) in horribly difficult circumstances. Her absent husband was an unreliable support, her work as a part-time teacher brought in little money, and she was forced to move her household frequently, staying one step ahead of her creditors; according to Gilman, they moved nineteen times within eighteen years.[6] If Gilman's childhood was unhappy, it was also the perfect preparation for a career as a social reformer, revealing to young Charlotte the hollowness of the Victorian pieties surrounding the supposedly sacred institutions of marriage, family, and home.

Mary Perkins, true to nineteenth-century ideals of womanhood, was highly religious, although her religious beliefs took heterodox form. In 1874, when Charlotte was fourteen, Mary moved the family into a Swedenborgian communal house in Providence, Rhode Island. Gilman hated the experience, and throughout her adult life she decried all social reform efforts based on cooperative living; she saw no advantage in multiplying the number of inefficient, dysfunctional families within one household. She also developed a distaste for "esoteric and occult" religion.[7] Emmanuel Swedenborg, an eighteenth-century Swedish mystic, was undeniably esoteric; he detailed his religious visions, which he believed had revealed a perfected form of Christianity, in his many complex and prolix books. His followers in the U.S. frequently combined his teachings with the occult doctrines of spiritualism, and the Providence group was headed by a woman who believed herself to be something of a psychic as well as a gifted interpreter of Swedenborg.

In reaction against the Swedenborgians, who would spend hours around the dining room table discussing fine points of the master's elaborate theology and speculating about the spirit world, the teenage Gilman decided to work out her own religious doctrine. Years later, in her autobiography, Gilman described the construction of her personal religion as a highly original and completely rational process. Of course, it was neither. Gilman's religious beliefs, like those of other late nineteenth-century spiritual seekers, combined available cultural resources with personal psychological needs. Her spiritual journey was remarkably close to that of her near-contemporary Edward Bellamy. Like Bellamy, she rejected the orthodox Calvinist theology of her more distant forebears. Again like Bellamy, she was influenced by Henry Ward Beecher's liberal Protestantism, which replaced doctrines of original sin and salvation of the elect with emphasis on a loving God who offered salvation to all. She absorbed Transcendentalism through Emerson and through her favorite poet, Walt Whitman, whose work expressed in vivid images the transcendentalist conviction that God is immanent within human beings and the natural world. ("Why should I wish to see God better than this day?" Whitman wrote. "I see something of God each hour of the twenty-four, and each moment then, / In the faces of men and women I see God, and in my own face in the glass.") Most importantly, independently of Bellamy but in remarkably similar terms, she embraced the idea of what Bellamy called the "dual life": the presence within everyone of both the individual ego or personality and a larger, all-encompassing world-self.[8]

Gilman, desperately unhappy in her personal life, had good reason to seize on the ideal of a grand, immortal common human spirit. The belief enabled her, at moments of greatest stress, to look at her suffering individual self as a thing apart. "My 'self' I was sorry for," she wrote in her autobiography. "When the suffering was extreme I would look at my self as if it were a little creature in my hand, and stroke it softly, saying, 'You poor little thing! You do have a hard time, don't you.'" More dispassionately, she proclaimed, "Human life is not personal, it is social." If the self were merely an illusory phenomenon, it followed that the purpose of life was neither individual salvation nor personal aggrandizement but service to the whole.[9]

Gilman worked out her self-denying religion of service to society during her teenage years and remained faithful to it throughout her life. Ironically, her liberal spirituality brought her to a position little different from that of her Puritan forebears: work was the means through which one realized the divine purpose. Puritans valued work in part because it could lead to worldly success, which in turn served as a sign of God's favor toward the individual believer. Gilman, in contrast, was professedly unconcerned with individual success. She argued that work was important precisely because it was not individual but collective, a form of social service. Work "is not a process of taking care of oneself," she insisted, "but a process of taking care of one another." In order to understand work rightly, humans had to transcend the fundamental intellectual error of the "Ego concept" and embrace the notion of the collective so that work was seen, not so much as altruism, but as "omniism."[10]

As a young adult, Gilman constructed an idealistic, intellectually consistent theory of work as world-service. The problem was that Gilded Age society offered painfully few opportunities for a woman committed to meaningful work. Of course, hundreds of thousands of poor women labored on farms or in factories, but this was not what a member of the Beecher family meant by *work*. Middle-class women had only a few options, and Gilman tried two of the most common. In July 1883 she took a position as governess to the son of a wealthy Providence family. The arrangement started promisingly enough, but within two months she was writing in her diary, "Morning in the boat with Eddie. . . . A despicable boy." Two weeks later, she quit. This left her with one other means of earning money. Gilman had a talent for drawing, and a cousin hired her to paint advertising cards for his soap company. She claimed that she found the commercial art work "amusing," but when someone told her that she could make a living as a painter of still lifes, the prospect seemed to her "a poor ambition, not conducive to my object—the improvement of the human race."[11]

Professionally ambitious but unfulfilled, Gilman took solace in her friendship with Martha Luther. The two young women met early in 1879, when Gilman was eighteen and Luther a year younger.

By that fall, they were fast friends. The relationship intensified over the next two years; at one point they bought matching bracelets to signify the "bond of union" between them. Such romantic friendships were common among nineteenth-century women. Middle-class women lived in a largely homosocial world, with much schooling still segregated by sex and little opportunity to socialize informally with men. As Edward Carpenter characterized the similar situation in Great Britain, "males and females . . . have been wont to congregate in separate herds, and talk languages each unintelligible to the other." Spending most of each day in female company, their contact with single men limited largely to the formal and rigidly supervised domain of courting, many young women developed deep emotional attachments to other women. Historian Lillian Faderman has observed that it is "virtually impossible to study the correspondence of any nineteenth-century woman . . . and not uncover a passionate commitment to another woman at some time in her life."[12]

Gilman's and Luther's romantic friendship was unexceptional within the context of late nineteenth-century New England. The word "lesbian" was unknown to most Americans, and friendships between young women were encouraged precisely because they were seen as morally pure, free of any possible taint of sexual desire. Gilman felt free to express her love in extravagant terms, as revealed in a series of letters that she wrote over a two-month period in 1881 when Luther left Providence on summer holiday. Gilman wrote ten- to twenty-page letters almost daily—letters filled with accounts of her activities, intense analysis of her interactions with family and friends, young-adult self-absorption, and, always, professions of love for her friend. Luther is her "kitten," her "little girl," her "pet and sweetheart!" "I could spend hours in cuddling if I had you here," she wrote. "O my little love!" she wrote in another letter. "I'd like to wind all round and round you and let you feel my heart."[13]

Although Martha Luther's side of the correspondence has not survived, it is clear that she understood her romantic friendship with Gilman as a step on the way to the ultimate romance of heterosexual marriage. At the same time that Gilman was writing passionate declarations of love, Luther was growing increasingly close to Charles A. Lane, a young man she met while on vacation. Gilman, however, had decided that she would never marry, the better to pursue her life's work of world service. With resolution remarkable for a largely self-educated twenty-one-year-old woman, she wrote Martha that she had determined to drop "my half-developed functional womanhood, and take the broad road of individuality apart from sex"; she was ready to claim the identity of "strongminded old maid." *"I have decided,"* she wrote, heavily underlining the words. "I'm *not* domestic and don't want to be."[14]

Gilman bravely envisioned turning aside from the common path of marriage and family. She could not imagine going without love and intimacy, however. Luther, she believed, could serve as substitute for the conjugal love she had renounced. "I'd be willing to bet five cents, if I was in the habit of betting," she wrote, "that you will make up to me for husband and children and all that I shall miss." Such pronouncements evidently startled Luther, and Gilman had to reassure her friend: "I think you misunderstood me a trifle," she explained in her next letter. "You are to be your own sweet lovely self, marry all you please, and be loved and cared for to your hearts content. But be your home as charming as it may, I am to have a night-key as it were, and shall enjoy in you and yours all that I don't have myself."[15]

Gilman fantasized that even if Luther were to marry, their friendship would continue undiminished. However, when Luther became engaged to Charles Lane in November 1881, less than two months after returning to Providence from vacation, Gilman was devastated; she felt as if a limb had been amputated. The next month she wrote, but did not send, a letter to Luther in the form of a long blank verse poem. After an introduction reflecting on all the pet names she called her friend, the poem continues:

> "My little girl!" *My* little girl! No more,
> Never again in all this weary world
> Can I with clinging arms & kisses soft
> Call you "my little girl!"

> "My darling!" O my darling! How my heart
> Thrills at the words with sudden quivering pain,
> Rises and beats against the doors of speech
> And sends hot tears and sobs that will be heard.

"Sweetheart!" You *were* my sweetheart. I am none,
To any man, and I had none but you.
O sweet! You filled my life; you gave me all
Of tenderness, consideration, trust,
Confiding love, respect, regard, reproof,
And all the thousand thousand little things
With which love glorifies the hardest life.

Think dearest, while you yet can feel the touch
Of hands that once could soothe your deepest pain;
Think of those days when we could hardly dare
Be seen abroad together lest our eyes
Should speak too loud. ** There is no danger now.

Gilman must have realized how powerful this poem is, how vividly it depicts the pain of being abandoned by the woman she regarded as the love of her life. Though she wrote "Unsent" on the manuscript, a week later, when Luther called on her, she could not resist reading the poem aloud to her friend and gaining the meager satisfaction of seeing her weep and ask for a copy. Luther did not break off her engagement, however, and Gilman realized that she had "lost . . . forever" a "perfect friendship." As she would throughout her life in the face of personal suffering, Gilman renewed her commitment to world-service. On the flyleaf to her diary for 1882, she wrote, "My watchword at 21—1882 *WORK!*" A few weeks later she added for good measure, "*Once and for all;* to Love and personal happiness—so called—*NO!*"[16] By that point, Gilman had reason to fortify herself with dramatic resolutions to embrace her self-sacrificing ideals; she had just met a devastatingly attractive young man.

{⸎⸎⸎W⸎⸎⸎}

Less than one month after she read aloud her passionate poem to a weeping Martha Luther, Gilman attended a lecture by the rising young Providence artist Charles Walter Stetson. The next day, she went with a friend to his studio. The twenty-three-year-old Stetson—only two years older than Gilman—was, with self-dramatizing flourish, living out the life of a New England bohemian artist: im-

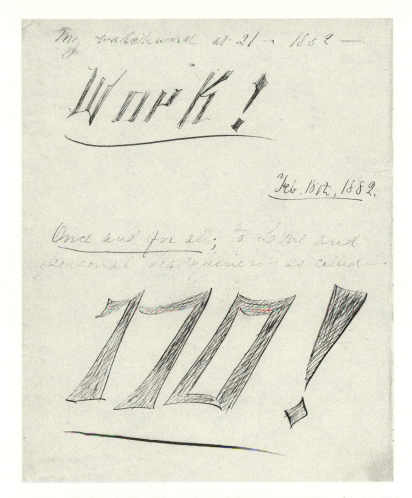

FIGURE 5.1 Charlotte Perkins Gilman, Journal, January 1, 1882–December 31, 1883. Schlesinger Library, Radcliffe Institute, Harvard University.

poverished and ambitious, morally high-minded even in the presence of the young prostitutes whom he hired to pose nude. He looked the part of the artist: slight, blue-eyed, with tousled blond hair. Friends told him that he resembled Keats, but his idol was Dante Gabriel Rossetti—like Rossetti, he fancied himself both painter and poet. He was immediately taken with Gilman, who was as strikingly good looking as he. "She has a form like a young Greek & a face also resembling a cameo," he wrote in his diary after her visit to his studio. "She has such a classic figure! She is moral, intellectual and beautiful!" Stetson was completely smitten by this

FIGURE 5.2 Charles Walter Stetson, ca. 1884, the year of his marriage to Charlotte Perkins. Schlesinger Library, Radcliffe Institute, Harvard University.

young woman who seemed to him to combine the "warm, soft, sensuous nature" of his models with moral purity and intellectual brilliance.[17]

The two young people's friendship advanced quickly. They spent hours talking about themselves and their feelings for each other, then would go home to write long letters and diary entries covering the same ground. Stetson felt as if he were living a dream: "To have

FIGURE 5.3 Charlotte Perkins, ca. 1884, the year of her marriage to Stetson. Schlesinger Library, Radcliffe Institute, Harvard University.

a *perfect* friendship with a woman who unites the highest type of intellect with a perfect physical nature is simply overpowering." Stetson avidly pushed the relationship forward, spurred by a combination of his intense admiration for the brilliant, unconventional Miss Perkins and his equally intense sexual drives. "My sexual desires are almost overpowering," he confessed to his diary. "I shall certainly die if my desires are not gratified in some way." Gilman posed for him—fully clothed—though the thoroughly chaste experience led Stetson to compose a throbbingly erotic sonnet:

> These many days I've tried to fix the face
> Of her I love on canvas . . .
> Most patiently did she sit, and I did trace
> And study the marvellous eye that's dark & bright,
> The curve from the wide clear brow's fair height
> Along the cheek to the eloquent lips' red place;
> And then adown the delicate smooth chin
> To the supple throat, until it was so lost
> In the hid and heaving breasts' cream white high mounds.[18]

Within weeks of their first meeting, Stetson was already happily imagining marriage. Gilman too imagined it, but the prospect was not, for her, a pleasant one. With Luther engaged and preparing to move away, Gilman welcomed the affection and admiration that she received from Stetson, and she was drawn to the handsome, gifted artist. She knew, however, that marriage to Stetson, unlike her romantic friendship with Luther, would require significant sacrifices. Luther could give her the love and intimacy she craved while still leaving her free for an as yet unrealized but deeply cherished career of world-service. Marriage to Stetson would mean giving up all dreams of significant work. Within their middle-class milieu, there were virtually no models of women who successfully combined marriage with an independent career, and in any case Stetson, for all his advanced ideas, found the notion absurd.

Throughout their courtship, Gilman struggled with her feelings. "Were I to marry," she told Stetson shortly after they met, "my thoughts, my acts, my whole life would be centered in husband and children. To do the work that I have planned I must be free." She tried to break off the romance after several weeks, writing Stetson that "much as I love you I love *WORK* better, & I cannot make the two compatible." Stetson, fired by ideals of romantic heroism, took her dismissal as a challenge: "My true love *shall* conquer," he declared in his journal. Stetson imagined their courtship as a knightly quest; for Gilman it was two years of "torture," a period of unrelenting emotional tumult. She told Stetson that she was torn between what she identified as her "frenzy for freedom" and her "woman's heart." Stetson was erotically charged by his lover's "startling contrasts." He noted how, despite her independence, "she likes to nestle by my side and depend on me"; she was an accomplished athlete, "yet she can be as soft & gentle as a weakly woman." For Gilman, her own contrasting desires—to serve the cause of humanity; to retreat from the world and be loved and cared for—were a source of pain. "Perhaps it was not meant for me to work as I intended. Perhaps I am not to be of use to others," she confessed to her diary in a dark moment. In a letter to Stetson she wailed, "Oh God! O God who made me! Help me to learn what I am, and to avoid a grievous sin!"[19] At this moment of crisis, Gilman turned to the religiously charged language of her Beecher forebears. Giving up her altruistic ideals of work in the world for marriage might be more than a mistake; it might be a sin against her God-given nature.

Gilman interpreted her anguish as a conflict between warring sides of her self, but she also understood that it involved what, a century later, would be termed the politics of gender. During her romance with Stetson she read two of the nineteenth century's most powerful works on the oppression of women: John Stuart Mill's *The Subjection of Women* (1869) and the letters of Jane Carlyle, Thomas Carlyle's brilliant, independent, and unhappy wife. She tried to negotiate a marriage that would enable her to maintain some degree of autonomy, but when she proposed separate residences, Stetson dismissed her "wild theory": "Of course I would not do that: and I would not think much of a man who would." During the first year of their courtship, Stetson signed with a flourish a pledge that Gilman had written: "I hereby take my solemn oath that I shall never in future years expect of my wife any culinary or housekeeping proficiency. She shall never be required, whatever the emergency, to DUST!" The pledge's playful tone undercut Gilman's serious aversion to conventional domesticity, and in any case Stetson doubtless made clear to her what he wrote in his diary: "Every one knows that I believe in the utmost freedom for women but that freedom is false which makes them rebel against the ties of home and love."[20]

Gilman had terrible forebodings about married life: "I anticipate a future of failure and suffering," she wrote a few months before her wedding. "Children sickly and unhappy. Husband miserable because of my distress; and I—!" However, powerful forces—cultural, economic, and psychological—combined to pressure her into marriage. Emotionally bruised after Martha Luther's marriage, she was lonely and hungry for love; she had little prospect of earning her own living; and her family and friends all expected her to marry. Moreover, she had internalized her society's view of marriage as woman's highest goal: "I ought not to complain of being offered the crown of womanhood," she wrote in one of her agonized letters to Stetson. He was convinced that "marriage and *home*" would cure her anguish.[21]

When they married at last, in May 1884, Stetson's optimism seemed warranted. Gilman's "warm, soft, sensuous" side was fully revealed. She wrote in her diary a detailed description of her wedding night that reveals how she stage-managed the event to turn what was often a brutal and shocking event for unprepared young women into a sacred ritual. She turned their marital bed into a "fairy bower" decorated with lace and flowers and made herself a crown of white roses. Then she washed and put on a thin white muslin robe fastened with a rosebud and girdled with a belt of velvet and pearl, along with white velvet slippers and a white snood. Once she was dressed, she went into the next room, where her new husband was waiting. "He meets me joyfully," she recorded afterward; "we promise to be true to each other; and he puts on the ring and the crown. Then he lifts the crown, loosens the snood, unfastens the girdle, and then—and then. O my God! I thank thee for this heavenly happiness!"[22]

In the days following, Stetson proved himself exceptionally willing, for a man of his era, to assist Gilman with household tasks. However, when she suggested, one week after their wedding, that he pay her for her domestic work, he responded angrily. "Mutual misery" ensued, and Gilman retreated to her bed and cried.[23] These were not the last tears she was destined to shed during her marriage.

Within a few weeks, the young couple conceived a child. Gilman had a miserable pregnancy; she was almost continuously ill for nine months. After their daughter, Katharine, was born in March 1885, Gilman experienced a breakdown. The term "postpartum depression" was unavailable to Gilman and her physicians, and in any case it scarcely conveys the seriousness of her mental illness and its lifelong consequences. Five months after Katharine's birth, Gilman recorded her symptoms in her diary: "Every morning the same hopeless waking. Every day the same weary drag. To die mere cowardice. Retreat impossible, escape impossible." Later, she said it felt as if she had become an "armless, legless, eyeless, voiceless cripple." Stetson, deeply concerned, borrowed money to send his ailing young wife on a five-month trip to Pasadena, California, where the family of her girlhood friend Grace Channing had relocated. Stetson invited his mother-in-law into his home to help care for young Katharine and, sobbing, put his wife on the train. Stetson may have been distraught at his wife's departure, but Charlotte's mood brightened as soon as the train's wheels began to roll westward. Once in California, she fell in love with Pasadena, then a small town set amidst orange groves. It seemed to her heaven on earth. Immediately after she returned to her husband and child in Providence, however, depression enveloped her, and life was once again a succession of "black empty days and staring nights."[24]

Finally, two years after Katharine's birth, the Stetsons determined that Charlotte should consult the nation's most prominent "nerve specialist," Dr. S. Weir Mitchell of Philadelphia. Mitchell was famous as the inventor of the "rest cure," a regime he developed to treat traumatized Civil War veterans and that he had extended to women suffering from the loosely defined ailment of "hysteria." The rest cure involved essentially infantilizing the patient: confining her to bed, feeding her fattening foods, and forbidding her even the mildest of mental stimulations such as reading. Remarkably, the treatment often worked. Its success can be explained, in the cases of many women, as a triumph for patriarchy: the enforced infantilization reconciled the middle-class patient to her normative gender role as wife and mother. However, other cases resist this interpretation. For example, four years before Gilman's treatment, Jane Addams, who went on to found Hull House, entered Mitchell's hospital. The ambitious young Addams was studying medicine at the Women's Medical College in Philadelphia but hated the work and developed illnesses that forced her to leave medical school and seek treatment from Mitchell. Like many nineteenth-century physicians, Mitchell was convinced that challenging intellectual work was detrimental to women's health, and he advised Addams—as the canny young woman no doubt suspected he would—to cease her medical studies. "I was very glad," she wrote later, "to have a physician's sanction for giving up clinics and dissecting rooms and to follow his prescription of spending the next two years in Europe."[25]

Mitchell's patriarchal prescriptions had less success with Gilman. Initially, the rest cure worked: the month of enforced rest, isolated from her husband and child, suited Gilman perfectly. When he discharged his patient, however, he warned her that she must "live as domestic a life as possible. Have your child with you all the time. . . . Have but two hours' intellectual life a day. And never touch pen, brush or pencil as long as you live." The single Jane Addams was advised to travel to Europe; Mrs. Stetson needed to assume a purely domestic role. Years later, Gilman wrote that she returned to Providence, followed Mitchell's directions rigidly, "and came perilously near to losing my mind." Stetson's diary confirms the seriousness of her decline: within days of returning home, his wife was suicidal, talking of "pistols and chloroform."[26]

In a frequently reprinted essay, Gilman wrote that she cured herself by casting Mitchell's advice aside and returning to work—"work, the normal life of every human being; work, in which is joy and growth and service." Gilman used her essay to advance her ideas about work as woman's salvation and also to explain her motivation for writing "The Yellow Wallpaper." This psychologically complex and artistically brilliant gothic story is an exception within Gilman's fictional oeuvre, which tends toward the highly didactic. The unnamed narrator, a hysterical woman confined to the children's nursery in a mansion rented to effect her rest cure, descends into utter madness. The story suggests that the rest cure is responsible for the narrator's insanity, and in her essay "Why I Wrote 'The Yellow Wallpaper'?" Gilman claimed that her work had convinced Mitchell to alter his treatment.[27] Yet both the story and Gilman's own experience are more complicated than her essay suggests. The Dr. Mitchell character in "The Yellow Wallpaper" is both the narrator's physician and her husband, blurring the distinction between medicine and marriage. And the story itself was written in Pasadena, where Gilman moved the year after completing Mitchell's treatment. Gilman cured herself only partly, as she claimed, by returning to the joy of working. Her recovery depended also on abandoning conventional married domesticity and separating from her husband.

Gilman stressed the importance of rejecting both marriage and Mitchell's patriarchal advice in a letter to Grace Channing, her closest woman friend during the years after Martha Luther's marriage. "O I *am* so much better!" she wrote in autumn 1887. "I decided to cast off Dr. Mitchell bodily, and do exactly what I pleased." She was also making plans, as Channing knew, to cast off Stetson. "When I leave Walter entirely out of my calculations, and make no attempt to fulfill my wifely duties toward him," she told her friend, "why straitway [*sic*] his various excellencies become visible again and he becomes a loved companion instead of a nightmare husband." Gilman invited Grace Channing to spend the summer of 1888 with her, Katharine, and a nursemaid in a rented house on the Rhode Island shore. Two weeks into the visit, she wrote Stetson frankly, "I'm not homesick a bit, don't think of missing you and am getting well so fast. . . . I haven't felt *unhappy* once since I left. . . . You are very dear to me my love; but there is no disguising the fact that my health and work lie not with you but away from you."28

That fall she and three-year-old Katharine left Stetson in Providence and traveled across the country to Gilman's beloved Pasadena. The Channings found her a tiny cottage near their home. Orange groves surrounded the house; roses and oleander and fragrant herbs grew in profusion; she alternated between swinging in a hammock and writing plays with Grace that would, the two young women were certain, make their fortune. Gilman's idyll was disrupted late in the year when Stetson joined them. He wanted to save their marriage, and he hoped that he could find a market for his paintings among wealthy Californians.

Gilman kept her husband at as much distance as could be managed in their diminutive home. Looking for ways to free herself from the domestic duties that she believed prevented her, along with other women, from doing significant work in the world, she arranged for the Stetsons to dine with Grace Channing and her family, in what was the first of her experiments in alternative housekeeping arrangements. Ever the dramatist, she also staged the next act of her relationship with Stetson, encouraging his romantic interest in her friend Grace. With her approval, the two took excursions and spent long hours together in Stetson's studio while he painted Channing's portrait. Grace and Walter are "great friends," Gilman noted several weeks after her husband's arrival, "which gives me sincere delight."[29]

Early in 1890, Stetson traveled east to be with his dying mother; he did not return to California. His departure left Gilman free to begin the next phase of her life as author, lecturer, and activist. Until then, she had published a total of about thirty pieces, but in 1890–91 she published thirteen short stories, two dramatic dialogues, twenty-three poems, and over thirty articles, in addition to delivering numerous lectures. When her uncle Edward Everett Hale, a prominent author, visited her in Pasadena early in 1891 he proclaimed, "You are getting to be a famous woman my dear!" Gilman's career seemed launched. As for her personal life, she had resolved after Stetson left, "I will shut the door of my heart again; and hang on it '*Positively* no Admittance except on Business!'"[30] Her resolution lasted just over a year; before she turned thirty-one she had entered into a tumultuous love affair that made her relationship with Stetson seem as placid as a paddleboat excursion.

◦──◦W◦──◦

Gilman met Adeline Knapp on a trip to San Francisco in May 1891. Knapp, a journalist, was known as Delle. Before long, Gilman gave her a private nickname: "Delight." Within ten days of meeting her, Gilman was in love; two weeks after that, they were sleeping together. It was common for friends, particularly women, to share a bed during the nineteenth century, but Gilman left little doubt that her relationship with Knapp was sexual. Years later, writing to the man who would be her second husband, Gilman confessed that Knapp possessed letters "most fully owning the really passionate love I had for her. I loved her, trusted her, wrote her as freely as I write to you. I told you that I loved her that way. You ought to know that there is a possibility of such letters being dragged out some day." She went on to imagine the newspaper headlines that might result if the letters ever became public: "Revelations of a Peculiar Past! Mrs. Stetson's Love Affair with a Woman. Is this 'Friendship'!"

At the time, though, Gilman reveled in the romance of her relationship with Knapp. After riding with her lover on the ferry between San Francisco and Oakland late at night, she confided to her diary her pleasure in the "calm delicious night, warm, starlit, with the light-engirdled bay all smooth, and we two happy together."[31]

After Gilman returned to Pasadena, the two women wrote to each other as many as five times a day. That fall Gilman moved to Oakland, settling in a boarding house where Katharine, now six years old, shared a room with Gilman's ailing mother and Gilman roomed with Delight. Throughout her marriage to Stetson, Gilman had been torn between the private world of her personal relationships to her husband and child and the public realm of world-service in which she longed to make her mark. Now, with Knapp, it seemed that she might have love and intimacy at the same time as she worked toward the betterment of humanity. The early 1890s, which had started so unpromisingly, proved a blissful moment for Gilman both personally and professionally. Unlike Martha Luther, Knapp had no interest in marriage to a man. Now it was possible for Gilman to imagine a lasting relationship with another woman, free of the oppressive patriarchal expectations that had ruined her marriage to Stetson. In addition, Gilman's poems in the *Nationalist* and its successor, the *New Nation*, had earned her a reputation as the poet laureate of Nationalism, and invitations to lecture to California Nationalist clubs and other progressive groups were pouring in. The Nationalist movement was at its peak in the early 1890s, when it seemed as if Bellamy's vision of a frictionless, egalitarian utopia might be realized in the new century. Gilman found herself at the center of what seemed a potentially world-changing social movement.

Unfortunately, this interlude of personal and professional happiness was brief. Gilman's always difficult relationship with her mother was worsened by the elder woman's illness, which was soon diagnosed as terminal cancer. When her boarding house manager left to attend a sick relative, Gilman took over the position in order to achieve some financial stability, a spectacularly bad decision that plunged her back into the midst of the domestic duties that had contributed to her breakdown during her marriage—except that now she was cooking and keeping house for five strangers in addition to her mother and daughter. Worst of all, Knapp proved to be as emotionally unstable as Gilman, though she lacked the latter's prized Beecher virtues of honesty and integrity. The two women began fighting frequently, with the violence verging on the physical. Knapp cursed, lied, drank heavily, and delighted in public scenes. On the last day of 1892, Gilman mournfully assessed the past year as one of "great and constantly increasing trouble. Poverty, illness, heartache, household irritation amounting to agony. . . . My last love proves even as others." Once more, Gilman believed that she was forced to choose between personal happiness and world-service: "Out of it all," she reflected, "I ought surely to learn final detachment from all personal concerns."[32]

Grimly, Gilman pushed forward with the divorce proceedings she first contemplated in 1891, shortly after she met Knapp and believed that she had found the friend with whom she could live for the rest of her life. The divorce took a full three years to achieve, since mutual incompatibility was not sufficient grounds during the 1890s; the Stetsons' amicable separation was regarded as collusion that rendered divorce impossible. In December 1892 Walter Stetson sued for divorce on the grounds of abandonment. A reporter at the Providence courthouse got hold of the story, and a sensationalized version of Stetson's suit was published in newspapers around the country. The headline of an article in Joseph Pulitzer's *New York World* gives the flavor of the coverage: "She Didn't Wear Corsets. Artist G. W. Stetson Seeks a Divorce from His Handsome Wife. He Says She Is a Crank on Dress and Physical Reforms. Mrs. Stetson Established a Literary Bureau and Had No Time to Devote to Her Husband—She Is Charged with Appearing in Public Without Corset, Waist-Belt or Boot Heels." All the coverage emphasized Gilman's deviations from the ideal of true womanhood, and William Randolph Hearst's *San Francisco Examiner*, which covered the case with special and salacious zeal, impugned Stetson's manhood as well: "G. Walt is not a muscular man, and somewhat undersized, so his complaint seemed to hint that his wife was rather the head of the household before she picked up her dress reform duds, her Bellamy writings and her muscular development and put off for California." Stetson issued a dignified statement, printed in a few newspapers, that defended his wife: "I am pained that the press seems so eager to speak ill of a woman of so much genius and sincerity of purpose."[33] The *Examiner* continued its mocking stories, and Gilman and Stetson wound up getting the worst of both worlds: they were ridiculed nationally, and the divorce was denied.

Given the hostile press coverage of the first suit for divorce, it took considerable courage for Gilman to file a second suit in early 1894 and to arrange to give up custody of her nine-year-old daughter. Gilman felt herself to be at a low point at the time. Her mother had died, in great pain, the year before. Delle Knapp had moved out and was spreading malicious gossip about her. Her writing and lecturing, however well received, earned her only a scanty and precarious income. Moreover, she had never recovered fully from her breakdown a decade before and was prone to bouts of severe "melancholia." Knowing that Grace Channing and Stetson intended to be married as soon as the divorce was final, Gilman determined to send Katharine across the country to live with them. The decision left her, she said, with a hole in her heart, though she acted with the best of intentions: "Since her second mother [Grace Channing Stetson] was fully as good as the first, better in some ways perhaps; since the father longed for his child and had a right to some of her society; and since the child had a right to know and love her father . . . this seemed the right thing to do." In spite of her own sense of justification, "furious condemnation" followed. A former neighbor in Pasadena slapped her in the face the next time they met; others were satisfied with labeling her an "Unnatural Mother."[34]

Gilman used the phrase as title for a short story she wrote at the time, "An Unnatural Mother" (1895). The story's protagonist, Esther Greenwood, is an unconventional young woman with an artist husband and an infant daughter. When a dam gives way above her village, she runs to warn the townspeople, leaving her own baby asleep. Her warning saves everyone in her village and in the two villages lower in the valley, but Esther and her child die in the flood. Afterward, village gossips label her an "unnatural mother." This literary parable both advances Gilman's ideas about the "larger motherhood" and dramatizes her self-justification for giving up Katharine to Grace and Walter Stetson. Gilman believed relinquishing custody of Katharine to be a necessary sacrifice in order to achieve her goal of advancing the human race through her work on behalf of Nationalism and women's rights. In any case, she expected that her daughter would return to her in a year or so. As it turned out, soon after Katharine's departure Gilman had no home for her to return to. For a period of five years, from 1895 to 1900, Gilman was, as she wrote in the visitor's book at one of her lecture sites, "At large."[35]

Gilman began her at-large years at Chicago's celebrated social settlement, Hull-House. Jane Addams, whom Gilman met in San Francisco, had invited her to become a resident. Gilman's stay was brief. She claimed uncongenial roommates, but there were multiple reasons for her early departure. Gilman thought of herself as a philosopher and sociologist, not a practical reformer, and Hull-House was dedicated to incremental reform. Its most celebrated resident in 1895, aside from Addams, was Florence Kelley, a compact tornado of a woman who had successfully pushed a factory reform bill through the Illinois legislature and then been appointed as the state's chief factory inspector. Gilman, in comparison, was a small, ornamental fish in a large, practical pond. She claimed to like being among folks greater than herself, but it must have galled her that the series of lectures she gave at Hull-House was poorly attended.[36]

Her self-esteem was restored the next year when she traveled to England as delegate to an international congress of trade unionists and socialists. Her book of poetry, filled with clever political verse, had recently been published in a British edition and was well received among English socialists. Gilman was taken up by the Fabians, who made her an honorary member, and she spent time talking with future prime minister J. Ramsay MacDonald and sparring verbally with George Bernard Shaw. "All these men are funny all the time," she marveled in her diary.[37] She dined with William Morris at his London house, where Jane Morris held up a great silver candelabrum so that the American visitor could see Rossetti's portrait of her in her glorious youth. Gilman delivered lectures and sermons across Great Britain, speaking on socialism in America to an audience in Morris's carriage house and preaching on "The New Religion" at a Labour Church. She made the visiting socialist celebrity's obligatory visit to rural Derbyshire, where Edward Carpenter measured her feet for sandals.

Returning to the U.S., Gilman continued her peripatetic life of lecturing and writing for another four years. The constant travel was wearing, and Gilman frequently sank into depressions that made it difficult for her to function. However, her "at large" years proved crucial to her development. Freed of domestic duties and childcare, she lived out the life of an economically self-sustaining, independent woman. At the same time, she found emotional sustenance in the communities of progressive women and men who hosted her on her lecture tours. Staying in the home of Toledo, Ohio's socialist mayor in the late 1890s, Gilman rhapsodized, "It's no wonder I love the world so. . . . The wildest dreams of socialism are only what I live in—to move freely among the people—to be loved and cared for everywhere—to ask for nothing and get much—that has been my life for near five years."[38] Gilman relished the combination of independence and community. During her years as a traveling lecturer, which corresponded to the years of Nationalism's decline, she worked out her own visionary ideas about gender, economics, socialism, and utopia and published a book that would, by the turn of the century, gain her a reputation as America's foremost feminist intellectual.

Gilman believed that her life had been split in two by her breakdown as a young mother: before, she had been at a peak of brilliance and self-discipline; afterward, she was left permanently "feeble-minded," her creativity hampered, unable even at her best to do sustained reading. She lived under "a heavy handicap," she emphasizes over and over in her autobiography, and there is no reason to doubt her suffering.[39] On the other hand, her self-described handicap proved extremely useful to Gilman: unable to do any serious research, she wrote her books and essays with extraordinary speed, turning out three thousand or more words in a single session, day after day. Her scant reading also enhanced her self-perception and public reputation as an original thinker. Gilman's nonfiction books and essays are largely devoid of quotations or citations, seeming products of her own untutored genius.

The only contemporary to whom Gilman acknowledged an intellectual debt was Lester Frank Ward, whom she described as "the greatest man I have ever known."[40] Ward, a founder of the discipline of sociology in the United States, is now little known even among sociologists, but in the late nineteenth century he was famous as an intellectual rival of British philosopher Herbert Spencer. Spencer, celebrated for his application of evolutionary theory to the social realm, coined the phrase "survival of the fittest" and was admired as the theorist of what became known as "social Darwinism." Spencer did not originate the latter phrase, but he was not in disagreement with the central tenets of social Darwinism as articulated by its most avid American proponents: any attempt to ameliorate the negative effects of laissez-faire capitalism by redistributing resources from rich to poor was an unjustifiable interference with natural processes. Spencer believed that a loosely defined process of "evolution" favored the fittest with prosperity at the same time as it rid society of the least able through ultimately benign means of disease, poverty, and starvation.

Ward, like Spencer, believed it perfectly appropriate to apply to the social world evolutionary ideas that had been developed to explain biological processes—in that sense he, too, was a social Darwinist. Ward argued, however, that evolution worked differently in the biological and in the social realms. Social evolution, he argued, was shaped by conscious human control. In Ward's terms, it was "telic," directed toward an end point of human perfection. Human beings were uniquely able to control their own evolution, and thus social reform was not, as Spencer would have it, a violation of natural processes but rather a necessary part of humanity's ongoing development.[41]

Ward's "reform Darwinism" provided crucial intellectual inspiration and support to Gilman and other turn-of-the-century reformers. What particularly attracted her to Ward, however, was another dimension of his analysis of social evolution, his "gynaecocentric theory." Spencer, along with other nineteenth-century intellectuals, took it for granted that human evolutionary progress was driven by the male of the species. The male, in the discourse of the era, was the "race type," the initiator of all improvement in the human race, while the female's utility within the evolutionary scheme was limited to reproduction. Ward turned Victorian sexual theorizing on its head, arguing that the female was the "race type," while the male was an afterthought useful principally for his sperm.

Ward explained his gynaecocentric theory at length in a ponderous scientific tome that Gilman most likely never read. She discovered Ward's work through a brief article that he contributed to a popular magazine. On the basis of those few pages, Gilman proclaimed his theory "the greatest single contribution to the world's thought since Evolution." Ward's suggestive essay served as foundation for Gilman's own theoretical superstructure, which she elaborated over the course of her career. In brief, Gilman seized on Ward's idea that human society had originated with "gynaecocracy," or matriarchy. She theorized that during the prehistoric "matriarchate," society had been shaped by the essential female characteristics of nurturance and self-sacrifice. Individualism was almost nonexistent, and decisions were made for the good of the tribal group as a whole. In biological terms, human advancement was dependent on female sexual selection. Males, naturally more aggressive, would fight among themselves to win the regard of a female, who would then mate with the victor, assuring the progress of the species through her choice of the fittest male. The women of the matriarchate further originated all human industry. While men were hunting and fighting, or "pranc[ing] and prophesy[ing] as 'medicine men'"—no Carpenterian celebration of the intermediate sex for Gilman—women developed the arts crucial for social evolution: agriculture, cooking, weaving, and pottery, among others.[42]

The matriarchal idyll was destroyed when men abrogated women's power of sexual selection. At a certain point in human history—Gilman was strategically vague about details—the male realized that his superior strength offered an as-yet unseized advantage. Why should he battle with other men for a woman's favor, when he could use his aggression and strength to subdue a potential mate? As Gilman succinctly put it, the prehistoric male concluded that it was "easier to fight a little female, and have it done with, than to fight a big male every time."[43] This realization, the crucial turning point in human history, transferred the power of sexual selection from women to men, destroyed the matriarchate, and subjected women to men under a patriarchal social structure that had persisted from prehistory to the present.

This gynaecocentric theory of human origins was at the heart of Gilman's lifelong utopian project. Starting in 1898, she devoted her writing to explaining the unfortunate consequences of maintaining in the modern age a prehistoric and unnatural "androcentric"—i.e., male-centered—social structure. She offered an alternative that would not only liberate women but free humanity to realize its evolutionary utopian destiny. In 1898 Gilman published *Women and Economics*, her first nonfiction book, which would become an international best-seller. The heart of her argument in *Women and Economics*, as well as in her subsequent nonfiction books and essays, centers on her observation that human beings constitute the only species in which the "sex-relation" between females and males is also an economic relation, with women economically dependent upon men for their survival. This unnatural dependence led, she argued, to women being "over-sexed." The term had nothing to do with female sexual desire. Rather, Gilman meant that women's economic dependence on men had resulted, through a process of social evolution, in excessive sexual differentiation, so that female markers of sexual attraction had flourished at the expense of their purely human traits. Women's dress and ornamentation, their deformation of their bodies with tight-laced corsets and high-heeled shoes, their narrow focus on romance, home, and family—all were distortions of women's humanity fostered by their need to attract a mate in order to survive economically.[44]

Innumerable other social theorists had commented on the extreme sexual differentiation of the nineteenth century, but to them it signified the era's advanced civilization. Intellectuals such as Alpheus Hyatt and G. Stanley Hall argued that "divergence of sex is a marked characteristic of progression among highly civilized races" and that attempts to lessen sexual differentiation—such as coeducation and woman suffrage—were not only misguided but actually "degenerative" in effect, with the potential to hinder humanity's evolutionary progress.[45] Women's rights activists greeted *Women and Economics* with such exuberance because Gilman, using the same prestigious scientific discourse as the leading male intellectuals, offered a compelling counternarrative that linked human progress to women's independence.

Gilman was praised by women's rights leaders, and her book was read by thousands in the women's movement despite the fact that her focus on economic issues diverged from some of the movement's major emphases. Whereas the movement's principal unifying goal was female suffrage, Gilman gave little attention to winning the vote in any of her best-known works. For her, women's full participation in the economic sphere was the key to independence. The Women's Christian Temperance Union, the largest American women's organization by far during the late nineteenth century, was based on the premise that women's alleged moral purity, once fully unleashed in the public sphere, would purge the world of (male-initiated) vice. Gilman, in contrast, argued that woman's nature, far from being superior to man's, had been distorted by her economic subjection and that the mass of women were "weak and little" creatures "with the aspirations of an affectionate guinea pig."[46] Gilman was sympathetic to many of the WCTU's goals, but she imagined a transformed society in which temperance was only a minor element. Her all-encompassing vision was both wildly idealist and solidly materialist, her utopianism both grandiose and tantalizingly attainable. At the heart of her thinking lay two images, one reassuringly Victorian, the other coolly modern: the World-Mother and the kitchenless house.

Gilman had no desire to restore the matriarchate. As a good progressive, she looked not to a restoration of the past but toward a future when the patriarchate would be succeeded by the age of humanity. She believed, however, that the two sexes had inherently different orientations based on their evolutionary histories. Men, with their primary prehistoric vocations of hunting and fighting, were naturally turned toward combat and self-expression, or competition and individualism. Women, whose central life experience was giving birth, naturally embraced love and service. Under the patriarchate these maternal virtues were limited to the woman's immediate family, but in the coming age of humanity, women would rise into "the larger motherhood of the world" and become "World-Mothers." Once women shared fully in governing, the world's governments would be shaped by motherhood, "and that would mean," Gilman explained, "care, nurture, provision, education."[47]

Gilman's poetic idealization of the mother-spirit necessary to reach humanity's utopian potential was balanced by her prosaic attention to the material conditions of domestic life. Throughout her career Gilman advocated for the construction of kitchenless apartments and houses, which would, she argued, not only liberate women from household drudgery but advance human evolution. From her reform Darwinist perspective, Gilman perceived the private home as the most primitive of human institutions. The work of human males had evolved from mere hunting and fighting into thousands of highly specialized occupations, but women, for the most part, were confined to the same domestic tasks of cooking, cleaning, and childcare as their primitive ancestors. Gilman believed that all women had the potential to be world-mothers, but actually raising children was another matter—childcare, along with cooking and cleaning, needed to be placed in the hands of experts. Gilman, who shared the Progressive faith in scientific expertise, argued that the average woman knew nothing about nutrition and little about child-rearing, and that even seemingly unskilled cleaning tasks were best handled by professionals. Apartment hotels already existed in which a professional woman could take her meals in the hotel dining room while a maid cleaned her room—why not multiply such buildings throughout every city?

The sheer inefficiency of the private home offended Gilman's progressive-evolutionary sensibilities. In New York City alone, there were hundreds of thousands of isolated families, in each of which an untrained woman spent her entire day cooking and cleaning and looking after her young children. What could be easier than to open one or more professional cookshops, laundries, and childcare facilities in every block? Gilman had no fondness for communal living— her teenage experience with the Swedenborgians had taken care of that—but the compact nature of urban living should make it a simple matter to deliver cooked food directly to each apartment. As for the suburbs, Gilman imagined kitchenless cottages, each connected by a covered walkway to the local dining hall. Alternatively, cleverly insulated packaging could enable delivery of hot meals directly to each family.[48]

Gilman's vision of the kitchenless home was inspired by Bellamy's *Looking Backward*. For all his Victorian gender conventionality, Bellamy understood that the only way every citizen in his utopia could contribute to the commonweal as a worker in the industrial army was if women were freed from domestic tasks. In his imagined Boston of the year 2000, the Leetes usher Julian from their kitchenless dwelling to the local dining hall, where a male waiter takes their order, leaving the women free to listen to another of Dr. Leete's interminable monologues. The gender equality discussed—if incompletely shown—in *Looking Backward* drew Gilman, along with thousands of other women's rights activists, into the Nationalist movement. Over the course of the 1890s, however, Gilman developed her own feminist utopian program that drew upon Nationalist ideas but inverted Bellamy's conviction that if socialism were established, women's freedom would follow. Instead, Gilman combined Nationalism, reform Darwinism, and her materially oriented feminism into a distinctive path toward utopia. The first step, she argued, was to liberate women from the kitchen and nursery by professionalizing and socializing cooking and childcare. Once women were no longer confined to the home, they could contribute, as men had ever since the elimination of the matriarchate, to human evolution. How could humanity expect to advance toward the ideal socialist future if half of humanity is kept "tied to the starting-post," Gilman asked. "The human race," she stated, "has moved only half as fast and as far as it rightly should have done" had not women been trapped within primitive domesticity. Once woman is no longer relegated to the role of "house-servant," she will advance humanity through her labor as "world-servant."[49]

The path to utopia lay through the kitchenless home—Gilman first outlined her material feminist utopia in *Women and Economics* and then at greater length in *The Home* (1903). She then began to show rather than tell. Starting with "A Woman's Utopia" (1907), Gilman wrote a succession of utopian fictions that emphasized women's economic independence and freedom from domestic duties as the foundation of a transformed future. Before she could enter this period of utopian creativity, however, she had to get her own house in order. When she published *Women and Economics*, Gilman was still an itinerant lecturer with no fixed address, and, for all the nurturance provided by her socialist hosts, she was a fundamentally lonely woman. For six years, at the same time as she was developing her ideas about the utopian potential of the Motherspirit, she saw her own child infrequently. She wanted to establish a home with Katharine, but her peripatetic life seemed to make that impossible. Her attempt at conventional domesticity with Walter Stetson had been a disaster, as was her effort to form an alternative family with Delle Knapp. Was it possible to find a life-partner who could provide stability for her and Katherine, who would enable her to combine domestic security and independence, to have both intimacy and freedom? At the same time as she was working out her utopian feminism, Gilman was moving tentatively toward an unconventional but rewarding second marriage.

Early in 1897, during her at-large years, the thirty-six-year-old Gilman decided to drop into the New York City office of her first cousin G. Houghton Gilman, a lawyer with a modest solo practice. "You haven't the slightest idea who I am," she said as she entered. "Yes, I have," he replied immediately, "you're my Cousin Charlotte." Although it had been nearly two decades since they had last seen one another, Houghton was unlikely to have forgotten his cousin. When he was twelve and she nineteen, he had developed a crush on her. Gilman must have recognized his infatuation, since after their youthful visit she had sent him a series of jovial, mildly flirtatious letters: "What Ho!" she addressed him; "O long suffering youth!"; "Oh guileless infant." Now, at twenty-nine, the guileless infant was still visible behind the enormous soup-strainer moustache that he had grown in a futile attempt to look older. The cousins' friendship was immediately rekindled. Houghton's mother and his older sister had died within weeks of each other when he was twelve, tragedies that must have intensified his pleasure in the attention from an older female relative. For Gilman, the reconnection gave her the chance to ignore a succession of failed relationships and to become, once again, the attractive, self-confident young woman who enjoyed a teasing friendship with her adoring younger cousin. She picked up right where she had left off, playfully addressing him in her letters as "Pleasing and Desirable Cousin" and "Elegant Youth."[50]

Soon after their re-encounter, back on the road again, Gilman began sending him long letters almost daily. Within a few months they declared their love for each other. For the next two and a half years, until they married, Gilman continued her lengthy letters, extraordinary documents that chronicle her love for Houghton, her feminist insights, and her efforts to reconcile the two—to construct

FIGURE 5.4 George Houghton Gilman in 1897, the year he and Charlotte renewed their relationship. Schlesinger Library, Radcliffe Institute, Harvard University.

a relationship that would be personally satisfying and also serve as a model for an egalitarian future. The letters veer wildly between passionate declarations and stern admonitions as Gilman struggles one moment to fan Houghton's love, the next to warn him about her personal shortcomings or her commitment to world-service or the unconventionality of the marriage that she was imagining for them.

"How ever *can* you love me Houghton!" she wrote him at one point. "Such a mess as I am!" Gilman was well aware of her personal contradictions, and she wanted Houghton to know all sides of her. With extraordinary insight for someone in the pre-psychiatric era, she understood that her "brain-sinking melancholy" was "a good honest disease" that no amount of personal happiness could cure. "Nothing touches it," she warned Houghton, "not Love even." She told him frankly about her love affair with Delle Knapp, but she also assured him of her heteroerotic desire: "Sweetheart! You shall kiss me anywhere you want to and all you want to as soon as ever there is a chance. I will wait till you are exhausted and then begin operations on my own account." She explained to him, as she had tried to do with Walter Stetson, that her mission of world-service was more important to her than private life and rejoiced that he understood "to the full" that "I am a world-worker and must be—that I simply give you the part that stays at home, and that I shall go right on thinking, writing, lecturing, and travelling when I must." Yet she also freely revealed her insecurities and her occasional desires to be his "little kitten," his "little girl" who wanted only to come into his arms and rest.[51]

Gilman found in her young cousin a quietly remarkable man who could cuddle her when she wanted but who also accepted her position as a leading public intellectual and her need for a radical new form of domesticity. Gilman understood, with prescient clarity, that the personal is always political, that if her failed marriage to Stetson demonstrated the oppressiveness of patriarchal traditions, a successful life with Houghton had the potential to model new modes of relationship. A year before their wedding, she wrote him that the task ahead of her was "to prove that a woman can love and work too. To resist this dragging weight of the old swollen woman-heart, and force it into place—the world's Life first—my own life next. Work first—love next." With her materialist attention to the ways in which women's freedom was dependent on domestic institutions and routines, she warned Houghton that the danger for her lay in "the household machinery. We must try to live like two friendly bachelors in apartments." In a somber mood, she pleaded with him: "Houghton—as you value my life, my sanity, my love; use your clear mind and strong will to work out such plan of living as shall leave me free to move as move I must. You will have to give up a certain ideal of home [but] . . . *I must not* focus on 'home duties'; and entangle myself in them."[52] Gilman was staking everything on this marriage: not only was it a chance, as she approached forty, to find personal stability and happiness, but it was also an opportunity to demonstrate to the world that it was possible to have a marriage in which work was as important to the woman as to the man, and home meant no more to her than to him.

In her autobiography, Gilman devotes a total of two sentences to her second marriage:

> I returned to Chicago June 8th [1900], and on the eleventh went to Detroit, as usual to the house of a friend, where I was met by my cousin, G. H. Gilman of New York, and we were married—and lived happily ever after. If this were a novel, now, here's the happy ending.[53]

Gilman slyly subverts literary convention; far from ending with her marriage, the book continues for another fifty pages, detailing her continuing public career. Gilman could represent her life with Houghton only by ironizing the conventional novelistic treatment of marriage as the final climactic event of a woman's life—and by omitting details such as the fact that her fifteen-year-old daughter came to live with her and her new husband in their New York apartment. However, all the evidence suggests that the marriage was indeed a happy one—including the fact that, once married, she commenced an extraordinarily productive period of writing that included multiple utopian fictions.

Over a ten-year period, Gilman produced a remarkably large body of utopian work: three novels, a novella, and a flock of short stories. Almost all of these, like *Looking Backward*, place the ideal society in the future, differing from Bellamy's novel principally in the interval required to effect the utopian transformation. *Moving the Mountain* (1911) is set thirty years in the future, "A Woman's Utopia" (1907) only twenty. Both works, like the utopian short stories Gilman turned out during the same period, depend on two mechanisms to initiate radical change in a short period. The first is the figure of the enlightened capitalist. Gilman never abandoned entirely her commitment to Bellamyite socialism, but her association with the American Fabian movement brought her into contact with socialists who made room in their vision for what now is called "social entrepreneurship"—business people who want to do well by doing good, investing money and energy into projects designed to improve society as well as to generate profit. The capitalist godfather in "A Woman's Utopia" is conservative New Yorker Morgan Street, in love with reformer Hope Cartwright. Street, about to go traveling around the world for twenty years, leaves Cartwright and her friends $20 million to realize their cockeyed schemes. On his return, he is startled to find that they have succeeded in turning New York into a utopia by investing his money into housing complexes with kitchenless apartments, where cleaning is done by commercial services and childcare is managed by experts.[54]

The second utopian mechanism is religion. Both "A Woman's Utopia" and *Moving the Mountain* devote extensive attention to the new religion of the future. It has no name—it's just "Living" and "Life," a character in "Woman's Utopia" explains—but it is essentially the post-Christian spirituality of personal denial and service to the larger, social self that Gilman worked out as a teenager. The last news from the outside world that the narrator of *Mountain* hears before thirty years of isolation in Tibet is that Mary Baker Eddy had died and that "another religion had burst forth and was sweeping the country, madly taken up by the women." Gilman had no fondness for Christian Science doctrine, but she could admire its female founder, the gender equality of its clergy, and its rapid spread during Eddy's lifetime. Why should not her rational religion of world-service enjoy the same sort of popularity?[55]

Between 1907 and 1913, Gilman wrote numerous variations of the same utopian blueprint: the ideal society could be achieved peacefully in a remarkably short time if only women were freed from the household to work in the world and to promote the new religion of social service. Then in 1915 she broke the mold with *Herland*, a fantasy that combines the plot of Tennyson's *The Princess* (1847) with the conventions of the masculine adventure tale. Three chums since college—Terry, Jeff, and Van the narrator—have joined a scientific expedition to a remote part of the globe, where their native guides tell them fearsome stories of a land inhabited only by women, located at the crest of an inaccessible mountain range. Fired with desire to be the first to explore this mythic woman-land, the three men decide to return on a secret expedition of their own.

Terry, a wealthy pilot, brings along a disassembled biplane, which they put together and launch from a lake just below the mountainous cliffs that shelter the hidden women. Once in the air, they spy signs of civilization and decide to land in a remote area miles from the city they have glimpsed. The three men are armed and confident; however, the natives have told them that no man who ventured into the mountains ever returned, and the explorers advance warily—just in case.

The first people the three friends encounter as they explore this brave new world are three beautiful young women, who will reappear later as the men's love interests. The volatile Alima fascinates Terry, a high-testosterone womanizer who enjoys the challenges of a difficult courtship. Jeff, a courtly southerner, is attracted to the sweet Celis, while Van forms an easy friendship with intelligent, curious Ellador. However, before the couples pair off, the men, upon their landing, first pursue the three women, intending to capture these native specimens. The athletic young women, in their sensibly reformed dress, easily outrun the men, who upon arriving at the town are surrounded by a phalanx of unarmed but well-disciplined women who capture and chloroform them.

The men wake up inside a remote fortress, where they are placed under a gentle house arrest and provided with tutors who teach them the Herland language. They try to escape but are recaptured, then are granted their liberty in exchange for a promise not to attempt another escape. At this point Van, the narrator, addresses his readers frankly: "It is no use for me to try to piece out this account with adventures. If the people who read it are not interested in these amazing women and their history, they will not be interested at all."[56] Van's announcement signals a change in genre, from masculine adventure tale to utopian exposition. Fortunately, the ensuing exposition is handled gracefully. Since each of the three male protagonists has a tutor as well as a love interest, there are multiple potential expositors, thus avoiding the necessity for a Dr. Leete or Old Hammond to go on at numbing length. And the fantastic nature of Gilman's premise seems to have liberated her from the obligation to treat at length many of the concerns of other utopian fictions, including her own earlier ventures that purported to portray an America of two or three decades hence.

Herland gives remarkably little attention to the topics that dominate earlier utopian fictions from Thomas More on, including work, the economy, and government and politics. The three female love interests work as foresters; there's a Morrisian nod to artisans' pride in their handicrafts; but aside from these bits of casually dropped information, the novel offers little sense of what people do for a living—or of what it means to make a living in Herland. It's not clear how the economy is organized, how goods are produced and distributed, or how people are compensated for their labor. Herland appears to be technologically and industrially advanced—the men are transported in electric cars over an extensive system of paved roads—but in Van's enamored descriptions, Herland's verdant landscape is free not only of air pollution but of factories and, indeed, of the sight of any workers not engaged in agricultural pursuits. The treatment of government and politics is similarly scanty. One Herlander refers to the Land Mother—"what you call president or king"—but it is not clear how she is appointed or elected, or if elections even exist. Politics is almost certainly nonexistent. When Terry balks at the "evident unanimity" of everyone in Herland, Jeff explains that this is because women are "natural cooperators" and compares Herland to an ant colony or beehive, with each working for the good of all.[57]

With the areas of labor, economics, government, and politics casually dismissed, Gilman felt free to explore her own idiosyncratic utopian interests, such as house pets. She devotes a section to the cats of Herland, which have been trained not to hunt birds and bred not to yowl. She gives several pages to dogs—rather, to the three men's explanation of canines, which do not exist in Herland. The women are horrified by what they hear—nearly as horrified as a dog-loving reader of *Herland* is likely to be by the women's defamiliarizing summary of what they have learned: that dogs are kept indoors as prisoners and taken out for meager exercise on a leash, are susceptible to the violent madness of rabies, and, even when healthy, are liable to bite children. Gilman's hostility to keeping dogs as pets is linked to a larger, Carpenterian interest in animal rights. Herlanders have eliminated all domesticated animals because of the cruelty inherent in slaughtering them for food or even obtaining milk. The men's auditors turn white as they listen to a description of "the process which robs the cow of her calf" and beg to be excused; any interference with the natural processes of mothering is horrific to them.[58]

Mothering, of every sort, is at the center of Herland society, from biological processes of conception and birth to child-rearing and education, from social theories of mother-love as the basis of community to religious conceptions of a universal "Mother Spirit." The word "mother" or its variants appears over one hundred times in this brief novel—more than enough to make the hypermasculine Terry fume with exasperation. He is the first to ask outright, once the men have mastered the Herland language, "Are there no men in this country?" The answer is no: for the past two millennia the women of Herland have reproduced parthenogenetically, bearing only daughters. Absent men, Herland society has been shaped by a communal maternalism. Women are fond of their own children, but they regard each child as the child of all. "We each have a million children to love and serve," Van's tutor explains to him. Gilman, keenly interested in economics, must have felt no need to explain Herland's economic system because it seemed to her so obvious: these "natural cooperators," whose "whole mental outlook" is collective, have no use for the individualism and competitiveness inherent in capitalism. Instead, a motherly state evidently assures every citizen's basic needs.[59]

This socially diffused motherliness is reinforced by Herland's religion, a "Maternal Pantheism." Under the gentle but pointed questioning of his sweetheart Ellador, Van is forced to admit that the "Hebrew God" of Western religions reflects the patriarchal family structure, with a father/ruler who is both loving and cruel, kind and jealous. Herlanders originally conceived of a Mother Goddess, but over their history this anthropomorphized figure has turned into an impersonal, uplifting force, the essence of mother-love "magnified beyond human limits." *Herland* served Gilman as a testing ground for ideas she would develop more fully a few years later in *His Religion and Hers* (1923), which locates the origins of Judeo-Christian religion in the prehistoric patriarchal past, when the human male was principally a hunter and warrior. His religious ideas were "death-based," developed in response to men's frequent experience of death and intended to counter their primal terror of extinction with a promise of eternal survival to the pious individual. The religion of the future, once women's equality is achieved, will be "birth-based," arising from women's experience of motherhood, centered not on the individual's survival in the afterlife but on present service to others.[60]

Herland is, in many ways, an extended challenge to its era's widely held conceptions of women's essential nature. According to the gynaecocentric theory that Gilman had borrowed from Ward and elaborated over the course of her career, conventional femininity was merely a response to women's subjection by men after the matriarchal period of human prehistory. Dependent upon men for economic survival, women developed a fascination with physical adornment, a swooning interest in heterosexual courtship, and an intense devotion to the private home and family. In Gilman's language, they were "over-sexed," their supposedly feminine traits developed at the expense of the human characteristics that they share with men. Freed of any reliance on men, the women of Herland aren't "*womanly*," according to Terry, which to him means that they are indifferent to his sexual swagger. The sociologically inclined Van realizes that what he has always thought of as "feminine charms" are "not feminine at all, but mere reflected masculinity—developed to please us because they had to please us."[61]

With no need to please men, the women of Herland are, to a certain extent, androgynous, their hair cut short, dressed in sporty leggings and tunics, capable of every physical and mental task required in an industrially advanced civilization. At the same time, Gilman insists on their differences from men—differences centered on women's "maternal instinct."[62] She repeats the phrase; the novel's entire premise depends on the idea that everything in an all-female society, from food to religion, would be shaped by women's inherent motherly feelings.

Gilman held to her theory of women's instinctive maternalism despite her own experiences as a mother. After Katharine's birth, she was so overwhelmed by depression that she could not bear to hold her baby. Later, when Katharine was nine, Gilman sent the child across the country to live with her father and stepmother and then saw her only occasionally for the next six years. *Herland* provided its author with a chance to reconcile the contradictions between her utopian celebration of maternal feeling and her personal experience of mothering. It turns out that although every woman in Herland is capable of giving parthenogenetic birth, only an elite is entrusted with rearing children. Collectivized and professionalized childcare was as central to Gilman's utopian vision as the kitchenless home. Her commitment to professional childcare came in part from her conviction that women, like men, owed it to the world to work outside the home and in part from her self-exculpating belief that, as Van's Herland tutor explains to him, the raising of children is so important to the future of the race that it must be entrusted to professionals.

Gilman derided the smallness, the possessiveness of the average woman's conception of motherhood: *my* children, *my* family, *my* home. She argued for a "Wider Motherhood" with the same zeal that Edward Carpenter brought to his advocacy of the Larger Socialism. Herlanders see every child as theirs, the entire population as one family, the nation as home. And as mothers in the widest sense, they are obsessed with improving their families and home. When the men first arrive in Herland, they are impressed by the way in which every inch of the land is carefully tended, the carefully groomed forests filled with fruit trees and hardwoods, the entire landscape one "enormous garden." Later, they learn that the population is just as carefully groomed and tended. Herland, it turns out, is a eugenic paradise.[63]

{━━━━━━━}

The now discredited pseudoscience of eugenics is generally perceived as being linked at best with political conservatism, at worst with totalitarianism. In the late nineteenth and early twentieth centuries, however, virtually every American progressive accepted some combination of eugenic ideas. A commissioner of the newly established American Eugenics Society boasted in 1922 that eugenics aimed for "progressive improvement in vigor, intelligence, and moral fiber of the human race. It represents the highest form of patriotism and humanitarianism."[64] If conservative eugenicists rejected any aid to the "unfit" poor as an interference with the project of breeding a better human race, progressives—who subscribed to

Lamarckian theories of evolution—saw their reform activities as a form of eugenic intervention: uplifting the poor of one generation would, thanks to the inheritance of acquired traits, lead to a raised level of intelligence and morality in succeeding generations.

Progressives, for the most part, embraced what was called "positive eugenics": not only "getting desirable people to breed," in the words of Theodore Roosevelt, but improving the environment in order to develop desirable—and inheritable—traits. They also accepted the need for some degree of "negative eugenics," defined by Lester Ward as "preventing the mental and physical defectives of society from perpetuating their defects through propagation." Ward, Gilman's intellectual hero, assumed that no one could disagree with this admirable goal. In an address later published in the *American Journal of Sociology*, he acknowledged the necessity for a program of negative eugenics before adroitly moving to the topic of positive eugenics. Speaking in 1913, Ward said that in the thirty years since Francis Galton had introduced the term "eugenics," the idea had "set the world on fire, and now seems to engross the attention of all classes." Many people, he said, "see in eugenics the regeneration of mankind."[65] Ward was one of them. He devoted his address to proving that humanity could be uplifted through a progressive version of eugenics—i.e., improving both current and future generations through reforming the environment.

Gilman, like many turn-of-the-century feminists, integrated eugenic ideas into her evolutionary conception of social reform. She took from Ward and other reform Darwinists the concept of "social evolution," the notion that human society was undergoing an inevitable process of change, directed toward an end point of perfection—although, as Nancy Cott dryly observes, reform Darwinists tended to argue that "the inevitable nonetheless had to be shaped." In the preface to *Women and Economics*—subtitled "A Study of the Economic Relation Between Men and Women as a Factor in Social Evolution"—Gilman melded evolutionary and eugenic discourses, proclaiming that her purpose was to convince "the thinking women of to-day" of "their measureless racial importance as makers of men."[66]

The thought of their measureless racial importance is never far from the mother-worshipping consciousness of Herland's inhabitants. A carefully devised eugenic regime is at the heart of their national origin story. Herland began some two thousand years ago, when a combination of natural and political disasters wiped out all the men. The women, isolated in their mountain aerie, expected their society to die out within a generation, when a miracle happened: one young woman gave birth. Over the next few years, she gave birth to four more children, all girls, and her five daughters in turn each bore five girls, so that within a few generations, the country was fully repopulated. As Val Gough points out, the miracle of parthenogenesis is a necessary plot device, yet it also beautifully illustrates Gilman's cherished theory, first articulated twenty-five years before in her popular poem "Similar Cases," that conservatives have it all wrong: you *can* change human nature.[67]

Herlanders' parthenogenetic reproduction was so successful that they soon reached a population crisis, but their innate sense of Wider Motherhood quickly provided a solution: a system of voluntary birth control, with most women limiting themselves to one child. Although all the women are virgins, conception nevertheless carries an erotic charge. Van's tutor tells him that "before a child comes to one of us there is a period of utter exaltation." When a woman senses the onset of this thrilling exaltation, she takes the Herland equivalent of a cold shower, throwing herself into her work. Selflessly devoted to the good of all, Herlanders willingly give up motherhood, their highest desire, in order to sustain the society. Furthermore, once Herland achieved a stable population, the women decided that, since they were restricted in quantity, they would "set to work to improve that population in quality." In pursuit of that goal, they employ both positive and negative eugenics. Positively, they honor the women deemed most fit as "Over Mothers," encouraging them to bear more than one child. In addition, they "breed out . . . the lowest types" by requiring undesirable young women to renounce motherhood.[68]

Gilman gives little sense of the regime of social control that enforces these eugenic programs, both positive and negative, but it is clear that Herland lacks the programs of forced sterilization that many U.S. progressives enthusiastically supported. In any case, most mothers in Herland are not allowed to rear their own children; the care of children, from infancy on, is entrusted to only the "most fit" women.[69] Gilman's eugenicism, like that of countless other progressives, was founded upon a blithely confused melding of hereditarian and environmental ideas. On one hand, progressives shared with the most conservative eugenicists a conviction that social evolution depended on encouraging those whom they regarded as the fittest to bear children, while restricting the right to propagate of those considered defective. At the same time, progressives believed that educational and environmental reform served as eugenic measures, raising up those judged to be below the norm and enabling them to pass on their newly acquired intellectual and moral traits to their children.

Gilman gave varying emphases to hereditarian and environmental forms of eugenics at different times in her career. At the turn of the century, she argued that "artificial selection"—breeding only from the "best types"—might be an effective way to achieve higher milk yields in cows or greater egg-laying in hens, but applied to the human realm, it was vastly inferior to education. The "more advanced" members of society could lift the less advanced immeasurably faster through exposure to "knowledge, culture, and refinement" than through the "slow current of heredity."[70] Yet only a few years later, in *Moving the Mountain*, her first full-length utopian fiction, she depicted the future United States as a chillingly ruthless eugenic state.

The United States of *Moving the Mountain*, which is set in 1940, has a federal Department of Eugenics that supervises the sterilization of those judged genetically defective. More drastic measures are a thing of the past. In conversation with an old friend who has become a professor of ethics, protagonist John Robertson learns that "moral sanitariums" have largely replaced prisons. When John proves skeptical about the widespread effectiveness of moral suasion, his friend, smiling, with "his fine eyes full of light," acknowledges that "sometimes we had to amputate, especially at first." "You mean you killed the worst people?" John asks. "We killed many hopeless degenerates, insane, idiots, and real perverts, after trying our best powers of cure," his friend calmly explains, before going on to describe the wonders of the reforming sanitariums.[71]

Most Gilman scholars deal with the creepily efficient eugenic regime depicted in *Moving the Mountain* by simply ignoring the novel. Other scholars have tried to explain away the book—and Gilman's broader commitment to eugenics—as an unfortunate lapse in her otherwise admirable feminism.[72] This won't work. Eugenics is at the center of Gilman's progressive feminist program of reform. As she emphasized at the beginning of her most widely read book, *Women and Economics*, Gilman wanted women to wake up to their measureless importance as makers of the next generation. Gilman stressed women's supposedly natural maternalism throughout her work—nowhere more strongly than in her utopian novels—for both moral and biological reasons: in social terms, women's maternal love for their children could serve as the model for the religion of love and service that Gilman saw as the basis of the utopian society to come, while women's biological capacity for childbearing had the power to improve the race if only it could be intelligently directed and controlled.

But what does it mean to "improve the race"? Gilman used variants of the phrase repeatedly in her work.[73] Frequently she added the adjective "human," but often "race" was unmodified, leaving the possibility that the signified is actually the "white" race. Van, the narrator of *Herland*, is careful to tell us that these utopian women are "white." "There is no doubt in my mind," he adds, "that these people were of Aryan stock, and were once in contact with the best civilization of the old world."[74] The reference to "Aryan stock" reveals Gilman's intense interest in racial theory. The "Aryan" race was an invention of nineteenth-century French aristocrat Arthur de Gobineau, who took a term that until then had been used only by philologists and applied it to the European upper class in an effort to assert their racial superiority. His principal work, *The Inequality of Human Races* (1853–55) was not fully translated into English until 1915, the year Gilman was serializing *Herland*. Gilman seized on the novel term.[75]

Over her career, Gilman, like many middle-class Americans of her era, became increasingly concerned with fine distinctions of race. Her own origins were safely Anglo-Saxon; on the second page of her autobiography she notes her descent from Ethelred the Unready. Later, she says that her "large, undiscriminating love of Humanity" was originally "without a shadow of race-prejudice or preference" but that her ideas changed after she settled in New York City with her new husband, Houghton Gilman.[76] Her years in New York pushed race toward the center of Gilman's feminist utopian project, but not in the ways readers today might expect. Remarkably, she expressed no particular animus toward black Americans. Instead, as revealed in *With Her in Ourland* (1916), the sequel to *Herland*, she believed that America's progress toward utopia depended on controlling the new immigrants from southern and eastern Europe.

Racial and ethnic differences are at the center of *With Her in Ourland*, in which Van and Ellador travel to the United States. The entire novel is an extended equivalent of Julian West's dream-return to 1887 Boston, when he is horrified by the now-defamiliarized city. Van's return is not nightmarish, but traveling about the country with Ellador is, he admits, "sometimes painful. It was like carrying a high-powered light into dark places." The darkest of all the places they visit is New York City, which according to Ellador is "stuffed . . . with the most ill-assorted and unassimilable mass of human material that ever was held together by artificial means." When Van weakly protests, Ellador berates Americans for their failure to recognize that "the poor and oppressed were not necessarily good stuff for a democracy."[77]

Throughout *Ourland*, Gilman uses Ellador to lay out her racial views. Like a good progressive, Ellador is appalled by what she learns of the United States' treatment of Native Americans and Pacific Islanders. She regards the importation and enslavement of Africans as a terrible mistake, denounces prejudice against them as "silly [and] wicked," and says that in only a few generations black Americans have made "noble" progress. Once prejudice against them is eliminated, social evolution will soon do its work. "It's no problem at all," she assures Van.[78] The real problem preventing America from realizing its utopian destiny lies with the new European immigrants—particularly with the Jews.

Over her lifetime, Gilman saw patterns of immigration to the U.S. change radically. As late as 1895, when she was in her thirties, a majority of immigrants to the U.S. came from northern Europe, as did 80 percent of foreign-born residents. However, in the early twentieth century, average annual immigration increased to a total of nearly one million immigrants each year between 1900 and 1914, with over 70 percent of those immigrants coming from central, eastern, and southern Europe. The change was particularly noticeable in New York City, where by 1920 immigrants and their children constituted just under 80 percent of the population. Jews, who had once constituted a small proportion of New York's population, now made up nearly 30 percent of the total.[79]

With Her in Ourland treats at length what Ellador calls "the Jewish race question." She offers numerous justifications for anti-Semitic prejudice, including Jews' "morally degrading" religion and their "race egotism." Ellador is certain that African Americans will reach equality with whites in a few generations. The Jews, however, are another matter. She believes that the prejudice against them is fully justified, and the only way for individual Jews to get on the social evolutionary train for utopia is to "leave off being Jews" and to intermarry with Gentiles. The forthright anti-Semitism of *With Her in Ourland* illuminates the racial ideology that underlies *Herland* as well. Gilman's maternal utopianism was founded on a racially homogeneous conception of the national family.[80]

Herland became the most popular of Gilman's utopian fictions in part because it does not foreground the eugenic regime that is directly addressed in *Moving the Mountain* or the nativism and anti-Semitism that permeate *With Her in Ourland*. In addition, its fantastic premise of a long-hidden all-female society enabled Gilman to sidestep the difficult question facing her predecessors Bellamy and Morris: how can the United States or Great Britain become utopia? Morris foresaw the necessity of a workers' revolution, but Bellamy rejected that path. Nationalism appealed to large numbers of Americans in a way that Marxist socialism never did precisely because it offered a peaceful model of social change in opposition not only to Marxist theory but to the violent labor struggles of the Gilded Age.

Gilman's fidelity to the Nationalist model of nonviolent social transformation is evident in her first two major utopian fictions, "A Woman's Utopia" and *Moving the Mountain*. In both, a painless transition to utopia is achieved when Americans, led by women, abandon egoism for the new religion of "socioism."[81] *Herland*'s maternal religion is essentially identical to socioism, but the novel, written and published in 1915, during the second year of the Great War in Europe, acknowledges the problem of human violence in a way that none of Gilman's earlier fiction does. Whereas Gilman's first utopian fictions are set in a near-future U.S., *Herland*'s fantastic all-female utopia originated in the distant past, some two thousand years ago. As the men learn from their tutors, at that time the nation contained both women and men and, like many ancient societies, was slave-holding. The nation had access to the sea, and the ensuing contact with other peoples led to frequent warfare. During one campaign on the plain below their mountainous plateau, a volcanic eruption killed the entire force of fighting men and in addition filled up the mountain pass, cutting off Herland from the rest of the world. Almost the only men left alive were slaves, who rose in revolt and slew all the country's surviving men and boys, intending to subjugate the women. However, the women, vastly outnumbering the slaves, turned against them and killed every remaining male.

At the start of World War I, Gilman, along with many American feminists, declared herself a pacifist. Yet at the same time she wrote a narrative that depicts revolutionary violence, directed by women, as a necessary and creative force. Mark Van Wienen has argued convincingly that *Herland* participates in the "peace through strength" discourse that suffused American politics in 1914–16.[82] Woodrow Wilson ran on the slogan "He kept us out of the war" in 1916, yet at the same time Wilson and other progressives pursued a policy of preparations for war that were, they argued, necessary to maintain America's peaceful neutrality. Gilman may have stressed a nurturing maternalism as the central philosophy of Herland, yet her utopia's origin story is centered on women's capacity for violence. Its survival proves to be equally dependent on the precise application of force. The tightly disciplined actions of the women who surround, disarm, chloroform, and imprison the three male explorers when they first arrive in Herland suggest a practiced drill. Some never-acknowledged regime of civil defense seems to have been maintained in Herland for just such a moment as this. Later in the book, when Terry tries to rape his partner, other women quickly spring to her aid and efficiently bind Terry and incapacitate him with their ever-ready chloroform.

Gilman's first utopian fictions smoothly elided problems of violence, but *Herland*, composed amid news from the bloody trenches of Europe, depicts both justified revolutionary violence and the ongoing problem of sexual violence against women. *Herland*'s sequel, *With Her in Ourland*, written in 1916 as the violence in Europe intensified, directly confronts the Great War: Ellador insists on visiting France and on surveying the battlefields from an airplane. The episode forms a very minor part of the novel—Gilman gives much more attention to problems of immigration than to the cataclysm of the Great War—yet the war seems to have diminished her optimism. Whereas her first utopian novels depict the arrival of the millennium in only twenty or thirty years, *Ourland*, her final utopian work, is much more ambiguous. Ellador and Van make no attempt to convert Americans to Herland's utopian ideals. Instead, at the novel's conclusion, they retreat to Herland, where they will raise their newborn son. Herland, after two thousand years, will again have both men and women among its citizens, but there is no suggestion of when, if ever, the transformed Herland might have an effect on Ourland. Charlotte Perkins Gilman's motherly utopia was deferred into the indefinite, unforeseeable future.

{⚬⚬⚬W⚬⚬⚬}

With Her in Ourland, completed at the end of 1916, was Gilman's last utopian fiction. The world war, which reduced the audience for utopian fiction in Britain and America, presumably played some part in her turn away from the genre, but there were many other reasons, some of them personal and pressing. *Ourland*, like most of Gilman's other utopian works, had been published in the *Forerunner*, a one-woman journal that Gilman began in 1909. The venture was always economically precarious, and the magazine folded in December 1916. Once it was gone, she had trouble placing her work. With few new works in print, she found it increasingly difficult to book lectures, which were both her major source of income and her primary means of keeping her name before the public. When the

League of Women Voters conducted a poll in 1923 to determine the twelve greatest living American women, sixty-three-year-old Gilman did not make the cut. Two decades earlier, she had been widely celebrated as the nation's most important woman intellectual; now she wrote to a friend, "Guess I'm a has-been."[83]

All the last utopians were has-beens by the 1920s. Nationalism ceased to be a serious political movement after the 1896 U.S. presidential election, and *Looking Backward* became a literary curiosity. Morris's version of revolutionary socialism had been tamed and absorbed into the Labor Party, where the focus was on electoral victories, not visions of an arcadian Nowhere. Carpenter's works were largely out of print, not to be revived until the gay rights movement of the 1970s and 1980s. The 1920s proved inhospitable to utopian speculation. It was an era of rising affluence, increasing consumption, and commercialized leisure, a time when the pleasures of private life were paramount for many.

Women as well as men embraced the individualistic culture of consumption. The powerful women's movements in both the U.K. and U.S. largely dissipated in the 1920s, following Britain's Representation of the People Act of 1918, which extended the franchise to the majority of women over thirty, and the 1920 ratification of the Nineteenth Amendment, which gave American women the vote. Women's suffrage had always been a minor part of Gilman's program; she saw it as merely one element within her larger utopian vision. She imagined that the enfranchised women of the twentieth century would set aside old ideals of women's devotion to home and family in favor of work in service to the larger world. As it turned out, the generation of middle-class women who came of age in the early twentieth century did turn away from earlier ideals, but not in the manner that Gilman had hoped. Instead, young women of the new century rejected the Victorian image of pure womanhood in favor of new ideals of self-realization and individual freedom, including personal pleasure, sexual indulgence, and immersion in the burgeoning culture of commercial goods and leisure. Gilman was aghast. The twentieth century, she wrote, should be "the woman's century, the first chance for the mother of the world to rise to her full place, her transcendent power to remake humanity, to rebuild the suffering world—and the world waits while she powders her nose." In a private letter, she dismissed young women as "painted, powdered, high-heeled, cigaret smoking idiots."[84] The World-Mother was out, the Flapper was in.

In disgust with jazz age New York, Gilman fled to Connecticut in 1922, the year she turned sixty-two. Her husband had inherited a family house in Norwich, and Gilman relished the chance to escape a city that now seemed to her "hideous."[85] During her first years in Norwich, until demand for her lectures dried up entirely, she escaped the New England winters by touring in warmer climates, culminating with a few weeks in Pasadena, where Katharine had settled with her husband and two children. The relationship between mother and daughter was generally affectionate, if sometimes testy—not unlike that between many women and their adult children. In Norwich, Gilman led a quiet, circumscribed life. She tended her large garden, visited neighbors, took walks with Houghton. With little demand for her essays on current topics, in 1926 she decided to write an autobiography, although she approached the task with scant enthusiasm—her destiny as a Beecher was to improve society, not troll through memories. The autobiography reveals Gilman's thin-skinned insecurity; she recalls slights from her childhood and boasts about the importance of her work. Gilman placed the manuscript with an agent, but publishers were uninterested. She set it aside and did not pick it up again until 1935, when the breast cancer that had been diagnosed over three years earlier was rapidly advancing. With scant energy for revising, she wrote a brief final chapter. She noted the death of her husband Houghton the year before and her decision to move back to Pasadena and to settle close to her daughter, Katherine. Her old friend Grace Channing, now Walter Stetson's widow, moved in with her. She declared herself content. "The one predominant duty" in life, she wrote, "is to find one's work and do it." At that, she declared proudly, she "had striven mightily."[86]

Upon her diagnosis with cancer, Gilman, who had long supported euthanasia, began accumulating bottles of chloroform. Now, she declared that she had not the least objection to dying, but she "did not propose to die of [cancer]." In the final chapter of her autobiography, she wrote that it seemed to her "the simplest of human rights to choose a quick and easy death in place of a slow and horrible one." Ever the Beecher, she was determined to turn even her death into an opportunity for reform. She excerpted two paragraphs from the manuscript of her autobiography's final chapter, titled them "A Last Duty," and left them as a suicide note, with instructions that the document be distributed to the newspapers. "Believing this open choice to be of social service in promoting wiser views on this question," she wrote, "I have preferred chloroform to cancer."[87] On August 17, 1935, Charlotte Perkins Gilman poured chloroform onto a towel and placed it over her face. Her work was done.

CHAPTER SIX

After the Last Utopians

The Anti-Utopian Twentieth Century

Early on the morning of July 1, 1916, some 120,000 British troops waited anxiously in their trenches near the River Somme in northern France. During the preceding week, the British had launched over a million and a half shells toward the German lines, climaxing with a barrage of more than 224,000 shells in the last hour before the attack. The rumbling of the explosives was heard and felt in London, over three hundred miles away. At precisely 7:30 a.m., officers blew on whistles, signaling the start of the offensive, and the soldiers, most of them untested volunteers, clambered over the top and began walking toward the German lines at a steady pace.

Only half of them would return unharmed. By day's end, some 21,000 British troops were dead and 36,000 wounded. The toll among officers was even higher: three-quarters were killed or wounded. That night, back in their trenches, the survivors could hear the moaning of wounded men in no-man's-land, caught in the barbed wire or lying in shell holes. For weeks afterward, as the battle continued, soldiers would come across the corpses of men who had been wounded on the first day, wrapped in their waterproof ground cloth, their Bible or a letter from home grasped in one hand. By the time the Battle of the Somme concluded in mid-November, over one million men among the British, French, and German forces had been killed or wounded—a significant proportion of the thirty-seven million total casualties during the First World War.[1]

Among the casualties was the sort of utopian idealism exemplified in the lives and works of Edward Bellamy, William Morris, Edward Carpenter, and Charlotte Perkins Gilman. The very idea of progress was bloodied by the industrialized warfare of 1914–18. Progress had led to the machine gun, barbed wire, poison gas, armored tanks, and aerial warfare, to a mode of total war that obliterated distinctions between soldiers and civilians—some seven million of the war dead were noncombatants. The idealism that had inspired this War to End All Wars seemed, by the conflict's end, hollow and childish, its epitaph composed by Ernest Hemingway in a celebrated passage of *A Farewell to Arms* (1929):

> I was always embarrassed by the words sacred, glorious, and sacrifice and the expression in vain. We had heard them, sometimes standing in the rain almost out of earshot, so that only the shouted words came through, and had read them, on proclamations that were slapped up by billposters over other proclamations, now for a long time, and I had seen nothing sacred, and the things that were glorious had no glory and the sacrifices were like the stockyards at Chicago if nothing was done with the meat except to bury it.[2]

The slaughter that took place across Europe during World War I profoundly challenged the progressive idealism that underlay both the war's rationale and the utopianism that had flourished in the century preceding the conflict. The war called into question the notion of inevitable progress that was at the ideological heart of British and American culture throughout the nineteenth and early twentieth centuries, the faith in a better world to come that inspired the utopian imaginations of Bellamy, Morris, Carpenter, and Gilman. Their fervent optimism seemed a relic of a naïve past, and the utopian writings of all four fell out of favor.

Yet at the same time that World War I challenged utopian idealism, the war and its aftermath helped propel the totalitarian projects of Soviet Communism and German Nazism, both of which embodied a ruthless version of utopianism. Both Stalin and Hitler envisioned an ideal society: Hitler imagined a racially pure Germany animated by Aryan strength and virtue, Stalin an ideologically homogeneous society dedicated to the workers' state. If the Great War shook many progressives' confidence in the possibility of a uto-pian future, it suggested to the Bolsheviks and Nazis methods for establishing utopia with great speed. As historian Eric Weitz has pointed out, World War I exposed Europeans to previously unimagi-nable levels of bloodshed and demonstrated that entire populations could be motivated to accept and engage in massive projects of vio-lence for political ends. In the years following the war, both Ger-mans and Russians embraced emotionally stirring, nationally trans-formative utopian visions. The Nazis foresaw a thousand-year Reich populated by a racially purified and eugenically fit populace, while Bolsheviks promoted the ideal of a "new Soviet man" and "new So-viet woman" inhabiting a harmonious, egalitarian socialist republic. Most nineteenth-century utopians imagined that the ideal society would evolve over the course of generations, but the Nazis and Bol-sheviks, shaped by the Great War, were convinced that violent purg-ings of the population could transform an entire society within a matter of years.[3]

The catastrophic failure of both of these projects and the rev-elation, in the 1940s and 1950s, of the full extent of the Nazi Ho-locaust and Stalinist terror contributed to the twentieth-century turn against utopia. "Our history," Robert Elliott generalized in the preface to his highly regarded 1970 study of utopian literature, "has made confident visions of the wholesale reconstitution of so-ciety, like those of the nineteenth century, impossible."[4] If the late nineteenth century was a high point of utopian literature, the twentieth century saw the triumph of the literary dystopia, exem-plified by three critically acclaimed and now canonical novels: Yevgeny Zamyatin's *We* (1924), Aldous Huxley's *Brave New World* (1932), and George Orwell's *Nineteen Eighty-Four* (1949).

There's an argument to be made that these three modern classics have been mislabeled for decades, that they aren't actually dysto-pian novels but rather *anti-utopian* fictions. The distinction is im-portant. As Lyman Tower Sargent explains, traditional dystopian fiction is monitory—that is, it extrapolates from the present in order to warn readers about the dangers of an existing trend.[5] Perhaps the clearest example of dystopian fiction is one of the genre's foundational texts, H. G. Wells's *The Time Machine* (1895). The book is a sort of dark brother to Bellamy's *Looking Backward*. Both writers were appalled by late nineteenth-century class divisions, and both feared a workers' revolution. Bellamy, in response, created an egalitarian utopia; Wells took present trends to a horrifying extreme. Wells's time-traveling narrator arrives in a future England in which the bourgeoisie have evolved into the Eloi—beautiful, weak, and pleasure-loving creatures whose every want is supplied by the brutal Morlocks, underground-dwelling descendants of the industrial-era working class. The narrator helpfully spells out for readers that these two species represent the "working out to a logical conclusion [of] the industrial system of to-day."[6] The narrator, a pleasure-loving bourgeois himself, is not terribly bothered by this system until he discovers that the Morlock survive by cannibalizing the Eloi—a literal reversal of the way in which the nineteenth-century upper classes fed metaphorically off the labor of workers. Wells, who like Bellamy was a reform-minded socialist, crudely but effectively appropriated the utopian form, in which a narrator travels to a transformed future, to warn his readers of the dangers of class inequality.

There's a monitory side to *We, Brave New World*, and *Nineteen Eighty-Four* as well; all three raise alarms about disturbing trends in contemporary society. At the heart of all three books, however, is an attack on utopian thinking itself, which, as Sargent explains, makes them more anti-utopian than dystopian. *We* and *Nineteen Eighty-Four* both attack the utopian vision that underlay the Bolshevik revolution and the Soviet state. Yevgeny Zamyatin, author of *We*, was a committed socialist who was twice exiled to Siberia by the czarist regime. Initially, he welcomed the overthrow of the czar, but he quickly became disenchanted with the Bolsheviks' authoritarian tendencies and in 1921 completed the manuscript of *We*. This brilliant, brief, highly stylized novel, set in the twenty-sixth century, is cast in the form of a diary by citizen D-503, who is responding to the supreme leader's call for comrades to write compositions on the greatness and beauty of the all-powerful world state. Initially, D-503 writes of the glories of his life as a citizen whose every action, from eating to sleeping to sex, is minutely regulated by the Tables of

Hours, his adherence to the regime easily monitored since he, like all citizens, lives in a building whose walls are entirely made of glass. The comforting regularity of this life devoid of any disturbing freedom is interrupted by his encounter with I-330, a beautiful woman who becomes his lover and recruits him into a group of rebels. The rebels are defeated and captured, and D-503 is lobotomized, making it easy for him to betray his comrades and to watch dispassionately as I-330 is tortured. She refuses to utter a word, but D-503 knows that "we" will win; for, as he says in the novel's final words, "Reason must prevail."[7]

George Orwell appropriated the plot of *We* for *Nineteen Eighty-Four*, published three years after he first read Zamyatin. Both books are, at their heart, an attack on the utopian vision that underlay the Soviet regime, its dream of wiping clean the social and political slate by eliminating all enemies and creating a society of perfect equality, devoid of bourgeois concepts of individuality and privacy. In the formulation of Ruth Levitas, dystopias are the dark side of hope, and offer some hope for a way out. Anti-utopias attribute the darkness to utopian thinking, and tell us the exits are ambushed.[8] Wells's time traveler returns from the dystopian future to warn his auditors of the shape of things to come, implicitly offering a possibility of change. In contrast, *We* and *Nineteen Eighty-Four* shut down all hope. At the end of each novel the protagonist, his mind altered and his will crushed, has betrayed his lover and given all the affection of which he is capable to his totalitarian leader.

Brave New World's ending is equally bleak: John Savage, the rebel protagonist, has hanged himself, and his dangling body turns like a compass, pointing, regardless of which way it rotates, to a totalitarian future. The totalizing utopian vision that provoked Aldous Huxley's novel is, however, very different from that behind Zamyatin's and Orwell's. *Brave New World* is a speculation on one central, provocative question: What if the most powerful weapon of modern totalitarianism were not pain but pleasure? Huxley's immediate inspiration for *Brave New World* during its composition in the early 1930s was not Stalinist Russia or Nazi Germany but the United States in the heyday of the Roaring Twenties.[9]

In 1926 Huxley had embarked on a round-the-world voyage from England to India and across the Pacific to California. The celebrated young writer was welcomed grandly in Hollywood: taken to night-clubs, ushered onto a movie set, and accompanied on a beach walk by Charlie Chaplin. Eleven years later, Huxley would move to Los Angeles and would live in the U.S. for the remainder of his life; however, on this initial visit he was as much repelled as fascinated. He regarded Los Angeles as the epitome of American anti-intellectualism and materialism, a place where pretty young flappers and hustling young men gave themselves over to mindless pleasures. His description of the "great Joy City of the West" in his travelogue *Jesting Pilate* is a tour de force of satiric disdain:

> And what joy! The joy of rushing about, of always being busy, of having no time to think, of being too rich to doubt. The joy of shouting and bantering, of dancing and for ever dancing to the noise of a savage music . . . The joy of loudly laughing and talking at the top of the voice about nothing. (For thought is barred in this City of Dreadful Joy and conversation is unknown.) The joy of drinking prohibited whisky from enormous silver flasks, the joy of cuddling provocatively bold and pretty flappers . . . The joy of going to the movies and the theatre, of sitting with one's fellows in luxurious and unexclusive clubs, . . . of being always in a crowd, never alone. . . . The joy in a word, of having what is technically known as a Good Time.[10]

The brave new world of Huxley's novel is remarkably like 1920s Los Angeles. The citizens of his great Joy City (London six hundred years in the future) are never alone, rushing off in groups to go to the feelies, to play Electro-Magnetic Golf, to dance in the Westminster Abbey nightclub. Kept perpetually youthful-looking until death thanks to medical innovations, they maintain their promiscuous lifestyles courtesy of sex-hormone chewing gum and their placid demeanors with the aid of soma, a drug that offers all the benefits of hip-flask whiskey, minus the hangover.

Brave New World was a response to the utopian promise of twentieth-century consumer culture. More explicitly than either Zamyatin or Orwell, Huxley laid his anti-utopian cards on the table, offering as his novel's epigraph a passage by the twentieth-century Russian philosopher Nikolai Berdyaev:

> Utopias appear much more realizable now than we would have believed earlier. We find ourselves currently facing an agonizing question: How

to avoid their definitive realization? . . . Utopias are realizable. Life pro-
gresses towards utopias. And perhaps a new century is beginning, a
century when intellectuals and the cultivated class must imagine means
of avoiding utopias and returning to a non-utopian society, less "perfect" and more free.[11]

Huxley's brave new world is a perfect and perfectly controlled utopia, a Joy City in which the party never ends and any musings about
freedom are quickly swept away, never allowed to occlude the sunshine of Good Times.

George Orwell, who had been Huxley's pupil at Eton during the
older writer's brief, disastrous stint as a French teacher, delighted in
belittling his former master's novel. He wrote in 1943 that Huxley's
"completely materialistic vulgar civilisation based on hedonism"
was a danger past. Huxley, who outlived Orwell, had the last word
in a 1958 essay: "It now looks as though the odds were more in favor
of something like *Brave New World* than of something like *1984*."[12]
In the early twenty-first century, the contest between their bleak
visions of the future—unchecked hedonistic consumerism or repressive police state—may be too close to call. What is certain is that
both *Nineteen Eighty-Four* and *Brave New World* are, at heart, attacks on utopianism itself. By the 1950s, both novels were cultural
touchstones, required reading for secondary school students and
central texts of the anti-utopian twentieth century.

The Utopian Twentieth Century

During the fifty years following World War I, no utopian fiction
reached a sizable audience, sparking imaginative hopes in the way
that the work of Bellamy, Morris, Carpenter, and Gilman had done.
Walden Two, B. F. Skinner's novel about a utopian community designed by a benign behavioral psychologist, attracted some interest
when it was published in 1948, but it soon went out of print, and it
was not until later republications that the book attracted a wide
readership.[13] During the 1950s in both the U.S. and Great Britain,
the dominant visions of the future involved the containment of the
Soviet threat and the worldwide spread of democratic, free-market
values. Then the 1960s arrived—and with them a surge of utopian

energy. In an influential article, Lyman Tower Sargent argued that utopianism has three distinct faces: literature, social theory, and communities. All three thrived during the period that historians call the long 1960s, from the late 1950s through the 1970s.[14]

The explosion of communal settlements was the most obvious sign of 1960s utopianism. For over a hundred years after the surge of Owenite and Fourierist communities in the 1840s and 1850s, the communalist movement seemed moribund. Recent historians have complicated the narrative of the supposed death of the commune after 1860—a variety of communities, such as the small urban Swedenborgian group in which Charlotte Perkins Gilman lived as an adolescent, were founded in every decade from 1860 on—but it's true that the number of settlements declined drastically, their ambitions were limited, and there was little public awareness of communal alternatives to the traditional household. The sudden creation of thousands of hippie communes was one of the most striking, widely noted aspects of late 1960s and 1970s culture. It's difficult to determine precisely how many communes were established during the period—many left no written records, others dissolved and reformed, and problems of definition plague any effort to compile a census (e.g., should every group of young adults who shared a house be counted as a commune?). A low estimate is that in the U.S. alone there were at least 10,000 communes during the movement's peak in the early 1970s. Other scholars conclude that the actual total is in the tens of thousands, involving up to 750,000 Americans.[15]

Was every commune established during the period an expression of utopianism? In an influential study published in 1972, at the height of the modern communal movement, Rosabeth Moss Kanter argued that the hippie communes represented a retreat from utopia. The hippies wanted to establish alternative families, not alternative versions of society, and she claimed that the new communes, unlike those founded by the nineteenth-century Owenites and Associationists, looked backward toward a romanticized past rather than forward toward a transformed future. The argument has some validity, but Kanter's binary classifications—communes are either successes or failures, either forward-looking utopian experiments or regressive retreats from the larger culture—ignore the tensions that exist within any intentional community between the desire to serve as a shelter from the world at large and the urge to stand as a model of a better society.[16]

The history of the Farm—the largest and best-known of the hippie communes, established in rural Tennessee in 1971—serves as a challenge to Kanter's reductive thesis. On the one hand, the Farm was conceived as a sort of New Age retreat, a community intended to foster members' spiritual growth. It had its origins in a weekly class held in San Francisco during the late 1960s led by Stephen Gaskin, a charismatic spiritual teacher. Gaskin preached a cosmopolitan spirituality that made connections between the mystical traditions of the world's religions and the ego-shattering experience of psychedelic drugs with which most of his listeners were familiar. In 1971 he led a caravan of old school buses, filled with over three hundred of his followers and their families, from California to Tennessee in order to establish an egalitarian, pacifist, and environmentally sustainable community that would shelter its members from a society that they regarded as corrupted by materialism, militarism, and competition.[17]

Yet from its beginning, the Farm was not only a retreat for its residents but also a force for change in the world at large. The destination slot on the front of the Greyhound Scenicruiser that they bought and refurbished after arriving in Tennessee read "Out to Save the World." This was not an example of hippie irony. When the Farm was less than three years old and this collection of young people was still struggling to grow food and sustain themselves in a difficult rural environment for which nothing in their middle-class upbringing or liberal arts education had prepared them, Gaskin founded Plenty International, a social service organization that came to be known as the Hippie Peace Corps. After a 1976 earthquake killed 23,000 people and left one million homeless in Guatemala, residents of the Farm went to the country and became a major force in relief work. Among other efforts, they used their experience as vegans to establish a soy dairy that helped combat malnutrition in the devastated country and that, forty years later, is still in operation. Later in the 1970s, when the lack of medical care in the South

Bronx became a national scandal, Farm members moved to the impoverished New York borough and started a free ambulance service.

The Farm's tripartite emphasis on fostering personal growth, serving those in need, and creating a community that could stand as a model for a transformed world was not unique within the Sixties counterculture. Two epoch-defining works of social theory—the second of Sargent's three utopian faces—argued that the counterculture had the potential to lead to a transformation of both individual consciousness and society as a whole. The first of them was Theodore Roszak's *The Making of a Counter Culture* (1969), which is generally credited with originating the term "counterculture." The book concludes with an ecstatic utopian paean to the new "consciousness of life" that, Roszak argues, is embodied by Sixties youth culture. The bulk of Roszak's work, however, is a shrewd and nuanced appraisal of the mid-twentieth-century radical thinkers who laid the groundwork for the counterculture: Herbert Marcuse, Norman O. Brown, Alan Watts, Allen Ginsberg, Timothy Leary, and Paul Goodman. Roszak, an American historian who lived in England during much of the 1960s, had the advantage of proximity to the radical European movements of the era, and he observed how the Parisian young people who took to the streets in May '68 were shaped by France's long tradition of worker revolts. The students imagined that they would be joined by workers in a political revolution that would overthrow capitalism and establish a people's republic. In contrast, the lack of a strong radical tradition in the U.S. meant that American youths focused on a revolution in consciousness rather than in the political structure. This could lead, Roszak argued, to a political end, but one "sought by no political means."[18]

Roszak recognized that the 1960s counterculture was a minority movement within American society, even among the young, but he believed that it represented the only serious challenge to the militaristic, environmentally destructive, and humanly repressive technocratic culture that had dominated U.S. society since the end of World War II. A better future might be taking shape, but it was, he warned, an "excessively fragile" possibility.[19] *The Making of a Counter Culture* is a utopian work, but its utopianism is tentative and provisional.

No such hesitation is to be found in another major work of Sixties social theory, Yale law professor Charles A. Reich's *The Greening of America* (1970). In many ways, Reich's analysis agreed with Roszak's. Both writers believed that the Sixties youth counterculture possessed a transformative potential that relied not on conventional political strategies but on a change in consciousness, a rejection of repressive conformity, and a commitment to both the liberated self and the human community. Reich, however, rejected Roszak's nuanced analysis and tentative predictions in favor of a prophetic style that seems as if it's meant to be read aloud to rock music. "There is a revolution coming," he writes in the book's opening chapter. "It will not be like revolutions of the past. It will originate with the individual and with culture, and it will change the political structure only as its final act. . . . It is now spreading with amazing rapidity. . . . It promises a higher reason, a more human community, and a new and liberated individual. Its ultimate creation will be a new and enduring wholeness and beauty."[20]

It is highly unlikely that Reich was familiar with Edward Carpenter's theory that humanity had progressed from simple consciousness to self-consciousness and was on the verge of a transition to cosmic consciousness. However, he too developed a three-phase history of consciousness. Reich argued that Consciousness I, which originated in the nineteenth century, focused on self-advancement. Consciousness II, a creation of the early twentieth century, upheld the conformist values of a bureaucratic society. Consciousness III, arising with the youth counterculture, represents "the energy of enthusiasm, of happiness, of hope." It "rejects the idea that man's relation to man is to be governed primarily by law or politics, and instead posits an extended family in the spirit of the Woodstock Festival." Reich breezed past the messy details of political and economic change and posited instead that once America's youth conveyed "the great liberating process of recovery of self" to their fellow citizens, "the power of the Corporate State will be ended, as miraculously as a kiss breaks a witch's evil enchantment."[21]

The Greening of America is as grandiose and quirky as anything by Edward Carpenter or Robert Owen or Charles Fourier but, thanks to the media environment of late twentieth-century America, it quickly reached a vast audience that nineteenth-century utopian theorists could only dream of. A long excerpt from the book was published in the *New Yorker*, and the resulting publicity drove it to the number one spot on the *New York Times* best-seller list.[22] A half-century later, the book seems wildly naïve, but its immense contemporary success testifies to the widespread utopianism of the Sixties. The utopian speculation represented by *The Greening of America* spilled over, during the 1970s, into an outpouring of utopian fiction that rivaled the surge following the publication of Bellamy's *Looking Backward*.

The new utopian literature of the 1970s was a significant departure from *Looking Backward* and other turn-of-the-century fictions. *Looking Backward*, *News from Nowhere*, and *Herland* were all based on the model of More's *Utopia*, which in turn was based on the philosophical dialogue as established by Plato. *Utopia*, along with the books it inspired, was pre-novelistic, to borrow a term from Bakhtinian theorist Carl Freedman.[23] That is, the dialogue and plot in these works is little more than a flimsy drapery covering an essentially monologic form, in which a single character, standing in for the author, explains the structure of the ideal society. In contrast, utopian fiction of the 1970s is more science fiction than Platonic dialogue. Taking full advantage of the fantastic conventions of science fiction, these works plunge readers into alternative worlds with complex characters engaged in a variety of conflicts. Tom Moylan invented the term "critical utopias" to describe this new body of work; the term suggests both a critique of previous utopian fictions and intratextual arguments about the imagined society.[24]

The 1970s critical utopias include Ernest Callenbach's popular *Ecotopia* (1975), a male-centered fantasy set in San Francisco and the Pacific Northwest, which have seceded from the United States in order to form a more perfect countercultural union, but the best and most enduring of the 1970s utopian novels came out of that decade's feminist movement. Seventies feminists produced a significant body of utopian literature, which falls broadly into two camps identified by Angelika Bammer. On one side are separatist works such as Joanna Russ's novel *The Female Man* (1975) and Sally Miller Gearhart's *The Wanderground* (1979), which portray women-only societies inspired by the many lesbian communes established in the

1970s. On the other are gender-free utopias in which differences between women and men have been largely obliterated.[25]

Marge Piercy's *Woman on the Edge of Time* (1976) is the best-known of the latter. The inhabitants of Mattapoisett, the twenty-second-century Massachusetts village where much of the novel is set, are androgynous in appearance and dress and language. Biology, in Mattapoisett, is no longer destiny: all babies are conceived and gestated in vitro, in large facilities. Piercy boldly reconceives *Brave New World*, in which the baby factories are a tool not only of population control but of control over the population. In her novel, the factories are a technology of sexual equality, established as part of "women's long revolution." As one character explains, "as long as we were biologically enchained, we'd never be equal. And males never would be humanized to be loving and tender. So we all became mothers." In this brave new world, every child is assigned three co-mothers, at least one of each sex, all of whom, thanks to a nifty bit of bioengineering, are capable of breast-feeding the baby. Piercy embraces technologies of human liberation, but the dominant tone in Mattapoisett is of a casual, Edward Carpenter–like simple life. Culturally compulsory heterosexuality has disappeared, and most persons are bisexual.[26]

Piercy's novel is widely regarded as a twentieth-century utopian masterpiece. Its only peer is Ursula Le Guin's *The Dispossessed* (1974). Like other critical utopias of the period, *The Dispossessed* owes much to second-wave feminism. It owes even more, however, to William Morris and to Morris's admirer Peter Kropotkin, the great anarchist theorist and author of *Mutual Aid* (1902). Anarres, the planet on which the novel is set, is an anarchist utopia that resembles Morris's Nowhere.[27]

The Dispossessed is, in many ways, a continuation of Kropotkin's and Morris's emancipatory political projects. Like *News from Nowhere*, it is fueled by outrage at the persistence of poverty in an affluent society, a fundamental distrust of state power, and a dual commitment to communal solidarity and individual freedom. The people of Anarres, like the inhabitants of Morris's Nowhere, inhabit a sexually open utopia in which the words for *work* and *play* are the same. Yet at the same time as *The Dispossessed* extends Morris's idyllic utopian vision, the novel also contradicts it. For all its utopian qualities, Anarres is a wasteland, an arid planet whose inhabitants, anarchist rebels who fled the planet Urras two generations ago, can barely scratch out enough food and other necessities to sustain themselves.

The novel's protagonist is Shevek, a brilliant Anarresti physicist with the potential to contribute world-changing theoretical insights. Repeatedly, however, Shevek runs up against the limitations of Anarresti culture. The anarchist society of Anarres is supposedly devoid of hierarchy or repression, but the communal authorities have forbidden direct contact with Urras, lest Anarresti citizens pick up decadent ideas. *The Dispossessed* has unresolved debates at its core. The novel is centered not on a struggle between good and bad social visions but on the tensions between the opposing goods of collective solidarity and individual freedom.

The novel's plot is spurred by Shevek's choice of freedom over solidarity: he resolves to leave Anarres for Urras. He is the first person ever to do so, an act widely regarded as a betrayal of the culture's deepest values. Once on Urras, he is initially delighted by what he finds, but he is soon disillusioned by the society's materialism, militarism, and sexism. Repulsed by the inequality and repression that surrounds him, Shevek flees the university and arranges to return to Anarres.

The Dispossessed ends as Shevek is about to set foot on Anarres after his return from Urras. Most of the utopian fictions of the 1970s resist formal closure; Le Guin's novel is exceptionally open-ended. We're left with a string of questions: Will Shevek survive attempts on his life by the Anarresti who regard him as a traitor? If he does, will he be able to change his society in any significant way? More fundamentally: Can an anarchist system combine solidarity and freedom? Can Anarres, committed to an unchanging ideal of fellowship, even be considered a utopia? Isn't Urras, flawed but beautiful and vibrantly dynamic, closer to a paradise? More than any other writer of the 1970s, Le Guin reconceived the utopian novel in both formal and thematic terms. Morris, her great predecessor, subtitled *News from Nowhere* "An Epoch of Rest," signifying its roots in Arcadian romance and the ideal of a timeless, unchanging bucolic retreat. Le Guin's original subtitle was "An Ambiguous Utopia," suggesting irresolution and an unceasing struggle to create a better world.

The Dispossessed stands at the apex of its era's earnest, ambiguous utopian experimentation. With hindsight, it is evident that the novel also appeared near the movement's terminus. With the election of Margaret Thatcher in 1979 and Ronald Reagan in 1980, the long 1960s and the attendant widespread receptiveness to utopian speculation were essentially over. The slogan of the 1980s could well have been Thatcher's famous pronouncement, "There is no alternative"—no alternative to consumer capitalism, to free-market economic theory, to the paradigm of unlimited growth and the culture of triumphant individualism. The adjective "utopian" was returned to its diminished connotations of midcentury: "foolishly unrealistic," "naïve," "impossible." Utopian fiction continued to be produced during the 1980s, but no single work gained either a wide audience or critical acclaim. The finest speculative fiction of the decade was Margaret Atwood's *The Handmaid's Tale* (1987), a grim dystopian tale inspired by the era's resurgent religious fundamentalism and antifeminist backlash. The last utopians and their twentieth-century successors seemed outmoded and irrelevant. The collapse of Soviet communism at the end of the 1980s and the seeming triumph of the West spurred widespread speculation about the end of history—that is, the end of any serious challenge to neoliberal economic and political ideals.[28] With history at an end, what need could there be for the sharp critique and unfettered speculation of utopian literature, theory, and practice?

Utopianism in the Twenty-First Century

The terrorist attacks of September 11, 2001, destroyed not only the World Trade Center but also any remaining intellectual prestige of the end-of-history social theory of the 1990s. The attacks demonstrated the continuing power of grandiose, inherently violent utopian visions akin to those that had animated Hitler and Stalin in the twentieth century. Al-Qaeda, the Islamic State, and other extremist groups imagine a transformed future, with the Caliphate restored, Israel erased, and Sharia law dominant. The governments of the United States, Great Britain, and other Western democracies denounced the extremists' violent utopianism, but they also instituted repressive measures involving arrests, detention, and torture as well as programs of surveillance that extend far beyond suspected terrorists and that threaten the privacy of virtually everyone in society. Suddenly, Orwell's *Nineteen Eighty-Four* gained a new immediacy. Big Brother, it turns out, *is* watching us, and there has been a widespread realization that, as Margaret Atwood writes, "Thoughtcrime and the boot grinding into the human face could not be got rid of so easily after all."[29]

References to Orwell became ubiquitous in early twenty-first-century American and British culture. No significant utopian literature has been produced since 9/11, but dystopian literature and film have flourished. Dystopian fiction has become a dominant genre in young-adult fiction, with the *Hunger Games* series of novels and films the most prominent example. The *Hunger Games* series has little of the political seriousness that underlies the great twentieth-century works of Zamyatin, Huxley, and Orwell. It is inspired less by a public fear of state power than by the private anxieties of adolescence. As Laura Miller points out in a perceptive analysis of young-adult dystopias, *The Hunger Games* makes little sense as a political critique, but read as "a fever-dream allegory of the adolescent social experience," it becomes perfectly intelligible.[30] Still, twenty-first-century pop-culture dystopias are not entirely apolitical. Even if they focus on adolescent angst, their futuristic milieus of panoptic surveillance, repressive government, and brutal military and police forces are inspired by post-9/11 trends.

Those political trends have drawn a remarkable number of contemporary authors to the dystopian genre. The early twenty-first century has proven to be a golden age for dystopian fiction. Since 2001, scores of critically esteemed authors of serious literary fiction have used the dystopian form to sound a warning not only about terrorism and the repressive security state but also about income inequality and economic insecurity, the ongoing oppression of women, and environmental devastation. The last topic has fostered an entire dystopian subgenre known as "cli fi"—fiction about climate change.[31] Outstanding examples abound, including Nathaniel Rich's *Odds Against Tomorrow* (2013), an alternately witty and terrifying combination of romantic comedy and catastrophe fiction set in a New York City destroyed by a hurricane, and the genre's magnum opus, Margaret Atwood's *MaddAddam* trilogy: *Oryx and Crake* (2003), *The Year of the Flood* (2009), and *MaddAddam* (2013). Atwood's richly imaginative novels portray a dystopian future marked not only by human-initiated climate change but also by grotesquely increased income inequality, widespread child pornography, and pervasive human trafficking. Above all, Atwood's novels interrogate humanity's responsibility for the extinction of thousands of species and the scientific hubris underlying genetic engineering and biotechnology. The *MaddAddam* novels recall the greatest speculative fiction of the nineteenth century, Mary Shelley's *Frankenstein* (1818). Atwood's Crake is a twenty-first-century Victor Frankenstein, a brilliant megalomaniac who desires a godlike control over the human and natural worlds.

Atwood is a critic and theorist of speculative fiction as well as a practitioner, and she noted in a 2007 essay that dystopian visions of a totalitarian future tend to fall into two camps, the hard and the soft. The hard visions look back to *Nineteen Eighty-Four*, the soft to *Brave New World*. "Would it be possible for both of these futures," she speculated, "to exist at the same time, in the same place? And what would that be like?"[32] Not long after she posed the question, Gary Shteyngart answered it in *Super Sad True Love Story* (2010). If Atwood's *MaddAddam* trilogy recalls Mary Shelley, Shteyngart's brilliant, corrosive, and frequently hilarious novel recalls Jonathan Swift. His dystopian satire is set in a near-future New York City whose population is divided between the elite and the LNWIs, or Low Net Worth Individuals. New York's elite and the youthful strivers who long to join them are oblivious of the ways that marketers and social media have bound them in the "soft" restraints of self-absorption, envy, and perpetually unsatisfied desire, and they are only dimly aware of the "hard" security state that monitors LNWIs and dissidents and, when necessary, ruthlessly eliminates those who challenge its authority.

The speculative fiction of Rich, Atwood, Shteyngart, and their many peers performs one of the two principal functions of the utopian literature of earlier eras: it estranges readers from current reality, revealing the many forms of violence and exploitation that underlie everyday life. However, it does not address utopian writing's other primary purpose: to offer hope for the future. Utopian optimism is hard to find in contemporary literature or social theory. Since the end of the long 1960s, bold utopian visions have been largely missing in American and British culture.

The absence has not gone unremarked. Historian Russell Jacoby has published two books lamenting the loss of what he calls the "visionary impulse" in contemporary society and promoting what he calls "iconoclastic utopianism." Unfortunately, the iconoclastic utopian thinkers he champions—Martin Buber, Ernst Bloch, Gershom Scholem, and T. W. Adorno—were all born in the nineteenth century and stopped publishing well before the end of the twentieth, offering scant hope for a contemporary utopian revival.[33] The prominent Marxist literary critic and theorist Fredric Jameson has discussed utopian writing throughout his long career, but his most celebrated pronouncement on the topic is a postmodern koan from a 1977 essay: "Utopia's deepest subject, and the source of all that is most vibrantly political about it, is precisely our inability to conceive it."[34] Jameson argues, that is, that all utopian fictions are fundamentally failures. Their ultimate utility lies not in their portrayals of a better future but in their revelation of the limitations of our collective imagination as a result of our confinement within capitalist ideology. Jameson's theory of the inevitable failure of utopian literature is intellectually bracing, but it is unlikely to restore utopianism to a central place in contemporary culture.

Krishan Kumar, one of the most prominent figures in the field of utopian studies, published an essay in 2010 on "The Ends of Utopia."[35] The deliberate ambiguity of the title suggests that Kumar may be subverting the end-of-utopia narrative, but he agrees that literary utopia is exhausted as a genre, that social theory has retreated from utopian speculation, and that truly utopian ventures are difficult to identify in contemporary culture. His essay ends with a lament for the loss of utopia and a tentative hope for its revival. Kumar's essay functions as a sort of funeral oration for utopia. He does not deny the possibility of some future resurrection, but he makes clear that, for now, there is little to be done except to shed some tears, embrace the other mourners, and silently file away.

Yet perhaps it is premature to compose utopia's obituary. Kumar is correct that literary utopias of the sort that Bellamy, Morris, Carpenter, and Gilman offered are no longer prominent. Utopian social theory still exists, but its audience is limited.[36] That leaves the last of Sargent's three faces: what he defines as community, which I broaden to the concept of *lived utopianism*—living out some portion of a transformed future in the here and now. The moment for grand-scale utopian imagining may be past, but the visionary temperament is a human constant. If utopian desire is no longer expressed in literature and in theories of an alternative world, how is it manifested in contemporary life?

The answer may be found in what Davina Cooper calls "everyday utopias." Cooper, an ethnographer as well as a legal and cultural theorist, explores six contemporary British sites and activities, ranging from Hyde Park Speakers' Corner to the practice of public nudism, that bring utopian visions into daily reality. She argues that with utopian novels in short supply, utopianism needs to be reconceived as an orientation toward belief in the possibility of other, better worlds. Seen that way, examples of utopianism abound.[37]

Contemporary everyday utopias cover a broad spectrum. What French philosopher Louis Marin famously called "degenerate" utopias, such as Disneyland and cruise ships, are fantasies of escape, with one foot planted in Cokaygne, the medieval dreamland of leisure and effortless abundance, and the other firmly planted in contemporary consumer culture.[38] Conservative intellectuals offer a utopian vision in which free-market principles suffuse every aspect of life. Historian Daniel Rodgers has suggested that belief in "the market" became, in effect, a form of utopianism starting in the late twentieth century. "You know, there really is something magic about the marketplace when it's free to operate," Ronald Reagan cheerily announced in 1982—a perspective that still dominates much of our political discourse.[39] A third major form of contemporary social dreaming comes out of Silicon Valley and relies on the transformative power of science and technology. Inventor and futurist Ray Kurzweil promotes the concept of "the singularity"—a future era when human and machine intelligence will merge, becoming "trillions of times more powerful." In the singularity, "human aging and illness will be reversed; pollution will be stopped; world hunger and poverty will be solved."[40] The singularity is a contemporary version of Francis Bacon's Salomon's House in *New Atlantis* (1627), with Bacon's faith in science and technology ramped up to warp speed.

The degenerate utopias of consumer culture, the free-market utopias of the political and economic elite, and the techno-utopias of scientists and engineers are powerful and widespread varieties of contemporary utopianism. My interest, however, is in the utopian tradition exemplified by Bellamy, Morris, Carpenter, and Gilman. That tradition, as defined in the introduction, rests on four pillars. First, it is radically democratic, with a commitment to economic egalitarianism. Next, it is antipatriarchal, supportive of women's independence and open to new forms of family and community. It has a powerful environmental dimension, with a love for nature and a commitment to simple living. Finally, it has its roots in a progressive spirituality that regards the divine as immanent within humans and the natural world.

I went looking for contemporary everyday utopians who share those commitments. They can be found across the U.S. and Great Britain. In most cases, these contemporary utopians are unaware of their parallels to Bellamy, Morris, Carpenter, and Gilman. I wanted to investigate contemporary utopianism, not because I expected to have stimulating conversations about nineteenth-century writers, but because the progressive values that the last utopians advocated remain as important now as then. The contemporary utopians I encountered, like their predecessors, embrace optimistic, transformative visions of the future. Their utopianism, however, unlike that of their nineteenth-century predecessors, is partial. I use the term *partial* in two senses, derived from Kwame Anthony Appiah's notion of partial cosmopolitanism.[41] First, their utopianism is *partial* as in incomplete—not for them the utter transformation of society embraced by the last utopians and, malevolently, by twentieth-century totalitarians. Second their utopianism is *partial to*, or preferential; they have selected some aspect of transformative change on which to pin their utopian dreams. In the remainder of this chapter, I explore three forms of contemporary utopianism, one partial to community, another to education, and the last to food.

Some theorists would claim that what I call partial utopianism isn't really utopian at all, arguing that utopian dreaming is defined by its vision of a totally transformed world. Howard Segal labels all

visions that "seek changes in only one or two components" of life
"false utopias."[42] That's a defensible position, but it leads to a conceptual dead end for anyone who believes that utopian dreams are
crucial to a better future. Partial utopianism is the only vital democratic, egalitarian, and nonviolent utopianism that exists in contemporary British and American culture. The last utopians' heirs are
wary of the grand imaginative visions of their nineteenth-century
predecessors; their utopianism is experiential and modest. These
social dreamers are, nonetheless, committed to living out some portion of a transformed future in the here and now.

COMMUNITY

It's not easy to get to the intentional community on the isle of Erraid
in the Scottish Hebrides. Traveling by train from Glasgow, you head
north into the Highlands, gaining elevation quickly, then skirting
along the shore of narrow Loch Lomond. The train turns west at
Crianlarich, traveling along Loch Awe and Loch Etive before arriving, three hours after departure, at Oban. In Oban, a picturesque
town on the Firth of Lorn, it's a short walk past woolen stores and
whiskey shops and fish stands to the ferry, which lands, forty minutes later, at Craignure on the isle of Mull. Once there, you board
the bus to Fionnphort, no matter the driver's joshing that you can't
get on unless you pronounce the destination correctly. (It's *Finny-
furt.*) Fionnphort lies at the far end of the Ross of Mull, a long,
thinly populated peninsula jutting into the Atlantic. From Fionnphort, it's a short drive to the dock where the Erraid community has
a dinghy that can transport you across the strait separating the tiny
island from Mull. After all that, you'd best stay a while. Most visitors
to Erraid remain at least a week; most of the residents have been
there for years.

People visit Erraid for many reasons. I went because I had the
sense that the community there has been extraordinarily successful
in addressing the problem that absorbed William Morris: the alien-
ating nature of modern labor. Erraid's visitor program is called
"Love in Action," an abbreviation of the slogan, "Work is love in
action." Val, an Erraid resident, frequently repeated that slogan at
attunement. "Attunement" is Erraid's term for the group meeting at

the start of every work session. Each morning, the visitors sat on cushions in the community's small meeting room along with the eight adult residents, who explained their work projects for the day: "It's time to clean the chicken coop, and I can use one helper"; "I need two mates to split firewood"; "I'm whitewashing the interior of cottage three." We'd join hands and meditate in silence for a while, then go around the circle and say which job we were drawn to. Late in the week we were joined by a new visitor, an amiable American who tried to demonstrate his good nature by saying that he'd be willing to do any of the jobs. Roger gently corrected him: "What do you want to be doing?" The residents of Erraid believe that work assignments can be delegated without imposing authority, that people can be trusted to choose freely the tasks that need completion. They also believe that the work itself can be a source of spiritual nurture, a lesson in present-mindedness. In the garden, where I worked most days, Val would hold another attunement before we began our tasks. We would stand near the toolshed and the cold frames and hold hands while Val, in her graceful Scottish accent, brought our attention to the present moment: "Feel the sun on your face" (or, this being Scotland, "Notice the mist on your skin"). "How strong is the breeze today? Listen to the different birdsongs. Can you hear the sheep bleating?" To a surprising degree, her gentle exhortations carried over to the work itself. I found myself deeply attentive to the loose consistency of the soil as I pulled up carrots, the vegetables' varying shape and weight and color, the unexpected burst of scent as my trouser leg brushed an oregano plant.

Working on Erraid recalled Morris's utopia, where people freely choose their tasks and young men embark on a spell of road-mending for the sheer pleasure of using their muscles in the open air. Morris himself had nothing but contempt for the communal experiments that popped up occasionally in Great Britain and America during the late nineteenth century. They "are of their nature non-progressive," he wrote; "at their best they are but another form of the Mediaeval monastery, withdrawals from the society of the day, really implying hopelessness of a general change."[43] Bellamy and Gilman were similarly dismissive. It's not so easy, however, to dismiss the intentional communities of twenty-first-century Great Britain and America. For one thing, there are so many of them: several dozen in the U.K. and over 1,700 in the U.S.[44] The common perception is that communal living essentially vanished after most of the hippie communes established in the 1970s folded, but intentional communities are thriving. Erraid is typical in its small size, but I also visited two large communities that keep a waiting list for applicants: Twin Oaks in Virginia, with more than a hundred residents, and Findhorn, on Scotland's northeast coast, home to more than four hundred people. At all three communities, I expected to encounter mostly aging baby boomers—I'd imagined lots of gray ponytails—but the population skewed young, and I met dozens of people in their twenties and thirties who are trying out community life after college or who want to raise their children in a place that provides some relief from the isolation and pressure-cooker tensions of the nuclear family.

Morris saw communes as withdrawals from society, and there's no question that isolation is part of the appeal. Everyone at Erraid savors its remote tranquility, and both Twin Oaks and Findhorn are in beautiful, out-of-the-way locations. Like many contemporary communities, however, they face outward as much as in and regard themselves not just as refuges but as educational institutions and agents of social change. The Internet has simplified outreach, and large communities such as Twin Oaks and Findhorn have extensive websites filled with lists of publications and conferences and with information designed to encourage visitors.[45]

Findhorn is particularly committed to education and outreach. The community began in 1962 when Dorothy Maclean, Eileen Caddy, and Eileen's husband Peter moved into a small caravan—the British term for what Americans call a trailer—near the village of Findhorn on Scotland's northeastern coast. All three were spiritual seekers, and they promoted both their cosmopolitan spirituality and their remarkable success with gardening, attracting an increasing number of countercultural settlers to the caravan park. Over the years, the community outgrew the original caravans, and in the 1980s they began construction of what became the Findhorn Ecovillage, a development of attractive houses with tiny carbon footprints. They also established the Findhorn Foundation, now a United Nations–recognized NGO in the field of environmental sustainability. In a typical year, more than three thousand people from over forty countries travel to Findhorn for courses and workshops on the environment and on spirituality. During the three days I spent at Findhorn, I talked with residents and visitors from Scotland, England, Australia, the United States, Italy, Spain, and Japan.[46]

The adjective "utopian" was applied to communes from their heyday in the 1840s well into the late twentieth century. Whenever I asked a resident of Erraid or Findhorn or Twin Oaks if the term "utopian" applied, the first response was generally laughter. "Hell, no, this ain't utopia!" exclaimed Julia, an American who had lived at Erraid for four years and who had returned for a visit during the week I was there. The Hebridean winters are brutal, living quarters are tight, the children can be annoying, and personal frictions between the few adults are inevitable. "But," Julia added, "it's more utopian than other places."

Robert Owen regarded New Harmony as a model that would be replicated until the entire society was organized on similar lines. It's hard to find anyone today who imagines that mainstream American or British society will transform itself along communal principles, but successful communities continue to serve as models. Historian Donald Pitzer has written widely about what he calls "developmental communalism," a scholarly version of what the community residents I talked with generally called the "ripple effect."[47] Pitzer, like the residents, argues that the progressive social experiments enacted in intentional communities are frequently adopted by society as a whole in succeeding years. He points to nineteenth-century communards' experiments in universal education, democratic governance, and women's rights that were later integrated into American and British life. Some people I talked with at Findhorn were convinced that the humanistic spirituality practiced there is the wave of the future; others were more skeptical. But everyone I met at Findhorn was certain that the environmental practices they had adopted—the innovative wastewater treatment facility, the massive wind turbines located just off the beach, the small, environmentally friendly houses—would have to spread in order for our society to survive.

Sustainability was also a frequent topic of conversation at Twin Oaks in rural Virginia, although there the talk was less about purchasing a new electric vehicle than about keeping the community's fleet of aging clunkers running. Twin Oaks is less physically polished than Findhorn—in essence it's an Appalachian farm, not a Scottish village—but it's nearly as old (established in 1967) and has been fully as influential. Twin Oaks was established to prove the feasibility of B. F. Skinner's utopian novel *Walden Two* (1948). Its founders combined Sixties back-to-the-land communalism with midcentury behaviorist psychology. The behaviorism was soon abandoned, but they have maintained other aspects of Skinner's vision: his planner/manager form of government, in which policies are set by a small, rotating group of planners rather than through the consensus decision-making employed in most communities; his system of work credits; and his belief in income-sharing, with most needs being met by the community and profits from participation in the larger economy divided equally among residents.

Twin Oaks' approach to work is as innovative as Erraid's, but, in line with its Skinnerian origins, it is rational and bureaucratic rather than spiritual. Everyone is obligated to earn forty-two credits a week, with each credit equal to an hour of work, but the work can be done at any time, and few people specialize in one job. Calvin, who showed me around Twin Oaks on the second day of my visit, pulled out one member's worksheet for the coming week as an example. This member would be doing eight different jobs that week, tasks as diverse as washing dishes, cleaning house, weeding the garden, giving a tour, and working in one of the community's two major income-producing enterprises: weaving hammocks (they produce a few thousand a year) and making tofu (two thousand pounds daily). In exchange, the community provides meals, housing, and access to a wealth of shared resources: cars, bicycles, computers, tools, sports equipment, and a large clothing exchange known as Commie Clothes (for Community Clothes)—plus seventy-five dollars a month. "We increase sustainability by not spending a lot," Calvin told me somewhat ruefully. He acknowledged that money can be a source of tension. The community's economic equality is not perfect: members with valuable skills, such as construction, can take on outside work during their free time and use that money for travel, and those who come from affluent families have options for small luxuries unavailable to members from working-class backgrounds. An egalitarian ethos pervades the community, however, and since members' only private space is their bedroom in a shared residence, there is scant opportunity for conspicuous consumption. Life in Twin Oaks is remarkably stress-free. "We don't worry about all the things that people outside worry about constantly," Valerie, a twenty-year resident, told me over lunch. "Rent, food, healthcare, bills, debt—none of that is a problem here."

Twin Oaks' income- and resource-sharing schemes are widely known; the community has been the subject of multiple documentaries, numerous books, and hundreds of articles in the popular and scholarly press.[48] Among feminists and their allies, it's also known for its commitment to gender equality. Economists have long recognized the gendered distortion inherent in the capitalist system: work traditionally considered "feminine," such as housecleaning and childcare, is not considered economically valuable and is unaccounted for in conventional economic models. At Twin Oaks, childcare gets the same work credit as fixing the engine on a pickup. A resident with a baby automatically gets forty hours a week of labor credits, so that if she washes dishes for two hours a week, she's done. "But nobody uses all forty hours," Carrie, a recent college graduate, told me. "You want to do other things, and other residents are eager to do childcare." It's not just women doing the childcare. The community encourages people to try jobs that go against the gendered grain, so that men frequently cook and look after children, while women work as carpenters and auto mechanics. Twin Oaks has eliminated the structural inequalities that oppress women, and the community works against even linguistic inequality. Starting in the 1970s, some residents began replacing gendered pronouns—he/she, his/hers—with "co" and "cos": e.g., "Where's Alana? I think co left cos work gloves here." When I asked Valerie about gender equality at Twin Oaks, she said the community is far from perfect. "There's a cultural hangover of sexism that both the men and the women here suffer from. But at least in terms of labor, we're equal."

J. C. Hallman, a writer whose cheeky, entertaining account of his three-week residence at Twin Oaks appears in his book *In Utopia* (2010), arrived with a theory that the community's emphasis on gender equality was inspired by Charlotte Perkins Gilman's *Herland*. It turned out that no one there had read the book.[49] Despite that, in an inevitably imperfect, stuttering fashion Twin Oaks is trying to live out a Gilmanesque program of gender equality as well as the ideals of simplicity, community, and economic equality advocated by her and the other last utopians.

Twin Oaks' commitment to those ideals was evident throughout my three-day visit. Most significantly, I found that even the briefest residence in a community dedicated to the simple life could defamiliarize the everyday world more effectively than the greatest of utopian fictions. Retrieving my car from the distant field where I had parked it on arrival, I pulled away from Twin Oaks and began driving through rural Virginia, a landscape little different from the low, wooded hills in which the community is set. But within an hour I was on the outskirts of Fredericksburg, surrounded by strip malls and big-box stores. This common American landscape struck me with sudden, nightmarish power. I looked around as if viewing everything for the first time, repulsed by the casual ugliness of the huge asphalt parking lots and the utilitarian buildings; the slick, strident commercialism of the massive signs outside Walmart and Target and the dozens of fast-food restaurants; and the underlying dependence of it all on cheap oil and low-wage labor. Like Julian West awakening in nineteenth-century Boston near the end of *Looking Backward*, I found that a few days in an alternative society had estranged me from my surroundings and exposed the dystopian ugliness and injustice of everyday life.

Relatively few people can upend their life, set aside their career, and move into an intentional community such as Erraid, Findhorn, or Twin Oaks. That's why the cohousing movement has generated so much interest since the 1990s, when it migrated from Denmark to the U.S. and U.K. Cohousing communities, a compromise between a commune and a conventional neighborhood, physically resemble a condominium or a small suburban development, depending on location. Residents own their private units or houses, but the community also has a large common space and some degree of resource sharing. The community is designed and governed by the residents, who generally meet once a month or so to make decisions and frequently come together for a shared meal in the common kitchen and dining room.[50]

I arranged to visit Takoma Village Cohousing in Washington, D.C., on a Monday, the day when residents gather for their weekly shared dinner. Before dinner, I chatted with Steve Pretl on his small front porch. Takoma Village, which was built in 2000, looks like a particularly handsome condominium development. It's large for cohousing, with forty-three attached units in a U-shape. In the center are lawns and gardens with specimen trees and shrubs: serviceberry trees, a tricolor beech, blue atlas cedars, and lots of clematis and wisteria artfully climbing up the buildings. It was early June, and as we drank our iced tea a string of neighbors passed by: young women, children, a family on bicycles. All of them greeted Pretl by name, and I was reminded of the T-shirt I'd seen earlier on a Takoma Village resident: "Takoma Village Cohousing. The Old-Fashioned Community of the Future."

That was pretty much how Pretl, who was retired and in his seventies, saw it. "I used to have a house in the suburbs," he told me. "Then, after I got divorced, I moved into an apartment downtown. What those two places had in common was no sense of community. Living in a place like this makes it a lot easier to get help. If you need a ride to pick up your car at the mechanic, or your kid has an accident and you have to go to the emergency room and need someone to look after your other children, there's always someone you can call on. Plus there's the Monday-night dinners and the celebrations. We just had a party to welcome a new family. We have house concerts, and of course there are cookouts on Memorial Day and the Fourth of July and Labor Day."

Pretl walked me to the common area so he could pick up his mail—the clustered mailboxes were designed to increase opportunities for casual conversations among residents—then led me upstairs to talk with Ann Zabaldo, one of the community's founders. Zabaldo became a cohousing activist in the early 1990s, when the movement was just getting established in the U.S. In conversation, she was quick to place cohousing in a historical perspective. "For much of the twentieth century," she said, "there was a John Wayne effect in American culture: 'I don't need to depend on anybody.' With postwar affluence, people had the money to buy a house in the suburbs.

Everybody was busy putting up a fence. That meant families got isolated, and women in particular got isolated. I see cohousing as a way of transforming society back into what we say we are, recovering ideals of liberty, equality, justice. We're just living into American values."

"Utopia" is not in the vocabulary of most cohousing residents, but the pioneers who have developed some 170 communities in the U.S. and U.K. since the 1990s are consciously trying to live out some portion of a transformed future in the here and now. They don't engage with issues of economic justice or spirituality—it's telling that in terms of issues like zoning and tax codes, communes are frequently classified as monasteries, while cohousing is treated like condominiums—but they embrace the simple life and environmental sustainability. Cohousing apartments and houses tend to be small, since the common area generally has bedrooms for guests and spaces for parties and games. Residents share tools and, frequently, a hot tub or sauna or pool. They give each other rides, plant vegetable gardens together, and put up solar panels. In addition, they model forms of community that have attracted utopian thinkers for centuries. The member of Goodenough Community in Seattle who said that she was drawn to it because the conventional nuclear family "seems very *dry*" is unconsciously echoing the British communitarian who, in 1839, said that he and other Owenites were seeking "bigger homes for ourselves and our families."[51]

{⊷⊶ W ⊶⊷}

People who live in intentional communities, whether communes or cohousing, can be considered full-time everyday utopians—that is, they live out, on a daily basis, some portion of utopian idealism. There are also part-time utopians: people who live for a matter of days or weeks in temporary communities that come together around transformative ideals. One of the best-known temporary utopias is Burning Man, an annual weeklong gathering held in the Nevada desert. Established in the 1980s as a small countercultural art event that climaxed with the burning of a giant wooden figure, Burning Man now caps attendance at 50,000 people. Burning Man is often covered in the media as an ecstatic, drug-fueled party carried on to the beat of techno music. That's not entirely wrong, but it's incomplete. Burning Man is part party, part serious experiment in living out an alternative future. Its ten foundational principles, heavily publicized among participants, include "radical inclusion" and "communal effort"—that is, anyone is welcome, but everyone contributes to the community. Burning Man is structured as an alternative to mass culture and consumer capitalism. It relies on a "gift economy" that recalls William Morris's Nowhere. There's nothing for sale at the Burning Man site except for ice and coffee, and Burners, as attendees are known, freely offer one another art works, theatrical performances, massages, food. Burning Man's founder, artist Larry Harvey, has called it a "utopian experiment" in "decommodification," a participatory community that nurtures creativity and marginalizes consumption.[52]

Burning Man is held in the high desert, on an ancient lake bed that serves as a blank canvas on which to paint this temporary utopia of commerce-free art and self-expression. It is also a landscape that, as the event's "Survival Guide" states, "is trying its best to kill you."[53] Daytime temperatures regularly hit one hundred degrees, at night it can plunge into the forties, and dust storms fueled by hundred-mile-an-hour winds are a regular occurrence. I passed up an invitation from my cousin Ethan, a longtime Burner, to join him at Burning Man. But I visited another famous temporary utopia, an encampment that aimed at nothing less than the transformation of the American economy.

It was raining hard on the afternoon in late October 2011 when I arrived at Occupy Wall Street. Zuccotti Park, Occupy's site, is remarkably small, well under an acre, and only by the standards of lower Manhattan could it be considered a park. The entire site is paved in granite slabs, with a sprinkling of small trees poking through the stone. The Occupy protestors had pitched small tents and strung up an array of tarps that were only moderately effective against the steady rain and offered no protection against the day's biting cold. I was bent over, trying to take notes while keeping the ink from bleeding off the damp page, when I looked up to see a man

I vaguely recognized: a big guy with a round face and black-framed glasses wearing a Sundance Film Festival cap. He nodded to me, and I walked over to introduce myself. It was the filmmaker Michael Moore. He'd obviously just arrived and, with everyone hunkering out of the rain, had not yet attracted attention. Pointing to my notebook, he asked me who I was writing for. I explained that I was an academic researching a book about utopia. Moore broke into a grin and opened his arms wide: "Congratulations! You're there."

Of course, he was kidding. But not entirely. There were plenty of negative aspects to the Occupy Wall Street encampment. As I quickly discovered, Zuccotti Park had lots of earnest graduate students keen to talk about politics, but it also had a contingent of drug-users, a fair number of young men eager to provoke violent confrontations with the police, and a scattering of single-issue cranks. Yet this temporary community also had utopian dimensions. Occupy Wall Street and the other Occupy movements that arose around the U.S. and abroad in the fall of 2011 provided thousands of participants and millions of observers on television and other media an opportunity to encounter a working anarchist society.

Occupy Wall Street, crammed into a granite wedge between skyscrapers, might not have physically resembled William Morris's pastoral utopia, but its organizing principles were the same. The general assembly that took place each evening was the equivalent of Morris's *Mote*, the group of citizens who gathered to settle community policies by a lengthy, difficult, but radically democratic policy of consensus. The mainstream media pinned the label "anarchist" on the "black bloc" demonstrators in Occupy Oakland who covered their faces with black bandannas, smashed property, and attacked police. But political hooligans are only one small wing of anarchism. The activists at the heart of the Occupy movement were closer to Peter Kropotkin, the nineteenth-century advocate of small-scale, nonviolent anarchist communities.

Even the briefest visit to Occupy Wall Street provided the opportunity to witness mutual aid in action. During the period that I spent hanging out at the media tent, I encountered a stream of people volunteering to help. An immigration attorney in a downtown office had come with a tray of green-tea rice balls for the people working in the tent; a woman who owned a printing business was looking for a way to offer her services; a yoga teacher wanted to lead a workshop. A few yards away, at a tent labeled "Comfort Station," volunteers were giving away ponchos, socks, and dry clothing to anyone in the rain-sodden crowd who needed them. Activist Cindy Milstein wrote that even if not everyone participating in Occupy understood anarchist principles, they were "doing anarchism."[54]

The Occupy movement was frequently criticized for not putting forward clear demands, but the criticism ignores the movement's underlying philosophy. Anarchist theorist David Graeber, a London School of Economics professor who served as a sort of intellectual godfather of the Occupy movement and who was on hand in New York during the movement's crucial early weeks, argues that it was an example of "prefigurative politics."[55] According to this political theory, the way to achieve a more egalitarian society—one that Graeber calls "horizontal" rather than "vertical"—is not to issue demands or press for progressive policies but to enact horizontal practices in the here and now. Although no one used the term, Graeber and other Occupy activists were promoting a lived utopianism. They may not have achieved the specific policies that some of those associated with the movement wanted to demand, such as forgiveness of student loans or the establishment of a global financial transaction tax, but they demonstrated that an alternative, leaderless community animated by the desire for economic justice and principles of mutual aid could survive, at least for a period of weeks, even in the glass and steel canyons of global capitalism's heartland.

⟨━━◈W◈━━⟩

Edward Carpenter had a direct influence on another form of temporary utopian community that was first initiated in the late twentieth century and that continues today: gay men's retreats. On a sunny Sunday in August, I joined a group of two dozen British men for the last day of their annual weeklong summer retreat in Scotland. When they first met, in the 1980s, the event was known simply as Gay Men's Week. Now it has become the Edward Carpenter Community, a group with a mailing list of about eight hundred men that holds several events a year, some at a hostel in the Lake District and others at Laurieston Hall, an intentional community in the Scottish borderlands that rents out space.[56]

I arrived at Laurieston Hall too late to take part in the early-morning meditation group, yoga class, or loch swim that began each day of the retreat, but I joined the line dance group, and before lunch I wandered into the Archers workshop, which turned out to be three men lounging in the living room while listening to a BBC radio soap opera about farmers. They were a bit embarrassed about it—"It's the sort of show our grannies listen to"—but they good-naturedly made room for me on the sofa. For most of the day, I was outdoors, where men took advantage of the unusually warm weather to sunbathe and read and chat.

It turned out that few of the men in the Edward Carpenter Community, or ECC as it's usually known, are familiar with Carpenter's ideas about the "intermediate sex" and its role as utopian vanguard. They know him only as a gay contemporary of Victoria and Albert. But Will, one of the community's founders, said there's nevertheless a utopian dimension to the ECC. The retreats, he said, are about "looking for deeper human relationships." Repeatedly, people told me that they saw the ECC as an alternative to the superficiality and hypersexuality of the commercial gay scene of bars and clubs. "People think a group of gay men getting together in a house for a week would be about rampant sex," Steve, who has been coming to ECC retreats for thirteen years, told me. "But that's not it. It's about being together openly and honestly. This is about dropping the armor. If being gay means competition, clubs, putting on a persona, then I'm not gay—I'm a man who has sex with men. But this is a gay community where men can be themselves."

For a time during the 1980s, the ECC founders thought that they might establish a gay men's intentional community devoted to the simple life, a re-creation of Carpenter's home at Millthorpe. That did not work out, although Peter, a founding member, told me that in the early years of the ECC there was a strong connection to Carpenterian practices such as vegetarianism and sandal-wearing. Now, that has lessened, and men admitted to me that they occasionally escaped the regime of vegetarian meals at Laurieston Hall by ducking out to the nearby town of Castle Douglas for a pork sandwich. Yet the connections to Carpenter and Millthorpe remain. The men at ECC retreats come together to establish, for one week, a cooperative egalitarian community of same-sex-loving men.

{≈≈≈≈}

Carpenter's utopian sexual theorizing has been enormously influential among another group established about the same time as the ECC: the Radical Faeries. The Radical Faeries is a loosely knit group organized around "sanctuaries"—rural retreat spaces throughout the U.S. as well as in Australia, Canada, and France. A few sanctuaries function as year-round intentional communities, while others serve as sites for occasional gatherings.[57] I attended the annual Walt Whitman Gathering at a Faerie sanctuary in Vermont, along with more than one hundred other men, ranging in age from twenty-somethings to seniors. Bambi, one of the Faeries, a big, bearded guy who would look like a lumberjack if lumberjacks wore T-shirts and long skirts, told me that the Whitman gathering was originally called the Memorial Day gathering until one year a faerie showed up with a jarful of dirt from Whitman's gravesite and mentioned that the poet's birthday was May 31. Right then, everyone decided to ditch "Memorial Day"—a holiday constructed around military observances—for a celebration of a figure whom Faeries, from the beginning, regarded as an ancestor.

The late activist intellectual Harry Hay, one of the founders of the Radical Faeries, was very familiar with both Whitman and Carpenter. In an autobiographical reminiscence, he said that his dawning moment of gay consciousness came in 1923, when he was eleven, and the librarian at the local public library left her desk for a period, long enough for him to use her key to open the locked glass case where he'd glimpsed a book titled *The Intermediate Sex*. In Hay's flamboyantly mythicized account, his first reading of Carpenter's book was a "shattering" moment, "full of glitter and glisten and fireworks in my head and tumult of thunder and trumpets in my blood." He'd discovered that he "wasn't the *only* one after all," that there were other boys and men who loved their own sex.[58]

Later, in 1950, Hay cofounded the Mattachine Society, one of the world's first homosexual rights organizations. The Sociétés Mattachines of Renaissance France were groups of unmarried men whose performances at folk festivals satirized the established hierarchy, a carnivalesque Feast of Fools. The name reflected Hay's armchair anthropological theorizing, directly inspired by Carpenter's work. Like Carpenter, he believed that homosexuals had occupied a special role not only in European folk culture but also in traditional tribal societies, serving as honored priests, healers, and artists. Having spent time in the American Southwest as a teenager, working alongside Native Americans, Hay was particularly interested in the Berdache or "Two-Spirit" role among Indians, men who challenged conventional gender roles and frequently served as ritual leaders.

Following the Stonewall uprising of 1969, Hay threw himself into the Gay Liberation movement, but during the 1970s he grew increasingly uneasy with what he called the "dominant Gay Assimilationist Culture." Not for Harry Hay the idea that homosexuals were just like everyone else except for what they did in bed. He proudly declared, "We are a Separate People with . . . a different consciousness which may be triggered into being by our lovely sexuality." Hay's sexual theorizing, like Carpenter's, had a utopian core. He was uninterested in straightforward claims for civil rights. Instead, Hay insisted that gays had unique qualities that, once recognized, could help transform society. The heart of homosexuals' different consciousness was a recognition of the inequality inherent within patriarchy, which led to what Hay called "subject-object" relationships between men and women. Gay people instead created "subject-to-subject relationships of equals." He declared in a manifesto: "What we, a Cultural Minority, a separate Sub-species whose time has come, bring to share with the Hetero Community is this subject-SUBJECT consciousness."[59]

By 1976, Hay was convinced that the gay liberation movement had gone astray. The assimilationist strategy of pursuing equal rights involved turning a blind eye to broader inequalities in society—a stance that Hay, a former Communist and lifelong political radical, could not accept. That year he wrote, "It is time gay liberation regenerates itself into the gay fairy family of loving-sharing equals." Three years later he and three friends issued a call for the first "Spiritual Conference for Radical Fairies," held in Arizona.[60] *Fairy* for Hay was not only a way for gay men to appropriate a term that had been used for decades to belittle them; the word was also

linked to folk myths and rituals and signified the realm of playful
spirituality suppressed by both the dominant culture and gay as-
similationists. He soon changed the spelling to *faerie*, the better to
evoke mythic associations.

That spirit of playfulness, love of myth and ritual, and openness
to cosmopolitan spirituality was evident at the Whitman gathering
in Vermont. I'd heard that the Faeries were into cross-dressing, but
that's only partially true. Half of the men who had gathered on the
rural mountaintop wore jeans and T-shirts. The other half wore
outfits that looked as if they'd been put together from raids on
their mothers' closets, the local Salvation Army, and a theatrical
costume shop. Endora—a Faerie name; many but not all participants choose one—complemented his heavy black beard with a pink
and red dress. Later in the day, for a change of costume, he added
a padded red brassiere on top of the dress. Wave wore high boots,
black tights with a white codpiece, a striped shirt, and a black hat
with an enormous rakish brim; the effect was a swashbuckling cross
between Romeo and Bluebeard. Many, like Bambi, wore T-shirts
with a skirt or kilt. No one was trying to look like a woman. Rather,
men were playing with gendered conventions, challenging notions
of masculinity, and giving into the delight in dress-up that is social-
ized out of most males by adolescence.

During the day, men worked in the garden, went skinny dipping
in the nearby river, and enjoyed the unexpectedly warm sun. They
also attended informal workshops. Before lunch, I participated in a
shamanic spirit session, where we were encouraged to connect with
an animal spirit guide. Afterward, there were talks about Walt Whitman and Edward Carpenter. The Radical Faeries attract a fair number of intellectuals, and the talks drew a large crowd of men who
chatted knowledgeably about Whitman, Carpenter, and Harry Hay.
But the Radical Faeries are not principally a discussion group. The
Faeries gather to dress up, have fun in the outdoors, and participate
in rituals that aim to connect participants to the earth, to gay ancestors, and to one another. A highlight of the Whitman gathering is a
nighttime ritual in which participants move from one informal
shrine to another scattered across the mountaintop while reciting
portions of Whitman's verse, a celebratory gay version of walking
the Stations of the Cross.

Sociologist Peter Hennen has analyzed Faerie culture using Max Weber's theory of "re-enchantment," arguing that the Faeries are making a "deliberate attempt to revive and nurture a magical community of meaning in the wake of late capitalism's increasing rationalization."[61] Faeries are highly conscious of building not only alternative communities but also alternative families; the standard greeting to newcomers is "Welcome home."

Faerie culture has a significant anarchist dimension, and at morning gathering Calamus, one of the event's organizers, talked about Emma Goldman and her anarchist ideals of community without hierarchy. Like other contemporary partial utopians, most Radical Faeries don't use the word "utopia," but Faerie sanctuaries are temporary utopias of equality and simplicity based in an earth-centered humanistic spirituality. For most Faeries, gatherings no doubt function principally as a retreat, a safe space apart from the world at large, but a number of men talked to me about the ripple effect, how they carried the spirit of Faerie gatherings back into the world. Those familiar with Harry Hay said they agreed with his notion that gay culture has special gifts to offer to the larger society, and Endora wrote me after the event that he believes that "faeries are Utopian in similar ways to Carpenter—that queer folks have an evolutionary and specific role to play in human history."[62]

EDUCATION

Education is at the heart of all utopian imagining. Utopia depends on the notion of human plasticity, the idea that humans can be, if not perfected, then at least brought closer to an ideal. Full-blown utopian fictions tend to suggest that once economic and political institutions are transformed, human beings will change along utopian lines, and a transformed educational system will ensure that successive generations maintain and improve utopian social structures. But one powerful strand of partial utopianism maintains that the way to change society as a whole is through education: transformed human beings will create the society of the future.

Among the last utopians, only Bellamy and Morris described in detail their ideal educational system. A large chunk of Bellamy's *Equality*, the sequel to *Looking Backward*, is set in a school. It's a grim place. Children rise, one after another, to recite improbably long and articulate defenses of Nationalist ideology. Just as Bellamy was unable to imagine an alternative to the Victorian nuclear family, he was incapable of envisioning a school that did anything beyond perfecting the most inflexible features of nineteenth-century pedagogy. Morris's imagination roamed farther. In his utopia, schools as such have been abolished, and the people of utopia are unfamiliar with the word *education*. As for learning, that's a different matter. Dick boasts to Guest that all the children learn to swim and ride and cook, and most of them can do useful tasks such as thatching and carpentering and mowing. Under prodding, he adds that children learn to read simply from having so many books lying about. Once able to read, they can easily teach themselves whatever else they want to know without formal schooling.

Morris's ideas about education anticipated the child-centered approaches of major twentieth-century educational progressives such as Maria Montessori, John Dewey, and A. S. Neill, the founder of Summerhill. The philosophy of all three contains a strong utopian dimension, but the person most successful in creating a system of education along Morrisian lines was the eccentric Austrian philosopher Rudolf Steiner, founder of the Waldorf schools. Steiner, born into a working-class family in 1861, developed his ideas independently of the progressive philosophical movements that nurtured his contemporaries Montessori and Dewey. The most powerful influence on the young Steiner was Theosophy, the occult religious movement begun in 1875 by the charismatic Russian Helena Blavatsky. Theosophy, one of the most successful new religious movements of the nineteenth century, attracted people dissatisfied with the scientific rationalism of industrial modernity. It challenged materialist views of reality with an emphasis on mystical apprehension and an insistence on the divine unity of humanity and the natural world. Steiner served as leader of the German Theosophical Society for twelve years until a dispute with Blavatsky's successor, Annie Besant, led him to resign and to begin elaborating his own system of spiritual philosophy, which he dubbed Anthroposophy.[63]

Anthroposophy was only incidentally a philosophy of education. Steiner saw it as a comprehensive system of thought that could ultimately transform all of society, and he initiated anthroposophical systems of medicine, agriculture, architecture, and the arts. He laid out his basic educational theories in a 1907 essay, "The Education of the Child in the Light of Spiritual Science." His idiosyncratic view of psychology relied on the medieval theory of the four humours, but his theory of child development prefigured, albeit in a non-empirical fashion, Jean Piaget's later work. Steiner believed that children went through three "births": the second occurred around age seven, when they lost their milk teeth, and the third seven years later, at puberty. He classified the first seven years of life as the period of will, the next seven as the time of feeling, and the third as the age of thought, and he argued that schools need to take account of the child's unfolding faculties.[64]

In 1919 a wealthy anthroposophist, owner of the Waldorf-Astoria cigarette factory in Stuttgart, invited Steiner to start a school based on his theories. The first Waldorf school opened its doors that fall, with 191 children of factory employees and 65 children whose parents were well-off followers of Steiner. It quickly attracted attention as one of the most successful progressive schools in Europe. The Stuttgart Waldorf school, which enrolled children across twelve grade levels, was the only comprehensive school in Germany open to children from all social classes; at the time, fewer than 10 percent of German students attended secondary school. Steiner abolished grades and educational tracking and brought girls and boys together in a school that offered all children an equal education and that was run not by a top-down hierarchy but by a council of teachers. Other Waldorf schools soon opened in Germany and, by the end of the 1920s, there were Waldorf schools throughout Europe, in England, and in the United States.[65]

Currently there are more than a thousand Waldorf schools worldwide, with 136 in the United States and 30 in Great Britain.[66] The Waldorf school near where I live, like the majority, enrolls children from prekindergarten through eighth grade. During the two days that I spent at the school, talking to multiple students and teachers and parents, I didn't hear any references to Anthroposophy, and Steiner himself insisted that there should be no indoctrination. Instead, the adults talked about the three stages of childhood and

Steiner's emphasis on educating the hands and heart as well as the head. The attention to hands is the most obvious and distinctive feature of Waldorf education. Like the children of Morris's utopia, Waldorf students devote large portions of their day to arts and craftwork. "No man can be a real philosopher who cannot darn his socks," Steiner said, and Waldorf schools take him literally.[67] In a fifth grade handwork class, boys and girls were knitting colorful socks. I also observed children carving linoleum blocks, singing, cooking, gardening, and dancing.

The children I spoke with had little idea of Steiner's educational theories, but they enjoyed being in a school that puts as much emphasis on arts and crafts, music and movement, as on arithmetic and reading. None had heard of William Morris, but they were receiving an education that Morris, who hated his schooling at Marlborough and Oxford, might have enjoyed. Morris was dismayed by the way that schools replicated the hierarchical divisions of nineteenth-century society, not only separating social classes but dividing individuals' intellectual and creative faculties. Morris wanted a world in which everyone could be both artist and worker, in which thatching a roof or mowing a field was valued as much as painting a canvas or translating Homer. Morris died decades before Waldorf schools began promoting education of the head, heart, and hands, but he might well have recognized the slogan's utopian aptness.[68] Jennifer Rosenstein, one of the teachers, told me, "There's a transformational impulse behind Waldorf education. It arose in Germany in 1919, just after Europe had experienced this terrible war. Steiner was asking, 'How can we create an education so that generations to come won't be led into another war like this?'" When the Nazis came to power in the 1930s, they recognized the transformative potential of Waldorf schools and shut them down. "Education toward freedom" is a Waldorf catchphrase, a sentiment that did not sit well with Nazi ideologues. Peter Sheen, another teacher, said ardently, "We're not educating for today but for tomorrow." The success of Waldorf schools suggests that he is not the only person who imagines that in a transformed future, more boys and girls might be spending part of their school days dancing or knitting socks or carefully lifting worms out of a compost bin in order to spread the rich humus underneath the tomato plants.

FOOD

The first utopia was a garden. The myth of Eden has persisted for millennia, its image of ease amidst beauty and plenty a perpetual lure. With Plato arose a competing myth, the *polis*, or ideal city, an image of perfect order that Thomas More adopted for *Utopia*, with its geography of identical symmetrical cities, and that Edward Bellamy drew on for his vision of a futuristic Boston. An intellectual tension between Eden and the ideal city has existed throughout the history of utopian thought, though the garden seemed more attractive to all the last utopians save Bellamy. Edward Carpenter's self-sufficient smallholding at Millthorpe served as a utopian ideal to a generation of cultural progressives dismayed by the mechanization and specialization of modernity.[69]

During the early twentieth century, with the development of a process for the production of synthetic nitrogen fertilizers, industrial modernity's conquest of the garden began in earnest. The combination of increased mechanization, new hybrid seeds, and chemical fertilizers, pesticides, and herbicides revolutionized agriculture worldwide. In 1935, 25 percent of Americans lived on the nation's 6.8 million farms; now that's down to under 2 percent of the population on just over 2 million farms.[70] Yields, particularly for commodity crops, increased dramatically. To take corn as an example, in 1900 one acre yielded 25 bushels; now it's 120 bushels.[71] Unquestionably, the industrialization of agriculture has a utopian dimension, with its vision of science and technology vastly increasing productivity, eliminating hunger, and enabling millions of people to escape the hardships of farmwork. Techno-utopians point to the fact that in 1940 the average American farmer fed 19 people, while today each farmer feeds 129 fellow citizens.[72] Meanwhile, the price of food has fallen dramatically, and the average American household spends under 10 percent of its income on food, less than half of what it spent only fifty years ago.[73]

The dystopian dimensions of the industrial food system have become increasingly clear, however. The environmental consequences of what one critic has called the regime of "chemotherapy on the land" have been profound, poisoning lakes and waterways and decimating wildlife.[74] Moreover, the system is heavily reliant on cheap oil: the American food system uses almost one-fifth of the nation's fossil fuel energy, which comes out to four hundred gallons of oil per person each year.[75] Cheap food also comes at the cost of animal welfare, with millions of chickens, pigs, and cattle confined in appalling conditions that, inevitably, lead to pathogens in the food system which kill children and the elderly.[76] Food system workers are routinely exploited and abused, exposed to dangerous machinery and toxic chemicals.[77] Consumers' health has also been affected by the spread of cheap fast food, with dramatic spikes in chronic diseases linked to diet, including obesity, type 2 diabetes, heart disease, stroke, and at least a third of all cancers.[78] Finally, industrial agriculture has devastated rural life, emptying out small towns, enriching a few large corporations and landowners, while forcing most farmers into grinding cycles of indebtedness.[79]

In response to this environmental, animal, and human devastation, a number of alternative food movements have arisen in the U.S. and U.K. in recent decades. These movements are diverse, focusing variously on the environment, public health, animal welfare, workers' rights, and gastronomy.[80] The most visible of the food movements is the campaign for local, sustainable food that was inaugurated in the 1970s by the Americans Frances Moore Lappé, Wendell Berry, and Alice Waters. Lappé, author of *Diet for a Small Planet* (1971), advocated a vegetarian diet that, she argued, could not only improve consumers' health but heal the environment, protect animals, and lead to a more just global economy. Berry, a Kentucky poet and farmer, issued a series of manifestos that called for the nation to return to its Jeffersonian, agrarian roots of small, independent farmers. Waters set off a culinary revolution when she established Chez Panisse, her Berkeley, California, restaurant that relied on local, high-quality suppliers. Through her books and public activism, she became the godmother of the farm-to-table movement, helped provide the intellectual underpinnings of the international Slow Food movement, and was instrumental in establishing the school gardens that are now widespread across the U.S. and U.K.[81]

The sustainable food movement inspired by Lappé, Berry, and Waters has achieved striking successes. Direct, local sales by farmers are the fastest-growing sector of the food industry. Since the 1990s, the number of U.S. farmers' markets has increased almost five times, while community supported agriculture (CSA), which involves farmers selling directly to consumers, increased from two U.S. farms in 1986 to over twelve thousand farms in 2012; total direct sales from farmers to individuals totaled over \$3 billion in the same year.[82]

Statistics, however, cannot convey the utopianism that pervades the sustainable food movement. Movement activists, both farmers and consumers, enact some of the same values that animated the last utopians. The thousands of high-minded, well-educated young people who have turned to sustainable farming as a career are engaged in the sort of simple-life idealism that turned Cambridge don Edward Carpenter into a Derbyshire market gardener. Millions of farmers and consumers are working to create small-scale local economies and build a sense of community through their participation in farmers' markets and CSAs. Profoundly influenced by the movement for gender equality, they have rejected the notion of farming as men's work; there are nearly one million women farmers in the U.S., 30 percent of the total.[83] In addition, many are inspired by an earth-centered spirituality that sacralizes the land and invests farm labor with a sense of higher purpose.

As fully as the activists in the Occupy movement, participants in the sustainable local food movement—ranging from farmers to occasional diners at farm-to-table restaurants—are engaging in prefigurative politics and lived utopianism, enacting a portion of a transformed future in the here and now. The movement's generally implicit utopianism is explicitly expressed in the intense lyricism of some of its most popular texts, such as Barbara Kingsolver's *Animal, Vegetable, Miracle* (2007), which invests her family's Virginia farm with the same lush exoticism that nineteenth-century travelers bestowed on tropical Polynesia.

Food activists' often fervent utopian rhetoric has provoked a backlash, with three principal criticisms leveled at the sustainable local food movement. The first is that the movement's overwhelmingly white and middle-class activists are oblivious to the ways in which their racial and class positions shape their perspectives.[84] Another common criticism is that organic agriculture cannot be productive enough to feed the entire planet.[85] Finally, critics charge that "Vote with Your Fork"—a food movement slogan popularized by Michael Pollan—promotes feel-good consumerism but neglects the hard work of political change. In a witty food movement take-down, Nicholas Sabloff sums up this critique: "Sooner or later, politics, in all its incremental and often unappetizing details, will have to take a seat at the table if the food movement is ever going to serve up something greater than personal satisfaction for the few who can afford it."[86]

All three critiques have some validity. The first, however, ignores the way in which the 1970s food movement—populated largely by participants in the decade's overwhelmingly white, middle-class counterculture—spawned multiple twenty-first-century food movements, many with leadership and members composed primarily of people of color. The urban gardening movement, for example, arose in response to the existence of "food deserts," areas without easy access to fresh foods or even to a conventional grocery store. Will Allen, one of the movement's American leaders, left his career as a professional basketball player to buy a derelict plant nursery in Milwaukee's largely African American north side and established a large garden that provided food and jobs to people in the community—an effort that led to a MacArthur "genius" grant for Allen and that inspired the creation of thousands of urban gardens across the U.S.[87] Or consider La Via Campesina (Spanish for "the way of the peasant"), an organization that claims to represent some two hundred million people worldwide and that promotes the concept of "food sovereignty," challenging corporate hegemony and strengthening local, democratically controlled food systems.[88]

Food movement critics who argue that it is impossible to feed the world's seven billion people exclusively through organic agriculture have a point, but they conflate "organic" and "sustainable" agriculture, as if the two were identical. In fact, many proponents of sustainability recognize that organic agriculture—particularly the version regulated by rigid U.S. standards—is only one version of sustainable farming and acknowledge that it is impractical for much of the world. Instead, they argue that different food systems are needed in different locations, and that there are multiple paths to sustainability, including the thoughtful, limited use of new seed varieties and of chemical fertilizers and pesticides. A massive, years-long study of agricultural technology, begun in 2002 by the World Bank and the United Nations, concluded that a shift in the current technological paradigm was called for and that food insecurity could be addressed at the same time as both developed and developing countries adopt sustainable agricultural systems.[89]

Finally, it is fair to say that many food movement activists are not politically engaged, but only if the "political" is narrowly defined. Certainly, electoral politics and government policymaking play a crucial role in the future of food. Wenonah Hauter, executive director of Food and Water Watch, is an especially articulate proponent of this view, and her book *Foodopoly* argues that in order to break up the corporate-controlled industrial food system, activists need to turn their attention to overhauling the Farm Bill, revising antitrust regulations, and agitating for a constitutional amendment to overturn the Supreme Court's *Citizens United* decision, which allows corporations to make unlimited contributions to political campaigns.[90] Hauter's policy-oriented agenda is crucial, but it is also, taken alone, uninspiring. The most powerfully appealing aspect of the sustainable local food movement is that it is not focused solely on long-term goals but is anchored in the immediately pleasurable present—in the earthy smell and deep scarlet of a freshly picked heirloom tomato, the unctuous texture of a goat's milk cheese, the intense aroma of fried bacon from a locally raised pig, or the hoppy tang of a craft-brewed beer. The acts of growing, protecting, and consuming local foods belong, in part, to the world of Cokaygne, the medieval utopia of purely sensuous pleasure, but they are also forms of prefigurative politics, enacting everyday utopias of shared delight.

Such everyday utopias are as close as a nearby farmers' market— or perhaps as close as a rundown block in the heart of Trenton, New Jersey, a once-thriving industrial city that is now one of America's poorest urban centers. I spent a Saturday morning working in Trenton's Gandhi Garden, a community garden established in a vacant lot by a group of artists who rented studio space in the building next door. When the artists moved into the building on East Hanover Street, the lot was littered with abandoned automobile tires. They decided to make sustainable art out of this unpromising medium, and I spent much of the morning stacking tires and filling them with a mixture of topsoil and compost to make rubber-ziggurat planters.

During a break, I talked with Will "Kasso" Condry, a graffiti artist who painted the colorful mural that gives the garden its name: a giant representation of Gandhi, framed by a cityscape, is featured next to the apocryphal quotation, "You must be the change you wish to see in the world." Condry, a Trenton native, is a big, solidly built African American man in his thirties with hip black-framed glasses and a ready smile. I asked him why he and the other artists decided to start a garden. "Well, a garden is about rebirth, renewal, rejuvenation, isn't it? I think of us as alchemists, turning crap into gold. I have to admit, I'm not a born gardener. My father had a garden, but I hated when he made me work in it. Now it's different. If you can grow your own food, that's power. We're showing people in the neighborhood that you can rely on yourselves. Plus, gardening forces you to organize with other people to get things done."

Condry is one of an increasing number of urban gardeners who see their plots not just as oases amidst asphalt or a cheap source of good food but as a locus of empowerment, a means for creating self-reliant communities. Inner cities, food activists argue, have a special interest in creating a better food system as a way to combat low-income food deserts where fresh fruits and vegetables are hard to find but corporate-supplied junk food is abundant.

Bronx resident Pam Phillips brings a broad political perspective to her food activism. I met Phillips at a food justice workshop held as part of a Barnard College conference on women and utopia. When Phillips and co-organizer Gwen Beetham opened the event by announcing that there were cupcakes available on a table at the back, a stampede ensued. As people returned to their seats, Phillips and Beetham held up a package of Little Debbie cupcakes in order to make a point: the modestly sized cupcakes on the back table, from an organic, artisanal bakery in lower Manhattan, cost $2.45 each. The two enormous cupcakes encased in a Little Debbie wrapper sold for $1.99 at a local bodega. Phillips explained, "We don't have organic cupcakes in my neighborhood. What we have in abundance are pizza joints, Chinese restaurants, liquor stores, and bodegas that sell junk food like Little Debbie." As a graduate student at the New School, Phillips had one foot in the academy and the other in community activism. "In my neighborhood," she explained, "people don't know the terms 'food inequality' or 'food justice.' People don't put a label on what they're experiencing. But they're living it." Few people in Phillips's community were food activists, but she believed in the possibility that they could one day be part of a better, fairer, more sustainable, and more delicious food system.

CODA

The question that he frames in all but words
Is what to make of a diminished thing.

—ROBERT FROST[91]

One hundred years after the publication of *Herland*, the final significant work by one of the last utopians, utopianism itself is, to borrow Robert Frost's phrase, "a diminished thing." During the quarter-century before World War I, utopian fiction flourished, and millions of people were familiar with the utopian visions of Edward Bellamy and his peers. Now utopianism has to be sought out at the cultural margins—at a rural commune, a protest encampment, a private school, a community garden. And the question remains whether this sort of partial utopianism can be considered utopian at all. Tom Moylan argues that utopian thought is necessarily "totalizing"; the speculative analysis needed to work out how society could be reconfigured "requires that the entire system, in all its interlocking parts, be taken into account."[92] If the only utopian visions are total ones, then utopian thinking in the twenty-first century is moribund.

Yet perhaps the most important feature of the contemporary utopianism traced here is its wariness of totalizing visions. Like Bellamy, Morris, Carpenter, and Gilman, these contemporary utopians are committed to economic justice and gender and sexual equality; they want a simpler life of fulfilling labor in a community that exists in harmony with the natural world; and they are committed to realizing their goals through nonviolent, democratic processes. They are distrustful, however, of the uniformity that accompanied their nineteenth-century predecessors' grand visions, the certainty that everyone shares the same desires, the downplaying—or denial—of difference.

Contemporary partial utopianism is more modest in its claims, more sensitive to human variety. It is also more open to a charge leveled against Morris and Carpenter—that of nostalgia. All of the contemporary movements I've traced might be accused of having one eye on a rose-tinted past, of longing for a time when small farmers and their families worked the land under unpolluted skies, when large numbers of people lived in tight-knit communities of equals. The accusation of nostalgia can serve as a conversation stopper, signifying the naïve embrace of an imagined past. As Charles Maier wittily put it, "Nostalgia is to longing as kitsch is to art"—that is, a crude attempt to craft a shapely product designed to appeal to a broad and undiscerning audience.[93]

Cultural theorist Svetlana Boym argues, however, that nostalgia comes in two very different varieties. "Restorative nostalgia" is the dangerous effort to impose on the present an idealized conception of the past, to shape an entire society in line with a shared dream of a simple and harmonious bygone era. The Nazis' vision of a Thousand-Year Reich involved restorative nostalgia, as did the Kampuchea imagined by the Khmer Rouge. More recent and less brutal nostalgic projects of national restoration include the efforts to "Make America Great Again" and, in the U.K., to "take back control" from the European Union. Yet politically significant nostalgia need not involve the imposition of a crudely simplified version of the past. Boym identified what she called "reflective nostalgia," a flexible and dynamic mode of thought that looks to the past for practices that can be adapted to bring about a better future. Boym contested the idea that nostalgic longing and critical thinking are mutually exclusive. The past, she noted, can open up "a multitude of potentialities."[94] Architects of co-housing developments look beyond the suburban sprawl of contemporary America to less affluent urban neighborhoods of a century ago in which residents shared common space, if only an alley, and pooled resources to get by. The Radical Faeries construct rituals inspired by a past when, they believe, same-sex-loving men and women were respected as priests and healers. Waldorf educators look to a time when children were integrated into the daily activities of largely self-sufficient households, joining in gardening and cooking and mending; but, drawing on modern conceptions of gender equality, they engage both boys and girls in those tasks. Food movement activists take inspiration from a past of small farms and backyard gardens, adapting older practices to suit an urbanized society.

In a brief, provocative essay, political theorist Norman Geras has argued that utopian dreaming is essential because "the realities of our time are morally intolerable."[95] That is, we manage to get on with our daily routines only because we live with moral blinders in place. Otherwise, we couldn't bear to read the daily news, with its tales of poverty and war and police brutality, its warnings of global climate change and reports of mass incarceration, its stories of violence against women and LGBTQ people, its transcriptions of the nakedly racist and nativist rhetoric permeating political discourse. The last utopians refused moral blinders. Their defamiliarizing stories and poems exposed the intolerable realities of their day and offered visions of a transformed future.

Contemporary partial utopians are living out possibilities for a transformed future in their communities, their schools, and their everyday lives. Edward Bellamy, William Morris, Edward Carpenter, and Charlotte Perkins Gilman believed fervently in the transformative possibilities of the utopian imagination. They understood that utopianism is essential to society, that without it, we're reduced to resigned acceptance of a morally intolerable status quo. Their contemporary heirs live in a moment when powerful political optimism is in short supply. Yet what was true during the last utopians' era is true today: visions of a transformed world, along with efforts to live out some portion of it in the here and now, are crucial to a better future.

Introduction

1. See Karl Marx, *The Communist Manifesto* (1848; New York: Norton, 1988), 75–85; Friedrich Engels, *Socialism: Utopian and Scientific* (1880; New York: International Publishers, 1935).

2. See chapter 1 for a discussion of nineteenth-century Fourierist and Owenite communities.

3. Henry George, *Progress and Poverty* (San Francisco: W. M. Hinton, 1879); Marie Howland, *Papa's Own Girl* (New York: J. P. Jewett, 1874); Ismar Thiusen [John Macnie], *The Diothas; or, A Far Look Ahead* (New York: G. P. Putnam's Sons, 1883).

4. See Lyman Tower Sargent, *British and American Utopian Literature, 1516–1985: An Annotated, Chronological Bibliography* (New York: Garland, 1988).

5. *The Collected Letters of William Morris*, ed. Norman Kelvin (Princeton: Princeton University Press, 1987), 2:353.

6. My definition of "utopia" is shaped by numerous authors, particularly by Jay Winter's discussion of transformational political thinking in *Dreams of Peace and Freedom: Utopian Moments in the Twentieth Century* (New Haven: Yale University Press, 2005) and by Lyman Tower Sargent's definition of utopianism as the transformation of the everyday in *Utopianism: A Very Short Introduction* (Oxford: Oxford University Press, 2010).

7. Zygmunt Bauman, *Socialism: The Active Utopia* (New York: Holmes & Meier, 1976), is a powerful theoretical exploration of the links between socialism and utopia. Two important secondary sources for understanding British socialism in this period are Stanley Pierson, *British Socialists: The Journey from Fantasy to Politics* (Cambridge: Harvard University Press, 1979); and Stephen Yeo, "A New Life: The Religion of Socialism in Britain, 1883–1896," *History Workshop* 4 (1977): 5–56. These can be supplemented with Mark Bevir, *The Making of British Socialism* (Princeton: Princeton University Press, 2011); and Anna Vaninskaya, *William Morris and the Idea of Community: Romance, History and Propaganda, 1880–1914* (Edinburgh: Edinburgh University Press, 2010). A good starting point for research on non-Marxist U.S. socialism is Nick Salvatore, *Eugene V. Debs: Citizen and Socialist* (Urbana: University of Illinois Press, 1982).

8. Barbara Taylor, *Eve and the New Jerusalem: Socialism and Feminism in the Nineteenth Century* (New York: Pantheon, 1983), is a classic study of the links between socialism, utopianism, and feminism.

9. On nineteenth-century post-Christian liberal spirituality, see Leigh E. Schmidt, *Restless Souls: The Making of American Spirituality* (New York: HarperSanFrancisco, 2005); and *American Religious Liberalism*, ed. Leigh E. Schmidt and Sally M. Promey

(Bloomington: Indiana University Press, 2012). On the religion of socialism, see Yeo, "A New Life."

10. Edward Carpenter, "A Note on 'Towards Democracy,'" in *Towards Democracy* (New York: Mitchell Kennerley, 1922), xix–xx. On the simple life, see David E. Shi, *The Simple Life: Plain Living and High Thinking in American Culture* (New York: Oxford University Press, 1985).

11. Richard Powers, *Three Farmers on Their Way to a Dance* (New York: William Morrow, 1985), 44.

12. See Eric D. Weitz, *A Century of Genocide: Utopias of Race and Nation* (Princeton: Princeton University Press, 2015).

13. K. R. Popper, *The Open Society and Its Enemies*, vol. 1: *The Spell of Plato* (London: Routledge, 1945), 138–48.

14. John Gray, *Black Mass: Apocalyptic Religion and the Death of Utopia* (New York: Farrar, Straus and Giroux, 2007), 17; Frédéric Rouvillois, "Utopia and Totalitarianism," in *Utopia: The Search for the Ideal Society in the Western World*, ed. Roland Schaer, Gregory Claeys, and Lyman Tower Sargent (New York: New York Public Library and Oxford University Press, 2000), 331.

15. G. D. H. Cole, introduction to *Stories in Prose, Stories in Verse, Shorter Poems, Lectures and Essays*, by William Morris (London: Nonesuch Press, 1934), xvi.

16. Margaret Atwood, the *MaddAddam* trilogy (*Oryx and Crake* [New York: Nan A. Talese, 2003]; *The Year of the Flood* [New York: Nan A. Talese, 2009]; *MaddAddam* [New York: Nan A. Talese, 2013]); Gary Shteyngart, *Super Sad True Love Story* (New York: Random House, 2010); Howard Jacobson, *J* (London: Jonathan Cape, 2014).

17. I adapt the term *lived utopianism* from religious studies, in which *lived religion* has been an important field of study since the late 1980s; see *Lived Religion in America*, ed. David D. Hall (Princeton: Princeton University Press, 1997). Tom Moylan uses the term in "To Stand with Dreamers: On the Use Value of Utopia," *Irish Review* 34 (2006): 1–19. My articulation of lived utopianism is influenced by Sheila Rowbotham, *Edward Carpenter: A Life of Liberty and Love* (London: Verso, 2008), 105.

18. Davina Cooper, *Everyday Utopias: The Conceptual Life of Promising Spaces* (Durham: Duke University Press, 2014), 9, 82, 3.

19. See Susan M. Matarese, *American Foreign Policy and the Utopian Imagination* (Amherst: University of Massachusetts Press, 2001); Thomas Peyser, *Utopia and Cosmopolis: Globalization in the Era of American Literary Realism* (Durham, NC: Duke University Press, 1998); Jean Pfaelzer, *The Utopian Novel in America, 1886–1896* (Pittsburgh: University of Pittsburgh Press, 1984); Kenneth M. Roemer, *The Obsolete Necessity: America in Utopian Literature, 1888–1900* (Kent, OH: Kent State University Press, 1976); and Robert Francis Shor, *Utopianism and Radicalism in a Reforming America, 1888–1918* (Westport, CT: Greenwood, 1997).

20. Despite their titles, Dohra Ahmad's *Landscapes of Hope: Anti-Colonial Utopianism in America* (New York: Oxford University Press, 2009) and Matthew Beaumont's *Utopia Ltd.: Ideologies of Social Dreaming in England, 1870–1900* (Leiden: Brill, 2005) treat both American and British writing, as does Beaumont's *The Spectre*

of Utopia: Utopian and Science Fictions at the Fin de Siècle (Oxford: Peter Lang, 2012). Chris Ferns's *Narrating Utopia: Ideology, Gender, Form in Utopian Literature* (Liverpool: Liverpool University Press, 1999) stretches from the Renaissance to the late twentieth century but devotes special attention to Bellamy, Morris, Gilman, and their contemporaries. Krishan Kumar's *Utopia and Anti-Utopia in Modern Times* (Oxford: Basil Blackwell, 1987) is a massive and masterly study of the period from 1888 through the 1970s, prefaced by a lengthy survey of utopian writing from its beginnings in the classical era.

21. Ahmad, *Landscapes of Hope*, 68.

22. Stanley Pierson discusses Carpenter and utopianism in "Edward Carpenter: Prophet of a Socialist Millennium," *Victorian Studies* 13 (1970): 301–18.

23. Milan Šimečka, "A World with Utopias or without Them?" in *Utopias*, ed. Peter Alexander and Roger Gill (London: Duckworth, 1984), 175; Lucy Sargisson, "The Curious Relationship between Politics and Utopia," in *Utopia Method Vision: The Use Value of Social Dreaming*, ed. Tom Moylan and Raffaelle Baccolini (Oxford: Peter Lang, 2007), 31; Karl Mannheim, *Ideology and Utopia* (1936; London: Routledge, 1997), 192.

24. Ernst Bloch, *The Principle of Hope*, trans. Neville Plaice, Stephen Plaice, and Paul Knight, 3 vols. (1954–59; Cambridge: MIT Press, 1986).

25. Oscar Wilde, "The Soul of Man under Socialism" (1891), in *The Soul of Man under Socialism and Selected Critical Prose*, ed. Linda Dowling (London: Penguin, 2001), 141.

Chapter One. Locating Nowhere

1. Mark Bevir, *The Making of British Socialism* (Princeton: Princeton University Press, 2011), 36–38; *Charles Booth's London*, ed. Albert Fried and Richard M. Elman (New York: Pantheon, 1968); B. Seebohm Rowntree, *Poverty: A Study of Town Life* (1901; New York: Garland, 1980); Gordon M. Fisher, "From Hunter to Orshansky: An Overview of (Unofficial) Poverty Lines in the United States from 1904 to 1965," U.S. Census Bureau, October 1993, revised August 1997, www.census.gov/hhes/povmeas/publications/povthres/fisher4.html#N_1_.

2. Robert Blatchford, *Dismal England* (1899; New York: Garland, 1984), 102; Jacob A. Riis, *How the Other Half Lives* (1890; New York: Dover, 1971), 41.

3. Nell Painter provides a vivid overview of American labor strife from 1877 through World War I in *Standing at Armageddon: The United States, 1877-1919* (New York: Norton, 1987), 1–71. Two books focus on the year of the Great Strike: Robert V. Bruce, *1877: Year of Violence* (Indianapolis: Bobbs-Merrill, 1959); and Michael A. Bellesiles, *1877: The Year of Living Violently* (New York: New Press, 2010). Numerous works have focused on Haymarket and the Great Upheaval; two of the best are Paul Avrich, *The Haymarket Tragedy* (Princeton: Princeton University Press, 1984); and James R. Green, *Death in the Haymarket* (New York: Pantheon, 2006).

4. H. M. Hyndman quoted in Gareth Stedman Jones, *Outcast London* (Oxford: Oxford University Press, 1971), 345; "Howells to James," October 10, 1888, in *Letters,*

Fictions, Lives: Henry James and William Dean Howells, ed. Michael Anesko (New York: Oxford University Press, 1997), 272.

5. John Tosh, *A Man's Place: Masculinity and the Middle-Class Home in Victorian England* (New Haven: Yale University Press, 1999), 8.

6. Frank E. Manuel and Fritzie P. Manuel, *Utopian Thought in the Western World* (Cambridge: Harvard University Press, 1979), 24.

7. Karl Kautsky, *Thomas More and His Utopia*, trans. H. J. Stenning (1888; London: A. & C. Black, 1927), 170; Thomas More, *Utopia*, trans. Paul Turner (New York: Penguin, 2003), 25. Turner's highly colloquial translation replaces More's Utopian proper names, such as *Hythloday* and *Anyder*, with English equivalents, such as *Nonsenso* and *Nowater*. A more conventional translation, with the Latin text and excellent scholarly apparatus, can be found in the 1995 Cambridge University Press edition edited by George M. Logan, Robert M. Adams, and Clarence H. Miller; see also Logan's fine Norton Critical Edition (New York, 2011).

8. More, *Utopia*, trans. Turner, 5.

9. Desmond Lee uses the phrase "magnificent myth" in his translation of *The Republic* (New York: Penguin, 2003), 115.

10. Krishan Kumar, *Utopianism* (Minneapolis: University of Minnesota Press, 1991), 1–19.

11. Two collections of utopian literature offer selections from Hesiod and most of the other writers mentioned: *The Faber Book of Utopias*, ed. John Carey (London: Faber & Faber, 1999); and *The Utopia Reader*, ed. Gregory Claeys and Lyman Tower Sargent (New York: New York University Press, 1999). The quotation from *Works and Days* is from *Faber*, 9.

12. See J. F. C. Harrison, "Millennium and Utopia," in *Utopias*, ed. Peter Alexander and Roger Gill (London: Duckworth, 1984), 61–66; and Ernest Tuveson, *Millennium and Utopia: A Study in the Background of the Idea of Progress* (New York: Harper & Row, 1964).

13. "The Land of Cokaygne," trans. A. L. Morton, in Morton, *The English Utopia* (London: Lawrence & Wishart, 1952), 218, 220; "The Big Rock Candy Mountain," in Marie Louise Berneri, *Journey through Utopia* (London: Routledge & Kegan Paul, 1950), 318.

14. More, *Utopia*, trans. Turner, 56.

15. Ruskin quoted in Arthur F. Kinney, *Humanist Poetics: Thought, Rhetoric, and Fiction in Sixteenth-Century England* (Amherst: University of Massachusetts Press, 1986), 86; Stephen Duncombe, "Introduction," *The Open Utopia*, accessed May 15, 2017, http://theopenutopia.org/full-text/introduction-open-utopia.

16. Tomasso Campanella, *The City of the Sun*, trans. Daniel J. Donno (Berkeley: University of California Press, 1981).

17. Francis Bacon, "New Atlantis," in *Francis Bacon: The Major Works*, ed. Brian Vickers (Oxford: Oxford University Press, 2002), 480. My contrast between *New Atlantis* and *City of the Sun* is quite different from the Manuels' interpretation of seventeenth-century utopianism, which stresses these works' similarities; see *Utopian Thought*, 205–21, 243–88.

18. Louis-Sebastien Mercier, *Memoirs of the Year Two Thousand Five Hundred*,

trans. W. Hooper (Richmond, VA: N. Pritchard, 1799); Mercier's eighteenth-century English translator explains in his preface that he thought it preferable to round up Mercier's title date of 2440. On Mercier, see Robert Darnton, *The Forbidden Best-Sellers of Pre-Revolutionary France* (New York: Norton, 1995), 118–36.

19. Chris Jennings, *Paradise Now: The Story of American Utopianism* (New York: Random House, 2016), 206.

20. See Karl Marx, *The Communist Manifesto* (1848; New York: Norton, 1988), 75–85); Friedrich Engels, *Socialism: Utopian and Scientific* (1880; New York: International Publishers, 1935); and Arthur Bestor, "The Evolution of the Socialist Vocabulary," *Journal of the History of Ideas* 9.3 (1948): 259–302. Vincent Geoghegan provides a valuable brief introduction to the utopian socialists in *Utopianism and Marxism* (London: Methuen, 1987), 8–21.

21. See Henri Saint-Simon, *Selected Writings on Science, Industry, and Social Organization*, ed. Keith Taylor (New York: Holmes & Meier, 1975); and Manuel and Manuel, *Utopian Thought*, 581–640.

22. Robert Owen, "Report to the County of Lanark," in *A New View of Society and Other Writings*, ed. Gregory Claeys (London: Penguin, 1991), 276. The Great Truth was printed on the cover of every issue of *The Crisis*, a periodical edited by Robert Owen and his son Robert Dale Owen in 1832–34. The most recent biography is Ian Donnachie, *Robert Owen: Owen of New Lanark and New Harmony* (East Lothian, U.K.: Tuckwell, 2000). The best brief introduction to Owen's life and work is Donald E. Pitzer, "The New Moral World of Robert Owen and New Harmony," in *America's Communal Utopias*, ed. Pitzer (Chapel Hill: University of North Carolina Press, 1997), 88–134. The New Lanark Trust, through its excellent management of the New Lanark World Heritage Site, offers visitors a vivid sense of life in Owen's mills during the early nineteenth century.

23. Engels, *Socialism*, 42, 43.

24. On Owenite communalism, see in addition to Pitzer, "New Moral World," Arthur Bestor, *Backwoods Utopias: The Sectarian Origins and the Owenite Phase of Communitarian Socialism in America, 1663–1829*, 2nd ed. (Philadelphia: University of Pennsylvania Press, 1970), 60–229; and J. F. C. Harrison, *Quest for the New Moral World: Robert Owen and the Owenites in Britain and America* (New York: Scribner's, 1960). On women and Owenism in Great Britain, see Barbara Taylor, *Eve and the New Jerusalem: Socialism and Feminism in the Nineteenth Century* (New York: Pantheon, 1983); on women and American Owenism, see Carol A. Kolmerten, *Women in Utopia: The Ideology of Gender in the American Owenite Communities* (Bloomington: Indiana University Press, 1990).

25. Jonathan Beecher and Richard Bienvenu's extensive introduction to *The Utopian Vision of Charles Fourier* (Columbia: University of Missouri Press, 1983) offers a good biography, and their volume provides the best selection in English of Fourier's writings.

26. On Fourier's complex philosophy, see, in addition to Beecher and Bienvenu's introduction to *Utopian Vision*, Jonathan Beecher, *Charles Fourier: The Visionary and His World* (Berkeley: University of California Press, 1987).

27. *Utopian Vision of Charles Fourier*, 275–76.

28. On Brisbane, see Carl Guarneri, *The Utopian Alternative: Fourierism in Nineteenth-Century America* (Ithaca, NY: Cornell University Press, 1991).

29. Fourier's most detailed writings on sexuality remained unpublished until 1967, when they appeared under the title *Le Nouveau monde amoureux* (Paris: Editions Anthropos). This volume has not been translated into English, but Beecher and Bienvenu include a generous selection in *Utopian Vision of Charles Fourier*, 329–95.

30. Emerson quoted in Guarneri, *Utopian Alternative*, 130.

31. *The Correspondence of Emerson and Carlyle*, ed. Joseph Slater (New York: Columbia University Press, 1964), 283.

32. Nathaniel Hawthorne, *The Blithedale Romance* (New York: Bedford, 1996), 43, 44; *Selected Letters of Nathaniel Hawthorne*, ed. Joel Myerson (Columbus: Ohio State University Press, 2002), 86. There is a vast historical literature on Brook Farm. Chris Jennings offers a brief, entertaining overview in *Paradise Now*, 188–235; the fullest recent account is Samuel F. Delano, *Brook Farm: The Dark Side of Utopia* (Cambridge: Harvard University Press, 2004).

33. "Rebecca Codman Butterfield's Reminiscences of Brook Farm," ed. Joel Myerson, *New England Quarterly* 65 (1992): 624–27; Guarneri, *Utopian Vision*, 60; F. O. Matthiessen, *American Renaissance: Art and Expression in the Age of Emerson and Whitman* (New York: Oxford University Press, 1941), viii.

34. Kumar, *Utopia and Anti-Utopia*, 95.

35. The best introduction to George's life and work is John L. Thomas, *Alternative America: Henry George, Edward Bellamy, Henry Demarest Lloyd and the Adversary Tradition* (Cambridge: Harvard University Press, 1983). On his British reception, see Elwood P. Lawrence, *Henry George in the British Isles* (East Lansing: Michigan State University Press, 1957).

36. Henry George, *Progress and Poverty* (1879; Garden City, NY: Doubleday, Page, 1925), 403–4, 549.

37. Lawrence Gronlund, *The Cooperative Commonwealth* (1884; Cambridge: Harvard University Press, 1965).

Chapter Two. *Edward Bellamy's Orderly Utopia*

1. Edward Bellamy, Delta Kappa Epsilon questionnaire, August 1887, MS Am 1181, Houghton Library, Harvard University; W. D. Howells, "Two Notable Novels," *Century Illustrated Monthly Magazine* 28 (August 1884): 632–34.

2. Arthur Lipow, *Authoritarian Socialism in America: Edward Bellamy and the Nationalist Movement* (Berkeley: University of California Press, 1982).

3. Lyman Tower Sargent, *British and American Utopian Literature, 1516–1985: An Annotated, Chronological Bibliography* (New York: Garland, 1988).

4. Arthur Morgan interviews with Ames Carter (June 2, 1939) and Jeanette E. Sanderson Sackett (June 3, 1939), MS Am 1182, Houghton; Frederick Bellamy quoted in Mason A. Green, "Edward Bellamy," MS Am 1181.10, Houghton; Maria Bellamy to Edward Bellamy, March 26, 1871, MS Am 1181, Houghton. No reliable modern biography of Bellamy exists; my discussion is based on materials in the Houghton Library.

The best account of Bellamy's life is in John Thomas, *Alternative America: Henry George, Edward Bellamy, Henry Demarest Lloyd and the Adversary Tradition* (Cambridge: Harvard University Press, 1983).

5. Edward Bellamy, "Religion," MS Am 1181.4, Houghton; Bellamy, "Autobiographical Sketch," MS Am 1181.4, Houghton.

6. Green, "Edward Bellamy," MS Am 1181.10, Houghton; Bellamy, "The Marshals of Napoleon," MS Am 1181.4, Houghton; Bellamy, "Autobiographical Sketch," MS Am 1181.4, Houghton.

7. Green, "Edward Bellamy," MS Am 1181.10, Houghton; Frederick Bellamy, address to Boston Bellamy Club, March 29, 1916, MS Am 1181, Houghton.

8. On nineteenth-century Chicopee, see John Robert Mullin, "Bellamy's Chicopee: A Laboratory for Utopia?" *Journal of Urban History* 29.2 (2003): 133–50; and Vera Shlakman, *Economic History of a Factory Town* (1935; New York: Octagon Books, 1969).

9. Edward Bellamy, "How I Wrote 'Looking Backward'" (1894), in *Edward Bellamy Speaks Again!* (Kansas City, MO: Peerage Press, 1937), 218.

10. "The Barbarism of Society" is missing from Bellamy's papers, but he quotes the speech at length in "How I Wrote 'Looking Backward,'" 218–21.

11. Edward Bellamy, "Second Lyceum Address," MS Am 1181.4, Houghton; Zygmunt Bauman, *Socialism: The Active Utopia* (New York: Holmes & Meier, 1976). Howard Quint, *The Forging of American Socialism* (Columbia: University of South Carolina Press, 1953) remains a valuable guide to late nineteenth-century American socialism; see also Paul Buhle, *Marxism in the United States: A History of the American Left* (London: Verso, 2013).

12. Edward Bellamy, "Eliot Carson" notebook, MS Am 1181.6, Houghton.

13. Toby Widdicombe and Herman S. Preiser have collected forty-two of Bellamy's *Springfield Daily Union* editorials in *Revisiting the Legacy of Edward Bellamy* (Lewiston, NY: Edwin Mellen, 2002); the quotations are from pages 214 and 189.

14. Edward Bellamy, Notebook #4, MS Am 1181.6, Houghton; Bellamy, "Autobiographical Sketch," MS Am 1181.4, Houghton.

15. In *The Feminization of American Culture* (New York: Knopf, 1977), Ann Douglas offers an analysis of gender and religion in the nineteenth-century U.S. congruent with Bellamy's view. Douglas's influential but controversial analysis has been challenged by many scholars; for a representative response, see David S. Reynolds, "The Feminization Controversy: Sexual Stereotypes and the Paradoxes of Piety in Nineteenth-Century America," *New England Quarterly* 53.1 (1980): 96–106. My interpretation of Bellamy, which emphasizes changes in white middle-class masculinity, is influenced by Gail Bederman, "'The Women Have Had Charge of the Church Work Long Enough': The Men and Religion Forward Movement of 1911–12 and the Masculinization of Middle-Class Protestantism," *American Quarterly* 41 (1989): 432–65. For broad discussions of post–Civil War masculinity, see Michael Kimmel, *Manhood in America: A Cultural History*, 3rd ed. (New York: Oxford University Press, 2011); and Anthony Rotundo, *American Manhood: Transformations in Masculinity from the Revolution to the Modern Era* (New York: Basic Books, 1994).

16. For Comte's influence on Bellamy and, more generally, on American religious liberalism, see Gillis Harp, *Positivist Republic: August Comte and the Reconstruction of American Liberalism, 1865–1920* (University Park: Pennsylvania State University Press, 1995). Bellamy's admiration of Beecher is expressed in the "Eliot Carson" manuscript at Houghton; on Beecher and religious liberalism, see Debby Applegate, *The Most Famous Man in America: The Biography of Henry Ward Beecher* (New York: Doubleday, 2006).

17. Numerous writers have noted Bellamy's debt to Emerson; the most incisive analysis is Jonathan Auerbach, "'The Nation Organized': Utopian Impotence in Edward Bellamy's *Looking Backward*," *American Literary History* 6.1 (1994): 24–47.

18. Edward Bellamy, "The Religion of Solidarity," in *Selected Writings on Religion and Society*, ed. Joseph Schiffman (New York: Liberal Arts Press, 1955), 3, 4.

19. Edward Bellamy, "The Dual Life," MS Am 1181.4, Houghton.

20. Ralph Waldo Emerson, "Self-Reliance," in *Emerson's Prose and Poetry*, ed. Joel Porte and Saundra Morris (New York: Norton, 2001), 121, 123; Bellamy, "Religion of Solidarity," 8–9.

21. Bellamy, "Religion of Solidarity," 26.

22. Edward Bellamy, Notebook #3, MS Am 1181.6, Houghton.

23. Ibid.

24. Ibid. On women and nineteenth-century freethought, see Susan Jacoby, *Freethinkers: A History of American Secularism* (New York: Metropolitan Books, 2004).

25. Edward Bellamy, "Eliot Carson" Notebook, MS Am 1181.6, Houghton.

26. Ibid.; Bellamy, Notebook #1, MS Am 1181.6, Houghton.

27. Edward Bellamy, "Why I Wrote 'Looking Backward'" (1890), in *Edward Bellamy Speaks Again!*, 199, 200.

28. Ismar Thiusen [John Macnie], *The Diothas; or, A Far Look Ahead* (New York: Putnam, 1883). A minor controversy arose over whether Bellamy had "plagiarized" *The Diothas*. Arthur Morgan, Bellamy's first biographer, expended considerable energy arguing that he had not; see Morgan, *Edward Bellamy* (New York: Columbia University Press, 1944), 63–64, 240–41.

29. On Bellamy and Henry George, see Thomas, *Alternative America*.

30. Edward Bellamy, *Looking Backward, 2000–1887* (Cambridge: Harvard University Press, 1967), 118.

31. Jackson Lears, *Rebirth of a Nation: The Making of Modern America, 1877–1920* (New York: Harper, 2009), 1–11.

32. Bellamy, *Looking Backward*, 304.

33. Chris Ferns, *Narrating Utopia: Ideology, Gender, Form in Utopian Literature* (Liverpool: Liverpool University Press, 1999).

34. Bellamy, *Looking Backward*, 123.

35. Ibid., 122, 127; Jean Pfaelzer, *The Utopian Novel in America, 1886–1896: The Politics of Form* (Pittsburgh: University of Pittsburgh Press, 1984), 5. On late nineteenth-century "neo-Lamarckism," see Peter J. Bowler, *Evolution: The History of an Idea*, rev. ed. (Berkeley: University of California Press, 1989); and Mark Pittenger, *American Socialists and Evolutionary Thought* (Madison: University of Wisconsin Press, 1993).

36. See in addition to Lipow, *Authoritarian Socialism*, Matthew Beaumont, *Utopia Ltd.: Ideologies of Social Dreaming in England, 1870 1900* (Leiden: Brill, 2005), and *The Spectre of Utopia* (Oxford: Peter Lang, 2012); Edward K. Spann, *Brotherly Tomorrows: Movements for a Cooperative Society in America, 1820–1920* (New York: Columbia University Press, 1989); and Philip E. Wegner, *Imaginary Communities: Utopia, the Nation, and the Spatial Histories of Modernity* (Berkeley: University of California Press, 2002).

37. Bellamy, *Looking Backward*, 155. Some recent critics have argued that shopping and consumption are central to the novel; see in particular Matthew Beaumont, "Shopping in Utopia: *Looking Backward*, the Department Store, and the Dreamscape of Utopia," *Nineteenth-Century Contexts* 28.3 (2006): 191–209.

38. Edward Bellamy to Charles and Maria Bellamy, April 4, 1878, MS Am 1181, Houghton.

39. Frederick Bellamy, address to Boston Bellamy Club, Houghton.

40. Neil Harris, "Utopian Fiction and Its Discontents," in *Cultural Excursions: Marketing Appetites and Cultural Tastes in Modern America* (Chicago: University of Chicago Press, 1990), 150–73.

41. Edward Bellamy, *Equality* (New York: Appleton, 1897), 255.

42. Jackson Lears discusses post–Civil War producerist ideology extensively in *Rebirth of a Nation*. See also Rose Curraino, *The Labor Question in America: Economic Democracy in the Gilded Age* (Urbana: University of Illinois Press, 2011). Ron Howe notes the links between Bellamy and producerism in "Reconsidering Edward Bellamy in the Year 2000," in *Revisiting the Legacy of Edward Bellamy*, ed. Widdicombe & Preiser, 417–32.

43. Bellamy, *Looking Backward*, 197.

44. Edward Bellamy letters to Emma Bellamy, MS Am 1181, Houghton.

45. Bellamy, *Looking Backward*, 267.

46. Frances Willard to "Lilian," June 4, 1888, MS Am 1181, Houghton. On *Looking Backward*'s appeal to women's movement activists, see Mari Jo Buhle, *Women and American Socialism* (Urbana: University of Illinois Press, 1981); and William Leach, "Looking Forward Together: Feminists and Edward Bellamy," *Democracy* 2.1 (1982): 120–34.

47. David Bleich, "Eros and Bellamy," *American Quarterly* 16 (Fall 1964): 445–59.

48. Bellamy, *Looking Backward*, 293; Bellamy quoted in Joseph Schiffman, introduction to *The Duke of Stockbridge*, by Edward Bellamy (Cambridge: Harvard University Press, 1962), xxvii.

49. Bellamy, *Looking Backward*, 267. The case for *Looking Backward* as a technological utopia is made by Harris, "Utopian Fiction," and John F. Kasson, *Civilizing the Machine: Technology and Republican Values in America, 1776-1900* (New York: Grossman, 1976).

50. Bellamy, *Looking Backward*, 275. A number of critics have explored the religious foundations of *Looking Backward*. See in addition to Thomas, *Alternative America*, Wilfrid M. McClay, *The Masterless: Self and Society in Modern America* (Chapel Hill: University of North Carolina Press, 1994); Kenneth M. Roemer, *The Obsolete Necessity: America in Utopian Literature, 1888-1900* (Kent, OH: Kent State

University Press, 1976); Joseph Schiffman, introduction to Bellamy, *Selected Writings on Religion and Society*; and Michael J. Turner, "For God and America: The Religious and Moral Premises of Edward Bellamy's Socialism," *Journal of Religious History* 20.2 (1996): 185–209. Catherine Tumber identifies Bellamy's religious vision as "gnostic" in "Edward Bellamy, the Erosion of Public Life, and the Gnostic Revival," *American Literary History* 11.4 (1999): 610–41.

51. Bellamy, *Looking Backward*, 97.

52. Ibid., 298, 307; Darko Suvin, *Metamorphoses of Science Fiction* (New Haven: Yale University Press, 1979).

53. Bellamy, *Looking Backward*, 307, 309.

54. Auerbach, "The Nation Organized," 41; Jean Pfaelzer, "Immanence, Indeterminance, and the Utopian Pun in *Looking Backward*," in *Looking Backward, 1988–1888*, ed. Daphne Patai (Amherst: University of Massachusetts Press, 1988), 65.

55. Bellamy in Joseph Schiffman, "Mutual Indebtedness: Unpublished Letters of Edward Bellamy to William Dean Howells," *Harvard Library Bulletin* 12 (1958): 370; Bellamy quoted in Thomas, *Alternative America*, 267; Bellamy quoted in Cyrus Field Willard, "The Nationalist Club of Boston: A Chapter of History," *The Nationalist* 1 (May 1889): 5; Bellamy to T. W. Higginson, 28 December 1888, MS Am 1162.10, Houghton.

56. Cyrus Field Willard to Arthur Morgan, [August 1939], MS Am 1182, Houghton.

57. C. F. Willard, "A Retrospect," *Nationalist* 2.1 (December 1889): 6.

58. Charles Postel, *The Populist Vision* (New York: Oxford University Press, 2007), 226.

59. Edward Bellamy to Horace Scudder, August 25, 1890, MS Am 1181, Houghton; Bellamy quoted in Green, "Edward Bellamy," MS Am 1181.10, Houghton.

60. Edward Bellamy, "The Cradle of Liberty Rocked," *New Nation* 1.38 (October 17, 1891): 606–7.

61. On the relation between Nationalism and Populism, see Postel, *The Populist Vision*.

62. "The Omaha Platform" (1892), *History Matters*, http://historymatters.gmu.edu/d/5361, accessed June 26, 2016.

63. Edward Bellamy, *New Nation* 2.48 (November 26, 1892): 697.

64. Edward Bellamy to H. D. Lloyd, December 5, 1896, MS Am 1181, Houghton.

65. Edward Bellamy, *New Nation* 1.45 (December 5, 1891): 727; Bellamy, *New Nation* 3.1 (January 7, 1893): 1; MacNair, *Bellamy and the Nationalist Movement*, 121. For favorable mentions of the Socialist Labor Party, see *New Nation* 2.17 (April 23, 1892) and 3.13 (April 1, 1893).

66. Bellamy, *Equality*, 12, 20.

67. Carl Guarneri, "An American Utopia and Its Global Audiences: Transnational Perspectives on *Looking Backward*," *Utopian Studies* 19.2 (2008): 158.

68. Kenneth M. Roemer, "Getting 'Nowhere' beyond Stasis," in Patai, *Looking Backward, 1988–1888*, 126–46.

69. Bellamy, *Equality*, 43, 135–36.

70. Ibid., 365; Bellamy, *New Nation* 1.36 (October 3, 1891): 567.

71. See, for example, "Edward Bellamy Dead," *New York Times*, May 23, 1898: 7.

72. John Clark Ridpath, "Is the Prophet Dead?" (1898), in *Edward Bellamy Speaks Again!*, 247.

73. Daniel T. Rodgers, *Atlantic Crossings: Social Politics in a Progressive Age* (Cambridge: Harvard University Press, 1998).

74. Richard Hofstadter, *The Age of Reform: From Bryan to F. D. R.* (New York: Knopf, 1955).

75. Oscar Wilde, "The Soul of Man under Socialism," in *The Soul of Man under Socialism and Selected Critical Prose*, ed. Linda Dowling (London: Penguin, 2001), 141.

76. R. C. K. Ensor, *England, 1870–1914* (Oxford: Clarendon Press, 1936), 334; F. J. Osborn, preface to Ebenezer Howard, *Garden Cities of Tomorrow* (1898; Cambridge: MIT Press, 1965), 20–21; Nick Salvatore, *Eugene V. Debs: Citizen and Socialist* (Urbana: University of Illinois Press, 1982), 103, 150; Upton Sinclair quoted in Thomas, *Alternative America*, 355; Dewey and Beard cited in Arthur Morgan, *Edward Bellamy* (New York: Columbia University Press, 1944), ix. See Morgan's preface for multiple examples of his high opinion of Bellamy.

77. *The Papers of Martin Luther King, Jr.*, ed. Clayborne Carson et al. (Berkeley: University of California Press, 2007), 6:126, 123–24.

Chapter Three. William Morris's Artful Utopia

1. *The Collected Letters of William Morris*, ed. Norman Kelvin, 4 vols. (Princeton: Princeton University Press, 1984–96), 3:59; Morris, "Looking Backward," in *News from Nowhere and Other Writings*, ed. Clive Wilmer (London: Penguin, 2004), 354; Morris, "How I Became a Socialist," in *The Collected Works of William Morris*, 24 vols. (1910–15; New York: Russell & Russell, 1966), 23:279.

2. Morris, "Looking Backward," 354; Morris, *News from Nowhere*, ed. Stephen Arata (1891; Peterborough, ON: Broadview, 2003), 238.

3. Morris, *Collected Letters*, 4:268. Aside from the *Collected Letters*, the most important biographical sources are J. W. Mackail, *The Life of William Morris*, 2 vols. (London: Longmans, Green, 1899); Nicholas Salmon, *The William Morris Chronology* (Bristol: Thoemmes Press, 1996); and Fiona MacCarthy, *William Morris: A Life for Our Time* (New York: Knopf, 1995).

4. Morris, *Collected Letters*, 2:227.

5. Ibid., 2:227–28.

6. Ibid., 2:56.

7. Mackail, *Life*, 1:46; Georgiana Burne-Jones, *Memorials of Edward Burne-Jones*, 2 vols. (London: Macmillan, 1904), 1:95–96; MacCarthy, *William Morris*, 77.

8. Charles Dellheim, "Interpreting Victorian Medievalism," in *History and Community: Essays in Victorian Medievalism*, ed. Florence S. Boos (New York: Garland, 1992), 49. Dellheim's essay is an excellent introduction to the subject. See also Lorretta M. Holloway and Jennifer A. Palmgren, introduction to *Beyond Arthurian Romances:*

The Reach of Victorian Medievalism (New York: Palgrave Macmillan, 2005). The foundational text on the subject is Alice Chandler, *A Dream of Order: The Medieval Ideal in Nineteenth-Century English Literature* (Lincoln: University of Nebraska Press, 1970). The central works on Morris and medievalism are Joanna Banham and Jennifer Harris, eds., *William Morris and the Middle Ages* (Manchester: Manchester University Press, 1984); Margaret Rose Grennan, *William Morris: Medievalist and Revolutionary* (New York: King's Crown Press, 1945); Anna Vaninskaya, *William Morris and the Idea of Community: Romance, History and Propaganda, 1880–1914* (Edinburgh: Edinburgh University Press, 2010); and Marcus Waithe, *William Morris's Utopia of Strangers: Victorian Medievalism and the Ideal of Hospitality* (Woodbridge, U.K.: D. S. Brewer, 2006).

9. Morris, preface to "The Nature of Gothic," in *William Morris: Artist, Writer, Socialist*, ed. May Morris, 2 vols. (1936; New York: Russell & Russell, 1966), 1:292.

10. John Ruskin, "The Nature of Gothic," in *Unto This Last and Other Writings*, ed. Clive Wilmer (London: Penguin, 1997), 85, 87, 90.

11. Morris, preface to "The Nature of Gothic," 292; Morris, "The Aims of Art," in *Collected Works*, 23:85.

12. Morris, "The Churches of North France: Shadows of Amiens," in *Collected Works*, 1:349.

13. See Tim Barringer, Jason Rosenfeld, and Alison Smith, *Pre-Raphaelites: Victorian Art and Design* (New Haven, CT: Yale University Press, 2012).

14. Burne-Jones, *Memorials*, 1:99.

15. *Letters of Dante Gabriel Rossetti*, ed. Oswald Doughty and John Robert Wahl (Oxford: Oxford University Press, 1965), 1:319.

16. Morris, *Collected Letters*, 1:28.

17. Jan Marsh, *Jane and May Morris* (London: Pandora, 1986), 24. Marsh's dual biography is the most complete account of the life of Jane Burden Morris. It can be supplemented with *The Collected Letters of Jane Morris*, ed. Frank C. Sharp and Jan Marsh (Woodbridge, U.K.: Boydell, 2012); and Wendy Parkins, *Jane Morris: The Burden of History* (Edinburgh: Edinburgh University Press, 2013).

18. Rossetti quoted in Jan Marsh, *Dante Gabriel Rossetti: Painter and Poet* (London: Weidenfeld and Nicolson, 1999), 222; Morris, *Collected Letters*, 2:228. Webb's elevations are reproduced in Jan Marsh, *William Morris and Red House* (London: National Trust, 2005), 30. Marcus Waithe offers a sophisticated analysis of Red House in *William Morris's Utopia of Strangers*, 33–50.

19. Mackail, *Life*, 1:165.

20. Ibid., 1:164; Morris, *Collected Letters*, 2:228.

21. Mackail, *Life*, 1:154–55.

22. Alfred Tennyson, "The Palace of Art," in *Poems of Alfred Lord Tennyson* (Oxford: Oxford University Press, 1910), 61; Morris, *Collected Letters*, 1:38; Mackail, *Life*, 1:170.

23. Morris, *Collected Letters*, 1:133.

24. Rossetti quoted in Marsh, *Dante Gabriel Rossetti*, 310.

25. See Marsh, *Dante Gabriel Rossetti*, 338–40; and Marsh, *Jane and May Morris*, 74–82.

26. Florence S. Boos, "Unprintable Lyrics: The Unpublished Poems of William Morris," *Victorian Poetry* 53.2 (2015): 193.

27. Morris, *Collected Letters*, 1:91.

28. Morris, "Gossip about an Old House on the Upper Thames," in *William Morris: Artist, Writer, Socialist*, ed. May Morris, 2 vols. (1936; New York: Russell & Russell, 1966), 1:371; Mackail, *Life*, 1:231

29. Morris, *Collected Letters*, 1:218.

30. Morris, *Collected Letters*, 2:229.

31. Morris, *A Journal of Travel in Iceland, 1871*, in *Collected Works*, 8:28; *Collected Letters*, 1:198.

32. The most detailed account of Morris's involvement in the Eastern Question Association is E. P. Thompson, *William Morris: Romantic to Revolutionary*, rev. ed. (New York: Pantheon, 1977), 202–25; see also MacCarthy, *William Morris*, 378–86.

33. Morris, *Collected Letters*, 1:352, 359.

34. J. Bruce Glasier, *William Morris and the Early Days of the Socialist Movement* (London: Longmans, Green, 1921), 104–5.

35. Morris, "Art of the People," in *Collected Works*, 22:42. The term "Whig history" was coined by Herbert Butterfield in *The Whig Interpretation of History* (London: G. Bell and Sons, 1931).

36. Morris, "Art of the People," in *Collected Works*, 22:33; Morris, "The Hopes of Civilization," in *Collected Works*, 23:68; Morris, "The Lesser Arts," in *Collected Works*, 22:6.

37. Morris, "Art and the Beauty of the Earth," in *Collected Works*, 22:171; Morris quoted in W. R. Lethaby, *Philip Webb and His Work* (Oxford: Oxford University Press, 1935), 94–95; Morris, "The Lesser Arts," in *Collected Works*, 22:26.

38. MacCarthy, *William Morris*, 463.

39. Ibid.

40. H. M. Hyndman, *England for All* (London: E. W. Allen, 1881), n.p. The best starting point for the early history of British socialism remains Stanley Pierson, *Marxism and the Origins of British Socialism* (Ithaca, NY: Cornell University Press, 1973). It can be supplemented with Pierson, *British Socialists: The Journey from Fantasy to Politics* (Cambridge: Harvard University Press, 1979); Tony Wright, *Socialisms: Old and New* (London, Routledge, 1996); and Mark Bevir, *The Making of British Socialism* (Princeton: Princeton University Press, 2011). Vaninskaya challenges Pierson's central arguments in *William Morris and the Idea of Community*, 137–74. Thompson places Morris within the history of early British socialism in sometimes numbing detail in *William Morris*, 274–639.

41. Morris, *Collected Letters*, 2:236.

42. Morris's lecture was published under the title "Art under Plutocracy," in *Collected Works*, 23:172, 190; Mackail, *William Morris*, 2:127.

43. *The Collected Letters of George Gissing*, ed. Paul F. Mattheisen et al., 9 vols. (Athens: Ohio University Press, 1990–97), 2:349.

44. Morris, "Art and Socialism," in *Collected Works*, 23:213; Morris, *Collected Letters*, 2:202.

45. Morris, *Artist, Writer, Socialist* 2:276; emphasis in original.

46. Morris, *Collected Letters*, 2:686.

47. Ibid., 2:363, 349.

48. [William Morris and E. Belfort Bax], "The Manifesto of the Socialist Party," *Commonweal*, February 1885: 1.

49. Morris, *Artist, Writer, Socialist*, 2:276.

50. Peter Kropotkin, "Anarchism," in *The Essential Kropotkin*, ed. Emile Capouya and Keitha Tompkins (New York: Liveright, 1975), 110. This edited collection provides the best introduction to Kropotkin; see also Stephen Osofsky, *Peter Kropotkin* (Boston: Twayne, 1979).

51. Morris, *Artist, Writer, Socialist*, 2:325.

52. Karl Marx, preface to the second (1873) edition, *Capital* (New York: Cosimo, 2007), 1:21.

53. Morris, "The Society of the Future," in *Artist, Writer, Socialist*, 2:454–55.

54. Ibid., 456.

55. Morris, preface to "The Nature of Gothic," in *News from Nowhere and Other Writings*, ed. Wilmer, 367.

56. Morris, "How We Live and How We Might Live," in *Collected Works*, 23:18.

57. Morris, "Society of the Future," 462.

58. Ibid., 457.

59. Ibid., 461–62. "Art, Wealth, and Riches," which also reflects Morris's environmentalism, is another important utopian essay of the 1880s; see *Collected Works*, 23:143–63.

60. Morris, *The Pilgrims of Hope*, in *Collected Works*, 24:402.

61. Morris, *A Dream of John Ball*, in *Collected Works*, 16:218, 219.

62. Morris, "Looking Backward," 354, 357, 358.

63. Morris, *News from Nowhere*, 54.

64. Ibid., 213, 95–96.

65. Morris, "Looking Backward," 194; Morris, "The Art of the People," in *Collected Works*, 22:33.

66. Morris, *News from Nowhere*, 89.

67. Ibid., 78, 80.

68. My ideas about Morris's challenge to hierarchy build on Northrop Frye, "The Meeting of Past and Future in William Morris," *Studies in Romanticism* 21.3 (1982): 303–18.

69. Morris, *News from Nowhere*, 122, 134; *Collected Letters*, 2:669; Peter Kropotkin quoted in Trevor Lloyd, "The Politics of William Morris's *News from Nowhere*," *Albion* 9.3 (Autumn 1977): 278. There is an extensive literature on Morris and anarchism; good starting points include Florence S. Boos and William Boos, "The Utopian Communism of William Morris," *History of Political Thought* 7.3 (1986): 489–510; Ruth Kinna, "Morris, Anti-Statism and Anarchy," in *William Morris: Centenary Essays*, ed. Peter Faulkner and Peter Preston (Exeter: University of Exeter Press, 1999), 215–28; and Lyman Tower Sargent, "William Morris and the Anarchist Tradition," in *Socialism and the Literary Artistry of William Morris*, ed. Florence S. Boos and Carole G. Silver (Columbia: University of Missouri Press, 1990), 71–73.

70. Morris, *News from Nowhere*, 130–31.

71. Ibid., 175, 174.

72. Jan Marsh, "*News from Nowhere* as Erotic Dream," *Journal of the William Morris Society* 8.4 (1990): 19; Morris, *News from Nowhere*, 64.

73. Morris, *News from Nowhere*, 185; Marsh, "*News from Nowhere* as Erotic Dream," 20, 22.

74. Morris, *News from Nowhere*, 184, 179.

75. Ibid., 104.

76. Morris, *Collected Letters*, 2:584–85; *News from Nowhere*, 104.

77. Morris, *Collected Letters*, 2:404, 545. See Florence S. Boos and William Boos, "*News from Nowhere* and Victorian Socialist-Feminism," *Nineteenth-Century Contexts* 14.1 (1990): 3–32.

78. Morris, *News from Nowhere*, 107; Ruth Levitas, "Utopian Fictions and Political Theories: Domestic Labour in the Work of Bellamy, Gilman, and Morris," in *A Very Different Story: Studies on the Fiction of Charlotte Perkins Gilman*, ed. Val Gough and Jill Rudd (Liverpool: Liverpool University Press, 1998), 81–99.

79. Bernard Shaw, *Collected Letters*, ed. Dan H. Laurence, 4 vols. (London: Max Reinhardt, 1965–88), 2:697.

80. Morris, *News from Nowhere*, 190.

81. Ibid., 228.

82. Ibid., 239, 240–41.

83. Ibid., 249.

84. Ibid.

85. Ibid., 132.

86. Ibid., 174.

87. Graham Hough, *The Last Romantics* (London: Duckworth, 1949), 108.

88. Morris, "The Society of the Future," in *Artist, Writer, Socialist*, 2:460.

89. Chandler, *Dream of Order*, 228; Krishan Kumar, *Utopia and Anti-Utopia in Modern Times* (Oxford: Basil Blackwell, 1987), 126.

90. Arata, introduction to *News from Nowhere*, 44; Thompson, *William Morris*, 791. The italics are Thompson's; the quotation is Thompson's translation from Miguel Abensour's University of Paris thesis.

Chapter Four. Edward Carpenter's Homogenic Utopia

1. E. M. Forster, terminal note to *Maurice* (New York: Norton, 1987), 249. Nicola Beauman discusses Carpenter's influence on Forster extensively in *Morgan: A Biography of E. M. Forster* (London: Hodder & Stoughton, 1993), 207–10. Beauman dates Forster's first visit to Millthorpe in 1910 (233–34). Forster's most recent biographer dates the visit 1912; see Wendy Moffat, *A Great Unrecorded History: A New Life of E. M. Forster* (New York: Farrar, Straus and Giroux, 2010), 112. I follow Forster's own dating in the note to *Maurice* and P. N. Furbank's account in *E. M. Forster: A Life* (New York: Harcourt Brace Jovanovich, 1978), 256.

2. Forster, terminal note to *Maurice*, 249.

3. Edward Carpenter, *The Intermediate Sex* (1908; New York: Mitchell Kinnerley, 1921).

4. Jessica Rutherford, *The Prince's Passion: The Life of the Royal Pavilion* (Brighton: Brighton & Hove City Council, 2003).

5. Edward Carpenter, *My Days and Dreams* (London: George Allen & Unwin, 1916), 13. In my account of Carpenter's life, I have relied on this autobiography and on Sheila Rowbotham's definitive biography, *Edward Carpenter: A Life of Liberty and Love* (London: Verso, 2008).

6. Carpenter, *My Days and Dreams*, 46, 47.

7. Edward Carpenter, *Narcissus and Other Poems* (London: Henry S. King, 1873), 3–4.

8. Sir Mountstuart E. Grant Duff, *Notes from a Diary, 1851–1872*, 2 vols. (London: John Murray, 1897), 1:78.

9. Edward Carpenter, "Self-Analysis for Havelock Ellis," in *Selected Writings*, vol. 1: *Sex*, ed. David Fernbach and Noël Greig (London: GMP, 1984), 290.

10. The literature on Victorian homosexuality is vast. A good starting point is H. G. Cocks, "Secrets, Crimes, and Diseases, 1800–1914," in *A Gay History of Britain*, ed. Matt Cook (Oxford: Greenwood World, 2007), 107–44. Cocks's entire body of work is useful; see especially *Nameless Offenses: Homosexual Desire in the Nineteenth Century* (London: I. B. Tauris, 2003.) Jeffrey Weeks's pioneering work remains valuable; see *Coming Out: Homosexual Politics in Britain from the Nineteenth Century to the Present* (London: Quartet Books, 1977); *Sex, Politics, and Society: The Regulation of Sexuality since 1800*, 2nd ed. (New York: Longman, 1989); and "Discourse, Desire, and Sexual Deviance: Some Problems in a History of Homosexuality," in *The Making of the Modern Homosexual*, ed. Kenneth Plummer (London: Hutchinson, 1981), 76–111. A good sourcebook is *Nineteenth-Century Writings on Homosexuality*, ed. Chris White (London: Routledge, 1999).

11. Walt Whitman, "Meeting Again," in *Poems by Walt Whitman*, ed. William Michael Rossetti (London: John Camden Hotten, 1868), 290–91. Rossetti gave this title to the poem, which is titled "When I Heard at the Close of the Day" in *Leaves of Grass*. On the Carpenter-Whitman relationship, see Carpenter's *Days with Walt Whitman* (New York: Macmillan, 1906); Michael Robertson, *Worshipping Walt: The Whitman Disciples* (Princeton: Princeton University Press, 2008), 167–88; and Eve Kosofsky Sedgwick, *Between Men: English Literature and Male Homosocial Desire* (New York: Columbia University Press, 1985), 201–17.

12. Carpenter, "Self-Analysis," 290.

13. Carpenter quoted in Horace Traubel, *With Walt Whitman in Camden*, 9 vols. (various publishers, 1906–96), 1:160; available at www.whitmanarchive.org.

14. Walt Whitman, "Song of Myself," in *Leaves of Grass* (New York: n.p., 1855), 29; available at www.whitmanarchive.org.

15. Carpenter quoted in Traubel, *With Walt Whitman*, 3:416; Carpenter quoted in Walt Whitman, *The Correspondence*, ed. Edwin Haviland Miller, 6 vols. (New York: New York University Press, 1961–77), 3:82n. On *Leaves of Grass* as a new bible, see David Kuebrich, *Minor Prophecy: Walt Whitman's New American Religion* (Bloom-

ington: Indiana University Press, 1989); Herbert Levine, "'Song of Myself' as Whitman's American Bible," *Modern Language Quarterly* 48 (1987): 145–61; and Robertson, *Worshipping Walt*.

16. Carpenter, *Days with Walt Whitman*, 18.

17. Carpenter quoted in Gay Wilson Allen, *Walt Whitman as Man, Poet, and Legend* (Carbondale: Southern Illinois University Press, 1961), 158; Carpenter quoted in Jonathan Ned Katz, *Love Stories: Sex between Men before Homosexuality* (Chicago: University of Chicago Press, 2001), 324. Katz (321–29) offers a detailed analysis of Gavin Arthur's multiple accounts of his visit to Carpenter. See also Martin G. Murray, "Walt Whitman, Edward Carpenter, Gavin Arthur, and *The Circle of Sex*," *Walt Whitman Quarterly Review* 22 (2005): 194–98. Katz (329) summarizes Ginsberg's gay lineage.

18. Carpenter quoted in Rowbotham, *Edward Carpenter*, 56.

19. Carpenter, *My Days and Dreams*, 103, 104.

20. Edward Carpenter, note to *Towards Democracy* (New York: Mitchell Kennerley, 1922), xviii. Carpenter discusses Cosmic Consciousness in *From Adam's Peak to Elephanta* (London: Swan Sonnenschein, 1892), 151–61.

21. Havelock Ellis in *Edward Carpenter: In Appreciation*, ed. Gilbert Beith (London: George Allen & Unwin, 1931), 47. See the extended comparisons of Carpenter's and Whitman's poetry in Andrew Elfenbein, "Whitman, Democracy, and the English Clerisy," *Nineteenth-Century Literature* 56 (2001): 76–104; Kirsten Harris, *Walt Whitman and British Socialists* (New York: Routledge, 2016), 30–64; and M. Wynn Thomas, *Transatlantic Connections: Whitman U.S., Whitman U.K.* (Iowa City: University of Iowa Press, 2005), 161–91.

22. Edward Aveling was the first to label Carpenter the "English Walt Whitman" in his review of *Towards Democracy* in *Progress: A Monthly Magazine of Advanced Thought* (September 1883): 61.

23. Edward Carpenter, "Towards Democracy," in *Towards Democracy* (New York: Mitchell Kennerley, 1922), 24, 23.

24. Ibid., 3, 5.

25. Ibid., 10.

26. Ibid., 27–28.

27. Fenner Brockway quoted in Stanley Pierson, "Edward Carpenter, Prophet of a Socialist Millennium," *Victorian Studies* 13.3 (1970): 301.

28. Carpenter, "Towards Democracy," 20, 5.

29. Ibid., 21, 24.

30. Ibid., 4, 34.

31. Martin Green, *Prophets of a New Age : The Politics of Hope from the Eighteenth through the Twenty-first Centuries* (New York: Scribner's, 1992).

32. Carpenter, *My Days and Dreams*, 164.

33. Ibid., 240.

34. Walt Whitman, "Are You the New Person Drawn toward Me?" in *Complete Poetry and Collected Prose* (New York: Library of America, 1982), 277; Henry D. Thoreau, *Walden* (1854; Princeton: Princeton University Press, 1973), 298. See Arthur

Versluis, *American Transcendentalism and Asian Religions* (New York: Oxford University Press, 1993).

35. Carpenter, *My Days and Dreams*, 106. Paul Marshall analyzes Carpenter's mysticism at length in *Mystical Encounters with the Natural World: Experiences and Explanations* (Oxford: Oxford University Press, 2005), 116–29.

36. Ponnanbalam Arunachalam quoted in Antony Copley, *A Spiritual Bloomsbury: Hinduism and Homosexuality in the Lives and Writing of Edward Carpenter, E. M. Forster, and Christopher Isherwood* (Lanham, MD: Lexington Books, 2006), 44.

37. Carpenter, *From Adam's Peak to Elephanta*, 176, 198.

38. William Knight, *Memorials of Thomas Davidson* (London: T. Fisher Unwin, 1907), 19; see Kevin Manton, "The Fellowship of the New Life: English Ethical Socialism Reconsidered," *History of Political Thought* 24.2 (2003): 282–304.

39. Edward Carpenter, "Correspondence," *Commonweal*, December 12, 1891; Bernard Shaw, "The Illusions of Socialism," in *Forecasts of the Coming Century*, ed. Edward Carpenter (Manchester: Labour Press, 1897), 167.

40. William Morris, *A Dream of John Ball*, in *The Collected Works of William Morris* (New York: Russell & Russell, 1966), 16:230.

41. Robert Blatchford, *The New Religion* (Manchester: Clarion Press, 1897), 3.

42. Fred Brocklehurst quoted in Stephen Yeo, "A New Life: The Religion of Socialism in Britain, 1883–1896," *History Workshop* 4 (1977): 51. Yeo's essay is an excellent introduction to ethical socialism. See also Mark Bevir, *The Making of British Socialism* (Princeton: Princeton University Press, 2011), 215–316; Manton, "Fellowship of the New Life"; Stanley Pierson, *British Socialists: The Journey from Fantasy to Politics* (Cambridge: Harvard University Press, 1979); and Pierson, *Marxism and the Origins of British Socialism* (Ithaca: Cornell University Press, 1973), 140–73. Anna Vaninskaya offers a powerful revisionist history of socialism during this period in *William Morris and the Idea of Community: Romance, History, and Propaganda, 1880–1914* (Edinburgh: Edinburgh University Press, 2010), 137–203.

43. *The Complete Letters of Oscar Wilde*, ed. Merlin Holland and Rupert Hart-Davis (New York: Henry Holt, 2000), 1197.

44. Lewis H. Morgan, *Ancient Society*, ed. Leslie A. White (1877; Cambridge: Harvard University Press, 1964), 467. Carpenter was not the only socialist taken with Morgan: Friedrich Engels expanded Marx's notes on Morgan into the influential *Origin of the Family, Private Property, and the State* (1884).

45. Edward Carpenter, *Civilisation: Its Cause and Cure* (1889; London: Swan Sonnenschein, 1908), 26, 29, 44.

46. Ibid., 41, 45, 46.

47. "Fabiana," *To-day* 11 (February 1889): 55; Bernard Shaw, preface to Stephen Winsten, *Salt and His Circle* (London: Hutchinson, 1951), 9, 12; Hyndman quoted in Winsten, *Salt and His Circle*, 64; Rowbotham, *Edward Carpenter*, 144.

48. Edward Carpenter, *Love's Coming-of-Age* (London: Swan Sonnenschein, 1909), 11. On Victorian marriage manuals, see Joanna Bourke, "Sexual Violence, Marital Guidance, and Victorian Bodies," *Victorian Studies* 50.3 (2008): 419–36.

49. Carpenter, *Love's Coming-of-Age*, 35, 42, 29, 30–31, 66.

50. Ibid., 43, 54.

51. Ibid., 40, 38.

52. Ibid., 64; Isabella Ford quoted in Rowbotham, *Edward Carpenter*, 220; Sedgwick, *Between Men*, 214. See Rowbotham 210–28 for discussion of Carpenter's involvement in the women's movement.

53. Carpenter, *Love's Coming-of-Age*, 3; *My Days and Dreams*, 98, 97, 98, 94–95, 97.

54. Michel Foucault, *The History of Sexuality*, vol. 1: *An Introduction* (New York: Vintage, 1990), 43. See also the works on Victorian homosexuality cited earlier.

55. Carpenter, *My Days and Dreams*, 196. On the Wilde trials, see Richard Ellmann, *Oscar Wilde* (New York: Knopf, 1988), 435–78.

56. See Ralph M. Leck, *Vita Sexualis: Karl Ulrichs and the Origins of Sexual Science* (Urbana: University of Illinois Press, 2016).

57. On the sexologists, see Heike Bauer, *English Literary Sexology: Translations of Inversion, 1860–1930* (New York: Palgrave Macmillan, 2009), and two books edited by Lucy Bland and Laura Doane: *Sexology in Culture: Labelling Bodies and Desires* (Chicago: University of Chicago Press, 1998) and *Sexology Uncensored: The Documents of Sexual Science* (Cambridge: Polity, 1998). Chris Waters provides an interpretive overview in "Sexology," in *The Modern History of Sexuality*, ed. H. G. Cocks and Matt Houlbrook (New York: Palgrave Macmillan, 2006), 41–63.

58. Edward Carpenter, *Homogenic Love* (Manchester: Labour Press, 1894), 16–24.

59. See Ivan Crozier's critical edition of *Sexual Inversion* (New York: Palgrave Macmillan, 2008) and Joseph Bristow, "Symonds's History, Ellis's Heredity: *Sexual Inversion*," in Bland and Doane, *Sexology in Culture*, 79–99.

60. *The Letters of John Addington Symonds*, ed. Herbert M. Schueller and Robert L. Peters (Detroit: Wayne State University Press, 1969), 3:483.

61. The quoted term comes from Bauer, *English Literary Sexology, passim*.

62. Carpenter, *Love's Coming-of-Age*, 42; Carpenter, *Intermediate Sex*, 14.

63. Carpenter, "O Child of Uranus," in *Towards Democracy*, 386–87. Brackets in original.

64. Carpenter, *Intermediate Sex*, 65, 36, 102, 108–9, 114.

65. Ibid., 107.

66. Carpenter, "A Mightier Than Mammon," in *Towards Democracy*, 375, 372, 374.

67. William A. Pannapacker, "'The bricklayer shall lay me': Edward Carpenter, Walt Whitman, and Working-Class 'Comradeship,'" in *Mapping Male Sexuality*, ed. Jay Losey and William D. Brewer (Madison, NJ: Fairleigh Dickinson University Press, 2000), 294; Ruth Livesey, "Morris, Carpenter, Wilde, and the Political Aesthetics of Labor," *Victorian Literature and Culture* 32.2 (2004): 611.

68. Carpenter, *Intermediate Sex*, 47–48, 13, 29, 30, 31, 34.

69. Whitman quoted in Traubel, *With Walt Whitman in Camden*, 1:223.

70. Valentine Cunningham quoted in Tony Brown, introduction to *Edward Carpenter and Late Victorian Radicalism* (London: Frank Cass, 1990), 11. On Victorian anthropology, see Thomas Hylland Eriksen and Finn Sivert Nielsen, *A History of An-*

thropology (London: Pluto Press, 2001), 16–53; Henrika Kulick, *A New History of Anthropology* (Oxford: Blackwell, 2008), 56–58; and G. W. Stocking Jr., *Victorian Anthropology* (New York: Free Press, 1987).

71. Carpenter, *Intermediate Types among Primitive Folks: A Study in Social Evolution* (London: George Allen, 1914), 58.

72. Carpenter, *The Art of Creation* (London: George Allen, 1904), 51.

73. Ibid., 71.

74. Ibid., 207; Edward Carpenter, *Pagan and Christian Creeds* (New York: Harcourt, Brace, 1921), 232.

75. Carpenter, *My Days and Dreams*, 126, 127, 129.

76. Carpenter, *Intermediate Sex*, 14; *My Days and Dreams*, 96.

77. Carpenter, *My Days and Dreams*, 163.

78. Edward Carpenter, *England's Ideal* (London: Swan Sonnenschein, 1887), 103.

79. Furbank, *E. M. Forster*, 258.

Chapter Five. Charlotte Perkins Gilman's Motherly Utopia

1. See Ron Howe, "Reconsidering Edward Bellamy in the Year 2000," in *Revisiting the Legacy of Edward Bellamy*, ed. Toby Widdicombe and Herman S. Preiser (Lewiston, NY: Edwin Mellen, 2002), 424.

2. Charlotte Perkins Gilman, "Human Nature," in *Charlotte Perkins Gilman: A Nonfiction Reader*, ed. Larry Ceplair (New York: Columbia University Press, 1991), 53.

3. Charlotte Perkins Gilman, "Her Memories," in Carol Farley Kessler, *Charlotte Perkins Gilman: Her Progress Toward Utopia with Selected Writings* (Syracuse, NY: Syracuse University Press, 1995), 177; Gilman, *Human Work* (New York: McClure, Phillips, 1904), 63; Gilman, "Mother to Child," in *In This Our World*, 5th ed. (Boston: Small, Maynard, 1914), 142; Gilman, "Two Callings," in *The Home: Its Work and Influence* (New York: McClure, Phillips, 1903), xi.

4. Charlotte Perkins Gilman, *The Living of Charlotte Perkins Gilman* (1935; Madison: University of Wisconsin Press, 1990), 6. On the Beecher family, see Cynthia J. Davis, *Charlotte Perkins Gilman* (Stanford: Stanford University Press, 2010), 4–13. In my discussion of Gilman's life, I have made use of Gilman's autobiography, hereafter cited as *Living*. This revealing but unreliable work needs to be supplemented with Davis's thorough, judicious biography, which largely supersedes two earlier biographies: Mary A. Hill, *Charlotte Perkins Gilman: The Making of a Radical Feminist, 1860–1896* (Philadelphia: Temple University Press, 1980); and Ann J. Lane, *To "Herland" and Beyond: The Life and Work of Charlotte Perkins Gilman* (New York: Pantheon, 1990). Two scholarly editions are invaluable: *The Diaries of Charlotte Perkins Gilman*, ed. Denise D. Knight, 2 vols. (Charlottesville: University Press of Virginia, 1994); and *The Selected Letters of Charlotte Perkins Gilman*, ed. Denise D. Knight and Jennifer S. Tuttle (Tuscaloosa: University of Alabama Press, 2009). I have also made use of the Charlotte Perkins Gilman Collection at the Schlesinger Library, Harvard University, which is available online at www.radcliffe.harvard.edu/schlesinger-library/collection/charlotte-perkins-gilman. Everyone writing about Gilman's life faces the

difficulty of what to call her, since until her 1900 marriage to Houghton Gilman she published under the name Charlotte Perkins Stetson. Some scholars choose to call her "Charlotte"; I have used "Gilman" throughout.

5. Gilman, *Selected Letters*, 47, 46.

6. Gilman, *Living*, 8.

7. Ibid., 27. On Swedenborg, see Sydney E. Ahlstrom, *A Religious History of the American People*, 2nd ed. (New Haven: Yale University Press, 2004), 483–88.

8. Walt Whitman, "Song of Myself," in *Complete Poetry and Collected Prose*, ed. Justin Kaplan (New York: Library of America, 1982), 244–45; Edward Bellamy, "The Dual Life," MS Am 1181.4, Houghton Library, Harvard University.

9. Gilman, *Living*, 181–82; Gilman, "The Vision and the Program," *Forerunner* 6 (May 1915): 119.

10. Charlotte Perkins Stetson, "What Work Is," *Cosmopolitan* 27.6 (October 1899): 680; Gilman, *Human Work*, 59, 134. See Daniel T. Rodgers's incisive analysis of Gilman's ideas about work in *The Work Ethic in Industrial America*, 2nd ed. (Chicago: University of Chicago Press, 2014), 189–93.

11. Gilman, *Diaries*, 1:222; *Living*, 47.

12. Gilman, *Diaries*, 1:16, 58; Edward Carpenter, *Love's Coming-of-Age* in *Sex*, vol. 1 of *Selected Writings*, ed. David Fernbach and Noël Greig (London: GMP, 1984), 117; Lillian Faderman, *Surpassing the Love of Men: Romantic Friendship and Love Between Women from the Renaissance to the Present* (New York: William Morrow, 1981), 15–16. Faderman's study remains a valuable introduction to women's romantic friendships, along with Carroll Smith-Rosenberg's "The Female World of Love and Ritual: Relations Between Women in Nineteenth-Century America," in *Disorderly Conduct: Visions of Gender in Victorian America* (New York: Oxford University Press, 1986), 53–76. See also Martha Vicinus, *Intimate Friends: Women Who Loved Women, 1778–1928* (Chicago: University of Chicago Press, 2004).

13. Gilman, *Selected Letters*, 10, 11, 14.

14. Ibid., 12, 22, 13.

15. Ibid., 11–12.

16. Gilman, *Diaries*, 2:862–63; 1:97–98; flyleaf of Journal, January 1, 1882–December 31, 1883, Gilman Collection, Schlesinger Library.

17. *Endure: The Diaries of Charles Walter Stetson*, ed. Mary Armfield Hill (Philadelphia: Temple University Press, 1985), 25, 27.

18. Ibid., 48, 49, 104.

19. Stetson, *Endure*, 32, 63, 64; Gilman, *Selected Letters*, 48; Stetson, *Endure*, 153, 66; Gilman, *Diaries*, 1:246; Stetson, *Endure*, 154.

20. Stetson, *Endure*, 144; Gilman, *Diaries* 2:878; Stetson, *Endure*, 145.

21. Gilman, *Diaries*, 1:246; *Selected Letters*, 29; Stetson, *Endure*, 256.

22. Gilman, *Diaries*, 1:278.

23. Ibid., 1:280.

24. Ibid., 1:332; Gilman, *Living*, 91, 104.

25. Jane Addams, *Twenty Years at Hull-House* (New York: Macmillan, 1910), 65. The secondary literature on Mitchell and the rest cure is vast; I have benefited from

Judith A. Allen's sophisticated interpretation in *The Feminism of Charlotte Perkins Gilman*, which cites Addams's experience (Chicago: University of Chicago Press, 2009), 20–25.

26. Gilman, *Living*, 96; Stetson, *Endure*, 342.

27. Charlotte Perkins Gilman, "Why I Wrote 'The Yellow Wallpaper'?" *Forerunner* 4.10 (October 1913): 271.

28. Gilman, *Selected Letters*, 85–86; Gilman quoted in Stetson, *Endure*, 363–64.

29. Gilman, *Selected Letters*, 82.

30. Gilman, *Diaries*, 2:440; Gilman quoted in Hill, *Charlotte Perkins Gilman*, 160.

31. *A Journey from Within: The Love Letters of Charlotte Perkins Gilman, 1897–1900*, ed. Mary A. Hill (Lewisburg, PA: Bucknell University Press, 1995), 246; Gilman, *Diaries*, 2:457.

32. Gilman, *Diaries*, 2:507.

33. "She Didn't Wear Corsets," *New York World*, December 18, 1892, clipping in folder 282, Gilman Collection, Schlesinger Library; *San Francisco Examiner*, December 19, 1892, quoted in Hill, *Charlotte Perkins Gilman*, 197; "In His Wife's Defense," *Philadelphia Press*, December 24, 1892, clipping in folder 282, Gilman Collection.

34. Gilman, *Diaries*, 2:613; Gilman, *Living*, 163; Charles Lummis quoted in Davis, *Charlotte Perkins Gilman*, 163.

35. "An Unnatural Mother" was originally published in the *Impress* in 1895 and was reprinted as "The Unnatural Mother" in *Forerunner* 7 (November 1916): 281–85; Gilman, *Living*, 181.

36. Gilman, *Selected Letters*, 95. Hill offers a thorough and incisive discussion of Gilman's sojourn at Hull-House in *Charlotte Perkins Gilman*, 180–87. On Florence Kelley, see Kathryn Kish Sklar, "Hull House in the 1890s: A Community of Women Reformers," *Signs* 10.4 (1985): 658–77.

37. Gilman, *Diaries*, 2:633.

38. Gilman, *Journey from Within*, 307.

39. Gilman, *Living*, 101, 104.

40. Ibid., 187.

41. On Ward and Spencer, see Richard Hofstadter, *Social Darwinism in American Thought* (Boston: Beacon Press, 1992), 67–84; and Clifford H. Scott, *Lester Frank Ward* (Boston: Twayne, 1976), 88–99, 114–19.

42. Gilman, *Living*, 187; Gilman, *The Home*, 87. Ward explains his gynaecocentric theory at length in *Pure Sociology* (New York: Macmillan, 1903), 296–377; Gilman read his article "Our Better Halves," *Forum* 6 (1888): 266–75. Ward's sexual theorizing is discussed in Barbara Finlay, "Lester Frank Ward as a Sociologist of Gender," *Gender and Society* 13.2 (April 1999): 251–65. See also the analyses of the relationship between Ward and Gilman in Judith A. Allen, " 'The Overthrow' of Gynaecocentric Culture: Charlotte Perkins Gilman and Lester Frank Ward," in *Charlotte Perkins Gilman and Her Contemporaries*, ed. Cynthia J. Davis and Denise D. Knight (Tuscaloosa: University of Alabama Press, 2004), 59–86; and Cynthia J. Davis, "His and Herland: Charlotte Perkins Gilman 'Re-presents' Lester F. Ward," in *Evolution and Eugenics in American*

Literature and Culture, 1880-1940, ed. Lois A. Cuddy and Claire M. Roche (Lewisburg, PA: Bucknell University Press, 2003), 73–88.

43. Charlotte Perkins Gilman, *Women and Economics: A Study of the Economic Relation Between Men and Women as a Factor in Social Evolution* (1898; Berkeley: University of California Press, 1998), 60.

44. Ibid., 5, 54. For Gilman's articulation of the argument summarized in this paragraph, see *The Man-Made World; or, Our Androcentric Culture* (New York: Charlton, 1911), in addition to *Women and Economics*.

45. Alpheus Hyatt and G. Stanley Hall quoted in Gail Bederman, *Manliness and Civilization* (Chicago: University of Chicago Press, 1995), 137–38.

46. Gilman, *Women and Economics*, 168. On the late nineteenth- and early twentieth-century woman's movement, see Mari Jo Buhle, *Women and American Socialism, 1870–1920* (Urbana: University of Illinois Press, 1981); Eleanor Flexner and Ellen Fitzpatrick, *Century of Struggle: The Woman's Rights Movement in the United States*, enlarged ed. (Cambridge: Harvard University Press, 1996); Nancy F. Cott, *The Grounding of Modern Feminism* (New Haven: Yale University Press, 1987); and Jean V. Matthews, *The Rise of the New Woman: The Women's Movement in America, 1875–1930* (Chicago: Ivan R. Dee, 2003).

47. Charlotte Perkins Gilman, *His Religion and Hers* (New York: Century, 1923), 278; Gilman, *Man-Made World*, 189–90.

48. Gilman first outlined her vision of the kitchenless house and professionalized cleaning and childcare in *Women and Economics*, 225–94, then expanded it in *The Home*.

49. Gilman, *Women and Economics*, 330, 269; Gilman, *The Home*, 102–3. My analysis of Gilman's material feminism builds on Dolores Hayden, *The Grand Domestic Revolution: A History of Feminist Designs for American Homes, Neighborhoods, and Cities* (Cambridge: MIT Press, 1981).

50. Gilman, *Living*, 219; *Selected Letters*, 6, 7; *Journey from Within*, 41, 64.

51. Gilman, *Journey from Within*, 217, 71, 168, 133, 129, 214, 198.

52. Ibid., 285, 244, 175.

53. Gilman, *Living*, 281.

54. On American Fabians' interest in beneficent entrepreneurship, see Thomas P. Jenkin, "The American Fabian Movement," *Western Political Quarterly* 1.2 (June 1948): 113–23. Gilman's utopian and proto-utopian short stories have been gathered in Carol Farley Kessler, *Charlotte Perkins Gilman: Her Progress Toward Utopia with Selected Writings* (Syracuse, NY: Syracuse University Press, 1995); see especially "Aunt Mary's Pie Plant," "A Garden of Babies," "Her Memories," "Maidstone Comfort," and "Bee Wise." Gilman's novel *What Diantha Did* (1910; Durham: Duke University Press, 2005) is an engaging expression of her material-utopian feminism.

55. Gilman, "A Woman's Utopia," 144; *Moving the Mountain* in *Charlotte Perkins Gilman's Utopian Novels*, ed. Minna Doskow (Madison, NJ: Fairleigh Dickinson University Press, 1999), 51, 53, 39. For Gilman's generally low opinion of Christian Science, see *Living*, 242–43.

56. Charlotte Perkins Gilman, *Herland* (1915; New York: Pantheon, 1979), 49.

57. Ibid., 75, 67.

58. Ibid., 48.

59. Ibid., 111, 45, 71, 67, 97.

60. Ibid., 59, 113, 11; Charlotte Perkins Gilman, *His Religion and Hers*, 37–56.

61. Gilman, *Herland*, 58, 59.

62. Ibid., 57, 95.

63. Gilman quoted in Davis, *Charlotte Perkins Gilman*, 164; *Herland*, 11.

64. Irving Fisher quoted in Wendy Kline, *Building a Better Race: Gender, Sexuality, and Eugenics from the Turn of the Century to the Baby Boom* (Berkeley: University of California Press, 2001), 30. For introductions to eugenic thought in the U.S., see also Mark H. Haller, *Eugenics: Hereditarian Attitudes in American Thought* (New Brunswick: Rutgers University Press, 1984); and Thomas C. Leonard, *Illiberal Reformers: Race, Eugenics, and American Economics in the Progressive Era* (Princeton: Princeton University Press, 2016), 109–28.

65. Theodore Roosevelt quoted in Donald K. Pickens, *Eugenics and the Progressives* (Nashville: Vanderbilt University Press, 1968), 125; Lester F. Ward, "Eugenics, Euthenics, and Eudemics," *American Journal of Sociology* 18.6 (May 1913): 738.

66. Cott, *Grounding of Modern Feminism*, 119; Gilman, *Women and Economics*, lxxv.

67. Val Gough, "Lesbians and Virgins: The New Motherhood in *Herland*," in *Anticipations: Essays on Early Science Fiction and Its Precursors*, ed. David Seed (Liverpool: Liverpool University Press, 1995), 202.

68. Gilman, *Herland*, 70, 71, 69, 82.

69. Ibid., 83.

70. Gilman, *Human Work*, 377.

71. Gilman, *Moving the Mountain*, 136.

72. One of the few critics to offer an extended analysis of *Moving the Mountain* that takes into account the novel's eugenicism is Mark W. Van Wienen, *American Socialist Triptych: The Literary-Political Work of Charlotte Perkins Gilman, Upton Sinclair, and W. E. B. DuBois* (Ann Arbor: University of Michigan Press, 2012), 180–92.

73. See, for example, *Living*, 186; *Man-Made World*, 245; *His Religion and Hers*, 9; and "The Ethics of Woman's Work," in *Nonfiction Reader*, 79

74. Gilman, *Herland*, 54.

75. On the reception of Gobineau in the U.S., see Nell Irvin Painter, *The History of White People* (New York: Norton, 2010), 195–98.

76. Gilman, *Living*, 2, 284.

77. Gilman, *With Her in Ourland*, in *Charlotte Perkins Gilman's Utopian Novels*, 356, 320–21.

78. Ibid., 323, 358.

79. John Higham, *Strangers in the Land: Patterns of American Nativism, 1860–1925* (New Brunswick: Rutgers University Press, 2002), 88; Raymond L. Cohn, "Immigration to the United States," in *EH.Net Encyclopedia of Economic and Business*

History, available online at http://eh.net/encyclopedia/immigration-to-the-united-states, accessed January 15, 2015; Paul Ritterband, "Counting the Jews of New York, 1900–1991: An Essay in Substance and Method," in *Papers in Jewish Demography 1997*, ed. Sergio DelloPergola and Judith Even (Jerusalem: Hebrew University, 2001), 199–228.

80. Gilman, *With Her in Ourland*, 362, 363. Tracy Fessenden, Thomas Peyser, and Alys Eve Weinbaum have intensively analyzed Gilman's racial attitudes. See Fessenden, *Culture and Redemption: Religion, the Secular, and American Literature* (Princeton: Princeton University Press, 2007), 161–80; Peyser, *Utopia and Cosmopolis: Globalization in the Era of American Literary Realism* (Durham: Duke University Press, 1998), 63–91; Weinbaum, *Wayward Reproductions: Genealogies of Race and Nation in Trans-atlantic Modern Thought* (Durham: Duke University Press, 2004), 61–105. See also Louise Michele Newman's *White Women's Rights: The Racial Origins of Feminism in the United States* (New York: Oxford University Press, 1999), which locates Gilman's racial theories within a broad analytic history of the woman's movement of the time.

81. Gilman, "A Woman's Utopia," 149.

82. Van Wienen, *American Socialist Triptych*, 193–212.

83. Gilman, *Selected Letters*, 272.

84. Gilman, *Living*, 331; *Selected Letters*, 190.

85. Gilman, *Selected Letters*, 151.

86. Gilman, *Living*, 335.

87. Ibid., 333–34. See Davis, *Charlotte Perkins Gilman*, 394–97.

Chapter Six. After the Last Utopians

1. On the Battle of the Somme, see Adam Hochschild, *To End All Wars: A Study of Loyalty and Rebellion, 1914–1918* (Boston: Houghton Mifflin Harcourt, 2011), 195–214.

2. Ernest Hemingway, *A Farewell to Arms* (1929; New York: Scribner, 1995), 184–85.

3. See Eric D. Weitz, *A Century of Genocide: Utopias of Race and Nation* (Princeton: Princeton University Press, 2003). Weitz explores in detail the utopian projects of Cambodia's Khmer Rouge and of Serbian nationalists in addition to the USSR and Germany. In *Picture Imperfect: Utopian Thought for an Anti-Utopian Age* (New York: Columbia University Press, 2005), Russell Jacoby argues against the idea that these nationalist projects can be considered utopian.

4. Robert C. Elliott, *The Shape of Utopia: Studies in a Literary Genre* (Chicago: University of Chicago Press, 1970), x.

5. Lyman Tower Sargent, "The Three Faces of Utopianism Revisited," *Utopian Studies* 5.1 (1994): 1–37.

6. H. G. Wells, *The Time Machine* (New York: Henry Holt, 1895), 117. On Wells, see Krishan Kumar, *Utopia and Anti-Utopia in Modern Times* (Oxford: Blackwell, 1987), 168–223.

7. Eugene Zamiatin, *We*, trans. Gregory Zilboorg (1924; New York: Dutton, 1959),

218. David M. Bell offers a different view of the novel, arguing that it is anti-anti-utopian: *Rethinking Utopia: Power, Place, Affect* (New York: Routledge, 2017), 25–32.

8. Ruth Levitas and Lucy Sargisson, "Utopia in Dark Times: Optimism/Pessimism and Utopia/Dystopia," in *DarkHorizons: Science Fiction and the Dystopian Imagination*, ed. Raffaella Baccolini and Tom Moylan (New York: Routledge, 2003), 26. Tom Moylan discusses the distinctions between dystopias and anti-utopias in his important *Scraps of the Untainted Sky: Science Fiction, Utopian, Dystopia* (Boulder, CO: Westview, 2000). Gregory Claeys provides a comprehensive survey of dystopianism in *Dystopia: A Natural History* (New York: Oxford University Press, 2017). For valuable brief introductions to dystopian and anti-utopian literature, see Gregory Claeys, "The Origins of Dystopia: Wells, Huxley and Orwell," in *The Cambridge Companion to Utopian Literature*, ed. Gregory Claeys (Cambridge: Cambridge University Press, 2010), 107–34; and the essays by Artur Blaim and Krishan Kumar in *Dystopia(n) Matters: On the Page, on Screen, on Stage*, ed. Fátima Vieira (Newcastle upon Tyne: Cambridge Scholars, 2013).

9. On *Brave New World*, see Krishan Kumar, *Utopia and Anti-Utopia in Modern Times* (Oxford: Blackwell, 1987), 224–87. The best biography is Nicholas Murray, *Aldous Huxley* (New York: St. Martin's, 2003).

10. Aldous Huxley, *Jesting Pilate* (New York: George H. Doran, 1926), 300.

11. Aldous Huxley, *Brave New World* (London: Chatto & Windus, 1932), n.p. My translation from the French; ellipsis in the original.

12. *George Orwell: A Life in Letters*, ed. Peter Davison (New York: Liveright, 2013), 217; Aldous Huxley, *Brave New World Revisited* (New York: Harper, 1958), 2.

13. See Krishan Kumar, *Utopia and Anti-Utopia in Modern Times* (Oxford: Blackwell, 1987), 347–78.

14. Sargent, "Three Faces." On the long 1960s, see Arthur Marvick, *The Sixties: Cultural Revolution in Britain, France, Italy and the United States, c. 1958–c. 1974* (New York: Oxford University Press, 2000).

15. The low estimate comes from Donald E. Pitzer, *America's Communal Utopias* (Chapel Hill: University of North Carolina Press, 1997), 12; the high from Timothy Miller, *The 60s Communes: Hippies and Beyond* (Syracuse, NY: Syracuse University Press, 1999), xviii–xx.

16. Rosabeth Moss Kanter, *Commitment and Community: Communes and Utopias in Sociological Perspective* (Cambridge: Harvard University Press, 1972).

17. See *Voices from the Farm: Adventures in Community Living*, ed. Rupert Fike, 2nd ed. (Summertown, TN: Book Publishing, 2012); and two books by Douglas Stevenson: *The Farm Then and Now* (Summertown, TN: Book Publishing, 2014) and *Out to Change the World: The Evolution of the Farm Community* (Summertown, TN: Book Publishing, 2014). For brief overviews by sociologists, see Miller, *The 60s Communes*, 118–24; and Joseph C. Manzella, *Common Purse, Uncommon Future: The Long, Strange Trip of Communes and Other Intentional Communities* (Santa Barbara, CA: Praeger, 2010), 67–74. The Farm's extensive website is a rich source of information: www.thefarmcommunity.com.

18. Theodore Roszak, *The Making of a Counter Culture: Reflections on the Techno-*

cratic Society and Its Youthful Opposition (New York: Doubleday, 1969), 240, 267. On Roszak and *Making of a Counter Culture*, see Rosemary Deller, "Roszak, Theodore (1933–2011)," in *Encyclopedia of the Sixties*, ed. James S. Baugess and Abbe Allen DeBolt (Santa Barbara, CA: Greenwood, 2012), 2:573–74.

19. Roszak, *Making of a Counter Culture*, xiii.

20. Charles A. Reich, *The Greening of America* (New York: Random House, 1970), 4.

21. Ibid., 234, 384, 295.

22. See Rodger D. Citron, "Charles Reich's Journey from the Yale Law Journal to the New York Times Best-Seller List: The Personal History of *The Greening of America*," *New York Law School Law Review* 52.3 (2007/2008): 387–416.

23. Carl Freedman, *Critical Theory and Science Fiction* (Hanover, NH: Wesleyan University Press, 2000), 38–43.

24. Tom Moylan, *Demand the Impossible: Science Fiction and the Utopian Imagination* (New York: Methuen, 1986).

25. Angelika Bammer, *Partial Visions: Feminism and Utopianism in the 1970s* (New York: Routledge, 1991).

26. Marge Piercy, *Woman on the Edge of Time* (New York: Knopf, 1976), 98. For discussion of the novel, see Chris Ferns, *Narrating Utopia: Ideology, Gender, Form in Utopian Literature* (Liverpool: Liverpool University Press, 1999), 205–13; and Bammer, *Partial Visions*, 93–104.

27. Ursula Le Guin, *The Dispossessed* (1974; New York: HarperCollins, 2003). The large body of critical literature on *The Dispossessed* includes two books devoted to the novel: Tony Burns, *Political Theory, Science Fiction, and Utopian Literature: Ursula K. Le Guin and* The Dispossessed (Lanham, MD: Lexington, 2008); and Laurence Davis and Peter Stillman, eds., *The New Utopian Politics of Ursula K. Le Guin's* The Dispossessed (Lanham, MD: Lexington, 2005). See also Bell, *Rethinking Utopia*; Ferns, *Narrating Utopia*, 219–30; Freedman, *Critical Theory and Science Fiction*, 111–29; Moylan, *Demand the Impossible*, 91–120; Christine Nadir, "Utopian Studies, Environmental Literature, and the Legacy of an Idea: Educating Desire in Miguel Abensour and Ursula K. Le Guin," *Utopian Studies* 21.1 (2010): 24–56; and Raymond Williams, *Problems in Materialism and Culture* (London: Verso, 1980), 196–212.

28. See Francis Fukuyama, *The End of History and the Last Man* (New York: Free Press, 1992). For a sampling of responses to the end of history thesis, see *After History: Francis Fukuyama and His Critics*, ed. Timothy Burns (Lanham, MD: Rowman & Littlefield, 1994).

29. Margaret Atwood, *In Other Worlds: SF and the Human Imagination* (New York: Doubleday, 2011), 185.

30. Laura Miller, "Fresh Hell," *The New Yorker* (June 14 & 21, 2010): 135.

31. For an excellent brief introduction to cli fi fiction, see Rebecca Tuhus-Dubrow, "Cli-Fi: Birth of a Genre," *Dissent* 60.3 (Summer 2013): 58–61.

32. Atwood, *In Other Worlds*, 185.

33. Russell Jacoby, *The End of Utopia: Politics and Culture in an Age of Apathy* (New York: Basic Books, 1999), xiii; *Picture Imperfect*, passim.

34. Fredric Jameson, "Of Islands and Trenches: Naturalization and the Production

of Utopian Discourse," *Diacritics* 7.2 (1977): 21. Many of Jameson's essays on utopia are collected in *Archaeologies of the Future: The Desire Called Utopia and Other Science Fictions* (London: Verso, 2005).

35. Krishan Kumar, "The Ends of Utopia," *New Literary History* 41 (2010): 549–69.

36. David Harvey's *Spaces of Hope* (Berkeley: University of California Press, 2000) is a distinguished recent example of utopian social theory.

37. Davina Cooper, *Everyday Utopias: The Conceptual Life of Promising Spaces* (Durham: Duke University Press, 2014).

38. Louis Marin, "Disneyland: A Degenerate Utopia," *Glyph* 1 (1977): 50–66.

39. Ronald Reagan quoted in Daniel T. Rodgers, *Age of Fracture* (Cambridge: Harvard University Press, 2011), 41.

40. Ray Kurzweil, *The Singularity Is Near* (New York: Viking, 2005), n.p. On techno-utopianism, see Majid Yar, *The Cultural Imaginary of the Internet: Virtual Utopias and Dystopias* (New York: Palgrave Macmillan, 2014); and Howard P. Segal, *Technological Utopianism in American Culture* (Syracuse, NY: Syracuse University Press, 2005).

41. Kwame Anthony Appiah, *Cosmopolitanism: Ethics in a World of Strangers* (New York: Norton, 2006), xvi–xviii. Angelika Bammer employs the concept of partial utopianism to different effect in *Partial Visions*.

42. Howard P. Segal, *Utopias: A Brief History from Ancient Writings to Virtual Communities* (Malden, MA: Wiley-Blackwell, 2012), 6.

43. William Morris, *Why I Am a Communist* (London: Liberty Press, 1894), 2.

44. See the website of the Fellowship for Intentional Community: www.ic.org.

45. See www.twinoaks.org and www.findhorn.org.

46. See Manzanella, *Common Purse, Uncommon Future*, 43–54.

47. Donald E. Pitzer, "Developmental Communalism into the Twenty-First Century," in *The Communal Idea in the 21st Century*, ed. Eliezer Ben-Rafael, Yaacov Oved, and Menachem Topel (Leiden: Brill, 2013), 33–52.

48. For introductions to Twin Oaks, see Hilke Kuhlmann, *Living Walden Two: B. F. Skinner's Behaviorist Utopia and Experimental Communities* (Urbana: University of Illinois Press, 2005), 81–132; and Jyotsna Sreenivasan, *Utopias in American History* (Santa Barbara: ABC-CLIO, 2008), 373–78. Essential resources are the two books by cofounder Kat Kinkade: *A Walden Two Experiment: The First Five Years of Twin Oaks Community* (New York: Morrow, 1973) and *Is It Utopia Yet? An Insider's View of Twin Oaks Community in Its Twenty-Sixth Year* (Louisa, VA: Twin Oaks Publishing, 1994).

49. J. C. Hallman, *In Utopia: Six Kinds of Eden and the Search for a Better Paradise* (New York: St. Martin's, 2010), 53–99.

50. See the websites of the Cohousing Association of the United States (www.cohousing.org) and the UK Cohousing Network (cohousing.org.uk); Graham Meltzer, *Sustainable Community: Learning from the Cohousing Model* (Victoria, BC: Trafford, 2005); and Lucy Sargisson, *Fool's Gold? Utopianism in the Twenty-First Century* (New York: Palgrave Macmillan, 2012), 167–88. The most recent book by Kathryn McCamant and Charles Durrett, the architects who introduced cohousing in the U.S., is

Creating Cohousing: Building Sustainable Communities (Gabriola, BC: New Society, 2011).

51. Claudia Roach interviewed in *Visions of Utopia: Experiments in Sustainable Culture*, part 2, directed by Geoph Kozeny (Rutledge, MO: Fellowship for Intentional Community, 2009), DVD; Barbara Taylor, *Eve and the New Jerusalem: Socialism and Feminism in the Nineteenth Century* (New York: Pantheon, 1983), 245.

52. All quotations are from the Burning Man website: www.burningman.com, accessed July 21, 2014. See pages "The Ten Principles" and "La Vie Bohème: A History of Burning Man. A Lecture by Larry Harvey." My understanding of Burning Man as a temporary utopia has been shaped by Rachel Bowditch, *On the Edge of Utopia: Performance and Ritual at Burning Man* (Chicago: University of Chicago Press, 2010); Lee Gilmore, *Theatre in a Crowded Fire: Ritual and Spirituality at Burning Man* (Berkeley: University of California Press, 2010); and by conversations with Ethan Dunn.

53. "Survival Guide," www.burningman.com, accessed July 21, 2014.

54. Cindy Milstein, "Occupy Anarchism," in *We Are Many: Reflections on Movement Strategy from Occupation to Liberation*, ed. Kate Khatib, Margaret Killjoy, and Mike McGuire (Oakland, CA: AK Press, 2012), 297.

55. David Graeber, *The Democracy Project: A History, a Crisis, a Movement* (New York: Spiegel & Grau, 2013), 23, 233.

56. See www.edwardcarpentercommunity.org.uk

57. There is no central Radical Faerie organization, but the website www.radfae.org offers a collection of information and resources, plus links to sanctuary websites.

58. Harry Hay, *Radically Gay: Gay Liberation in the Words of Its Founder*, ed. Will Roscoe (Boston: Beacon Press, 1996), 257.

59. Ibid., 289, 6, 213.

60. Ibid., 214, 239–41.

61. Peter Hennen, *Faeries, Bears, and Leathermen: Men in Community Queering the Masculine* (Chicago: University of Chicago Press, 2008), 80.

62. David Edleson, email message to author, June 2, 2011.

63. See Heiner Ullrich, *Rudolph Steiner* (London: Continuum, 2008).

64. Rudolf Steiner, "The Education of the Child in the Light of Spiritual Science," in *The Education of the Child and Early Lectures on Education* (Hudson, NY: Anthroposophical Press, 1996).

65. Ullrich, *Rudolph Steiner*, 81–85.

66. For the U.S. see the website of the Association of Waldorf Schools of North America (https://waldorfeducation.org/); for the U.K. see the Steiner Waldorf Schools Fellowship (http://www.steinerwaldorf.org/steiner-schools/list-of-schools/), both accessed May 18, 2017.

67. Rudolf Steiner quoted in Roy Wilkinson, *Rudolf Steiner on Education* (Stroud, U.K.: Hawthorn Press, 1993), 125.

68. See Phillippa Bennett, "Educating for Utopia: William Morris on Useful Learning versus 'Useless Toil,'" *Journal of William Morris Studies* 20.2 (Summer 2013): 54–72.

69. See *Earth Perfect? Nature, Utopia, and the Garden*, ed. Annette Giesecke and Naomi Jacobs (London: Black Dog, 2012).

70. The historical statistic comes from R. Douglas Hurt, *American Agriculture: A Brief History*, rev. ed. (West Lafayette, IN: Purdue University Press, 2002), 405; the current statistic from USDA, "2012 Census of Agriculture," available at www.agcensus.usda.gov.

71. Paul K. Conkin, *A Revolution Down on the Farm: The Transformation of American Agriculture since 1929* (Lexington: University Press of Kentucky, 2008), 99.

72. Nicholas Sabloff, "Politics or Style? The Good-Food Movement," *Common Review* 8.4 (Spring 2010), 10.

73. USDA Economic Research Service, http://www.ers.usda.gov/data-products/food-expenditures.aspx, accessed July 30, 2015.

74. Hurt, *American Agriculture*, 380.

75. Barbara Kingsolver, *Animal, Vegetable, Miracle: A Year of Food Life* (New York: HarperCollins, 2007), 5.

76. See the USDA Animal Welfare Information Center, https://www.nal.usda.gov/awic.

77. See Arturo Rodriguez, "Cheap Food: Workers Pay the Price," in *Food, Inc.* (New York: Public Affairs, 2009), 123–48.

78. Michael Pollan, "The Food Movement, Rising," *New York Review of Books* (June 10, 2010), 31.

79. See the USDA "2012 Census of Agriculture," which notes that of the existing 2.1 million American farms, only 251,000, or 12 percent, account for 89 percent of all sales. The majority of farmers must take other jobs in addition to working their land.

80. See two overviews of American alternative food movements: Sandor Ellix Katz, *The Revolution Will Not Be Microwaved: Inside America's Underground Food Movements* (White River Junction, VT: Chelsea Green, 2006); and Pollan, "Food Movement, Rising."

81. On *Diet for a Small Planet*, see Maria McGrath, "Recipes for a New World: Utopianism and Alternative Eating in Natural-Foods Vegetarian Cookbooks, 1970–84," in *Eating in Eden: Food and American Utopias*, ed. Etta M. Madden and Martha L. Finch (Lincoln: University of Nebraska Press, 2006), 162–84. Berry's most influential book is *The Unsettling of America: Culture and Agriculture* (San Francisco: Sierra Club Books, 1977); for an assessment, see Kimberly K. Smith, *Wendell Berry and the Agrarian Tradition* (Lawrence: University Press of Kansas, 2003). On Waters, see Thomas McNamee, *Alice Waters and Chez Panisse* (New York: Penguin, 2007), and Janet A. Flammang, *The Taste for Civilization: Food, Politics, and Civil Society* (Urbana: University of Illinois Press, 2009), 173–210.

82. USDA, "National Count of Famers Market Directory Listings" (2014), available at www.ams.usda.gov; USDA, "2012 Census of Agriculture."

83. USDA, "2012 Census of Agriculture."

84. See Mary Rizzo, "Revolution in a Can: Food, Class and Radicalism in the Minneapolis Co-op Wars of the 1970s," in *Eating in Eden*, 220–38; and Jade Aguilar, "Food

Choices and Voluntary Simplicity in Intentional Communities: What's Race and Class Got to Do with It?" *Utopian Studies* 26.1 (2015): 79–100.

85. Robert Paarlberg, "Attention Whole Foods Shoppers," *Foreign Policy* (May/June 2010), 82. For a more extensive version of Paarlberg's argument, see *Food Politics: What Everyone Needs to Know* (New York: Oxford University Press, 2010).

86. Sabloff, "Politics or Style?" 8.

87. See Will Allen with Charles Wilson, *The Good Food Revolution: Growing Healthy Food, People, and Communities* (New York: Gotham Books, 2012).

88. See Nave Wald, "Towards Utopias of Prefigurative Politics and Food Sovereignty: Experiences of Politicised Peasant Food Production," in *Food Utopias: Reimagining Citizenship, Ethics and Community*, ed. Paul V. Stock, Michael Carolan, and Christopher Rosin (London: Routledge, 2015), 107–25.

89. See *Agriculture at a Crossroads*, ed. Beverly D. McIntyre et al. (Washington, DC: Island Press, 2009), the "Synthesis Report" of the International Assessment of Agricultural Knowledge, Science, and Technology for Development. For arguments that build on this report see Sarah Elton, *Consumed: Food for a Finite Planet* (Chicago: University of Chicago Press, 2013); and HRH the Prince of Wales, *The Prince's Speech: On the Future of Food* (Emmaus, PA: Rodale, 2012).

90. Wenonah Hauter, *Foodopoly: The Battle Over the Future of Food and Farming in America* (New York: New Press, 2012).

91. Robert Frost, "The Oven Bird," in *The Poetry of Robert Frost: The Collected Poems*, ed. Edward Connery Lathem (New York: Henry Holt, 1979), 120.

92. Tom Moylan, "To Stand with Dreamers," *Irish Review* 34 (2006): 10.

93. Charles S. Maier, "The End of Longing? Notes toward a History of Postwar German National Longing," in *The Postwar Transformation of Germany: Democracy, Prosperity, and Nationhood*, ed. John S. Brady, Beverly Crawford, and Sarah Elise Wiliarty (Ann Arbor: University of Michigan Press, 1999), 273.

94. Svetlana Boym, *The Future of Nostalgia* (New York: Basic Books, 2001), 50.

95. Norman Geras, "Minimum Utopia: Ten Theses," in *Socialist Register 2000: Necessary and Unnecessary Utopias* (London: Merlin Press, 2000), 42.

THE LAST UTOPIANS builds on several decades of work by schol-ars in the burgeoning interdisciplinary field of utopian studies. The literature in the field is vast; what follows is a highly selective intro-ductory guide for nonspecialists.

Utopia and Utopianism

Two eminent figures in utopian studies have written brief introduc-tions to utopian literature, thought, and practice. Krishan Kumar's *Utopianism* (Minneapolis: University of Minnesota Press, 1991) is an excellent starting point, although Kumar has been criticized for his insistence on the primacy of the literary utopia and his assertion that utopianism is a uniquely Western tradition. Lyman Tower Sar-gent disagrees with both ideas, as evidenced in *Utopianism: A Very Short Introduction* (New York: Oxford University Press, 2010). Sar-gent's book can be supplemented with his highly influential defini-tional essay, "The Three Faces of Utopianism Revisited," *Utopian Studies* 5 (1994): 1–37.

J. C. Hallman's *In Utopia: Six Kinds of Paradise and the Search for a Better Eden* (New York: St. Martin's, 2010) is primarily a cheeky, journalistic account of the writer's experiences in a half-dozen contemporary utopian ventures around the world. Along the way, he also provides a quirky, enjoyable, and perceptive intellectual history of utopia. Erik Reece's *Utopia Drive: A Road Trip Through America's Most Radical Idea* (New York: Farrar, Straus and Giroux, 2016) is less ambitious—Reece limits his account to East Coast sites within driving distance of his Kentucky home—but equally quirky and enjoyable. Gregory Claeys's introduction to utopianism, *Search-ing for Utopia: The History of an Idea* (London: Thames & Hudson, 2011), is more sober, although the many full-color illustrations make this book by an eminent political historian a pleasure to read. *The Story of Utopias* (1922; 2nd ed., New York: Viking, 1962) is the first book by Lewis Mumford, the great twentieth-century intellectual. Hurriedly written and full of flaws, it remains an important and entertaining introduction to the topic.

No one has accused *Utopian Thought in the Western World* (Cambridge: Harvard University Press, 1979), by Frank E. Manuel and Fritzie P. Manuel, of being entertaining, and critics have faulted the Manuels' failure to define their topic, which leaves them free to include lengthy chapters on writers, such as Leibniz and Kant, not usually associated with utopia. Nevertheless, this massive survey, which marches from the Hebrew Bible to Herbert Marcuse, provides detailed, erudite discussions of every major figure.

Frank Manuel edited a special issue of *Daedalus* in 1965 that was expanded and published as *Utopias and Utopian Thought* (Boston: Houghton Mifflin, 1966). A number of the essays remain valuable, particularly Northrop Frye's "Varieties of Literary Utopias." Of the many other collections of essays about utopia, two are particularly valuable as introductions: *The Cambridge Companion to Utopian Literature*, ed. Gregory Claeys (Cambridge: Cambridge University Press, 2010), and *Utopia: The Search for the Ideal Society in the Western World*, ed. Roland Schaer, Gregory Claeys, and Lyman Tower Sargent (New York: New York Public Library and Oxford University Press, 2000).

Two hefty anthologies of excerpts from utopian works also serve as useful introductions to the genre: *The Utopia Reader*, 2nd ed., ed. Gregory Claeys and Lyman Tower Sargent (New York: NYU Press, 2017), and *The Faber Book of Utopias*, ed. John Carey (London: Faber and Faber, 1999).

Utopian Studies

Three books offer introductions to the academic field of utopian studies. Ruth Levitas's *The Concept of Utopia* (1990; Oxford: Peter Lang, 2011) was the first and remains the most important book-length survey of the field. David M. Bell, *Rethinking Utopia: Place, Power, Affect* (New York: Routledge, 2017), is in part an effort to update Levitas. *Utopia Method Vision: The Use Value of Social Dreaming*, ed. Tom Moylan and Raffaella Baccolini (Oxford: Peter Lang, 2007) is an engaging collection of original essays by twelve major scholars, who were encouraged to reflect on the field of utopian studies and their own engagement with it.

Theorizing Utopia

Literary critic and theorist Fredric Jameson has devoted much attention throughout his career to theorizing utopia, a project that culminated in *Archaeologies of the Future: The Desire Called Utopia and Other Science Fictions* (London: Verso, 2005), which gathers several of his earlier essays and includes a lengthy new reflection. *Archaeologies* does not include two of Jameson's most often cited essays: "Of Islands and Trenches: Naturalization and the Production of Utopian Discourse," *Diacritics* 7.2 (1977): 2–21, and "The Politics of Utopia," *New Left Review* 25 (2004): 35–54. The journal *Utopian Studies* devoted a special issue (9.2 [1998]) to Jameson's work.

Jameson's great peer Terry Eagleton does not cite Jameson in his essay "Utopia and Its Opposites," *Socialist Register 2000: Necessary and Unnecessary Utopias* (London: Merlin Press, 2000), 31–40, but this brief essay brilliantly complements Jameson's work. Jameson combines his interest in utopia with attention to the genre of science fiction, a combination that is powerfully explored by Darko Suvin, who argues in *Metamorphoses of Science Fiction* (1979; Oxford: Peter Lang, 2016) that "utopia is not a genre but the sociopolitical subgenre of science fiction." Raymond Williams never devoted a book to science fiction and utopia but wrote frequently about each; his essays have been collected by Andrew Milner in *Tenses of Imagination: Raymond Williams on Science Fiction, Utopia and Dystopia* (Oxford: Peter Lang, 2010).

Political theorist Barbara Goodwin offers a powerful defense of utopianism as a challenge to both Marxism and liberal political theory in *The Politics of Utopia: A Study in Theory and Practice* (1982; Oxford: Peter Lang, 2009), co-authored with Keith Taylor. Ruth Levitas, author of *The Concept of Utopia*, followed that influential work with *Utopia as Method: The Imaginary Reconstitution of Society* (New York: Palgrave Macmillan, 2013), which builds on H. G. Wells's claim that "the creation of utopias . . . is the proper and distinctive method of sociology."

German philosopher Ernst Bloch's three-volume work on utopia, *The Principle of Hope*, was not translated into English until 1986 (Cambridge: MIT Press) but has been extremely influential. This massive, idiosyncratic, ambitious work aims to place utopia at the center of both politics and psychology; Bloch intended to extend Marx's project, which he regarded as incomplete, and overturn Freud's, which he saw as fundamentally wrong. The book is exhilarating to read, but those approaching it for the first time may appreciate a guide. Several books are devoted to Bloch's ideas on utopia; helpful brief overviews can be found in Carl Freedman, *Critical Theory and Science Fiction* (Hanover, NH: Wesleyan University Press, 2000), and Vincent Geoghegan, *Utopianism and Marxism* (1987; Oxford: Peter Lang, 2008).

Geoghegan's book is an important study of the complex relationship between utopia and Marxist political thought; see also Steven Lukes's excellent brief essay, "Marxism and Utopianism," in *Utopias*, ed. Peter Alexander and Roger Gill (London: Duckworth, 1984). Zygmunt Bauman's *Socialism: The Active Utopia* (New York: Holmes & Meier, 1976) remains, more than forty years after its publication, a brilliant analysis of the topic.

Late Nineteenth-Century Utopianism

Several books focus on the surge of utopian literature in the United States following the publication of Edward Bellamy's *Looking Backward*. Jean Pfaelzer, *The Utopian Novel in America, 1886–1896* (Pittsburgh: University of Pittsburgh Press, 1984), is an excellent, tightly focused study. Other notable books on the period include Thomas Peyser, *Utopia and Cosmopolis: Globalization in the Era of American Literary Realism* (Durham, NC: Duke University Press, 1998); Kenneth M. Roemer, *The Obsolete Necessity: America in Utopian Literature, 1888–1900* (Kent, OH: Kent State University Press, 1976); and Robert Francis Shor, *Utopianism and Radicalism in a Reforming America, 1888–1918* (Westport, CT: Greenwood, 1997).

Despite their subtitles, Dohra Ahmad, *Landscapes of Hope: Anti-Colonial Utopianism in America* (New York: Oxford University Press, 2009), and Matthew Beaumont, *Utopia Ltd.: Ideologies of*

Social Dreaming in England, 1870–1900 (Leiden: Brill, 2005), treat both American and British writing, as does Beaumont's *The Spectre of Utopia: Utopian and Science Fictions at the Fin de Siècle* (Oxford: Peter Lang, 2012). Other books with a transatlantic approach have an extended chronological range but give special attention to the late nineteenth century: Chris Ferns, *Narrating Utopia: Ideology, Gender, Form in Utopian Literature* (Liverpool: Liverpool University Press, 1999); Philip Wegner, *Imaginary Communities: Utopia, the Nation, and the Spatial Histories of Modernity* (Berkeley: University of California Press, 2002); and Krishan Kumar's classic *Utopia and Anti-Utopia in Modern Times* (Oxford: Basil Blackwell, 1987).

Contemporary Utopias and Dystopias

Lucy Sargisson, *Fool's Gold? Utopianism in the Twenty-First Century* (New York: Palgrave Macmillan, 2012), is a broad survey of contemporary utopianism. Davina Cooper, *Everyday Utopias: The Conceptual Life of Promising Spaces* (Durham, NC: Duke University Press, 2014), is more focused—it explores six British case studies—but, like *Fool's Gold*, is conceptually rich and stimulating. Majid Yar, *The Cultural Imaginary of the Internet: Virtual Utopias and Dystopias* (New York: Palgrave Macmillan, 2014), is an incisive brief introduction to one important strand of contemporary utopianism. In *The Last Utopia: Human Rights in History* (Cambridge: Harvard University Press, 2010), Samuel Moyn makes the argument that the human rights movement is "the most inspiring mass utopianism" of our time. The geographer and cultural theorist David Harvey grounds *Spaces of Hope* (Berkeley: University of California Press, 2000) in an analysis of the ravaged urban landscape of Baltimore, Maryland, yet argues, nevertheless, for the necessity of utopian visions, and in an appendix he boldly describes his own imagined utopia, Edilia.

On the utopian fiction of the 1970s, see two essential books: Angelika Bammer, *Partial Visions: Feminism and Utopianism in the 1970s* (1991; Oxford: Peter Lang, 2015), and Tom Moylan, *Demand the Impossible: Science Fiction and the Utopian Imagination* (1986; Oxford: Peter Lang, 2014).

Since the 1970s, as the audience for utopian fiction has fallen away, dystopian literature has surged. Tom Moylan, *Scraps of the Untainted Sky: Science Fiction, Utopia, Dystopia* (Boulder: Westview, 2000), is a foundational analysis. Gregory Claeys, *Dystopia: A Natural History* (Oxford: Oxford University Press, 2017), is the most recent and comprehensive study. See also two collections of essays: *Dark Horizons: Science Fiction and the Dystopian Imagination*, ed. Raffaella Baccolini and Tom Moylan (New York: Routledge, 2003), and *Dystopia(n) Matters: On the Page, on Screen, and on Stage*, ed. Fátima Vieira (Newcastle upon Tyne: Cambridge Scholars, 2013).

INDEX

Page numbers in **boldface** refer to illustrations.

A NOTE ON THE TYPE

{⟨≈⟩≋⟨≈⟩}

THIS BOOK has been composed in Miller, a Scotch Roman typeface designed by Matthew Carter and first released by Font Bureau in 1997. It resembles Monticello, the typeface developed for The Papers of Thomas Jefferson in the 1940s by C. H. Griffith and P. J. Conkwright and reinterpreted in digital form by Carter in 2003.

Pleasant Jefferson ("P. J.") Conkwright (1905–1986) was Typographer at Princeton University Press from 1939 to 1970. He was an acclaimed book designer and AIGA Medalist.

The ornament used throughout this book was designed by Pierre Simon Fournier (1712–1768) and was a favorite of Conkwright's, used in his design of the *Princeton University Library Chronicle.*